TODAY WE DIE A LITTLE

ALSO BY RICHARD ASKWITH

Feet in the Clouds: A Tale of Fell-Running and Obsession
Running Free: A Runner's Journey Back to Nature

Richard Askwith

TODAY WE DIE A LITTLE

The Rise and Fall of Emil Zátopek, Olympic Legend

YELLOW JERSEY PRESS
LONDON

1 3 5 7 9 10 8 6 4 2

Yellow Jersey Press, an imprint of Vintage,
20 Vauxhall Bridge Road,
London SW1V 2SA

Yellow Jersey Press is part of the Penguin Random House
group of companies whose addresses can be found at
global.penguinrandomhouse.com

First published by Yellow Jersey Press in 2016

www.vintage-books.co.uk

A CIP catalogue record for this book
is available from the British Library

ISBN 9780224100342

Typeset in India by Thomson Digital Pvt Ltd, Noida, Delhi
Printed and bound in Great Britain by Clays Ltd, St Ives plc

Penguin Random House is committed to a sustainable future
for our business, our readers and our planet. This book is made
from Forest Stewardship Council® certified paper.

Contents

Prologue

The curious incident

On a sun-scorched runway in Prague, a twin-engined Československé Aerolinie airliner is waiting for take-off from Ruzyně International Airport. More than a hundred young men and women, the finest athletes in the Communist state of Czechoslovakia, are bound for Helsinki, a seven-hour flight away, where the XVth Olympic Games will begin in nine days' time. But there is a problem. The brightest and best of them all, Emil Zátopek, is absent.

The greatest runner of his generation – perhaps of all time – is missing from the flight that is due to take him to the Games that will define his sporting life. He is at the height of his powers: twenty-nine years old, a world record holder, a reigning Olympic champion who has lost only one of his last seventy races at his specialist distances, with his sights set on an unprecedented and never-to-be-repeated clean sweep of endurance running events.

It is the most important journey of his life. And he is late.

At least, that is how it looks. Emil's wife, Dana, knows better. A javelin thrower with Olympic ambitions of her own, she is on the plane already, weeping. She knows the real reason why Emil is not beside her. She knows that he is engaged in a high-stakes game of 'chicken' that could not just end his career but quite plausibly see him sent to a labour camp.

It is Thursday, 10 July 1952. The Iron Curtain that fell across Europe at the end of the Second World War has grown more oppressive in recent years, especially in Czechoslovakia. The Communists seized power there in 1948; a ruthless secret service, the Státní bezpečnost (StB), has helped them keep it. By 1950, show trials had begun. The most notorious, the Slánský trial, is still being prepared, but already scores of enemies of the revolution, real and imagined, have been executed. Tens of thousands are under surveillance by the StB. And now, with the Soviet Union preparing to take part in its first ever Olympic Games, the shadow of Stalin looms ever larger over Czechoslovak life – literally so in central Prague, where the world's biggest statue of the Soviet dictator, eventually to be nearly thirty metres high (if you include the base), is under construction.

No one is immune from the obsessive and brutal enforcement of political conformity. Athletes of all kinds have been among those rounded up in the purges. You don't have to be guilty of anything: just out of favour. It is less than eight months since the entire national ice hockey team was arrested, on the evening of its departure to London to defend its world title. Twelve players were condemned to camps for, supposedly, contemplating defection (and, in some cases, singing disrespectful songs); the combined total of their sentences was seventy-seven years and eight months.

By those standards, the problem with Stanislav Jungwirth, Emil's teammate and a future 1,500m world record holder, is a trivial one. Stanislav himself is not in trouble. It is Emil's response to the problem that is potentially catastrophic. Stanislav's father is in prison for political offences – and that, the Party has decided, makes it inappropriate for Jungwirth junior to travel abroad, except to other Warsaw Pact countries. It is a modest restriction; unless, like Jungwirth, you are an Olympic athlete who has spent the past four years dreaming of Helsinki.

News of Jungwirth's exclusion emerged the evening before the athletes were due to fly, when they turned up at the Ministry of Sport to collect their travel documents. Jungwirth was devastated to find that there were none for him, but quickly accepted that making a scene would only make matters worse. But Emil was incandescent. 'No way,' he told the officials. 'If Standa does not go, nor will I.' Then he stormed out, leaving his paperwork behind him.

The next day, on the morning of the flight, Jungwirth implores Zátopek to calm down. Emil insists on standing his ground. He gives Jungwirth his team outfit and tells him to return it to the Ministry when he returns his own. Then he goes off to train alone at Prague's Strahov stadium.

The stand-off continues for days, by which time the plane has long since left without Zátopek. Dana is inconsolable: the stress causes her to lose her voice. It is barely a decade since her own father was taken away by the

Gestapo during the German occupation; he ended up in Dachau. Now her husband seems to have condemned himself to a comparable fate.

In Helsinki, Western journalists are told that Zátopek has tonsillitis.

* * *

More than seventy years later, on a wet Wednesday evening in January, I am sitting in an aeroplane on that same runway. It is a Wizz Air flight this time, delayed for well over an hour by one of those inscrutable problems to which budget flights are prey. Our destination is London Luton, and the passengers, far from being Olympic athletes, are mostly price-conscious tourists. But my head is full of thoughts of Olympic glory in Helsinki.

I have spent the past few days visiting Zátopek's old haunts and talking to people who knew him; the highlight was a long morning of memories, laughter and slivovice (plum brandy) with Dana herself. Now, on the homeward journey, I have just reached the end of my second Zátopek biography of the week and am wondering which one to begin afresh. They are all the reading matter I have, and today there have been many hours to kill.

The engine starts to hum with pre-take-off half-life. The air crew perform their safety drill, and I note with pleasure that I recognise several words. Maybe that teach-yourself-Czech audio programme is starting to work. Then I find myself thinking about the Jungwirth incident. I wonder if the puddled runway I can see through the window bears any resemblance to the view that Dana saw as she scanned the asphalt fretfully through an aeroplane window in the summer of 1952, wondering if Emil would appear.

Then a startling thought occurs to me. That incident with Jungwirth – where is it?

I check and double-check, but it isn't there: not in either of the biographies. As I write, they are the only lives of Zátopek available in the English language. Yet neither even mentions that stand-off on the eve of the Helsinki Games. Nowhere. Not a word.

The incident's absence is not just curious. It is revealing. In both cases, there are good reasons for the omission. One of the books was written in English; the other is a translation from Czech. One can be assumed to have left out the episode because it was not widely known in the West; the other because, under Communism, it was unmentionable. Yet it happened. Indeed, it is arguably one of the more significant episodes not just in Zátopek's life but in the history of sport. If that seems a bold claim, consider what it involved. First, the stature of the main protagonist: Emil Zátopek, a colossus of athletics who from the late 1940s to the mid-1950s bestrode his discipline as no other runner has ever done. Three of his Olympic golds were won at the same Games, in the space of eight days, in a distance-running grand slam that remains unique. He set eighteen world records, won five Olympic medals and, in the words of one otherwise staid official Olympic Games report, 'completely upset all previous notions of the limits of human endurance'. He did so by pioneering approaches to training that had hitherto been unthinkable, and that remain the basis of most serious distance-running training today. And he achieved all this with a grace and generosity of spirit that transcended sport.

For those too young to remember, this last point is easily overlooked. Zátopek was celebrated, globally, not just as an astounding athlete but as a shining ideal. This was a man from a small country, a simple soldier of austere habits, who achieved sporting heights few had dreamed of through a simple formula: the cheerful acceptance and mastery of pain. This was the man who, it was said, trained in army boots, in the snow, or jogged on the spot while on sentry duty, or ran carrying his wife on his back; a man whose training sessions were so intense that experts considered them all but suicidal. This was an athlete who was not just fast but heroically tough. A hard man, but also a man of infectious warmth and humour. A man who never gave up, never complained, and never forgot that, in words that will always be associated with his name: 'Great is the victory, but greater still is the friendship.'

His fellow Olympians worshipped him. The Englishman Gordon Pirie praised his 'magnificent character'; the Frenchman Alain Mimoun called him 'a saint'; Fred Wilt, the American, called him 'perhaps the most humble, friendly and popular athlete in modern times'; Ron Clarke, the Australian, said: 'There is not, and never was, a greater man than Emil Zátopek.'

Ordinary athletics fans were scarcely less enthusiastic. The Helsinki Olympics were supposed to be the Games of the Cold War, with two separate athletes' villages embodying humanity's bitter and terrifying ideological division. Zátopek did more than anyone to turn them, by sheer force of personality, into the Games of

Reconciliation, where athletes and spectators of all nations came together and celebrated their common humanity. They did so largely through celebrating him: his genius, his tenacity, his life-affirming exuberance.

Yet it almost never happened. Just over a week before the opening ceremony, after four years of unimaginably intense preparation, knowing that he was poised to make sporting history and would never get a better chance to do so, Emil Zátopek risked losing it all. He had worked all his life for this moment and now, for the sake of a friend, he was prepared to throw it all away.

I can think of only one other example of an athlete of such stature gambling so much – and, in doing so, showing moral greatness to match his physical gifts. That was when Muhammad Ali refused to be inducted into the US armed forces in 1967, during the Vietnam War. Like Zátopek, Ali was not just a talented athlete but one of breathtaking, sport-redefining genius – and huge personal charisma. Like Zátopek in 1952, Ali was at his physical peak when he took his stand. In taking it, he risked not just punishment and disgrace but also, most painfully, the loss of the best years of his sporting life. Ali took his gamble and, in sporting terms, lost. By the time he had won his appeal against his conviction for draft evasion and was allowed back into the ring, in 1971, his best years were behind him.

Zátopek's gamble came off; but it was no less a reckless one for that, and it is arguable that he paid a heavy price for it later, in 1968, when he, like Ali, defied a superpower and lost. If it hadn't worked – if the Communist authorities had called his bluff and condemned him to hard labour in the uranium mines instead of caving in at the last minute and sending him, with Jungwirth, to Helsinki – then he too would have forfeited his golden years: the years of miraculous achievement on which his claim to sporting immortality is founded. But whereas Ali's sacrifice is central to his legend, and is celebrated in countless books, films and documentaries, Zátopek's stand is forgotten; or, more accurately, lost – like the plan for 'exemplary punishment of Captain Zátopek' that was drawn up by officials as Zátopek and Jungwirth were taking off for Helsinki on a later plane, then hastily destroyed when news came back that Zátopek had just won his third gold medal.

How could that happen? As the Wizz Air plane finally heaves itself into the night sky, the riddle preys on my mind. How can a moment like that – a landmark in the history of sporting heroism – slip from collective memory?

In one sense, it hasn't. Most hard-core Zátopek fans are aware of it. But that just makes the paradox more perplexing. How can an event be both known and unknown? The answer, when I arrive at it, surprises me. Zátopek's whole life is both known and unknown, and for the same reason.

He was, for two decades in the mid-twentieth century, the most celebrated sportsman on earth. Even now, he remains exceptionally honoured, with his own statue (one of only four) outside the official Olympic museum in Lausanne. *Runner's World* named him the greatest runner of all time – over any distance – as recently as 2013. Yet the facts of his life as a human being are obscured, not just by barriers of time, language and ideology but, above all, by myth.

Every running enthusiast over a certain age knows something about Zátopek – or thinks they do. But much of it is no more than hearsay: legends and half-truths endlessly recycled and re-embroidered. Many of the most famous tales are simply false. Even those of us who idolise him – who see him, as I do, as a kind of patron saint of running – are liable to find, on closer inspection, that we know far less about him than we think.

Those who knew him best grow older and fewer in number each year. Old memories play tricks; as do the everyday habits of dissembling and concealment that four decades of Communist tyranny ingrained into most Czechoslovak lives, including Zátopek's. Primary sources, including official ones, cannot be assumed to be trustworthy; some tell outright lies. The rest is a sea of biographical confusion, in which solid facts can barely be discerned from the froth of rumour in which they float. So the truth dissolves, slowly. The legends persist: wonderful in their way but insubstantial, because they can be endlessly reinvented.

The bare facts of Zátopek's running are preserved in official archives. But the real worth of his victories is lost on all but his oldest admirers. As for his records: his fastest time for 10,000m would have earned him twenty-fourth place in the 2012 Olympics. Times and trophies quickly lose their power to excite. It is the human side of Zátopek's story that is still capable of brightening and energising lives, six decades after his prime and a decade and a half after his death. That is the story that matters. And that, despite all the millions of words that have been written about him, is slipping away.

Yet the reality of Emil Zátopek's life – the scarcely believable tale of his rise, fall and unfinished rehabilitation – is too important to be allowed to vanish. He was not just an Olympic immortal: he was a magnificent, if flawed, human being, who lit up the post-war world with the warmth of his personality during some of the chilliest chapters of modern history. His story was one of tragedy as well as glory, and his struggles were intricately interwoven with the troubled history of Europe itself. He was also, as the French writer Pierre Magnan pointed out, 'a man who ran like us' – an athlete who had to labour for his achievements as painfully as the rest of us do. In the words of the great coach Percy Cerutty, who considered him 'the most epoch-shattering athlete of this age', he 'earned, and won for himself, every inch of a very hard road'. Yet such was the greatness of Zátopek's heart that he found time even in the heat of his most agonising battles to relate to his rivals as fellow human beings; to make gestures of friendship and sportsmanship and playfulness that echo through the ages. He was magnificent in his running, but more magnificent still in his instinctive use of running as a medium for friendship. If ever an athlete's life was worthy of being preserved in print, it is his.

By the time I notice the orange lights of Luton through the aeroplane window, scattered like broken beads across the cold blackness below, I have made a resolution. I will not let his story dissolve any further. I will return to Emil Zátopek's homeland and try, as tirelessly as he used to train, to discover and record his true story. It is a daunting challenge. It was all a long time ago – in a faraway country of which I, like most Westerners, know little.

Much of the truth was concealed even then. But I must try, whatever the difficulties – because he deserves it.

Contemplating the task ahead, I feel an ache of apprehension deep in my stomach: the kind of fear you feel just before beginning a long-distance race. I feel, in short, a little like one of the forty-five men who stood with Emil Zátopek on the starting line of the Olympic marathon in Melbourne on 1 December 1956. It was one of those oven-hot days when marathon-running seems not just foolhardy but dangerous. Emil was past his best by then and, to make things worse, was not fully fit and was still recovering from injury. He looked around with a grim smile.

'Men,' he said, 'today we die a little.'

Then, still smiling, he began to run.

1

'Zá-to-pek! Zá-to-pek!'

Let us start at the summit: the golden minutes for which all his previous struggles can be seen as preparation, and from which all that followed might be seen as a descent. It is around 5.50 p.m., on 27 July 1952. The streets of Helsinki's Töölö district are buzzing, the pavements packed with excited spectators, chattering and cheering.

Some have been there all afternoon, revelling in the party atmosphere and the chance to see history made. The weather has been kind: still but not stifling. In the Olympic stadium, off Hammarskjöldintie, 68,700 people are buzzing too, their attention focused not on the track – where the 4 x 400m relay has recently finished – but on a huge electronic scoreboard which is providing periodic updates on the times and positions of the leading runners in the final event of the XVth Olympic Games: the marathon. The latest (and last) bulletin indicates that, with just over two kilometres to go, he is two and a quarter minutes ahead of his nearest rival.

For the next nine minutes or so, only those lucky enough to have good vantage points in the street really know what is going on. The rest fall back on rumour and imagination. But there does not seem to be a single person watching, in the stadium or out on the streets, who hopes for any outcome other than this: that Emil Zátopek should keep going for a few more minutes, all the way to the end.

The unanimity is startling. Sixty-nine different nations have sent athletes to the Games, and most have sent spectators too, although the majority of those watching are Finnish. Yet somehow everyone wants the Czechoslovak to win.

The unanimity is all the more startling when you consider the context. The world is divided, dangerously so, by an ideological iron curtain, still quite new, that stretches from the Baltic to the Adriatic. Two superpowers, one led by an increasingly deranged Josef Stalin, glower at one another across it. Helsinki has taken the unusual step of providing the 4,955 competing athletes with two distinct Olympic villages to reflect this divide: one for the Communist bloc and the other for the rest. George Orwell's line about sport being 'war minus the shooting' has rarely felt more apt.

Yet somehow, after two weeks of competition, it is ending with this: sports lovers of countless races, creeds and political convictions coming together in one joyous family, to celebrate the achievements and personality of a single extraordinary athlete.

It is not all Zátopek's doing. There have been gestures of goodwill from other athletes whose youthful instinct to fraternise has proved too strong for the ideological taboos that are supposed to restrain them. But somehow Zátopek has come to embody the idea that these Games are a celebration of our common humanity. Rumours about him have been slipping out all fortnight, not just about his sensational racing and insane training routines but also about his warmth, his sportsmanship, his spontaneous generosity. He is said to have given up his bed, the night before one of his big races, to a visiting Australian with nowhere to sleep. He gave his socks to his English rival Gordon Pirie. He shares his training secrets with anyone who cares to ask. His gregariousness has prompted him to learn half a dozen languages – some say more.

His public utterances have a wit that belies Western stereotypes of robotic Communist drones. On the track, he radiates decency and charm. He talks to rivals, offers pats of encouragement, takes his turn in the lead even when it is not in his interests to do so.

Yet somehow he has also found the steel not just to win but to win emphatically – some would say majestically. In the past eight days he has already won two Olympic golds, achieving the elusive distance-running double of winning both the 5,000 and the 10,000m. And now he is minutes away from completing a treble which everyone watching must realise will almost certainly never be achieved again – assuming that it can be achieved even once.

That is the history the crowds have come to witness. It is the biggest challenge of Zátopek's life, and it seems as though most of the world is holding its breath, willing him to succeed.

The odd thing is, the man who has elicited this unprecedented groundswell of goodwill is not some godlike being who skims over the ground with easy grace. He is small and a little ungainly. He has wide shoulders, a furrowed brow and an insect-like way of sticking out his elbows, especially the right one. A receding hairline makes him look older than his twenty-nine years.

As for his running style, he makes such a meal of it that people have been commenting on it for years: the way he grimaces as he runs, rolls his head, sticks out his tongue, claws at the air, clutches at his chest with his left hand, sometimes even seeming to swing his shoulders as he runs. Sportswriters love him for this, as it provides an excuse for some enjoyable phrase-making: 'He runs like a man who has just been stabbed in the heart'; '. . . as if there was a scorpion in each shoe'; '. . . as if tortured by internal demons'; '. . . as if he might be having a fit'; '. . . like a man wrestling with an octopus on a conveyor belt'. He is used to such criticisms, and has often laughed them off: 'I am not talented enough to run and smile at the same time.'

Those who understand such matters will point to the contrasting smoothness of his movements below the waist: the metronomic efficiency of his short, fast strides. None the less, it is hard to see how his upper writhings can be helping him. In fact, if appearances were all, he would be a laughing stock: an early precursor of such celebrated Olympic no-hopers as Eddie the Eagle and Eric the Eel.

But over the past week he has shown beyond all possible doubt that appearances are not everything. He is living, thrilling proof that what really matters is what is inside: the blazing spirit that allows a man, flesh and blood like the rest of us, to challenge the accepted limits of human aspiration.

This is, by the way, the first time he has ever run a marathon.

If that seems improbable now, it seemed improbable then. That's not to say no one expected him to be leading at this stage. His admirers believe that anything is possible where Emil is concerned. But there is something awe-inspiring about the fact that he is even trying. The audacity of the man: that is part of his greatness.

A flame of fresh information blows its way up Vauhtitie, and then round the corner into Hammarskjöldintie, gathering in intensity as it spreads. Zátopek is still leading; his lead is growing; he is almost in the stadium; he is coming.

Then, behind the flame, comes the roar of cheering – and, beyond that, the man himself.

Step by painful step, he drives himself forward to the stadium tunnel, vanishes, and then, to a longed-for fanfare of trumpets, emerges inside the arena, leaning almost forty-five degrees as he turns on to the track to minimise loss of momentum. The eruption of sound threatens to blow the skeletal runner off his feet. Nearly 70,000 people are standing, ecstatic, bellowing their approval; and the roar finally resolves itself into a chant in spine-chilling unison: 'Zá-to-pek! Zá-to-pek! Zá-to-pek!'

His grimacing face looks more agonised than ever. His sodden red vest clings to the outside of his shorts. His eyes seem glazed; his jaw is clenched. He looks tired: tired and empty as death. Every step seems a struggle – not in the sportswriters' sense but in a real, palpably excruciating way. You can almost feel the jarring in his battered legs as his thinly shod feet pound against the track. His whole body seems to be crying out: when will this stop? Yet not for one moment does he relax his rhythm.

The number of Czechoslovaks in the stadium can be counted in dozens. Yet each spectator is urging Emil Zátopek on with the fervour we usually reserve for our own most cherished national heroes. Among them are Paavo Nurmi and Hannes Kolehmainen, the Finnish founding fathers of modern distance running, and – although perhaps cheering with a shade less enthusiasm than most – the British marathon world record holder and pre-race favourite, Jim Peters, who was brought back to the stadium in the press coach after dropping out with six miles to go.

'Zá-to-pek! Zá-to-pek!' Emil could not slow down his rhythm if he wanted to. There may never before have been a moment when people from so many different nations have come together in such a joyous celebration of sporting achievement. One of them, Juan Antonio Samaranch, a future president of the International Olympic Committee, will still be talking about it half a century later: 'At that moment, I understood what the Olympic spirit means.' But for a British journalist, J. Armour Milne, even that is not enough: 'All of us shared the common conviction that we were witnessing the greatest happening in athletics history.'

As he crosses the line, the gaunt runner can just manage a smile: curiously boyish in its transparent relief. He waves away the photographers, hobbles off the track, sits on the ground and removes his shoes from his bloodied feet. For a moment he seems overwhelmed, oblivious to the fact that he has not only achieved an all but impossible third gold but also slashed more than six minutes off the Olympic record – the third record he has broken in eight days. Then he is back on his feet, shuffling towards the stands to be kissed tenderly on the mouth by the gold medal winner in the women's javelin – who also happens to be his wife. Someone gives him an apple, which he gobbles greedily. Then he waits at the finishing line to offer congratulations and slices of orange to his fellow runners, the first of whom arrives more than two and a half minutes behind the winner – and five of whom have, like Zátopek, broken the previous Olympic record.

Minutes later, the Jamaican 4 x 400m relay team, who not long before set their own Olympic record, pick Zátopek up and chair him around the stadium on a lap of honour without parallel in Olympic history. And then, some time afterwards, Zátopek is standing on the winner's rostrum, listening to the Czechoslovak national anthem being played in his honour for the third time in eight days.

The final notes melt into applause. Zátopek congratulates his fellow medallists and then embarks on a weary, joyful lap of honour. He can hear tens of thousands of Finns calling him by their own special name for him, 'Satu Peka' – except that this time they are chanting '*Näkemiin, Satu Peka*'. He has taught himself enough Finnish to know what this means. They are saying goodbye.

And Emil Zátopek, basking in the world's adulation after pulling off the greatest feat in the history of distance running, feels suddenly overwhelmingly sad, because—

But to understand that, you need to know how Emil got there.

2

The Kopřivnice kid

Let us start again, at the beginning, in Kopřivnice, a small industrial town on what is now the eastern edge of the Czech Republic.

Back then, in 1922, it was Czechoslovakia – bang in the middle of it; four years earlier it had been part of the Austro-Hungarian Empire. Those who lived in the town thought of themselves as Moravians. They still do.

It's quieter today than it was then. Twentieth-century Kopřivnice was dominated by the factory of central Europe's premier car manufacturer, Tatra, which generated employment, pollution and noise in increasing measures as the century progressed (but has since declined).

František and Anežka Zátopek came here in 1922, drawn by the factory's magnetism from the nearby village of Zašová. They were in their early forties, with four children to feed – Jaroš, Marie, František junior (Franta) and Bohumil (Bohuš) – and barely enough money to do so. (Their eldest daughter, Ludmila – born out of wedlock and referred to, if at all, as an 'aunt' – was married and living in Brno; their first son, Josef, had died in an ice-skating accident at the age of ten.) František, a carpenter and cabinetmaker, was a founder member of a housing co-operative, with whom he built a semi-detached house on the northern edge of town: one of four such houses at the bottom of 1 Května Street ('1 May Street'). Each had a decent-sized patch of land for livestock and fruit trees.

Perhaps it seemed like a time for new beginnings. Czechoslovakia itself was new, created from the ruins of the First World War in a spirit of democratic idealism. Its founding fathers believed passionately in national self-determination and social inclusion. The economy seemed healthy, and if the hard-pressed Moravian working classes had yet to feel the benefits, there was at least hope for the future.

The Zátopek children had barely settled in when Anežka gave birth to her seventh child, Emil Ferdinand, on a bed in the corner of the kitchen that doubled up as František's workshop. It was 19 September 1922. An eighth, Jiří, would follow two years later.

The extra mouths strained the family finances. Anežka had long since given up her old job as a labourer in the brick factory. František earned what he could at the Tatra factory – wood was still an important component of cars' bodywork – and topped up his wages with private commissions, making furniture. This kept him busy but didn't make him rich. There was food on the table, but not always much, and Emil grew up with a yearning for a full stomach that never quite left him. Czech families traditionally celebrate Christmas by dining on carp. The Zátopeks made do with cheap smoked fish, while a present might be no more than a piece of fruit picked from the garden and wrapped.

Emil, writing about his childhood in later life, made light of the poverty. The way he told it, the overcrowded house was a place of cheerful chaos. Names were muddled up; children queued for breakfast 'like a factory canteen'; soap stung their eyes as they filed past their mother for the weekly wash. But he never entirely forgot the hunger and insecurity, and his adult worldview would reflect this.

As often happens in large families, not all the siblings were close, emotionally or in age. Jiří was Emil's nearest ally. But weight of numbers left the younger brothers little choice but to be, at least, gregarious. Emil grew used to living in a group, mostly among people bigger, stronger and more dominant than him.

Surviving grandchildren and friends remember the Zátopek household as a stable, loving, disciplined one. Anežka was known for her skill with herbal remedies, and for her compassion for the sick: 'limitlessly loving' was how one former neighbour remembered her. One grandchild – Jiří's daughter Dana – spoke fondly of the special hiding place where, when funds permitted, Anežka kept chocolate treats for small visitors. 'She was so kind,' Dana told me. 'She was always working, always smiling, always trying to look after her children.'

František was more intimidating: a man of firm principle whose efforts to instil discipline in his children once caused Anežka to burn the leather belt with which he had just thrashed one of them. (He subsequently used his wooden carpenter's ruler.) But he also had a kindly, twinkling side, tweaking noses in jest or inviting small children to light his long pipe and sip the froth on his beer. Emil was devoted to him. The grandchildren knew him as 'beardy grandpa' – even when his beard had become a mere moustache – so Anežka, logically, was 'beardy grandma'. The couple's greatest pleasure was to gather the whole family round to sing Moravian folk songs. Emil continued to sing them all his life.

The garden was scarcely less packed than the house, with goats, hens and geese jostling for space among trees and beehives. Children were expected to do their bit for animal husbandry, and would get into trouble for failing to do so. Emil once allowed the goats to get stuck in the clay of a nearby brick-making site ('It was Bohuš's idea' was his excuse), and he was beaten at least once for helping himself to fruit. But the world beyond was, or seemed, a benign place. There were streets and fields to play in; they could swim in the River Lubina (notwithstanding the raw sewage that flowed into it a mile upstream); and the foothills of the Beskyd Mountains were near enough for occasional hiking adventures.

The children were discouraged from taking part in sport, especially the new craze of football: the risk of wearing out shoes and clothes was too great, while any spare energy would be better spent, in Mr Zátopek's view, working in the smallholding. They played anyway – 'with more passion than those who were allowed to', according to Emil, who often played football barefoot. But they knew where their priorities were supposed to lie, and in one crunch match, against a tough team of older boys from the local German school, Emil deserted the team shortly after half-time when the sounding of the Tatra factory hooter reminded him that he had forgotten to feed the bees. His best friend, Jaromír Konůpka, who was captain of the team ('I owned the football,' Konůpka explained), didn't speak to him for a week.

But Mr Zátopek had a point. As the hopeful 1920s faded into the grim 1930s, home-grown food became a vital part of the family's subsistence. The Great Depression sucked the life from Europe's economy, and Kopřivnice did not escape. Tatra workers who kept their jobs faced lower wages, and less job security. For a long time, Emil's brother Jaroš couldn't find work at all. When he finally did, his clumsiness as a driver resulted in an accident and a ruinous damages claim; in despair, he took his own life. Emil was about seven at the time; and the terrible event became another subject that was never referred to in the Zátopek household. The family was no less scarred as a result. Anežka's response was to become even more solicitous – some would say fussy – about her surviving sons' welfare. František took the more practical step of joining Czechoslovakia's fledgling Communist Party.

This didn't prevent him from being an upstanding member of the community. The Party was more concerned with opposing fascism than with active subversion in those days, and most of its 60,000 members did no more than pay their subscriptions. František was secretary of the local federation of allotment holders and breeders of rabbits and small farm animals; later, he would be chairman of the Kopřivnice Beekeeping Association. Politically, he was more of a trade unionist than a revolutionary: he had been active in the bitter struggle to establish an eight-hour working day at Tatra but was otherwise best known for collecting union fees from fellow workers. He was not allowed to do this at the factory but had to tramp from home to home instead. Emil often accompanied him.

František also took his children to meetings of the Federation of Proletarian Education (FPT) – later superseded by the slightly less radical Workers' Association of Physical Education (DTJ). These offered opportunities for physical education for workers' children, usually in a specially kitted-out room in the Amerika pub, where Emil became adept at gymnastic tricks such as somersaults and headstands.

But that was about the limit of his early sporting prowess. He was energetic – 'the biggest fidget in the class', according to one schoolfriend – and enjoyed running around, a trait which at least one teacher exploited by using him as an errand boy. But he was puny and uncoordinated: by conventional measures of masculinity, he was a weakling – especially after a neglected bout of appendicitis, when he was eight, necessitated an extended stay in hospital. In football, he just ran around, enthusiastically but uselessly. He didn't get into fights, except occasionally with Jiří, while his tactic of screaming loud and early to escape his father's beatings earned him the nickname 'Emil the cry-baby'.

Early photographs show a small, plump-cheeked boy, with large ears and narrow shoulders combining to make his head look unusually wide. There is nothing athletic about his appearance: just an intent, curious, slightly anxious expression, as if he were trying to understand something. But one school picture, taken when Emil was six, has an interesting detail. Emil, sitting cross-legged in the front row, is the only child without shoes – although his friends have arranged their legs in such a way as to conceal, almost, Emil's bare feet.

You would never have put him down as a future Olympian. Yet somehow, even then, he seems to have had an air of being special. Jiří, speaking two years after Emil's death, claimed, without resentment, that Emil was his parents' favourite. 'Emil was the smartest one. If someone did something wrong, it had to be investigated. But if it turned out that it was Emil who did it, everything was all right.' Jiří's son – also called Jiří – proudly drew my attention to the family tradition that Emil was never stung by bees. 'When my grandfather wanted something taken out of a hive, he didn't need special clothing. He just got Emil to do it.'

Young Jiří – a big, moustachioed, bear-like man of middle age who lives in the neighbouring village of Štramberk – seemed to glow with affection when he talked about his uncle. It would not be the last time I would notice such animation in those who were sharing memories of Emil with me.

Milan Špaček, a classmate who became a champion skier, spoke laughingly about Emil's reckless streak. He once saw him rescued from drowning, after braving a water-filled gravel pit without having learnt to swim. Later, Emil proved better than anyone at swimming underwater: 'He could hold his breath longer, and he was not so afraid of drowning as the rest of us.'

Jaromír Konůpka, a retired draughtsman who remained close to Emil all his life, also laughed at the thought of his friend's recklessness. He particularly enjoyed the memory of a school expedition to the Beskyds when Emil was thirteen. The pupils stayed in a hostel on Bílý Kříž, but were kept awake by the snoring of a much older boy, Pepa Štefků. Around dawn, Emil decided to solve the problem by – for some reason – emptying an entire jar of salt into Pepa's mouth. Pepa woke up and leapt out of bed in fury. Emil, wearing only his underpants, jumped out of the window in the nick of time; Pepa pursued him via the door. 'He had found a big stick and was shouting that he would "kill that bastard". First they ran around the meadow, then we saw them in the forest . . .' Konůpka genuinely seemed to think that murder had been a possibility – but Emil had the stamina to escape unscathed.

Konůpka said that the key to Emil's youthful character could be found in a single statement: 'I don't want to do it, but if I have to, then I'm going to show you!' Passed over at the age of ten for a starring clown's role in the DTJ's Christmas play, *The Circus Comes to Town*, Emil stole the show by giving the gymnastics performance of a lifetime in his bit part as a monkey. Another time, forced to do algebra against his will ('Please, sir, why are we learning such drivel as *a+b* squared when we are never going to need it in life?'), Emil saved face by swotting up furiously and confusing the teacher by coming top in a test for which he had originally refused to study.

Then there was the 'essay strike', which Emil organised at the municipal school, to which he had progressed at the age of eleven. The class were told to write on the theme: '*Komu se nelení, tomu se zelení*' (literally, 'He who is not lazy, gets the greens'). Emil declared the subject 'stupid' and, perhaps inspired by his father's political activities, persuaded around half the class to refuse to write it. The protest lasted several days. The inevitable climbdown was followed, ignominiously, by a Saturday spent writing the essay anyway. Emil exacted partial revenge by writing an enormously long one – five large pages of tiny script – which took his teacher the best part of Sunday to mark. Perhaps the last laugh was hers, though, because the proverb's message stayed with him for the rest of his life.

But there was more to the young Emil than mere stubbornness: there was also a startling independence of thought – a sense that things didn't necessarily have to be as they were. Notwithstanding the view of one of his teachers, Ladislav Buček, that: 'You'll never amount to anything in life', Emil seemed to feel that almost anything might be possible. Naturally left-handed, he taught himself to be right-handed – and if that could be changed, what couldn't? One much-repeated tale describes how he allowed a mosquito to bite him on the hand. Instead of brushing it off, he watched it closely, observing how it sucked up his blood. He wanted to learn. On another occasion, he is said to have stolen a wooden cup from a miserly stall-keeper at the market: not because he wanted it but because he wanted to see if he could evade the old man's obsessive security measures. Ota Pavel, the author and journalist who later became Emil's good friend, claimed that the young Zátopek's defining characteristic was that 'he tried everything differently'.

Emil's parents cherished hopes that he, perhaps alone among their children, might find a future beyond the Tatra factory. František thought that Emil could become a teacher, although it was far from clear how the fees for training college could be paid. Education had been in short supply when he and Anežka were growing up. Anežka had been taken out of school early so that she could be sent out to work. (The local priest was bribed to falsify her birth certificate.) But now, in the new Czechoslovakia, it was not unrealistic to dream that a bright, poor child might use education as an escape route to better things, and Kopřivnice was as good a place as any to do so.

Emil seems to have made the most of his nine years of free schooling. He was not particularly diligent, but he was bright, with unusual powers of memory. It was often noted by those who knew him in later life that he appeared to remember every single thing he was taught as a schoolboy.

When his class were told to memorise three verses from Karel Havlíček Borovský's poem, 'Král Lávra', Emil learnt all thirty-seven. He expected to be applauded when he recited them in front of his class. Instead, his classmates looked dubious – presumably fearing that he was making them look bad – while the teacher was simply stunned.

Emil would grow used to such dubious looks. They were the price to be paid for what would become a lifelong habit of doing things his own way. As a teenager, though, what he really craved (according to friends such as Ota Pavel) was the kind of peer approval that is given not to poetry reciters but to those who excel on the sports field; the only problem being that Emil didn't.

Yet there was one occasion when he did discover what it meant to bathe in sporting glory. A dozen local children decided to organise a race. It was an endurance race, or so they called it, around the block which included the Zátopeks' home. The rectangular circuit was about a kilometre in total; the idea was to go round it as many times as possible. They set off, old and young all jumbled up.

Most stopped after two or three laps; a few managed six or seven. But Emil, despite being by no means the eldest, just carried on running, lap after lap after lap.

The afternoon wore on, and still he kept padding along. The other boys applauded and then, as the number of laps reached double figures, grew bored. Some went home; others started a card game on the side of the road. Emil kept running, on and on as the afternoon faded to evening, until no one could keep track of how many laps he had run – thirty? forty? – and he could scarcely stand. Even his elder brothers joined in the congratulations. Emil considered this last detail so remarkable that he cherished the memory decades later.

The route is still there. Jog around it, as I did on a warm autumn afternoon, and you may share my sense that there is something mesmerising about the alternation of views from the quiet streets. In three directions, there are empty skies, with tree-topped hills occasionally appearing on the horizons between the low rooftops. But the south-western corner of the circuit is dominated by the railway and the giant chimneys – presumably belching smoke in Emil's day – of the Tatra factory.

It is fanciful to speculate that such views played any part in his deliberations about what to do when his schooling came to an end; yet they offer a neat analogy for the choice he faced. He could remain in Kopřivnice, work as a labourer for Tatra and accept the default fate that his family circumstances had prepared for him. Or he could set his sights on more distant, adventurous horizons.

Emil's brothers would all remain in Kopřivnice. But by the time Emil left municipal school, Tatra was laying off, not hiring. František, despite the financial obstacles, still hoped that Emil would become a teacher. Yet his son's application to the teacher training college in the neighbouring town of Příbor was rejected. He had achieved the necessary grades but, he was told, his ear for music wasn't good enough. This may have been a polite way of saying that the sons of impoverished carpenters were still unwelcome in the teaching profession; but it is also true that Emil's sense of pitch was less perfect than he liked to think. He was advised that, if he chose to stay on at school for another year and repeat the final grade, he would be allowed to apply again. Emil gave short shrift to the idea, saying that he wasn't stupid enough to repeat a class from which he had already graduated with honours.

Instead, following the example and advice of a friend's older brother, he took matters into his own hands. In the late summer of 1937, several weeks short of his fifteenth birthday, he caught a train to the city of Zlín, forty-five miles to the south-west, to seek his fortune.

3

Shoemaking

There was something miraculous about Zlín. For six centuries it had been just another anonymous central European town, on the bottom edge of Moravia, Then, in the four decades before Emil's arrival, it had been transformed by the crazed genius of one family: the Baťas.

A cobbler's son, Tomáš Baťa set up a small shoemaking company with his brother and sister when he was eighteen. It was 1894. Within a year the business was technically bankrupt. Tomáš's brother left to do military service, while Tomáš wrestled with the problem of not being able to afford to buy leather. Desperate, he started making shoes with canvas uppers instead. The innovation proved an instant bestseller. Tomáš Baťa built a small factory in Zlín. The business grew, and with it his ambition. He took time out to work in a factory in America, studying the production-line methods pioneered by Henry Ford. By 1912, back in Zlín, he had more than six hundred employees.

But mass production was just part of his vision. The same year, he began to build houses and flats for his workers. He believed that employees with a stake in a company's prosperity were more productive than those who were merely exploited. When the First World War broke out, he somehow obtained an exclusive contract to provide the Austro-Hungarian army with shoes. The company's size increased exponentially: by 1918 it employed 6,000 people. More or less the entire population of Zlín escaped conscription in order to meet demand.

By 1923 Tomáš Baťa was mayor of Zlín. There was a company library, a company kindergarten, a sports club, a cinema. Home-building expanded into town-planning, in conscious imitation of the British idea of the garden city. Cutting-edge architects such as František Gahura and Vladimír Karfík – and, later, Le Corbusier – were hired to ensure that this workers' utopia was created along the most rational lines. Everything was built in the same materials – mainly red brick and glass – and to similar, uniform dimensions, based on 6.15 x 6.15m modules.

In 1924, profit-sharing was introduced. In 1925, the Baťa School of Work was founded, initially as a shoemakers' apprentice school but before long as an establishment offering a secondary education to up to 1,500 students a year. The students financed themselves, working in the factory to cover the cost of their board and lodging before studying at night. The more they learnt, the more useful they were as employees. As Baťa put it: 'Every penny spent on our schools will pay back many times.'

Tomáš Baťa died in 1932. Thanks to his bold pricing policies, Baťa employees had escaped the worst of the Great Depression. The population of Zlín had increased tenfold in three decades – and well over half of the 26,350 inhabitants were Baťa employees. Tomáš's brother, Jan Antonín, continued the growth, and the all-encompassing – some would say overbearing – paternalism. When Emil arrived, the Baťa group employed 65,000 people worldwide, with dozens of factories and thousands of stores across Europe, America and Asia. A new headquarters, Building 21, was approaching completion in the centre of Zlín, with a tower – Czechoslovakia's tallest – whose most notable feature would be Jan Antonín Baťa's office-cum-elevator, which would allow him to keep watch on his staff on whichever of the sixteen floors he chose.

To capitalists, Baťa represented the ideal of private enterprise: utopian, innovative, constructive and as beneficial to workers as to investors. To the Communists who nationalised the company after the Second World War, the same facts had a different meaning. The company used its paternalism as a tool for exercising total control over workers' lives, turning them into units of productivity rather than autonomous human beings. Baťa's dominance of Zlín was unhealthy. It owned everything, including the police force, and anyone deemed subversive or insufficiently productive – including the old or unemployed – was liable to find themselves unwelcome in the city. The Baťa intelligence service, thinly disguised as the personnel department, pried shamelessly into everything. Zlín was, by one analysis, 'a totalitarian town'.

But two things were beyond debate. For young, poor Czechoslovaks seeking to make something of their lives from nothing, Zlín was an attractive proposition. And, if you did go to work in Zlín, you belonged to Baťa.

If Emil had been unaware of this last fact when his application to the School of Work was accepted in July 1937, it was rapidly made clear to him when he arrived that autumn. He was housed in a dormitory building on a hillside overlooking the town: the fourth of eight such buildings, which between them housed 6,000 students. The dormitory walls carried slogans such as 'The young eagles fly towards the sun' and 'Fight is the father of all'. There was a dormitory warden whose word was law. Morality was strictly enforced: bad language was punished with a fine, and young men were expected to sleep with their hands outside the bedclothes.

An alarm went off at 5.30 a.m., after which there were compulsory outdoor morning exercises. At 7 a.m., the apprentices began their shifts in the factory. These continued, barring a two-hour midday break, until 5 p.m. There was then an evening meal, followed by study until shortly before the 9 p.m. curfew. 'I always had to think for a while about where I was,' Emil claimed, 'because so many things in the boarding house were the same as in the factory.'

The first year's education was devoted to 'shoemaker's basic training'. More interesting subjects such as languages and science would come later. Meanwhile, there was the challenge of the factory work. Emil spent eight hours a day on the production line: initially 'ploughing' corrugations in crêpe soles but then, when he proved inept at this, putting lasts on to the conveyor belt: left, right, left, right, left, right, changing the sizes according to a strict plan. His workshop had to produce up to 2,400 pairs of shoes a day. If Emil faltered, the production line would falter too, and a red light would point the finger of blame. The midday break was often spent catching up.

For a fourteen-year-old boy, away from home for the first time, it must have been both overwhelming and disorienting. On one early visit home, Emil told his parents how exciting he found it all. Twenty years later he gave a starker account of the period: his new life seemed bleak, he wrote, and 'full of hustle and fear'. The camaraderie of the Kopřivnice streets had been replaced by adult anonymity, with thousands of ambitious students, steeped in Baťa's devil-take-the-hindmost ideology, and shouting overseers who were quick to remind grumblers that, for every student, there were ten unsuccessful applicants who would be only too pleased to take their place. 'I did not even have the courage to remember Kopřivnice, and the house and garden of my childhood, and my father's bees,' Emil wrote. And, like many an unhappy child away from home before and since, he kept the truth from his parents because 'I did not want . . . to make them grieve.'

On a wall of the factory, another of Tomáš Baťa's sayings was painted: 'There are 86,400 seconds in a day.' Perhaps little more need be said about Emil's first years in Zlín. Work, study, sleep; morning exercises and canteen meals: that was the sum of it. There was nothing for it but to conform. Emil did so, working unhappily but diligently; and learnt, if nothing else, some early lessons about the patient endurance of distress. Three times a year – Easter, summer and Christmas – he was allowed a brief visit home. The rest of the time he absorbed the Baťa philosophy that 'he who passes on to his co-worker a piece of work unfit to be continued cannot be considered an honest man.' A sense that hard work was the key to success became central to his being.

His excellent memory served him well in exams, which meant that, after the obligatory two years at the School of Work, he was able to progress to the next level of Baťa education: the Higher Industrial School. He was doing his daily shifts in the chemical research institute by then. The air was noxious, but the daily grind was a fraction less mindless. His evening studies, too, were beginning to stretch him more. If there still wasn't a great deal of joy in his life, it was better than the alternatives.

In the wider world, terrible events were afoot. While Emil studied and worked, a series of unthinkable catastrophes had befallen his country. First, soon after his sixteenth birthday, Kopřivnice had ceased to be part of Czechoslovakia – ceased, in fact, to be Kopřivnice at all. The town lay just inside an eastern tentacle of the Sudetenland, which was ceded to Nazi Germany in September 1938 under the Munich Agreement – whereby Britain and France abandoned their Czechoslovak allies to Hitler. Zlín remained part of Czechoslovakia, but the Zátopeks' home town was now part of the Third Reich, and reverted to its old German name, Nesseldorf.

Five months later, in March 1939, Nazi Germany invaded what remained of Czechoslovakia. The loss of the Sudetenland had rendered the country indefensible, and Hitler was in Prague within days. Slovakia, by prior arrangement, declared independence. The rest of the country became the German Protectorate of Bohemia and Moravia. Perhaps this was marginally preferable to being totally absorbed into Germany, but it soon became clear that the SS was in charge, and Jews, Communists, trade unionists and non-compliant students and journalists quickly felt the effects. (Emil's father, however, was not victimised: he had temporarily left the Party a few years earlier after a row with a local official.) Six months later, the world was at war – and thousands of young Czech men began to be forcibly deported to Germany to supply slave labour for the Third Reich. The Baťa factory was as good a place as anywhere to try to sit out the storm.

All Czech factories were required to put their production at the disposal of the Wehrmacht – and thus Baťa, for the second world war in succession, found itself supplying footwear for the soldiers of the Central Powers. Jan Antonín Baťa had fled to America; his employees and students just had to make the best of things. Radomír Luža, a resistance activist who worked briefly for Baťa while on the run from the Gestapo in 1942, later described how he watched all the workers of Zlín going to work and 'wondered why they were so eager to get to work to make boots for German feet . . . didn't they realise that they were co-operating with the Nazis . . .?' Some may have felt guilty that their jobs at Baťa guaranteed them better rations than the bulk of the Czech population (who had a daily allowance of about 1,600 calories each), but most will have been preoccupied with getting from one day to the next without being arrested or shot.

Even Luža conceded that 'no one could refuse to work, and whoever worked, worked for the Reich'. The factory was 'purged' by the Gestapo at least once, in February 1941, and everyone knew that the country was scattered with labour camps for those who refused to co-operate. Dozens of workers in other factories had already been shot – in Brno, in Plzeň, in Ostrava – while many more had been arrested or beaten for falling behind with output. Overt resistance would have been suicidal. Instead, with as much foot-dragging as they dared, the Baťa employees and apprentices continued to churn out shoes, while those who could continued their studies as well, watching the months slip past and hoping for better days ahead.

Such was the background when, in May 1941, one of the wardens, a Mr Linhart, issued an order for all able-bodied fourth-year students under his charge to take part in the race through the streets of Zlín that took place each year in honour of Tomáš Baťa. (Zlín's annual May Day celebrations would not have looked out of place in Moscow or Nuremberg.) Any enthusiasm that the young men in question might ordinarily have felt for such a challenge was negated by a general reluctance to do more than was absolutely necessary to please the company bosses; and Emil, at this stage in his life, was in any case not keen on sport.

According to Emil: 'The warden said, "On Sunday there is a race across Zlín. I am an athlete, and everybody from my group will run. Only those who are sick do not have to run."' Emil raised his hand and said, 'My knee hurts.' The warden was contemptuous and insisted on an examination by the company doctor, who – quite reasonably – declared Emil a malingerer. He was ordered to run.

Even then, on the morning of 15 May, Emil had one last try at wriggling out of it. He retired to the reading room with a chemistry book, hoping that his absence would not be noticed. It was. He was tracked down and escorted to the starting line on Tomáš Baťa Avenue.

He was eighteen. The next five minutes would set the path of his adult life.

The course measured 1,400m. There were around a hundred young men competing. Most set off vigorously, although many eased off once they were out of sight of the start. Some had friends waiting with coats around the first corner. The crowd of runners spread out – and Emil, having vaguely resolved that, if he was to run, he might as well do his best, found himself towards the front.

'The desire to win took over me,' he recalled many years later, 'and I ran with all my strength.' He could hear people cheering him on, and he began to imagine the cheers that might greet him if he won. He made himself breathe faster than usual, reasoning that his lungs needed extra oxygen; this is unlikely to have helped. As the finish approached, he weakened, and an experienced athlete, Honza Krupička, drew away. Emil came second.

It barely mattered. 'He's my boy!' shouted Mr Linhart, the hostel warden. 'He's from my group!' Friends rushed to congratulate Emil. Krupička joined them, and suggested to Emil that he should try training with the regular athletes in the sports stadium: 'You will see how you will improve.' Emil laughed this off: he had no intention of running again, he said. Yet there was something potent about this post-race euphoria. Describing the moment half a lifetime later, he wrote: 'I felt something then that I had wanted since childhood.'

The feeling was strong enough to encourage him to spend a few sessions training with Krupička and others in the stadium beside the power station. Then, a few weeks later, he was persuaded to race again, for the Baťa team in the Silver Reed championships for high school students, organised by *Lidové noviny* newspaper, in Brno.

Emil came second in the 1,500m, beating Krupička this time, and helping his team to victory. He later described it as a 'great joy' to do well in such a competition, 'with an official starter and official timekeepers.' His time, 4 minutes 20 seconds, sounds slow by today's standards but was impressive for a novice in 1941.

Winter came, and the visits to the stadium stopped. Emil assumed that his running career was over; work and studies once again dominated his life. The employment was not pleasant: some of the workshops were known as 'devil's islands' because of their foul air. But the chemistry studies interested him: Baťa took research and development seriously.

In the spring, some friends organised an athletics competition between two halls of residence. Emil, now living in Hostel No. 3, was urged to do his bit for the Higher Industrial School. 'It was not difficult to talk me into it,' he admitted.

He won both his races, at 1,500m and 3,000m, and the embers of his ambition were rekindled. That, he said, was when 'it was decided that I would stick with athletics permanently.' Perhaps more significantly, he made an impression on some of the more serious runners, members of the local athletics club, who were in the stadium to train. One of them, the famous Jan Haluza, invited him to run with him the following evening. Popularly known as 'Ali', Haluza was one of Czechoslovakia's leading athletes, a champion at 1,500m and cross-country. He had recently moved to Zlín, where he ran for the SK Baťa club and was beginning to transfer his expertise into coaching. Even Emil had heard of him. He accepted the invitation eagerly.

The next evening, Haluza took Emil through his paces on Zlín's 453m track. The session went badly, or so Emil thought. He felt that he was tensing up under the star's gaze. He had no idea what times he ran and was embarrassed to ask.

The next morning he was summoned from his 'devil's island' workplace to answer the telephone. It was Haluza, calling to encourage him to train again – and, perhaps, to compete for the club. Haluza also enquired after Emil's diet, sleeping patterns and general lifestyle – all of which, he explained, played an important part in a serious athlete's preparation. By one account, Emil was close to tears: it had been so long since anyone had shown any interest in his wellbeing.

It is tempting to say that things now began to look up for Emil, but that would be an overstatement. These were miserable times. In September 1941, Hitler appointed the monstrous Reinhard Heydrich as Reichsprotektor of Bohemia and Moravia, with a brief to suppress dissent and to exploit Czech resources more ruthlessly. SS oversight of activities in factories was stepped up. Back in what used to be Kopřivnice, meanwhile, anything could have been going on. Most of the time, Emil couldn't even be sure that his family were still alive. Emil had been able to make occasional visits – returning to Zlín on at least one occasion with a large food parcel from his mother – and some correspondence got through. But the channels of communication would soon be blocked.

On 27 May 1942 (less than two weeks after Emil had quietly won his second Baťa 'Race Through Zlín'), Heydrich was attacked in Prague by a British-trained team of Czechoslovak paratroopers. He died a week later. Grotesque reprisals followed. Entire villages were obliterated; thousands of men, women and children were slaughtered or packed off to concentration camps. And in Zlín, the iron rule – of the Gestapo and the Gestapo-approved Baťa management – became even more oppressive. Reports of arrests and executions featured regularly in the newspapers; the athlete and resistance activist Evžen Rošický, executed on 25 June, was perhaps the most prominent victim.

In this terrifying climate, evening sessions on the athletics track – a permitted but largely unsupervised activity – began to seem like a precious release for Emil: the only time he felt free. According to Haluza, 'No one had to force him to go to training. He would even have slept at the stadium. As soon as his work in the factory ended, he would come immediately to the track. He was never visibly tired and never lost his humour and optimism.' By another account, 'his tracksuit transformed him into a boisterous young man.' The resulting friendships saw him spending more time with a group of fellow running enthusiasts at Baťa who occupied Room No. 19 in Hostel No. 2.

Occupants of the dormitory included Jindřich Roudný, a future Olympic steeplechaser, and Jaroslav Přeček, a leading sprinter. The friends would train together, eat together or simply hang out together; they kept a notebook in the room, in which they would leave each other messages. Another book kept a record of swearing fines: one crown per curse. According to Roudný, some people found it easier to indicate anger by simply slapping a crown down on the table. (Not that they had many: most of their earnings went automatically into compulsory savings accounts.)

Emil was nicknamed Badger – possibly in reference to his prematurely receding hairline, which, when he was barely twenty, had begun to give his upper forehead the vertically striped effect of a badger. He was also known as Sonny, in tribute to his habit of tricking the cook, Jarda, into giving him left-overs earmarked for the janitor's dog, Sonny.

The friends discovered girls together, too. Nothing serious: this was 1942, and morals were strictly policed in Zlín. But Emil found that women were not immune to his charms. According to Jaroslav Přeček, he favoured girls who were able to bring him gifts of food, such as apples or cakes. 'He was always on the lookout for a girl who was from the butcher,' Přeček told a Czech TV documentary more than half a century later.

Emil's most lasting romantic relationship was with a serious-faced young woman called Jarmila Švehláková, with whom he exchanged letters. He seems to have told her that he loved her. By 1943, however, the relationship would cool. Emil told her that, on his teacher's advice, he had to avoid all distractions before his final exams at the Higher Industrial School. This meant that he could not see her for two months – which she took to mean that he didn't want to see her again at all. She was probably right. They would not meet again until after the war.

Meanwhile, Emil had been becoming increasingly consumed by a rival passion: for running. He cannot possibly have imagined the importance it would eventually assume for him. In the short term, however, it filled a gap, giving him something thrilling and immediate to live for.

Jan Haluza led him gently, teaching him the basic techniques of warming up, breathing and structuring a training session but also nudging him – without pushing him – into setting his sights ever higher. The result, as Haluza may have intended, was that Emil developed his own voracious hunger to improve. 'Emil was very inquisitive and always asking about things,' Haluza recalled towards the end of his life. 'He wanted to know about everything – feet, legs, how to place them on the ground, how to work the arms, how to hold the torso.' He would also experiment – for example, by varying the ratio of steps to breaths he took. Haluza considered Emil 'very teachable – at first maybe too much so. I had to calm him down.'

In races, there was no stopping him. At first, Emil and his trainer used to compete in the same events. On 18 July 1942 they raced over 3,000m in Zlín. Haluza won; Emil came second. The report in the next day's *Zlínské noviny* newspaper mentioned 'a wonderful performance by Zátopek'. Emil read it again and again, and kept walking happily around Zlín with the newspaper in his hand. Two weeks later, he came second in another race, this time at 1,500m, and earned another accolade – 'wonderful performance by Zátopek' – in the paper. He was then selected for the Zlín team that travelled to Prague to take part in a national 4 x 1,500m relay contest. Zlín not only won but set a new Czechoslovak record.

It was a cheering note on which to end the season, and Emil embarked on his winter training with a greater sense of purpose than the previous year. Most days he would run to the neighbouring village of Malenovice and back after work – a round trip of about eight kilometres. In very cold weather, he wore up to three tracksuits, one on top of the other. Once, he and his companions were mistaken for partisans; they fled into the night without waiting to see if the shouts of alarm came from civilians or soldiers. But the possible dangers of keeping fit seemed less significant in Emil's eyes than the benefits. It was thrillingly simple. The harder he trained, the faster he could run. And he wanted to run faster.

He ran for fun as well. Some attempted visits to Kopřivnice got him no further than Frenštát, on the Protectorate's border; so he stayed there instead, with his old schoolfriend Milan Špaček. Sometimes they went running together, on the trails of the nearby Javorník Beskyds, near Radhošť. Emil remembered from geography lessons that this was the true 'spine of Europe': a watershed dividing the Continent more permanently than any line the Nazis could arbitrarily impose. Water on the northern side ultimately found its way to the Baltic Sea; that on the south to the Danube and thence to the Black Sea. He and Špaček took childish delight in stopping to urinate on this spine. 'We would start peeing into the Black Sea, but we wouldn't finish, and then we would dash across and pee into the Baltic,' remembers Špaček. 'We were so foolish – we were proud that no one else had peed, while running, into both seas.'

Increasingly, however, Emil was running with more conventional targets in mind. In the spring of 1943, he was narrowly defeated by the great Tomáš Šalé in the Vítkovice Road Race. He also lost to Šalé over 1,500m on the track, and achieved good times, but no victory, in a couple of 800m races. The near misses frustrated him. Then, as the season was drawing to a close, he took part in a match between Bohemia and Moravia, in Prague. His race was over 1,500m, and his opponents were focused on defeating his fellow Moravian, Šalé. Emil ran his own race, was third as the last lap began and noticed that none of his rivals was accelerating. He decided to overtake, and was surprised to find himself with a clear lead with 200m to go. 'Suddenly I realised I'm coming first. All I have to do is keep going . . .'

When he boarded the train for Zlín later that night, Emil was already clutching a copy of the next day's newspaper, and there his winning time was written: 4:01.4. 'I never had the brains for mathematics,' he said later, 'but that number enchanted me. I kept reading it for the whole night.' What made him happiest of all was the thought that this first victory in a 'proper race' had been won through the patient application of hard work. 'I had started as an average athlete – a normal boy. It took me three years to win a race. I was glad that I endured those three years – that I did not give up. I thought that, if I train more, I will run even better.'

But 'more' didn't just mean more miles. It meant more intensity, more speed, more focus – above all, more thought. Just running lap after lap at sub-racing speed, which was what most of his clubmates did, somehow didn't seem the best way to prepare for the rigours of a race. As Emil later put it: 'Why should I practise running slow? I already know how to run slow. I want to learn to run fast.' So Emil had begun to experiment with a different approach. He would run much faster, at something approaching full speed, and slow down only when he could no longer continue at that pace – after which he would revert to a jog even slower than his clubmates' 'normal' training pace. Then, when he had recovered, he would accelerate again. The experiment produced rapid improvements. Gradually, over the next couple of years, he began to systematise it.

It is hard to be certain precisely how much of the method Emil now developed was original and how much he was taught. Haluza had planted the seeds, emphasising the importance of not just practising running but practising running fast: 'Speed is the foundation of athletics,' he taught. And it seems likely that, through Haluza, Emil must have been at least vaguely aware of the rudimentary methods of interval training with which other European runners and trainers had been experimenting. Haluza knew of the enthusiasm of the great pre-war Scandinavian and Finnish champions – notably Paavo Nurmi – for *fartlek*, or 'speed play': that is, the practice of varying high speeds with more relaxed tempos in the course of an off-road training run. He probably knew about the German coach Woldemar Gerschler's use of short-distance speed sessions to improve spectacularly the performance of middle-distance runners such as Rudolf Harbig. He may even have heard reports that the Polish runner Janusz Kusocinski had incorporated such sessions into his training for longer distance races. If so, he may have passed some of this knowledge on to Emil. It is unlikely, however, that much detailed information about these pioneers had reached Zlín. Their examples may have informed Emil's thinking. The thinking was his own.

Emil summed this up well in an interview published in the *Observer* in Britain twenty years later. 'I didn't know much. It wasn't possible to buy a book about Nurmi, but I found out that in order to be faster over 10,000m he ran 5,000m many times in training. And to be better at 5,000m he ran 1,500m many times. And to be better at 1,500m he ran four times 400m in training. Maybe this isn't true because I never spoke to Paavo Nurmi, but running is easily understandable. You must be fast enough – you must have endurance. So you run fast for speed and repeat it many times for endurance.'

Such were Emil's influences; but the regime that he now began to develop would eventually go far beyond anything that anyone had tried before.

The principles were simple. As he later put it: 'I'm not interested in how long I can hold out, but in how fast I can reach the finishing line.' So, on the one hand, Emil would learn to run with sustained pace by running fast over distances of, typically, between 200m or 400m; and, on the other, he would develop endurance by repeating the process, again and again. Instead of resting between these semi-sprints, as other early interval trainers had done, he would allow himself only whatever recovery he could achieve while running slowly over a short distance – perhaps 200m – before taking off at speed again.

Speed, in this context, is an elusive concept. The most plausible estimates I have seen, for these early sessions, suggest that he typically ran each 400m lap in about sixty seconds: slower than his lifetime best for a 400m race (56.2 seconds, in 1943) but much faster than the sixty-four seconds a lap that he could sustain without interruption for a 1,500m race. The fast 200m repetitions would probably have been done at around twenty-six to twenty-eight seconds. A 200m recovery jog might take twice that. But these are just numbers. An athlete with more raw speed than Emil would have found such sessions easier, and thus less beneficial. They are also just estimates – of sessions that were rarely timed, in conditions that bear no comparison to those in which runners train today. It may be more helpful to focus on the thought that, once he had burnt through his anaerobic resources in the first lap or so of a session, Emil would have had to strive to achieve similar results aerobically, fuelling his muscles with whatever oxygen he could take in as he ran. Whatever his speed, he would have been struggling at the limits of physiology, trying to squeeze more power from a body that was growing emptier with each stride – just as he might in a frantic end-of-race surge for the line.

That's the thing about this kind of training. The figures aren't the point. It's keeping up the effort that matters. If you do so, the repetitions soon start to feel like flat-out, merciless, lung-bursting sprints, as the fatigue accumulates. Objectively, you are probably slowing down. Subjectively, you might just as well be trying to achieve your fastest-ever time for the distance every time, such is the degree of self-torture required. Keep repeating the torture, if you can, and the gains in performance can be spectacular.

Later, as his body and mind adapted to this hitherto unimagined challenge, Emil increased the volume. He began to focus more on 300m and 400m sections, mixing them up in different ways on different days, while reducing the recovery jog (the 'interval') to 150m. He tried sessions of 10 x 300m and 10 x 400m; or, more usually, 'ladders' or 'pyramids', whereby the lengths of the sections would progressively increase in length and then decrease again – so that a typical session might consist of 100m, 200m, 200m, 300m, 400m, 400m, 300m, 200m, 200m, 100m.

The details sound arcane, but, taken together, these represented the beginnings of a radical new approach. Previously, athletes had faced a choice between the the

'Long Slow Distance' method, which developed stamina, for long-distance running; and speed-focused interval training, usually for middle-distance runners. Emil was in the process of choosing both: high-quality repetitions, performed in such volumes as to build endurance as well as speed. And whereas Gerschler had taught his interval-training athletes to rest between repetitions for as long as it took to get their heartbeat back below 120 beats per minute, Emil was merciless in limiting his recovery intervals to the time it took to jog 150m. If his body couldn't squeeze enough recuperation out of those few moments, tough: it would just have to learn.

Different permutations produced different effects. Emil took careful note, observing, comparing and experimenting with the same rigour that he applied to his chemistry studies. But it wasn't a complicated formula. All it came down to was this: quantity plus intensity, multiplied by implacable persistence, equals steadily improving performance. And pain, endlessly repeated, becomes endurable. Tomáš Baťa would have understood: success came from hard, high-quality, consistent work. The rest was just detail.

Sometimes Emil's experimentation verged on the absurd. Walking down the poplar-lined avenue from his dormitory building towards the Higher Industrial School, he tried holding his breath for the time it took to get from the first tree to the fourth. The next day he did the same again, and then the day after that he kept going to the fifth tree – and so on. The exercise continued for over a week until, pushing double figures, he passed out in mid-stride. It seems unlikely that he gained much physiological advantage from this self-inflicted torture, but it was all useful experience in operating at the absolute extremes of endurance.

The further Emil explored the boundaries of possibility, the less relevant to his training his fellow athletes in Zlín became. 'The first year we trained together,' recalled Jindřich Roudný many decades later, 'but soon I was not good enough. There was no athlete who was able to keep up with Emil.' Some doubted Emil's wisdom; or even, at times, his sanity. They told him that he would damage himself – as he did in the winter of 1943–44, when the ill-fitting football boots in which he did his off-track training left him with some kind of abscess that required hospital treatment. But Emil was convinced that, notwithstanding setbacks, his new approach would work. As he put it later: 'This method of training brought me improvement in those basic characteristics a proper endurance runner should have. I was becoming faster, and more persistent.'

Some people made a different criticism, one which would dog him throughout his athletics career. He ran, they said, in an absurdly tortured way. Surely a smoother running style would be more economical – and less ridiculous? Emil shrugged off such jibes. 'I will run with perfect style when they start judging races for their beauty, like figure-skating,' he would say. 'For now, I just want to run as fast as possible.'

He also had to negotiate the more mundane challenge – familiar to runners of all standards – of fitting his running regime around his working life. In 1943, he had graduated from Baťa's Higher Industrial School and was moved to employment in the inorganic chemistry department. There he spent his days grinding silica into a fine dust. Most of this was used for shoes but much of it ended up in the air, on clothes, and in Emil's lungs. He had had more than one tuberculosis scare in his life, most recently the previous summer, and his growing athletic ambitions added to his anxiety about the damage he might be doing to himself. But his tentative request for a transfer was met with the threat of a labour camp.

He also worried about malnutrition, given the enormous amounts of energy he was expending and the limited calories he was able to take in. He countered this risk by gorging on potato goulash, which was off-ration. It was horrible, he said, and sometimes he ate so much of it that he was sick, but he kept at it. 'Maybe I was overdoing it,' he wrote later, 'but that never occurred to me, maybe because I overdid everything at the time.'

In January 1944 he attended a physical education course at which he met Josef Hron, Czechoslovakia's most famous trainer. This led to an invitation from Hron to a training camp in Toušeň in May. Hron seems to have bolstered Emil's confidence in his new approach to training, while also suggesting to him that he should consider competing at a longer distance, such as 5,000m.

Emil had his doubts. His best time for 5,000m was fifteen minutes thirty-eight seconds – getting on for a minute faster than the year before but still twenty-four seconds slower than the national record (which itself was more than a minute slower than the world record, 13:58.2, set in September 1942 by the Swede Gunder Hägg). But Hron persisted, even urging Emil to commit to an attempt on the Czechoslovak record before the year was over.

Another seed had been left to germinate. Emil ran 1,500m again at the 1944 national championships in July, coming second to Václav Čevona, and at a meeting in Přerov in September he broke four minutes at the distance for the first time. That still wasn't enough to beat Čevona, though. Maybe it was time to explore a longer distance.

Early in September, Emil asked a clubmate, Mirek Zdráhal, to time him in training as he ran 2,000m as fast as he could. The outcome astounded them both. 'Emil! Emil!' Zdráhal shouted. 'You've broken a record.' Emil was doubtful, but subsequently confirmed from a reference work that his time, five minutes thirty-six seconds, was two seconds faster than the Czechoslovak record. He urged Zdráhal not to tell anyone, but word leaked out. The following day, he received a call from the head of the SK Baťa club, telling him that a proper record attempt, with spectators and an official timekeeper, had been arranged for that weekend. 'You can't just break records in the evenings,' Emil was told. 'It needs to be done in front of people, officially. Otherwise it won't be valid.'

In fact, when Saturday came, there were only a few dozen spectators. The Third Reich was crumbling, and people were losing even the limited appetite they had had under the occupation for public events. Some Baťa dormitories had been requisitioned as hospitals for Luftwaffe pilots; other Baťa factories, such as Chelmek in Poland and Ottmuth in Germany, had become part of the Nazi concentration camp network. Not far to the east, the Slovak uprising was raging, while young Czech men and women were still being deported in thousands to Germany as forced labour: Franta, Emil's older brother, was among them. These were desperate times, and the possibility of a small line of sporting history being written in the city's stadium will have interested only the most hardcore athletics fans.

Emil was glad of it. The distance this time was 3,000m – a more frequently run distance than 2,000m and thus, he feared, unlikely to have such a 'soft' record. He hoped he would not humiliate himself.

He didn't. He was fitter than he had ever been, and, whatever his doubts, he had planned for success, working out how fast he needed to run each lap. He kept rigorously to his schedule – and his time of 8:38.8 knocked more than three seconds off the existing national best. It was 16 September 1944, and the name 'Emil Zátopek' had made its first appearance in the record books.

Emil enjoyed the triumph, not least because several people gave him presents of precious food – a slice of bread and butter; a couple of apples – as a reward; more than half a century later, he said he could still remember the taste. But news of his success was greeted with coolness in the national press – as if Prague-based sports editors doubted the validity of a record set in Zlín. Meanwhile, Josef Hron sent Emil a message reminding him of their discussions of the 5,000m record, and the management at SK Baťa decided to make the most of Emil's form. A new record attempt, this time at 5,000m, was announced for the following Saturday.

Emil spent the week focusing on speed-work: he did 10 x 200m on Tuesday, and the same again on Thursday. By Saturday he was raring to go and, undeterred by a significantly larger crowd of spectators, he proceeded to run 5,000m in 14:55 – forty-four seconds faster than he had ever run it before – knocking twenty seconds off the national record. Jindřich Roudný, in second place, was one minute and forty-six seconds behind.

The sporting heavyweights in Prague could no longer ignore this Moravian upstart. Never before had a Czechoslovak run 5,000m in less than fifteen minutes; some doubted that Emil could really have done so. Letters of congratulation found their way to Emil in Zlín, as did an urgent invitation to take part in yet another record attempt, this time in Prague.

And so, on Saturday, 1 October, Emil – three hours after gorging himself on plum dumplings made by Josef Hron's grandmother – lined up for his third record attempt in as many weeks: this time at 2,000m again. By some accounts, there were whisperings beforehand about 'Zlín time', and as the starter's gun fired there were many among the Prague spectators who wondered if an unknown athlete such as Emil could really have made such spectacular progress in such a short time. Five minutes and 33.4 seconds later they had their answer: Emil had broken his third national record in sixteen days – and the name Zátopek was becoming familiar to athletics fans right across the Protectorate.

Back in Zlín, there were even more letters of congratulation. Among them was one from Kopřivnice. The family had read about his triumphs in the papers, wrote Emil's father, and: 'We are worried about your health, and so we have decided that you will stop it. It is time to hang up your running shoes. And write to us straight away . . .'

Emil was not sure how to respond to this but decided that, since the racing season was now over, he could truthfully reply that he was no longer racing. But he had certainly not hung up his shoes. On the contrary, he felt hungrier for training than ever, ready to step up his workload and aim for higher things: 'Even when it was raining or it was cold, even when I didn't feel like it, I always found a moment to go to the stadium and to run at least ten laps with alternating pace,' he recalled. It was one of those precious moments in a young life when anything seems possible.

Then the bombs began to fall.

4

The soldier

Allied bombers had been marauding in the Protectorate's southern skies for weeks, heading from newly conquered bases in Italy to attack major Nazi transport hubs, such as Brno, and centres of oil production, such as Přerov, just twenty-five miles to the north. So Zlín was prepared for the worst. When the sirens sounded, at around midday on Monday, 20 November, most people had time to rush to the shelters they had dug in the surrounding countryside.

Bad weather had diverted the B-24s and B-17s from their original target further north, but the skies over Zlín were clear, and undefended. The Americans rained destruction on Baťa's factories until they had no more bombs to drop.

The first thing that Jindřich Roudný did when the all-clear was signalled was run back to the dormitory buildings. Room 19 was still there, but it had not been spared. But Roudný soon realised, as he inspected the damage, that Emil had beaten him to it. In a fresh entry in their shared notebook, Emil explained that he had rushed there in the hope of finding that the book recording swearing fines had been destroyed, and had been disappointed to find that it hadn't.

Altogether, 60 per cent of the factories in Zlín had been damaged. The human toll – forty-three dead and about ninety injured – was light by the standards of the time, but the blow to the morale of the Baťa management and their Nazi overseers was heavy. Everyone knew the Allies were coming. The border village of Kalinov, near the Dukla Pass, had already been liberated, by a Soviet-trained Czechoslovak regiment, two months earlier. Refugees, escaped prisoners and fleeing Germans were flooding across the eastern borders, and the Czech resistance, quiescent for so long, was becoming more active. It was now a question of when, not if, the occupation would end.

For Emil, as for most people, the main goal was simply to stay alive. Training seemed less important than avoiding the last-minute atrocities of an increasingly desperate army of occupation. With an evening curfew in force, much of his winter training was done indoors. He trained by running on the spot: five-minute bursts of fast, low steps alternating with five-minute bursts of high, powerful kicks – 'like when a horse digs something up with its hooves'. The intensity of the sessions made up for the fact that the hostel no longer had any heating. Eventually, however, they resulted in a tear to Emil's left quadricep, and a break in his training – much to his room-mates' relief.

When he recovered, he resumed his indoor sessions, this time in Room 19, all but one of whose occupants was an athlete. The exception, an architect called Solnes, used to watch and laugh as the others joined in Emil's rudimentary aerobics class. When the caretaker complained, he was told that they were practising a dance, which placated him because, in Emil's words, 'the only thing they would tolerate at the hostel was culture'.

By spring, the Germans and their collaborators were planning for post-war survival. Incriminating documents were destroyed, many of them in a bonfire in front of Hostel No. 1. By the end of April, Soviet artillery could be heard. There were none of the usual city-wide celebrations of May Day. Finally, on 2 May, the Red Army arrived.

Emil was at the stadium, training, when the sirens sounded. He ran three 200m sprints, with jogs in between, before they fell silent. Realising that this was no ordinary warning, he gathered up as much kit as he could carry and ran to find his friends. Shooting could be heard in the streets. Hurrying through the Zálešná neighbourhood, he realised that the soldiers he could see were not Germans but Soviets.

Several days of chaos ensued, about which all that can be said with confidence is that most of Zlín's inhabitants, including Emil, welcomed the Russians; that many – probably including Emil – offered various kinds of support, from food and drink to help in digging trenches; and that, after some resistance, the Germans and their supporters melted away. But that makes it sound less messy and terrifying than it must have been. The city's war memorial commemorates thirty Soviet soldiers who died in Zlín's liberation.

Within a week, the war had ended. On 5 May Prague rose up against the occupiers; on 8 May Germany surrendered. It would be many months – years, even – before central Europe could truly be said to be at peace; but the worst was over and the future at least offered hope.

Meanwhile, Emil was sufficiently enthusiastic about what he had seen of the Red Army to tell friends he was tempted to become a soldier himself. The athletes among them advised against it: it would, they said, be fatal to his development as a runner.

But working in Zlín no longer seemed such a good idea either. The Baťa management, struggling to come to terms with their second ideological U-turn in six years, seemed less sympathetic than before to Emil's racing ambitions. The Zlín running track was pocked with shell craters. And every medical check-up he underwent produced the same warnings about the job-related dangers of silicosis.

Not long after the liberation, Emil repeated his request to be redeployed. His manager, Mr Pumprla, didn't even pretend to care. You were willing to do that work for the Nazis, Emil was told, so we're certainly not going to let you stop doing it now.

This angered Emil, and perhaps also prompted the thought that being a Baťa man might not be a helpful tag to carry through life in post-war Czechoslovakia. Baťa had campaigned energetically against Nazism in the pre-war years, and had helped many of its Jewish employees to escape Europe altogether. But the company's subsequent co-operation with the occupation, no matter how unwilling, now made it an easy target for criticism from its left-wing enemies. The factory directors had already been arrested, and their deputies put to sweeping the city streets. There was an obvious risk for its employees of being tarred with the same brush.

So when Emil noticed a series of public announcements calling for recruits to the Czechoslovak army – which had been reconstituted along with Czechoslovakia itself – the opportunity seemed too good to refuse. The notices mentioned that there would be scope for cultural and sporting development. 'I liked that very much,' Emil explained later. He would probably have faced compulsory enlistment before long anyway. In the meantime, the army was arguably the safest place to be. Less than three weeks after the liberation, on 20 May 1945, he joined up.

He was not disappointed. On the one hand, the disciplined, regimented life was hardly a shock to someone who had spent eight years at Baťa. On the other, the physical side of the training, which many recruits found tough, was for Emil sheer pleasure. 'It was like training for long distances,' he explained in a radio programme a few years later. 'Marches, jumps, runs, with full combat gear. I thought to myself: this is good, this is a workout.'

His unit, in the 27th Infantry Regiment, was based in Uherské Hradiště, a small, rather beautiful old town about fifteen miles south-west of Zlín, and he embraced military life there with enthusiasm. There was no fighting to be done: just 'training from dawn to dusk'. Highlights included drills in the forest, morning gymnastics, assault courses, night exercises, and 'marching and running all the time'. Emil tackled them all with the same intensity that he had applied to his interval training, while also learning 'how to train my will, self-control and persistence'. His sense that running was his calling was growing stronger, and his world-view was increasingly coloured by a runner's priorities. He had to resist the urge to put fitness before military discipline, however. At one point he earned a reprimand for giving his comrades a head start in a run and then overtaking them.

It was a challenge finding opportunities to race, but his commanding officer proved surprisingly sympathetic, especially after Emil had won the 3,000m (setting a new Czechoslovak record) in the military championships in Prague on 1 June 1945. Not only did Colonel Ingr give Emil leave of absence for approved races: he even made sure that he was provided with rations to take with him. Emil repaid him with a string of superb results. 'After the war, we competed more joyfully, and some of that joy could be seen in my performances. Almost with every race I set a new record . . .'

In July, Emil was allowed to return to Prague for the Czechoslovak national championships. He won the 5,000m (setting another Czechoslovak record, this time of 14:50.8). The next day, back at barracks, he was surprised to hear Colonel Ingr congratulating him for his achievement in front of the whole regiment.

Emil had originally intended to finish his military service as soon as the rules permitted. Now he changed his mind. He had no desire to return to Zlín, whose inhabitants had been fleeing in thousands to escape the anti-Baťa backlash. Meanwhile, it was obvious that a soldier's life suited him. That autumn, the army reopened its officers' training academy, with a specific though as yet undeclared brief to train up officers from working-class backgrounds. Emil was among the first to apply. He was accepted, and in October he moved to Hranice, in Moravia's Přerov district, to begin a two-year course.

Once again, he thrived. The disciplines of military life felt like luxury: regular meals, somewhere to sleep, a uniform, laundry, challenging work, fresh air and endless opportunities to exercise.

Sometimes he had a training partner: a local youth called Milan Švajgr, who would later represent Czechoslovakia over distances from 800m to 10,000m, made contact with Emil and suggested that they run together. They used to meet outside the barracks once or twice a week, for runs together on the broad, sandy path beside the Bečva river. Švajgr sensed, however, that such excursions were frowned on by Academy officials; and Emil didn't seem especially keen either. Fitting in proper running around other duties required more flexibility than that.

But there was a good running track at the academy, which Emil used – and, for evenings when the weather was bad, an indoor riding school, where the combination of deep sand and heavy military boots lent a difficulty to his exercise that hugely increased the training value of each stride he took. (The legend that he also trained in the academy's 800m-long corridor is implausible: there were too many breaks and steps in it for this to have made any sense.) When the days grew short, Emil ran round and round the grounds of the barracks in the dark, torch in hand – although this is said to have provoked at least one potentially life-threatening confrontation with a sentry. Such misunderstandings may have encouraged him to seek more isolated training environments in the woods nearby, where he could pursue his repetitions untroubled by those who did not understand why they mattered.

One way or another, though, he managed to maintain, and increase, his training regime – even if the only way to do so was by jogging on the spot while on sentry duty. By some accounts, he even experimented with training in a gas mask, but his main gimmick was volume. He later claimed to have doubled his workload in the course of 1946. By the time he set yet another Czechoslovak 5,000m record in June – 14:36.6, at an international meeting in Prague – he was typically doing 10 x 200m and 10 x 400m every day, all fast, tapering off only in the week before a competition (with complete rest the day before).

It seems unlikely that it was part of anyone's plan that Emil should bring glory to the army through his running. The war was barely over, after all, and the army's overwhelming need was for competent officers, not prestige. Indeed, at one point Emil got into trouble at the Academy for having too many athletics trophies among his possessions – a reprimand that prompted him to give away the next one he won to Josef Hron's grandmother. He then discovered that this was one of those trophies that the winner is supposed to return so that it can be awarded again the next year.

But competence was not the only concern. The new army was being built under the supervision of a new defence minister, Ludvík Svoboda, a covert Communist whose overwhelming strategic priority was to make Czechoslovakia's armed forces ideologically sound. This required the gradual easing out of the old, conservative officer class and its replacement by a new generation of young, working-class, Soviet-friendly officers. And the idea seems to have taken root fairly soon that Emil, in addition to embodying this new ideal of the 'officer class', might also make a good advertisement for it. Emil's superiors clearly discussed his exceptional abilities: he was once ordered to run seven kilometres cross-country with a message, and the same distance back with the reply, simply to settle a bet between two superior officers as to whether or not he could cover the distance within an hour. Despite his duties, therefore, Emil was permitted to race half a dozen times in June and July of 1946; he won all but two of his races and set new Czechoslovak records for 5,000 and 2,000m. Then, in early August, he won the 5,000m in the national championships again, which led to an invitation to represent his country in the European Championships in Oslo later that month.

The experience was short but intimidating. The Czechoslovak team was full of novices. Emil, who had never been abroad before, was not the only one to go pale with fright when the elderly Junkers-52 took off. On arrival in Norway, they realised that they did not even have matching tracksuits; for the opening ceremony, they paraded around the track in vests and shorts instead. At the start of the 5,000m, Emil realised the size of the challenge he faced. The Bislett stadium was packed with fans, cheering loudly for their various nations' heroes: Sydney Wooderson, British record holder for three miles; Viljo Heino, world record holder; Wim Slijkhuis, the 'flying Dutchman'; Evert Nyberg, the big Swede. Emil felt out of his depth – even after trying to reassure himself by touching Heino's leg for luck – and all four finished in front of him. The fact that Emil's time was yet another Czechoslovak record (14:25.8) did not prevent the odd pointed remark when he got home to the effect of 'Do you really need to go all the way to Norway to come fifth?'

Emil drew a more positive lesson: that 'what was enough for Czechoslovak standards would not be enough once I got to world competitions . . . so for me this meant that I should train more'. There was also the encouraging fact that, despite his failure to win, he had now run the 5,000m faster than Paavo Nurmi ever did.

'I still remember how elated I was,' he told a Slovak journalist forty-six years later.

In September Emil was selected to represent Czechoslovakia in the Allied Forces military championships in Berlin. Most of the competing nations had sent large teams. Emil was Czechoslovakia's sole representative. He left Hranice on a Friday, by train. By midnight, he was alone in the pitch-black ruins of Dresden – much of which had been reduced to rubble by Allied fire bombs eighteen months earlier. He slept briefly on a bench, caught another train at 3 a.m., and arrived in Berlin late on Saturday afternoon, terrified that he had missed his race. He was relieved to discover that the races he could see in progress were just qualifying events, and that the race proper was the following day.

Returning to the stadium on the Sunday after a few hours' sleep, he found it difficult to make anyone understand who he was. He knew barely any English, apart from 'I am from Czechoslovakia', but quickly recognised that people kept asking him the same question: 'Only one?' 'I understood the English word "one", so I deduced that they wanted to know if it was only me. So I enthusiastically replied: "Yes, only one!" And I was happy to have understood them.'

The organisers were less cheerful, as was the American soldier who had been deputed to carry the banner in front of the Czechoslovak team as the competitors marched around the track during the opening ceremony. 'He asked: "Only one?"', recalled Emil, 'and that I already knew. So I replied, "Yes, only one!" And I thought, see, boy, even with you I can make myself understood.' But the soldier was not happy; and when the one-man team behind the 'Czechoslovakia' banner provoked hoots of laughter from the crowd, Emil was not happy either. 'I was all red, ashamed. I thought to myself: I should have stayed at home.' Remarkably, a photograph of this moment has survived, and you can see him thinking it.

Emil almost missed the start of his race, because he could not understand what was being said on the public address system. But once the starting gun sounded he knew exactly what he was doing. The spectators watched in amazement as he surged into a huge and ever-increasing lead, unsure if this was great running or laughable misjudgement of pace. Eventually, as one runner after another was lapped, they began to cheer him, and there was a great roar when he lapped the man in second place. At the end, the organisers were bemused to find that Emil didn't seem particularly exhausted.

On the ceremonial lap that ended the championships, Emil's GI escort was the happiest banner-bearer on the track. And although Emil knew that the standards here were far below those of a top-level international meeting, the event seems to have provided a lasting boost to his confidence, both in his running ability and in his ability to thrive in the world beyond Czechoslovakia's borders.

That autumn he was transferred from Hranice to the tank training school in Milovice-Mladá, in central Bohemia, where he was attached for the remainder of his training to the 11th tank brigade. The upheaval may have been the final nail in the coffin of the romance he had been tentatively trying to rekindle, by post, with Jarmila Švehláková, who was still in Zlín. But he was re-united in Milovice with an old acquaintance. Ladislav Kořán, known to friends as Láďa, had been a promising competitive cyclist until the crackdown following Heydrich's assassination made cycling impossible. He had channelled his talents into running instead, and Emil had made friends with him when they raced in Prague. Shortly after Emil's arrival, they bumped into one another at the sports stadium near the barracks, and Kořán was able – with Emil's guidance – to unlock the potential that would turn him into an international athlete. Both were in the Czechoslovak team that travelled to London that autumn for the inter-services Britannia Shield. Emil won the cross-country, on Ascot racecourse, by 600m – despite the fact that many of those behind him took advantage of the thick fog to go around jumps rather than over them.

Soon afterwards, a winter of exceptional severity descended on central Europe. Emil decided to embrace the challenge and did most of his winter training outdoors. He had moved on from the sports stadium by now, having grown tired of the witticisms ('Who's chasing you?' etc.) of the footballers who shared it with him. Instead, he would run a couple of miles to some nearby woods and then do his training there. When the snow was too deep for normal running, he ran with great bounds instead. His army boots protected his ankles from unseen hazards; and the net effect was, of course, that his body was working even harder.

How hard? It is difficult to be precise. In his first forest excursions, Emil simply ran, exploring rather than training in a focused way; but he had soon grown tired of 'killing time without a goal'. So he found some grassy stretches on which to do his interval training. A typical session involved twenty sets of 'about 250m' and twenty of 'about 400m'. There was no accurate way of measuring the distances – but then he wasn't in the habit of timing himself. The units he was interested in were units of effort: hard to quantify but, for the runner with sufficiently ruthless honesty, unmistakably real. Muhammad Ali once remarked that, when he did sit-ups, he only started to count them when they began to hurt – 'because they're the only ones that count.' This seems to have been Emil's approach, too: he was raising his pain threshold. 'It's at the borders of pain and suffering,' he is supposed to have said, 'that the men are separated from the boys.' From now on, these would be the borders where he trained, every day of the year.

The fact that such sessions were often conducted in foul weather only added to the psychological benefits: there is a sense of empowerment that comes from facing down such discomforts (and in the days before weather-proof sportswear there was a lot of facing down required). Sometimes, when he got back late from training, his only means of washing was to pour cold water over himself in 'a bathroom hung with icicles.' He credited this for the fact that he never suffered from colds. But the benefits were not just physical. For Emil, it was all part of the same formula: load up the pain now, and you will be grateful later. In his words: 'There is great advantage in training under unfavourable conditions . . . for the difference then is a tremendous relief in a race.'

His subsequent performances bore this out. That Christmas, Emil beat the great Gaston Reiff in a cross-country race in Brussels, despite getting lost in mid-race. Conditions were so cold that Emil wore a copy of *Le Soir* as an improvised lining inside his vest. Afterwards, he made friends with some miners from Charleroi, undeterred by the fact that he knew barely a word of French.

One of the first things he did on returning home was obtain a French dictionary, which he proceeded to memorise, starting with 'A' and working his way towards 'Z'.

The Brussels trip was also notable for a rare ethical lapse on Emil's part. A Czechoslovak official upbraided him for charging too little for his travel expenses, and persuaded him to claim for a longer journey. When Emil did so, the official pocketed the extra money, and Emil was left feeling both ashamed and aggrieved. This appears to have been the last time he allowed himself to be tempted by the possibility of profiting financially from his running; it would not be the last time, however, that he allowed himself to be influenced in a way he would later regret.

For now, though, his main concern was bettering himself, continuing his exploration of the uncharted frontiers of human athletic possibility. It was a solo voyage, yet it was not lonely; in fact, the better Emil got, the more he relished the fact that running had a social side. The homesick youth who had come out of his shell on the running-track in Zlín would soon be forging friendships on running-tracks across Europe.

In the spring of 1947, he was part of a Czechoslovak cross-country team (Zátopek, Kořán, Roudný, Vomáčka, Zabloudil) that scored a resounding success over ten kilometres in the Allied Forces championships in Hanover. His abiding memory was of the post-race banquet, where he was congratulated by the wife of the garrison commander. She told him that, in all her years of watching racehorses, she had never seen a sight so beautiful as that of Emil, once again many hundreds of metres ahead of his rivals, running all alone back from the woods to the racecourse. The Czechoslovak athletes laughed at her infatuation. This was a notable departure from the prevailing view that Emil's running style was ugly.

But Láďa Kořán took away a different snapshot of that same trip. His memory was of Emil, before the race, mixing himself a drink consisting of lemon juice, water and the chalk used to mark lanes on the track. Emil explained that the lemon juice was to keep his vitamin C levels up, and the chalk was to boost his calcium levels to protect his teeth. Like so much else that he did, it was simultaneously absurd and logical.

A fortnight later, despite being exhausted from two successive nights of all-night tank exercises at Milovice, Emil achieved his best 5,000m time yet: 14:08.2 in the first Rošický Memorial Race (held in honour of the executed Resistance hero). He also made friends after the race with the Finns he had beaten, Väinö Koskela and Evert Heinström, and was invited to race in Finland a few days later. Emil ran at least twenty-five races that summer, at 5,000 and 3,000m. He won all but two and set three more Czechoslovak records. But none was so important to his development as the race in Helsinki.

It was, at one level, just an ordinary meeting, arranged in a spirit of international friendship. On the flight out, Emil enjoyed trying to speak to Koskela and Heinström in Finnish, despite not knowing any. By the time they landed he had ascertained (he thought) that Koskela was a farmer and Heinström an electrician. In athletic terms, however, he knew that he was taking a daunting step up. Finland was the home of his discipline: the land of Paavo Nurmi and of his great successors, Hannes Kolehmainen and Ville Ritola. It was also the home of that day's main opponent, Viljo Heino, Emil's conqueror in Oslo the previous year – European champion at 10,000m and the fastest 5,000m runner in the world.

As the starting gun was fired in the Helsinki stadium, Emil realised to his dismay that the capacity crowd was cheering unanimously for Finland. Panicked, he set off as quickly as possible, hoping to shake Heino off. Heino stuck to him, and they ran the first 1,500m in 4:08 – well inside world record pace for 5,000m. The next four laps were barely slower. This was suicidal. Then Heino struck properly, powering past Emil in the straight to loud applause. Emil felt helpless: it was 'a terrible uproar', he said later: 'not just applause – it comes from the belly.' Then he told himself: 'I will not give up so easily.' In the next straight, he took back the lead. In the straight after that, Heino overtook again. The crowd sensed a fight and roared even louder. Emil wrestled back the lead, then Heino took it back again. And so it continued, twice a lap, with the lead changing hands in each straight. The tactics were ludicrous – the two men were racing one another into oblivion, like two boxers slugging it out toe-to-toe – or, as one writer put it, 'like two foolish boys'.

By the final lap, Emil had nothing left. 'People were screaming,' he wrote later, 'and I felt desperate to think that I had travelled so far only to lose.' The pace had slipped but they were still running at the utmost extremes of their endurance. Heino was leading and Emil could only hang on behind. Still he refused to despair, even when he tried to attack with 200m to go, and nothing happened. Finally, fifty metres from the line, he made one last desperate effort – and felt himself draw level. This progress encouraged him, and that glimmer of encouragement somehow gave him the strength to push a little harder. He won the final sprint by half a stride.

Afterwards, the two men had to lean on one another to avoid collapsing. 'If I could have spoken his language,' said Emil, 'I would have said "Isn't it stupid. We are fighting for 5,000 metres and all that is between us is a few centimetres."' Their times were unspectacular – 14:15.2 for Emil and 14:15.4 for Heino – but the spectators knew that they had just witnessed an epic battle, and they applauded generously. They recognised in Emil a distance runner worthy of the Finnish tradition: someone with that most prized quality: fighting spirit, or '*sisu*'. They would not forget it.

The race had taken so much out of both men that Heino did not go to the post-race banquet. Emil went briefly, then walked down to the seafront and was sick on the beach. He barely slept, and was disturbed at dawn by Scandinavian journalists wanting to interview him. The media pestering continued throughout his homeward journey, by train and boat. After six years of running, he was an international celebrity.

But he also realised that he had come of age as a runner in a more important sense – and fifty years later, in an interview with *L'Équipe*, he would identify this as one of the races that had marked him most. If he could beat Heino, in Finland, in a race that he had seemed to be losing, what race couldn't he win?

Returning briefly to Milovice, he felt ready to aim higher still. In just over a year's time, the Olympic Games would be held, the first for twelve years. Now, surely, it was realistic to dream of making a mark there as well?

It was a bold dream – more extravagant than hindsight makes it sound. Czechoslovakia's all-time tally of Olympic track and field glory consisted of a solitary medal: František Douda's shot-put bronze in 1932. The great Olympic nations would laugh at the idea that a runner from this obscure little country might snatch a medal in a major track event. Yet the results and the record books suggested that Emil must have a decent chance.

First, though, there were other things to attend to: an international meeting in Enschede, at which he defeated another of his great rivals, Slijkhuis, over 5,000m; the Czechoslovak national championships; matches in Prague against Italy and France. The France match saw Emil defeat the highly rated Alain Mimoun, a French, Algerian-born ex-soldier who would become Emil's great friend and rival over the next decade. This was their first meeting. Emil won by nearly a minute, but afterwards congratulated Mimoun on his performance, before sharing several glasses of Russian champagne with him – and practising his French – at the post-match celebration.

Two days later, Emil was back at the Academy he had started off in, in Hranice, to graduate as Lieutenant Zátopek, officer of the Czechoslovak army. On a fine, summery day, General Svoboda himself inspected the new officers, while Rudolf Slánský, the influential General Secretary of the Communist Party, was also present, and made a point of shaking Emil's hand.

Emil seems to have given remarkably little thought to his graduation, or to the significance it might hold for his poor, hard-working parents. It was at their initiative rather than his that they joined the other families who came to witness the passing-out parade, on 17 August 1947, and his joy at being able to share this moment with them was tempered with a certain awkwardness: the last time Emil had seen them, on a visit home the previous year, there had been a slight falling-out. He had sneaked out for a training run and – despite his practice of putting on his running shoes in the street, just round the corner – word had got back to his parents, who were still firmly opposed to the whole idea of running. They cannot have been entirely oblivious to Emil's success – he was the most famous runner in Czechoslovakia – but at home the fiction was maintained that he had obeyed their command to give up running. Somehow he had never quite found the right moment to resolve the issue.

To add to the awkwardness, he had no way of keeping from his parents the fact that, as a newly commissioned officer, he was now entitled to six weeks' holiday. He could hardly say that he had no time to visit them. So he returned home with them to Kopřivnice, wrestling privately with the question of what to do about the race in Brno in which he was due to be competing the following day.

He made his escape by announcing that he wanted to take some of his father's honey to his 'aunt' (presumably his sister) in Brno, promising to return straight away. But one thing led to another. Having delivered the honey – and set a Czechoslovak record for 3,000m – he was immediately invited to Bratislava, where he set a record for 2,000m three days later; and while he was there he was informed that arrangements had been made for him to fly to Paris to compete at 5,000m at the World Student Games (for which his time at military academy qualified him). So off to France he flew – and while waiting for his event there he entered and won the 1,500m as well.

He then had a few days off before his next race, in Ostrava, so he stopped off in Kopřivnice, sheepishly, on the way. His family were pleased to see him: they seemed to have resigned themselves to the incessant demands that racing put on his time. Then something curious happened. Some of his old schoolfriends insisted that he join in a race they had organised on the local playing field. To do so, Emil tried to make some minor repairs to his spiked running shoes. His father offered to lend him some suitable tools and, as he was looking for them, Emil noticed that he had a drawer full of newspaper clippings. He leafed through them and realised with a shiver what they were: a father's proud collection, meticulously ordered, chronicling Emil's achievements all the way back to Oslo and beyond.

Emil expressed his surprise. 'Do you collect the results of races?' he asked.

His father was embarrassed. 'Only the international ones,' he blustered.

Then, more remarkable still, when the time came to go to the race in Ostrava, Emil found his mother getting dressed up to go out. He asked her what she was doing. 'I would like to see you run at least once,' she explained.

The reconciliation must have heartened him. It did not, however, prevent him from continuing his exhausting globe-trotting lifestyle. There was another trip to the UK in September, for the Britannia Shield. Emil won the cross-country, at RAF Halton, by two minutes. Then there was a hastily arranged trip to Belgium, where Emil lost narrowly to Gaston Reiff over 3,000m. (The arrangements were so hasty that Emil did the entire trip without a passport, and had to show the Czechoslovak border guards race reports from the papers before they would let him back into the country.) October brought a quick trip to Poland, during which he won races in Warsaw, Gdansk and Katowice and was shocked by the freezing temperatures and war-ravaged cities.

Then he returned to Milovice, this time as commissioned officer. He was commander of a tank platoon, with three tank crews under him. It would be a short-lived posting. None the less, it marked the beginning of the next phase of his life.

5

Beginnings

It wasn't just Emil who was starting afresh. Czechoslovakia itself was changing. The final avalanche was still a few months away, but the creakings were unmistakable.

Some would say that revolution had been inevitable since the liberation; ever since Eduard Beneš, Czechoslovakia's pre-war president and leader of its wartime government-in-exile in London, had returned in July 1945 to form a new national government. His plan, a simple return to the pre-war status quo, had much to be said for it, but his hopes proved naïve. The country was too traumatised, the nationwide epidemic of post-war score settling had been too savage. People wanted something bolder. As the Catholic newspaper *Lidová demokracie* put it: 'It is impossible to return to the capitalist system which prevailed here during the first twenty years of our republic . . . We stand on the threshold of a new economic and social order.'

So it was that, while elections in 1946 had confirmed Beneš as president of the reconstituted nation, they had also confirmed that the most dynamic force in Czechoslovak politics was the Communist Party, which secured 38 per cent of the vote.

The Communists had had a good war, opposing the Nazis, supporting the Soviet liberators and having nothing to do with the Western powers that had betrayed Czechoslovakia to Hitler in 1938. In contrast to the Soviet-backed Communist parties in other Eastern European countries, who simply seized power in the late 1940s, the Communist Party of Czechoslovakia (KSČ) – though equally Soviet-backed – had genuine popular support. Yet that support was not quite enough to form a government.

The result had been eighteen months of stalemate and escalating political crisis, during which the democratic parties struggled to form a workable coalition with the Communists – and the Communists, who had insisted on control of the interior ministry as the price for any co-operation, busied themselves setting up a new police force from which non-Communist personnel were excluded with increasing brazenness. It is unlikely that Emil was too bothered by this: he himself, though not a Party member, was a beneficiary of the similar process that was taking place, less overtly, in the army. Yet he must have sensed that a crisis was imminent. Everyone did.

That December, in the last days of calm before the storm, Emil flew to Algiers. He and other leading European athletes had been invited by the *Journal d'Alger* to compete in both a 5,000m and, on Christmas Day, a ten-mile cross-country race. Emil won both, and turned down a prize worth 12,000 francs for fear of breaking the rules on amateurism. He persuaded officials to give most of the money to a Belgian friend who had no chance of winning anything himself. 'If he gets disqualified,' Emil argued, 'it will make him more famous.' Emil was also offered 'expenses' on his return trip, via Paris, but, again, refused them, saying only that, if the newspaper insisted, he would welcome a bag of oranges, 'as we cannot get them in Prague'.

What he did bring back with him were vivid memories of Algiers itself. He wrote later about the shocking contrast between the city's rich quarter and the shanty town beyond the kasbah (where he nearly had his jacket stolen); and about the beauty of the Atlas Mountains and the sea; and of the pleasure of meeting up again with his friend Alain Mimoun, who took Emil to Surcouf, where he had grown up, and introduced him to the delights of seafood. Emil also struck up a friendship with one of the Barbary apes that came to molest the athletes as they dined. Where others brushed the pests aside, Emil allowed one to climb all over him and spend a long time sitting on his head, picking at his thinning hair. With characteristic curiosity, he groomed the ape's head in return – and yet another bond was forged.

By the time Emil returned to Czechoslovakia, time had almost run out for democracy. With the government in paralysis, the Communists were losing public support and the party's paymasters in Moscow decided that, rather than wait to lose that spring's elections, they should act while they could. As 1948 began, the Ministry of the Interior stepped up its abuses of the democratic process, deliberately provoking the resignations of unsympathetic non-Communist ministers. A general strike was organised in February, to devastating effect. Armed 'workers' militias', later renamed People's Militias, roamed the streets, discouraging opposition. Ludvík Svoboda, the defence minister, confined the army to its barracks. President Beneš, whose health was failing, was bullied into accepting a new Communist-led government; he resigned in May after refusing to sign the new constitution. The last non-Communist minister, Jan Masaryk, died in suspicious circumstances in March. Czechoslovakia became, to all intents and purposes, a one-party state. The constitution took effect on 9 May, but for the next forty-one years the coup – or semi-coup – would be referred to as 'Victorious February'.

Emil, back in Milovice, would have been less affected than many by these events. True, the army was immediately purged of non-Communist officers – around 1,200 were reported to have been removed from their positions over the next four months, while the proportion of Party members in the officer corps would double over the next four years. But most of this ideological cleansing would have been above Emil's pay grade and perhaps even beyond his knowledge. He himself had nothing to fear: he was in the vanguard of General Svoboda's new cohort of officers from working class or peasant backgrounds who by 1952 would constitute two-thirds of the army's commissioned personnel. And the Communist takeover would have been presented to those in the barracks as a necessary emergency action, with huge popular support, to prevent Czechoslovakia from being dragged back to the bad old days by the forces of reaction.

Emil himself was not actively involved in politics at this stage of his life, but he would certainly have seen Communism as preferable to fascism. It was less than three years since he had seen the Red Army drive the Nazis out of Zlín – while his father, brothers and school-friends were among those who brought the Tatra factory in Kopřivnice to a complete standstill during the general strike. He remembered the hunger of his childhood. Not least, he remembered the tragic fate of his brother, Jaroš. If a struggle was going on between the Communists and forces hostile to Communism, Emil knew which side he was on.

And so the old order changed, and Emil, seeming to fit in his training around his new officer's duties without too much difficulty, carried on much as before. He stuck to the same self-created regime of interval training, ratcheting up the intensity and quantity of his training as steeply as his body would stand. Meanwhile, within weeks of the Communist takeover, sporting success was moved several places higher on the list of national priorities. The Sokol organisation – which might loosely be described as a mass participation sports movement with Boy Scout and nationalist overtones – was taken over by the state, and in March 1948 all sports clubs and associations across Czechoslovakia were forcibly brought under its control. (Later in the year, Sokol itself would be abolished – just as it had been by the Nazis a decade earlier – and replaced with a centralised sports federation.) The army was encouraged to increase the emphasis it placed on physical education.

Emil, while continuing to perform his more conventional military duties, made the most of the new climate. Over the next five months, he laid down the foundations not just of his own future success but also, arguably, of the future of elite running. He described his methods as 'simple and primitive', with a focus on 'speed and stamina, speed and recovery' and the golden rule: 'Run fast and try to recover during the movement itself.' But the way he applied these simple principles was revolutionary. It would be more than a decade before sports scientists first defined the physiological principles underlying Emil's approach – and yet, as Láďa Kořán pointed out sixty-five years later, 'within a few years there wouldn't be a single top athlete who wasn't doing interval training – and Emil was the first'.

A purist might argue that he wasn't. There had been interval trainers before; there had even been a few who, to some degree, recovered in motion. But no one had done with these methods what Emil did with them, turning them into tools for developing stamina and applying them in volumes that no one had contemplated before. That was his real innovation: to tear up every scrap of received wisdom about the load of intense work that an athlete's body could endure. As Fred Wilt would write in his 1959 'bible' of post-war athletic methodology, *How They Train*: 'Before Zátopek, nobody had realised it was humanly possible to train this hard.' By the spring of 1948, Emil was typically doing 5 x 200m, followed by 20 x 400m, followed by another 5 x 200m, every day – or, on alternate days, 5 x 150m, 20 x 250m and 5 x 150m – mostly in the woods with his boots on; with about five miles of extra jogging to get to and from the relevant parts of the forest.

But perhaps the most remarkable thing about these training sessions was not the volume but how solitary they were. He had no coach, partly because no coach worth his salt would have approved of Emil's outrageously unorthodox methods. As for training partners, there were other serious runners around, but none who could run at the levels to which Emil now aspired. Láďa

Kořán, for example, seems to have trained with Emil only on the track. In any case, there was something to be said for solitary sessions: just the runner and the runner's pain, repetition after repetition of lung-bursting, run-for-your-life intensity, endured and overcome day after day, week after week, month after month, until Emil understood with every nerve in his body a truth first expressed by Jan Haluza: 'Pain is a merciful thing. If it lasts without interruption, it dulls itself.'

As spring turned to summer, he upped the workload, until he was doing the longer sessions every day. There were interruptions. Some were significant. He ran four 5,000m races between early May and late June; his quickest was a victory over Slijkhuis in Prague in 14:10 – his second-fastest time ever. More important was a cross-country victory, in April, in Spa in Belgium. It was a tough, rough course – runners had to drag themselves up one wooded hillside by their hands – but Emil won by such a prodigious margin that he was besieged afterwards by athletes and journalists demanding that he tell them his secret. Yet what really excited him about this race was the distance: exactly 10,000m.

He had been thinking for several months about adding this longer distance to his track repertoire. The international competition seemed less dangerous, while Viljo Heino's 1944 world record – 29:35.4 – must have seemed eminently attainable, given Emil's 5,000m best of 14:08.2. His Spa victory confirmed Emil in his resolve to try himself out as a 10,000m runner.

He did so in Budapest, on 29 May. He won easily, in 30:28.4, and knocked well over two minutes off the fifteen-year-old Czechoslovak record. Three weeks later, in Prague, pacing himself more confidently this time, he sliced off another fifty-one seconds. His winning time, 29:37.0, was only 1.6 seconds outside Heino's world record. This was a stunning beginning, and a major landmark in Emil's athletics career. In terms of his life, however, it wasn't even the biggest landmark of the month.

On 11 June, there was an international match against Belgrade in Zlín. Emil ran – and won – at the unusual distance of 4,000m. Before he did so, the organisers asked him to present a congratulatory bouquet to another Zlín athlete: a javelin thrower called Dana Ingrová.

Dana was new to the sport. She had previously been a handball player. Her father – although Emil did not initially realise this – was Colonel Antonín Ingr, Emil's former commanding officer at Uherské Hradiště, where the family still had their home. Photographs from around that time show Dana as a dark-haired young woman, seemingly brimming with vitality, with a thoughtful face – slightly feline in its beauty – and a warm, humorous smile. She worked in Zlín at a girls' physical education college and had taken up the javelin in the same way that Emil had taken up running: reluctantly. At her first session, she completely failed to master the technique that the coaches were trying to teach. In frustration, she tossed away the final javelin, grasping it instinctively like a pen – and the coaches decided that they had a major talent on their hands.

They were right. Six days before the match against Belgrade, in the same stadium, Dana had set a new Czechoslovak record of 38.07m, in a match against Katowice. Hence the congratulatory bouquet when she returned to her home stadium. Dana accepted it from

Emil politely. 'I was quite cool with him,' she recalls. 'I turned away, so that he wouldn't think I was swept away.'

Emil then ran his 4,000m. He won, naturally, and set a new Czechoslovak record; and, more impressively, set a new Czechoslovak record for 3,000m in the process. So he, too, had to be given a congratulatory bouquet, and Dana was ordered to present it. 'And this time,' says Dana, 'we did talk a little bit.'

Emil was not unattached at the time. He had been seeing a young hammer-thrower, Adéla Macháčková: they used to meet when he went to Prague. They had even discussed marriage. But that first double-encounter with Dana – who was a friend of Adéla's – put an end to that relationship.

Five days later, the athletes of Zlín – including Emil – travelled to a match in Bratislava, in what is now Slovakia. For the return journey, Emil managed to secure the seat next to Dana on the bus. It was a long journey, everyone was in high spirits, and Moravian folk songs – Emil's speciality – were sung. It went down well. They were not, perhaps, an obvious couple: Dana's family were comfortably off and suspicious of Communism – which had already seen Colonel Ingr hustled into early retirement. But she and Emil shared a love of music and a sense of fun, and the journey passed happily.

Close to midnight, the bus passed through a small town called Lanžhot – still more than fifty miles from Zlín. The athletes noticed a pub that was still open and demanded a toilet break. ('Everyone shouted "Pee! Pee!"', according to Dana.) Inside the pub some kind of party was going on. Emil was recognised, and the revellers insisted that the athletes join the celebrations. Emil was nominated to do a 'solo' dance and chose Dana as his partner. By the time the bus reached Zlín, a much longer journey had begun.

Not long afterwards, Dana was at work in Zlín when word reached her that 'the runner' had left something for her. It was a huge bouquet of flowers – the biggest she had ever seen. Dana already knew Emil well enough to assume that he must have won them, but it secured him another meeting. Emil asked her to the cinema, but Dana said that she was going home to see her parents. Emil announced that he would accompany her.

Outside her home in Uherské Hradiště that day, Emil was startled to see his former commanding officer. 'This is my father,' said Dana. It is hard to say which of the two men was most shocked. Emil quickly inveigled his way into the kitchen, where his (unfeigned) interest in the pancakes Dana's mother was making seems to have worked the necessary charm. But Colonel Ingr had his doubts. He was a thoughtful man, who had spent much of the Second World War in Dachau and Buchenwald because of his associations with social democracy. He liked Emil. He had liked him even when he was just another soldier under his command. But he also loved his daughter. Think very carefully, he told her, before you decide to link your life to that of such a celebrated man. His fame will become your burden as well as his, and there will be no escaping it. He was right; but, like most fatherly advice, it fell on deaf ears.

A little later, Emil and Dana went out again – and discovered something surprising. It came up in conversation that Dana had been born on 19 September. 'But that's my birthday!' said Emil. Dana insisted: 19 September

1922 – that is, not just the same day but the same year. Much incredulity ensued: 'I though he was playing a trick on me,' says Dana. So they arranged another date. This time, each brought along identity papers. It was true, they really had been born on the same day. It felt like destiny. 'We could have our wedding on the same day too,' said Emil.

Dana laughed and said nothing. She had already noticed Emil's habit of speaking without thinking; no doubt this was just another amusing thing that had popped into his head. Then they paid another visit to Uherské Hradiště.

It was late June, the sun was shining, and the avenue of linden trees outside the Ingrs' house was bright with blossom. Emil suggested they go swimming in the river. Dana's mother begged them not to. A family tragedy long ago had given her a horror of swimming. She suggested instead that they should gather some linden blossom for her. So Emil and Dana went outside and climbed a tree, and while they were up there Emil, after the usual joking around, became solemn.

'Would you like to marry me?' he said.

Dana felt suddenly apprehensive. 'Couldn't we just go on having fun?' she asked.

'But we can carry on having fun when we're married,' countered Emil.

Dana smiled and then 'evaded the question' with a joke: 'How many other girls have you asked this already?' But it was obvious that the question would not go away.

In the short term, though, there was limited time for exploring the matter further. Emil had his army duties;

Dana had her job. Above all, each was anxiously aware that the Olympic Games were due to begin in July.

For Dana, the challenge was simply to take part. When her romance with Emil began, she had yet to throw the Olympic qualifying distance of forty metres. The prospect of sharing such an adventure with Emil inspired her to redouble her efforts. Finally, with less than four weeks to go, she got there. On 1 July, in Prague, she set a new Czechoslovak record of 40.06m – winning not just the national championships but also a precious place on the plane to London. 'I qualified by the ears,' was how she put it.

But Emil was thinking of medals – and so, it seems, was the army. The final weeks before the Games saw him moved yet again, to a villa set aside for army athletes at Stará Boleslav – not far from Prague and many miles from Milovice. There was accommodation (the villa had been confiscated from a chocolate millionaire), a running track, and woods, and, above all, unlimited time, which allowed Emil to focus on his running with an intensity that even he had barely contemplated before, training up to three times a day. For one ten-day period he upped his sessions to 60 x 400m each day. These would, of course, have been slower than the sixty seconds per lap quoted earlier. After the first few repetitions he would have been closer to the seventy-four-second laps that are more usually cited as Emil's training norm – and even that might have been a struggle. But these laps were something much more important than fast: they were flat-out. Emil ran each one at his limits.

It seems unlikely that anyone had ever prepared for an Olympic Games with a workload of such size and brutality. Yet there was no one coaching him, no one urging him on: just a solitary twenty-five-year-old, hurling himself through the woods time after time, in the unwavering, almost religious conviction that the sacrifice must ultimately bring its reward.

At the beginning of July, the Sokol movement held the last great *slet* in its history: a three-day festival of mass exercises and sporting demonstrations to celebrate its ideals of bringing fulfilment to the young through patriotism and sport. Emil and Dana were among tens of thousands of young people who went to Prague for the celebration – although not among those who took advantage of the occasion to chant anti-Communist slogans. Afterwards they wandered over Charles Bridge, and were enchanted by the view of Prague Castle over the River Vltava – a panorama they had previously known only through postcards.

And then, just over a fortnight later, they were in Prague again, boarding a plane together, Emil carrying a large kitbag while Dana carried Emil's guitar, on their way to London for the biggest adventure of their life so far.

6

The lights come on again

You didn't have to be young and in love to find something magical about the XIVth Olympic Games of the modern era. It was a moment of innocent hope such as the world has not often known. London, the host city, still bore the scars of the Blitz; most of those visiting for the Games will have seen worse damage at home. The phrase 'Austerity Olympics' meant little then, but from today's perspective it is hard to think of a better description.

Years of war had left Britain all but destitute. Rationing was still in force, although athletes selected for the Olympics were, like coal miners, allowed up to 5,467 calories a day – more than twice the general allowance. The total budget for the Games was £730,000: equivalent in real terms – that is, as a percentage of GDP – to one-seventieth of the budget for London 2012. Some thought even this was excessive – but it was generally felt that London had done the right thing by taking on the burden when there were no obvious alternatives. And now that summer was here, and the capital buzzed again with the make-do-and-mend spirit that had helped to get Britain through the war, it was hard not to feel that, as Vera Lynn had once sung, the lights were coming on again all over the world.

The BBC paid £1,000 for the television rights. The gold medals were made from oxidised silver. The running track at Wembley stadium was a former greyhound track that had been converted by having 80,000 tons of cinders dumped on it. The wood for the diving boards was donated by the Canadians. Sponsorship came from Craven A cigarettes, with a few hundred pairs of free Y-Fronts thrown in for the British athletes, 90 per cent of whom were men.

Three years earlier, the world had been at war. Now, young people representing fifty-nine nations – 4,104 athletes in all – were coming together to do nothing more lethal than see who could be fastest, highest or strongest. Rarely has the Olympic ideal seemed more life-affirming.

Even so, it probably did no harm to be young and in love as well – and perhaps that is why no one ever caught the spirit of London 1948 more poetically than Emil, in his much-quoted observation (made nearly two decades later) that: 'It was a liberation of spirit to be there in London. After those dark days of the war, the bombing, the killing and the starvation, the revival of the Olympics was as if the sun had come out. Suddenly, there were no frontiers, no more barriers, just people meeting together.'

For Dana, and for many others on the Czechoslovak team, there was an additional thrill. It was the first time she had been abroad. 'I was a country girl,' she remembers, 'from a small town. I had read about Big Ben and Westminster Abbey and Buckingham Palace, but now I was seeing them in real life. It was overwhelming – like a dream.'

The Czechoslovak team managers were anxious that no one – or at least, not Emil – should get carried away by the excitement. They knew that Emil had a strong chance of winning his nation's first ever Olympic gold – and that such a triumph would represent a huge propaganda coup for a regime still struggling to establish its legitimacy. British newspapers seemed more interested in events such as the defection earlier that month of General Antonín Hasal (the fourteenth Czechoslovak general to defect since February) or an alleged plot to murder General Svoboda than they were in any positive aspects of the new People's Republic. Emil had the chance to change the narrative. It was crucial that he should not be distracted.

The team arrived in London on 26 July, three days before the opening ceremony. There was no Olympic village in the modern sense: just a variety of military barracks and other units of improvised accommodation scattered across the city. The men were mostly in barracks in West Drayton; the Czechoslovak women were in a small boarding school, St Helen's, in Northwood, more than eleven miles away.

This was frustrating for Emil and Dana but a relief to their team managers, who were worried that romance would soften Emil's focus. (They had toyed with the idea of excluding Dana from the team but decided that this would be counter-productive.) As it was, Emil was able to devote the short period between arrival and the opening of the Games to training on the Uxbridge track with an intensity that prompted Paavo Nurmi, visiting with the Finnish team, to remark that only Zátopek understood what training really was.

There was a problem, however, when the day of the opening ceremony arrived. Thursday, 29 July was burningly hot – some said the hottest day of the year – and the team managers were afraid that Emil might succumb to heatstroke. He was told to remain at the barracks. He protested – 'People at home will ask me what the Olympics were like, and I will have to tell them that I don't know, because I was sitting in the shade' – but was overruled. He was allowed, however, to accompany his teammates as far as the stadium. After they had left him, supposedly safe beneath the stands, he made friends with the Danish team. ('Are you really from Denmark?' he asked them, momentarily lost for sensible words.) He got most of the way through the entrance tunnel concealed among red-coated Danes, then insinuated himself into the back of his own team just as they were emerging on to the track. His managers spotted him and were about to explode in fury when Emil whispered: 'The King is looking at us. How can I go off now?'

It was a foolhardy act of defiance, and could well have had serious disciplinary consequences for Emil. But the fact remains that he was right. What is the point of the Olympics, or even of sport, if all you care about is who wins? As giant letters proclaimed from the Wembley scoreboard, quoting Baron Pierre de Coubertin, 'The important thing in the Olympic Games is not winning but taking part. The essential thing in life is not conquering but fighting well.' (That said, it is only fair to record that Emil is also reported to have said: 'What? Not to win? Ah, but I wish to win.')

So it was that both Emil and Dana were there for what then passed as an opening ceremony. A military band played. The competitors paraded. Speeches were made. King George VI declared the Games open, the Olympic flag was raised, 2,500 pigeons were released, and a twenty-one-gun salute was fired. A young, unknown athlete – John Mark, chosen to symbolise youth and hope – ran into the stadium alone and lit the Olympic flame. 'God Save the King' was sung. And that was that.

Just over twenty-four hours later, at 6.40 p.m., Emil stood on the same cinder track, at the starting line for the first Olympic athletics final for twelve years: the 10,000m. There were twenty-seven runners. It was another stifling day, and Emil had agreed in a pre-race conversation with his main rival, Viljo Heino, that it would be foolish to set off at a blistering pace.

But the race had been delayed by nearly two hours – thanks to some confusion over the positioning of the hurdles for some earlier heats – and when the gun was eventually fired, Heino, whether from the build-up of nerves or because it was now a little cooler, set off at something close to a sprint. Others followed, and Emil was soon among the backmarkers.

The temptation to accelerate must have been strong, but Emil had a plan. He knew, and had agreed with Karel Kněnický (his notional 'coach' while he was with the team), that seventy-one-second laps should be enough to produce a winning time. If he could stick to that pace, victory would follow, irrespective of Heino. But he needed to get it right.

To help him, a signal had been agreed. If the pace was correct, Kněnický, watching from the stands with the other Czechoslovak athletes, would wave a pair of white shorts each time Emil passed; if Emil needed to go faster, a red vest would be waved – a task delegated to Dana. So Emil stuck to his pace, and each of the first seven laps provoked the white shorts. Emil found this alarming, as each lap saw his rivals extending their advantage: first Heino, then Heinstrom, and then fourteen others before Emil's struggling figure, apparently way off the pace.

The eighth lap saw yet another flutter of white. Emil was nearly eighty metres behind. Had he, or Kněnický, muddled up the signals? It took considerable willpower to resist the urge to go faster.

And then, to his relief, on the ninth lap Dana waved the red vest. Emil allowed himself to move up the field, progressing rapidly from seventeenth to fifth place. His sudden surge, made more conspicuous by the fact that many of the runners in front of him were starting to tire, caught the spectators' attention. The best-informed among them will have known that, with 1948's best 10,000m time to his credit, Emil was a contender for gold, but to most people he was just a clumsy Czechoslovak whose acceleration appeared to be costing him a superhuman amount of effort. As for Emil's fans back in Czechoslovakia, it was at around this point that radio coverage of the race was abruptly cut off: the delay to the start of the race meant that its allotted time was over, and no one wanted to risk their job by messing with the schedule.

Back at Wembley, there was a buzz among the spectators: as the ninth lap ended, Emil took the lead. It was an intriguing sight. Was this a genuine medal contender – or just a comical foreigner, out of his depth among serious athletes, flailing his way to the front through a sudden burst of misguided enthusiasm?

Such condescension may have been ill-informed, but it was not inexplicable. The post-war world did not lend itself to the rapid dissemination of sporting information, and Emil's running style did little to encourage the idea that he was a potential world-beater. He was, as usual, grimacing and writhing, eyes screwed up and tongue occasionally protruding. As one observer put it: 'He looked . . . as if he might be having a fit. At the very least, he seemed about to drop out.'

The positive side of these contortions was that they made Emil extraordinarily exciting to watch. When Pierre Magnan wrote that Zátopek was a man 'who ran like us', I am pretty sure that this was what he meant. You could see the effort, see the suffering, see the sacrifice and the struggle of the inner will. Anyone who has ever tried any kind of endurance running can recognise these concepts. They are metaphorical octopuses which we all have to wrestle. To watch a runner compete at the highest possible level, and to get an almost physical sense of what he is feeling, is to be very involved indeed in a race. It is thrilling theatre.

And this is what seems to have happened on that warm Friday evening at Wembley. People noticed Emil, wearing the number 203, hit the front. They noticed his clawing and straining; and they noticed the small Czechoslovak contingent in the crowd (mostly teammates) chanting with growing enthusiasm: 'Zá-to-pek! Zá-to-pek!' A few non-Czechoslovaks joined in. Suddenly, Emil had the wind of the crowd's excitement in his sails.

In the tenth lap, Heino seized back the lead. Emil let him keep it briefly; then, seeing the red vest again, put in another surge, opening up a thirty-metre lead. This brought him close to the tail-enders, a lap behind.

Soon he was actually lapping other runners. Spectators, officials, even athletes struggled to keep track. Emil pressed on confidently, but with one nagging doubt in his mind: he had no idea where Heino was. He decided to ask a trackside official – he and Dana had taught themselves a little English in preparation for the Games – but it took him a while to remember how to formulate the question. Eventually, he asked: 'Where is Heino?' – and received the answer 'Heino is out'. Exhausted by his excessive early pace, and demoralised by Emil's second seizure of the lead, Heino had left the track after sixteen laps.

The final nine laps were a glorious demonstration of fearless, rampant dominance. Runner after runner was lapped (including the future marathon world record holder, Jim Peters). Heinström, too, dropped out: reduced to an exhausted stagger, he was ushered off the track by an official. Emil just kept on pressing. True, he found time to smile and pat Abdullah Ben Said gratefully on the shoulder when the French runner moved out of a lane to allow Emil to lap him more easily; but then he was off again, driving himself furiously forwards as if he were engaged in a desperate battle with an invisible rival just a pace or two behind.

In fact, he was so far ahead that the race officials became confused. The bell for the final lap was rung a lap early. Emil was composed enough to ignore it, and had enough in reserve to run a final lap of 66.6 seconds – the fastest of the race. He crossed the line in 29:59.6, lowering the Olympic record by twelve seconds. The runner-up, Alain Mimoun, was 47.8 seconds behind, with Sweden's Bertil Albertsson a further six seconds behind him. The irrelevance of the other placings was emphasised by the chaos of the official results. Positions were recorded for only the first eleven runners (two of which were later reversed) and times only for the first eight. Britain's Stan Cox, who came seventh, was later told that he should have come fifth as he had run an extra lap. Perhaps the most telling statistic was that all but two of the twenty-seven starters had either been lapped or failed to finish. Rarely has an Olympic victory been so crushing.

For the Czechoslovak team, the sound of their anthem being played as Emil stood on the winner's rostrum was overwhelmingly moving. 'We all had tears in our eyes,' according to Dana. Emil exchanged warm congratulations with Mimoun and Albertsson, then returned to the Uxbridge barracks feeling distinctly pleased with himself. Congratulatory telegrams were already arriving from Czechoslovakia. His insubordination at the opening ceremony was forgiven: as someone pointed out, Heino had stayed out of the sun, and look what it had done for him.

But there was limited time for self-congratulation. The Games had barely begun. The women's javelin final took place the following afternoon. Dana threw quite well: 39.64. It was not quite her best or the best she could have hoped for, but it earned her a respectable seventh place. Considering that a few weeks earlier she hadn't expected to go to the Olympics at all, and that on their arrival in London Emil had had to calm her nerves with the somewhat dispiriting words: 'Don't worry, not everyone who goes to the Olympics is a phenomenal athlete', this was a satisfactory outcome. She had not disgraced herself, or her country.

The Czechoslovak supporters were thus in good spirits when Emil lined up later that day for the 5,000m heats. Emil was in the second of the three heats, and had little to worry about. He and Erik Ahlden, the Swede, agreed that, since four of the twelve runners involved would go through, there was no point in overexerting themselves. They would save their best for the final.

For eleven and a half laps they did the bare minimum necessary. Then, with their nearest rivals 100m behind, Ahlden, perhaps seeking to steal a psychological advantage, powered into a dramatic lead. Emil, rashly, decided after a moment's thought that he was not going to allow this. The resulting last-lap battle was thrilling, reinforcing the previous day's impression that Emil was the most watchable athlete at the Games. Ahlden won – Emil had given him too much of a start – but only by 0.2 of a second, and Zátopek fever strengthened its grip on London. The Czechoslovak team management were less impressed. Emil had run his race nearly thirty seconds faster than most of the others who qualified – thirty seconds faster than he needed to. What on earth did he think he was doing?

The next day was a rest day. Emil and Dana went sightseeing, visiting the Houses of Parliament and St Paul's. And then came Bank Holiday Monday and the 5,000m final.

The golden summer weather changed abruptly. For much of the day, torrential rain pounded Wembley's cinder track. By the time of the final – just after 5 p.m. – it was little better than mud. Frenzied attempts to clear the puddles had little effect. Many spectators huddled beneath the stands for shelter until the last minute, then emerged into the downpour wearing makeshift hats of plastic or, in some cases, programmes. It is hard to imagine that many of the athletes were in high spirits as the cold rain lashed down on them on the starting line.

Väinö Mäkelä led for the first lap; then Emil took over, driving into the wind and rain while his rivals clustered behind him. He hoped that someone else might take on the burden of leading after a lap or two. No one did. So he pressed on, keeping the pace testing without ever really seeming to take it up to the next, destructive level. This was a high-risk strategy: Gaston Reiff and Wim Slijkhuis both had faster finishes than he did. If he wanted to beat them by front-running, he needed to stretch them to breaking point.

To most of the spectators it looked as though Emil was winning, and perhaps Emil, hearing the chants of 'Zá-to-pek!' ring out again, agreed with them. Later he confessed that his 10,000m triumph had left him 'puffed up like a frog'. Watching the old television footage, you wouldn't say that he looks complacent. The face still grimaces, while the miseries of the weather are obvious: every athlete's lower half is black with muddy cinders. Yet perhaps there is a lack of urgency about Emil's movements, and a lack of crispness to his foot placement. By his standards, he doesn't seem to be hurrying – and nor do those behind him.

With four laps to go, Reiff blasted Emil's comfort zone to pieces. The Belgian put on a dramatic spurt that became a 67.8-second lap: two seconds faster than the previous one. Soon he was thirty or forty metres ahead. Emil, demoralised, was unable to respond.

Sensing Emil's vulnerability, Slijkhuis passed him, too. With two laps to go, Slijkhuis was thirty metres ahead, with Reiff a further thirty metres ahead of him. Emil was clearly a beaten man. He was still clawing and flailing, but it felt as if he was going through the motions.

There were all sorts of possible explanation. He had tired himself out unnecessarily with that pointless sprint in his heat. His 10,000m gold had taken the edge off his desire. He was struggling with the slushy cinders. Or perhaps he simply didn't have the stomach for a fight when the weather was foul and the race wasn't going his way. Whatever the reason, he seemed to be running on treacle.

Then he woke up.

There is no other word for it. One moment Emil is asleep on his feet; the next, he isn't. Watching the old footage, I find myself imagining a small boy in Kopřivnice, running round and round the block in a kind of trance – and then suddenly thinking to himself: 'Right, now I'm going to run as fast as I possibly can . . .'

You can see him shaking himself into action, jerking his arms almost crossly, his eyes still screwed up as if he were in a world of his own. He later said that he asked himself at this point whether he had come to London just to run until he was tired, or whether he had come to win. He decided that, if nothing else, he would fight Slijkhuis for the silver. Closing in, he realised that Slijkhuis was tiring, and he began to suspect that Reiff, though still about fifty metres ahead, was tiring, too. And he realised that, as he put it, 'No one was wearing the gold medal yet.'

He began to sprint.

It was not, of course, a smooth, effortless glide. It was a Zátopek sprint: a thrashing, gesticulating life-or-death struggle – as if, to quote one sportswriter, he were 'possessed by devils'. By the time he had passed Slijkhuis, everyone in the stadium had noticed – everyone, that is, except Reiff.

Incredibly, Emil closed the gap. Forty metres, thirty metres, twenty metres – surely he wasn't actually going to do it? As with his previous races, there were only a few dozen Czechoslovaks in the stadium, but it felt like tens of thousands, most of them on their feet by now and shrieking with excitement. By the time Reiff was rounding the last bend, the screams were overwhelming. In the words of the BBC journalist Rex Alston: 'The roar of cheers from the crowd was almost deafening. Stride by stride he brought Reiff back to him.' Finally, Reiff looked around – and saw a whirling blur of red-vested Czechoslovak bearing down on him, scarcely ten metres behind. He roused himself into a desperate sprint, but Emil continued to close: nine metres, eight metres, seven . . . Harold Abrahams, Olympic gold medallist in 1924 and contributor to the official report of the 1948 London organising committee, described the spectacle as 'phenomenal'.

The line came too soon. Reiff was still a stride ahead as he crossed it. Another couple of metres and Emil must have overtaken. But a stride was enough. Reiff was Olympic champion, and Emil had to make do with silver. Their times, 14:17.6 and 14:17.8 respectively, were both inside the old Olympic record.

For most of those present, the result barely mattered, and the times even less. This was one of the gutsiest sporting performances most of them had ever seen. Shortly after the finish, Emil took off his shoes to relieve his sore feet. A few minutes later, he discovered that someone had stolen them – presumably as a souvenir of an unforgettable Olympic moment. It was a funny kind of consolation, but it did perhaps illustrate the extent to which Emil had fought his way into the hearts of thousands of spectators. His stubborn, never-say-die heroism appealed particularly to a British public for whom Churchill's speeches of wartime defiance were still fresh in the memory. In the Czechoslovak camp, however, it was a different matter. Everyone knew that Emil had messed up. How, they wondered (out loud), could he have been so stupid?

By any previous standards of Czechoslovak Olympic achievement, a gold and a silver medal was not a bad haul. But everyone knew that it could have been better. Especially Emil.

It was too late, though. Years later, Emil claimed to have consoled himself with the thought that he would do better next time – before realising that it would be four whole years before there was another Olympic Games. Then he turned his thoughts to Dana, and spent the remainder of their stay in London consoling himself with her company.

This wasn't always easy. What the athletes called the 'sharp eyes' were everywhere: Czechoslovak officials monitoring the athletes' movements to ensure that no one had any improper contact with decadent Westerners. But the 'sharp eyes' were sleeping when, two days later, Emil, still distraught and fretful, crept from his bed before dawn and slipped out of the Uxbridge barracks. Using a combination of bus, train, jogging and broken English, he found his way across west London to Northwood.

At about 6.30 a.m., he arrived at the gates of St Helen's. There was no one around. He whistled a pre-arranged signal: the opening bars of 'their' tune, the Moravian folk song '*V Zarazicách krajní dům*'. Dana looked out of the window and signalled that, if he climbed over the gate, she would meet him in the garden, by the swimming pool. They sat by the pool, talking in whispers. Dana said consoling things about the 5,000m – and Emil took the opportunity to show her his latest medal.

The medal was in its presentation case. 'When I opened the box,' says Dana, still aghast at the memory, 'it slipped from my hand – and fell into the pool.'

There was only one thing for it. Emil stripped to his underwear, dived in and retrieved it from the bottom. He was just trying to squeeze the water from his underpants, behind a tree, when the headmistress of St Helen's emerged – to see a naked Czechoslovak fumbling with his clothes while his girlfriend looked embarrassed nearby.

'She shouted something in English and pointed her finger,' said Dana, giggling like a teenager as she described the moment to me on her ninety-second birthday. 'We didn't understand, but we could tell what she meant. We felt so guilty. But we hadn't done anything.'

Emil tried clumsily to dress ('but you know how difficult it is to put your pants on when your backside is wet') before being chased out; tripped on the gate's bolt casing as he turned to wave goodbye; picked himself up; and left in ignominy. 'We were so embarrassed,' chuckles Dana.

Emil didn't dare show his face in Northwood again. Yet he and Dana were still able to snatch some moments alone – or more or less alone – in their remaining time in London. On one occasion, they spent much of a journey on the Underground trying to ruffle the composure of a respectable Englishwoman sitting opposite them by kissing passionately. They did eventually succeed in making her laugh.

Perhaps more significantly, there was a joint visit to a jeweller's in Piccadilly, where Emil bought two rings. Strictly speaking, they were not yet engaged, but the purchase left little room for ambiguity about their intentions. Characteristically, Emil did not think to ask if they could try the rings on. A few months later they realised that they did not fit, and the two rings were eventually melted down to make a single ring for Dana.

Bad weather dampened the appeal of sightseeing, but there were other distractions. On 3 August, Emil was among 300 competitors and officials who were guests of the King and Queen at an 'informal' party at Buckingham Palace. The King was effusive when Emil was presented to him: 'Czechoslovakia must have a remarkable army,' he is reported to have said, 'if its officers can run so fast.' Dr Karel Popel, manager of Czechoslovakia's canoe team, quipped back: 'Yes, and you should see how quickly our generals can run away.' This reference to the recent stream of military defections does not seem to have done much for Dr Popel's career back in Czechoslovakia, and he defected to the West himself a few years later.

And then, almost unnoticed, the end came. Like many teams, the Czechoslovaks did not stay for the closing ceremony, which was even more low key than the opening. Perhaps they were anxious about allowing their athletes to be exposed to more Western temptations than absolutely necessary. If so, they may have had a point. On the eve of their departure, Marie Provazníková, coach of

Czechoslovakia's gold medal-winning gymnastics team, announced that she would be remaining in London. Citing the 'lack of freedom' in her homeland, she became the modern Olympics' first political defector.

But Emil and Dana had other things on their mind: the magical fortnight behind them, the years that lay ahead; sport, love, and the possibilities of a new life together. Perhaps, too, there were echoes in their minds as they left Britain of the idea that Lord Burleigh, president of the British Olympic Association, had expressed in his speech at the opening ceremony: 'It is our firm belief that you are kindling a torch, the light from which will travel to the uttermost corners of the earth, a torch of that ageless and heartfelt prayer of mankind throughout the world, for peace and goodwill towards men.'

As the aeroplane carrying the athletes back to Czechoslovakia gained height over London, Dana looked out of the window. 'It was early in the morning. We were flying above yellow clouds. It was so beautiful. I was enchanted. I thought to myself that I had achieved a fat lot of good there. But I could try, I could really try. I told myself: now I will try to mean something in athletics.'

As for Emil, he wasn't even on the plane. He had already been sent off to Europe for his next race. Yet the resolution he took away from London with him cannot have been very different from the unspoken vow that Dana made as the plane soared away into the morning: 'If it is in my powers, I will do it.'

7

Love and death

Emil came home, by a roundabout route, trailing clouds of glory. Never before in its short history had Czechoslovakia won such global renown. If Emil had hoped to return to a normal military life, he was quickly disappointed: instead, he found himself committed to a whirlwind schedule of victory parades, public appearances and, not least, races.

There were press interviews; a sculpture to be sat for; a propaganda film to be made. There was a reception at Prague Castle, including an encounter with an effusive Klement Gottwald, Czechoslovakia's first Communist president. There was even indirect contact from the West, with a German shoemaker called Adolf Dassler (future founder of Adidas) reportedly making discreet enquiries about the possibility of supplying Emil with shoes.

Above all, there were autographs to be signed, thousands of them, and off-the-cuff speeches to be given: for example, when Emil was spotted visiting Kopřivnice on the weekend of its annual fair – and caused even more of a sensation than the 'headless woman'. He proved so good at public speaking, scripted or improvised, that

Party officials scrambled to recruit him to give morale-boosting addresses to workers' groups.

He was also promoted, to captain, and – after a brief extra tank course in Vyškov – moved to a job in Prague, as commander of a company in the newly created Army Sports Club (ATK). He worked mainly at the Strahov stadium, but struggled to fit his responsibilities around his travel commitments.

His post-Olympic victory tour took him to Brussels, Amsterdam, Ostend, Prague, Brno, Paris, Bucharest, Bologna and Milan, where he raced at distances from 3,000 to 10,000m. This twelve-race sequence included two defeats. Emil had a sore hip, and was struggling to cope with the endless media attention. Somehow among all this Emil and Dana found time to visit her parents in Uherské Hradiště. It was 19 September, their joint twenty-sixth birthday. In an ideal world this would have been their wedding day, but there had not been time. Instead, after a few celebratory drinks with friends, they returned to the house for Emil to ask Colonel Ingr formally for Dana's hand in marriage. Emil felt intimidated by this, especially when his former commanding officer asked him if he was sure he was sober. Emil attempted to prove him wrong by doing a handstand, but for some reason lacked his usual steadiness in the position. None the less, consent was granted, and the date was fixed for 24 October – a rare gap in the couple's hectic schedule.

Emil also had to get permission to marry from the army – and was shocked to have his request refused. The Ingrs, he was told, were not a suitable family. Dana's father – and, more importantly, her relative and godfather, the famous General Sergej Ingr – were associated with the democratic Beneš regime. It really wouldn't do for Czechoslovakia's new national hero to marry into such a family. But Emil was determined and said that, rather than give up Dana, he would give up the army. The army thought about this for a while and then – rather like Colonel Ingr – gave its assent, dubiously.

A month later, Emil and Dana returned to Uherské Hradiště for what can only be described as a celebrity wedding. They were slightly late, having gone cycling that morning and, while doing so, attempted to kiss. Valuable time had been lost patching up the resulting damage to Emil's uniform and Dana's knee. By the time they arrived, the square outside the church was so packed with people that Dana could barely fight her way through, despite an athletes' guard of honour forming an arch of javelins at the door. Inside, the crowds were so dense that people were standing on the pews. 'Everyone wanted to congratulate us,' according to Dana. 'My bridal bouquet disappeared in the crowd somewhere.' Several outfits were looking distinctly the worse for wear by the time all the guests had fought their way out again and joined the happy couple for the celebration dinner.

The only difficulty in Emil and Dana's immediate future was that there was no time for a honeymoon, and no immediate prospect of living together either. Dana was not yet able to leave her job in Zlín, while Emil was tied to Prague. The pain of separation was eased by the fact that, early in 1949, Emil was given an apartment: a two-bedroom flat at No. 8 U Půjčovny in central Prague. Perhaps this was less remarkable than it sounds to modern Western ears: it was owned via a housing co-operative, to which it would eventually be returned, and was a place to live rather than an asset. None the less, it was a handsome late wedding present. Western visitors to the first-floor apartment, which would remain the Zátopek home for nearly twenty-five years, tended to describe it as 'modest' or 'simple'. Yet for a poor boy from Kopřivnice who had never yet had so much as a room he could call his own and had been living in institutional accommodation since he was fifteen, it must have seemed like a palace.

This was, of course, part of the idea: part of a nationwide pattern whereby the Party rewarded those it favoured with privileges, positions and possessions. As one propaganda newsreel (showing Emil being driven past cheering crowds through the centre of Prague) put it: 'This is how the people reward those who are most faithful to them, who fight for society's glory.' It hardly needed spelling out that those whose attitudes or class backgrounds made them unsuitable for public employment were simultaneously losing their jobs and, in some cases, their accommodation. In the first few years of Communist rule, around 300,000 people were driven out of public life, including thousands of army officers.

Time for Emil to think about such matters was limited. If he wasn't travelling or racing, he was at his desk, trying to catch up with paperwork. By one account he was able to train only after dark, and had to climb a fence to get to the running track. Yet his appetite for self-improvement as a runner remained as voracious as ever. 'What you do when the stadium is full is important,' he said. 'But what you do when the stadium is empty is a thousand times more important.'

Medals or no medals, he still yearned to make himself faster, and he trained with obsessive persistence. 'When a person trains once, nothing happens,' he said. 'When a person forces himself to do a thing a hundred or a thousand times then he certainly develops in ways more than physical. Is it raining? That doesn't matter. Am I tired? That doesn't matter either. Willpower becomes no longer a problem.' That was part of his secret: he never spared himself.

But a 1949 article by the Prague-based Hungarian coach Klement Kerssenbrock also identified one other thing: the fact that, 'If Zátopek feels tired and has an idea that the speed is slowing down, he immediately tries to increase the pace.' This isn't rocket science; it's barely sports science; yet it may come close to explaining one of the most extraordinary adventures in sport. When the going got toughest, Emil got going: not just on the big occasions but every time, in repetition after repetition, day after day, month after month, until it became his instinctive reaction to the kind of pain that makes ordinary human beings give up. Emil even had a saying for it: 'When you can't keep going, go faster.' It was that simple, self-made instinct that raised him to a level beyond the mere elite. Everything else was detail.

In fact, it was not just ordinary human beings who were being left behind by Emil's relentless self-improvement. He and Dana were eventually allowed a quick honeymoon, in a hostel owned by the Czechoslovak Athletics Federation in the Vysočina region of the Bohemian-Moravian Highlands. It was comfortable, and offered a chance to rest and be together, but it wasn't especially private – in fact, they ended up inviting some friends from Brno to join them. There was also a German shepherd dog, owned by the woman who ran the hostel.

When the dog realised that Emil and Dana were going running every day, it agitated to go with them. So, each day, the three of them would head off on the mountain paths, jogging at first before Emil found somewhere to do more serious training. One day, the dog seemed to be lagging, distracted by its own agenda. Emil went back and chivvied it along. 'I don't know what he said to it,' laughs Dana, 'but suddenly the dog was in front and Emil was chasing it. It looked so confused!' The chase went on at full Zátopek speed, for mile after mile, culminating in a set of flat-out repetitions around a lake; and then, with more chasing, they all returned to the hostel.

That evening, the dog's owner was perplexed. 'I don't know what's wrong with this dog,' she said. It showed no inclination to eat or drink, let alone play. It just lay there, exhausted.

The next day, Emil came to fetch the dog for another excursion. When it realised who was there, it whimpered and crawled deep into the back of its kennel. It was a reaction with which a growing number of Emil's human rivals could identify.

When the new racing season arrived, Emil was pleased to find that his winter training had yielded dividends. There was a cross-country race in Horka u Jičína in April which he won narrowly after building up a huge lead, getting badly lost and then having to fight his way to the front from twenty-ninth position. He won a couple of 5,000m races, too, the second of which, in Warsaw on 9 May, yielded the impressive time of 14:10.2; and there was a 3,000m in Prešov three weeks later, which he also won. Then, on 11 June, he went to Ostrava to run the 10,000m in the Czech military championships.

Jaromír Konůpka, who had not seen Emil race before, made the short journey from Kopřivnice to watch him, and bumped into him beforehand at the Vítkovice stadium. 'I asked him how it was going to be. "Don't ask," he said. He said he had spent the morning being filmed in Zlín, and then had to stand all the way on the train. "I had two slices of bread and some cheese," he said. "And when the train stopped in Přerov I had a beer. So don't expect much . . ."'

But when the race started, Emil felt fine. There wasn't much competition, but, even so, he didn't hold back, and shortly after halfway he began to notice a certain excitement among the spectators. He wondered why: he was in no danger of being overtaken. Then the race announcer explained on the PA system that Emil had completed the first 6,000m faster than Heino had done at the equivalent stage of his 1944 world record of 29:35.4.

Spurred on by the crowd, Emil decided to go for it: his first world record. After 8,000m, he was still ahead of Heino's schedule. The cheering became hysterical. Czechoslovakia had never had a world record in running before. Emil, perhaps distracted, lost a little pace and found himself needing to run the final kilometre in less than three minutes. He could feel himself tiring – but his champion's instinct kicked in. He met the fatigue head-on with a fresh surge of effort which he maintained for two and a half laps. He crossed the line to rapturous applause, in 29:28.2. He had beaten Heino's record by seven seconds.

While officials hurried to telegraph the good news across the world, Emil made a gracious speech to those who had cheered him on, urging others to follow in his footsteps. Quite apart from the magnitude of his achievement, he seemed to be growing accustomed to his duties as a sporting figurehead, and he was handling his celebrity with a grace and ease that would soon become a central theme of the Zátopek legend.

Then there were more races, more travels; at times it must have seemed little more than a blur: a match against Romania in Ostrava; an international match in Stockholm; a four-race tour of Finland (including a 10,000m victory over Heino) in July; and a seven-race tour of Warsaw Pact nations that took in Moscow, Budapest, Sofia and Bucharest. Throw in a few races in Czechoslovakia and you have twenty-two track races from May to September, in eight countries, over distances from 1,500 to 10,000m. If war had broken out the Czechoslovak People's Army would have had to do its best without him.

It would be nice to dwell on all the races. Those who were there sometimes do. But all that really need saying here are three things. First: that's a lot of races. Mo Farah raced only eleven times in the whole of 2015 (and only five times at his specialist distances of 5,000 and 10,000m). The second is that Emil won all but one of them; and that, while most of the races were slow by his standards, he still managed three 5,000m times that were faster than the Olympic record-breaking 14:17.6 with which Gaston Reiff had snatched gold from him in London. And the third and most important thing is that, for Emil, it wasn't just about winning. He raced because he loved to race: to pit himself against the strongest opposition he could find and see who was best. And he did all this with a *joie de vivre* that brightened the process for all concerned. His growing mastery of foreign languages made him, in the words of British steeplechaser John Disley, a 'focal point' for conversation at international meetings. His warmth, good humour and interest in people made him more than an interpreter: he was a facilitator of friendship. Bill Nankeville, the British miler, considered him 'a wonderful man, terribly kind'. Unlike Disley, Nankeville didn't race against Emil, but he still appreciated the friendly glow of his personality.

Emil loved to talk: before, after and even during races. Perhaps he was making up for the solitude of his training. The chatter was largely inconsequential and often in a pidgin version of a half-learnt language; the details are mostly forgotten. But everyone remembered Emil's zest for human interaction: a witticism here, a word of encouragement there, a joke false start to entertain the crowd there. 'For me it was always about more than the victory,' said Emil later. 'I wanted to win, but not at all costs.'

His one defeat that summer was in the 1,500m in Přerov, a relatively obscure location in Moravia where he agreed to race as a personal favour to the organiser. Emil arrived at a railway station so packed with excited crowds that he could barely fight his way out of it, while the journey from station to stadium was such a struggle he almost gave up. Emil came third, behind Václav Čevona and Milan Švajgr – both specialists at the distance, unlike Emil. But the only person the crowd wanted to cheer was Emil, and local athletics fans still cherished the memory of his visit decades later.

It must have been tempting for Emil to bask in the same afterglow. In his past three months of racing, he had beaten Viljo Heino once and had beaten Väinö Koskela (world No. 2 at 5,000m) three times. He now had a sequence of fourteen consecutive victories at 10,000m – that is to say, every race he had ever run at the distance. Yet there was one small problem. In early September, news broke that Emil had ceased to be a world record holder. Running in Kuovola in Finland, Heino, who many people had assumed to be past his best, had shaved a whole second off Emil's time.

Emil professed himself unconcerned, suggesting that perhaps it was Heino's turn to hold the record for a while. His superiors felt differently. Later that month, there was a conversation with Colonel Václav Sábl, who was in charge of athletics at ATK Praha and may himself have been under some pressure from above, in which Emil was effectively ordered to bring the record 'back home'. Emil complained that he was too busy ('I was a company commander, so I can't train when I am supposed to be on duty'), and didn't have time to prepare. Colonel Sábl's response was a question: how much time do you need? The result was a three-week stretch in which Emil and two other athletes in his unit were excused all other duties. It was a rare privilege – some Westerners would say an unfair one – but also a huge responsibility. Colonel Sábl's intervention could be seen as support, or as something more threatening than that. Emil said at least once around this time that, when he raced in Czechoslovakia, he feared that, if he lost, he would be put in prison. Whether or not such fear was justified, there was an obvious implication that people in high places were disappointed that he had lost the record and would be still more disappointed if, now that these special arrangements had been made for him, he did not win it back.

The new record attempt was set for 22 October, in Ostrava. Emil's planned preparation involved two weeks of super-intense training, followed by a week's tapering off. For his first day of 'training leave' he did a modest 5 x 200m, 20 x 400m and 5 x 200m. For the second he increased the number of 400s to thirty, and thereafter he made it forty. His focus was primarily on pace; endurance wasn't really an issue by this stage of the season. Even so, it was a heavy load – and on the fourteenth day he developed bruising in his calf. He had no choice but to ease off more abruptly than he had planned, and rested altogether on the seventeenth and nineteenth days. By the twentieth day the calf seemed better, but it was, of course, too late for any more heavy training.

The record attempt was supposed to be unannounced, but news leaked out, and there were crowds awaiting him when he and his fellow ATK athletes arrived at Ostrava station. A car with a PA system accompanied them from the station to the barracks, drawing people's attention to the arrival of the great Zátopek. Emil, worried that the fanfare might undermine his hopes, spent the evening anxiously working out his schedule. He decided to aim for 70.5-second laps, which would yield a time of 29:23.0 – comfortably inside the record but more than five seconds inside his previous best.

The next day, a Saturday, was cold and blustery, but by 4 p.m. the wind had dropped. The Vítkovice stadium was packed with 20,000 people. Shortly before stepping on to the track, Emil was concerned to see a newspaper seller with a pack of posters pre-prepared to announce a 'special edition – Zátopek breaks world record'.

And then he was off. There were, of course, other runners, but there was no question of any pacemaking: no one else in ATK Praha was up to it. Yet the crowd's vociferous support provided a sense of urgency, and after a slow start Emil was able to stick fairly well to his 70.5-second laps – which he could monitor with the aid of a timekeeper who raised a flag at alternate seventy and seventy-one-second intervals. There was a minor crisis in the eighth kilometre, when he began to tire and, simultaneously, realised that he had slipped several seconds behind his own schedule, but the split times suggest that he was never in serious danger of falling behind Heino's pace. In any case, the spectators were not going to allow him to let the prize slip from his grasp, and their redoubled shouts helped to remind him to do what he did best – and respond to exhaustion by fighting back. Visibly gritting his teeth, he upped the pace. By the end of the ninth kilometre he had almost halved the deficit, and for the final laps he accelerated relentlessly. He finished with a near sprint for the final 300m, and crossed the line in 29:21.2 – six seconds faster than Heino's record.

The acclaim was huge, perhaps unlike anything he had experienced before. His Olympic medals had been won in London, before spectators who, however much they warmed to him, were not his countrymen. Here he was among his fellow army athletes, who hoisted him on to their shoulders, and among his fellow Moravians, including family and friends; and, not least, among tens of thousands of fans who had felt personally involved in the making of a new landmark in Czechoslovakia's sporting history. Once again, Emil made a dignified speech, reportedly praising 'the common struggle of all progressive human beings for peace and democracy'. There were more congratulatory messages and telegrams, too, including one from President Gottwald, while the approval of his military superiors was both obvious and gratifying.

The next morning, Emil visited Kopřivnice, where once again there were large crowds. He will have noted that building works were in progress for a new sports stadium named in his honour. Then he returned to Prague, where, according to Dana, he 'glowed like a meteor and couldn't fall asleep all night for excitement'.

Dana had been able to move to Prague by now, where she had found a job as a secretary for a sports magazine, *Ruch* (better known by its subsequent name, *Stadion*). She had struggled at first with the unaccustomed experience of living in a big city, and found it odd that, if she wanted to know what the weather was like, she had to go out on the balcony. But at least there was a balcony. There was also a maple tree outside, and a courtyard at the back, and friendly neighbours, including at least one fellow athlete, the discus thrower Jarmila Jamnická, with whom they socialised.

Inside, parts of the apartment came to look more like a gym than a home – one wall was lined with horizontal wooden exercise bars, which Emil had installed – reflecting the overwhelming priorities of the occupants. But it was, by all accounts, a happy home. After work, Emil and Dana used to train together at the Strahov stadium, at the top of the great hill that towers over Prague from the west bank of the Vltava. And afterwards, happily exhausted, they would jog home, down Strahov Hill, across Hradčany Square, through the grounds of Prague Castle – 'All the visitors had gone by then,' says Dana, 'and there were just the soldiers standing guard' – and then down the long, sloping, castle steps, chasing their shadows towards Klárov and the zigzagging alleys that would take them home. The hard cobbles cannot have been very comfortable for their plimsolled feet; none the less, says Dana, these twilight jogs were 'the most beautiful training I ever did'.

There were many such enchanted moments in those days. In November, there was another short holiday, this time in the Tatra Mountains. Much of it was taken up by the novelist František Kožík, who conducted interviews with Emil that would form the basis of a biography (published soon afterwards) that began life as *The Will to Victory* but was repeatedly adapted and expanded over the next five years to take into account Emil's multiplying achievements and fame. But there was also time for training, on wet roads in army boots, and for long walks with Dana which, according to Kožík, regularly degenerated into tree-climbing sessions and games of leapfrog. There was no dog to run with this time, but Emil did make friends with a flock of sheep, some of which seemed tempted to run with him but soon thought better of it.

Then, in spring, there was a trip to the Soviet resort of Sochi, on the Black Sea. It wasn't a holiday: like most things in their lives in this period, it was simply something they had been told to do. In effect, they were at a training camp, along with many other leading Soviet bloc athletes, and both took full advantage – for most of April – of the opportunities this offered. One report had Emil doing more than twenty-five kilometres' worth of fast 400m repetitions every day (which by June would increase to a staggering thirty-two kilometres' worth). The Soviet trainers watched and learnt, but Western experts were baffled by the reports that trickled back to them. 'I have yet to hear of any athlete who can manage anything approaching the Czech's programme,' wrote the editor of *Athletics Weekly* that spring. Yet Emil seemed to thrive on the workload, and he returned to Prague bearing tales not of hardship but of Sochi's unforgettable beauty, with the snowy mountain-tops of the Caucasus in one direction and, in the other, a shining sea in which it was warm enough to swim with dolphins. He was particularly enthused by the fact that the resort was populated not by 'millionaire drifters' but by factory workers and miners.

It is tempting to describe this phase of Emil's life as a golden one, but this would not be entirely true. Life was treating the Zátopeks kindly, but there were countless other Czechoslovaks for whom the years between the London Olympics of 1948 and the Helsinki Olympics of 1952 were anything but kind. The Communists' one-party state had quickly become a tyranny, in which the government's overwhelming priority was to eliminate threats to the Party's continuing dominance. By 1950, that policy had turned into what can only be described as a Terror. Those 300,000 'class enemies' driven out of public life were only the beginning. Less easily shrugged off are the tens of thousands – perhaps 200,000 in all by the end of the 1950s – convicted of political offences, of whom several hundred were executed and around 100,000 were sent to labour camps.

Few people knew the full extent of the Terror – perhaps not even all of its perpetrators. But it was hard for anyone to be totally unaware of it. Emil, for example, may not have heard of the execution of his fellow officer General Heliodor Píka, which took place on the day of Emil's first world record. But it would have been odd if the fate of his mentor, Jan Haluza, had passed him by. Haluza was arrested in Zlín in September 1948 for refusing to join the Communist Party and sent to a concentration camp at Jáchymov, where he would spend six years.

The Communists set up eighteen concentration camps in all. Those around Jáchymov were the most hellish, thanks to the mining town's deposits of uranium, for which the Soviet Union had an urgent appetite. Political prisoners offered a cheap solution to the challenge of getting the stuff out of the ground safely. It wasn't safe, but prisoners were expendable. They hacked out the radioactive rock with drills and pickaxes and loaded it on to trucks with their bare hands. Lung cancer was a common cause of death, as were bullets for would-be escapees. Life expectancy among prisoners was forty-two. But there were plenty more where they came from. The political prisoners were known as '*mukl*' – acronym-based slang for 'men marked for liquidation'.

It would be some years before the details of their ordeal became widely known, but most people must have had a notion that the camps existed, if only from the way that people kept disappearing. Ladislav Kořán was another one – Emil's friend from Zlín and Milovice and, in recent years, a fellow member of the Czechoslovak national team. Kořán combined his athletic gifts with a brilliant mind, which he applied to the field of electronics. In the late 1940s he developed a prototype for an instrument that would become one of the world's first electric guitars. (Later models of Blatenská Resonet guitars would be played by, among others, George Harrison of The Beatles and Led Zeppelin's Jimmy Page.) But the Communist coup put paid to Kořán's hopes of developing his own business, and so he tried to sell the company abroad. The next thing he knew, he was being tipped off about his imminent arrest for 'industrial espionage'. He fled the country in late 1949 but then, in April 1950, made the mistake of returning to fetch his family. He was picked up and sentenced to eighteen years. He would spend the next decade as a *mukl* in Jáchymov.

Information about specific cases circulated slowly: most people had learnt not to talk about them freely. But the wider shadows of totalitarianism were everywhere, from the city formerly known as Zlín (renamed Gottwaldov in 1949 in honour of the nation's slavishly Stalinist president) to the centre of Prague, where work was about to begin on that thirty-metre-high statue of Stalin, on the edge of the Letenské Gardens. You had only to look at a newspaper to realise that the press had long since ceased to be free – why else would there be all those gratuitous, sycophantic stories about the wonders of the Soviet Union? As for freedom of thought, you could be jailed for up to a decade simply for failing to tell the police about other people's disloyal intentions: this new offence was known as '*Věděl, nepověděl*' – that is, 'Knew, but didn't tell'.

And now, in case anyone was in any doubt, terror was brought to the top of the public agenda. The 'monster trials' of 1949–52 can be seen as a direct extension of the Stalinist purges in Russia. Soviet 'consultants' were sent to Czechoslovakia to oversee them. The idea was not just to eliminate opposition to the regime – although 178 victims were indeed executed as a result – but to cow the entire population. Special courts were set up for the purpose, and special crimes added to the legal code. Little attempt was made to disguise the fact that the accused had been tortured, physically and psychologically; or that nearly everyone involved in the trials – which were broadcast live – was reciting from a script.

The accused ranged from genuine dissidents to Party officials who had fallen from favour. The most shocking case, in June 1950, was that of Milada Horáková.

Horáková was a transparently decent politician. A democratic socialist and patriot, she had opposed the Nazi occupation and, as a result, had spent much of the Second World War in a concentration camp. Following the liberation, she had represented democratic socialism as an MP for the Česká strana národně sociální (which translates, misleadingly, as Czech National Socialist Party). She resigned in March 1948 but continued to campaign against the new post-democratic regime. She was arrested in September 1949, accused of plotting to overthrow the 'people's democracy' and tried, with twelve supposed co-conspirators, from 31 May to 8 June 1950.

The proceedings were broadcast not just on radio but on public address systems in the streets and in workplaces, so that everyone could hear Horáková condemned as a 'criminal mastermind' of a 'terrorist conspiracy'. At the same time, a vicious campaign of public condemnation was organised. The Central Committee of the Czechoslovak Communist Party organised public meetings at which people were urged to sign petitions calling for the harshest possible sentences for the 'traitors'. Those who refused soon realised that, in so doing, they were casting doubt on their own loyalty to the regime.

And so, like a grotesque precursor to the Ice Bucket Challenge, the campaign went viral. Hardly anyone dared refuse to join in: why would you, unless you were part of the conspiracy? Workers were asked to vote on motions calling for the death penalty. ('Somehow everyone's hand went up,' one former factory worker recalled.) Petitions were even taken into schools, and woe betide the parents of children who refused the invitation to sign. But the most visible manifestation of the campaign was a flood of letters, to newspapers and government offices, condemning the accused on behalf of individuals or groups. *Rudé právo*, the newspaper of the Communist Party, devoted entire pages to anti-Horáková correspondence.

Horáková, a politely spoken woman of forty-eight, conducted herself with courage and dignity, refusing to stick to her persecutors' script and insisting, 'I remain, on principle, firm in my convictions.' When, on 8 June, the inevitable death sentence came (for her and three others), Winston Churchill, Albert Einstein and Eleanor Roosevelt were among those who pleaded for clemency.

But the hate campaign continued, and the page that *Rudé právo* devoted to it two days later included the following letter:

> *The words used by the President when he spoke to ČSM Congress and quoted an old revolutionary song – 'Let the old, shameful world perish, so that a new life on Earth can begin' – are also our own thoughts, which lead us forward.*

After all, we are already building a new life. Yet monsters have been found, who wanted to destroy the road to socialism that we are building.

The behaviour of these spies and traitors is both shameful and foolish, because a people who have fought for better conditions in life will never give up their historical development and will never return to the old days. People are convinced of the benefits of socialism, of compliance and of cooperation, and will not ever allow their rights to be taken from them.

The subversives have condemned themselves by their actions – by their divisiveness and by their preparation of war against their own people.

This judgment is a warning to all who pursue nefarious goals within our Czechoslovak Republic. By working together we have built a better life, and anyone who wishes to disrupt our work together will meet the same fate as this group of spies and subversives.

This judgment was handed down by the entire Czechoslovak people.

As a member of the Czechoslovak army, I can see that the peaceful life that results from the hard work of all our workers and soldiers has been preserved by this judgment.

Captain Emil Zátopek

This is not something that one reads about very often in accounts of Emil Zátopek's life. When I first encountered it, I refused to believe it. I cannot imagine anything more out of tune with what I believe to have been his generous, gentle character. Yet it appeared. I have seen it in print in the *Rudé právo* archive, halfway down the left-hand column of page three of the issue of 10 June 1950.

Even now, I am not sure what to make of it. Did Emil write it? It is hard to believe. The voice is that of a party propagandist, not a playful-spirited sportsman. He certainly would not have written it spontaneously, or in isolation. Did he sign it, or agree to put his name to it? This is a different matter. The fact that it is mild compared with many of the letters *Rudé právo* published – it is not, for example, a call for the death penalty – raises the possibility that it might have been a negotiated compromise. I am not aware of Emil ever having been questioned about this, let alone having answered (although I have heard it said that he expressed approval when, nearly two decades later, a more humane Czechoslovak government retrospectively overturned the verdict against Horáková).

Asked about Emil's letter more than sixty years after it was published, Dana Zátopková insists that he never saw it, and may not even have been aware of it – although there was one time when, after President Gottwald had given a speech on the subject to which the Zátopeks and other athletes had been forced to listen, 'Someone ran up to Emil and asked him what he thought – and he said: "Don't ask me, ask Comrade Gottwald." But that was all.' Perhaps she is right, and that is all the authority he gave; we have no way of knowing. I suspect, however, that it is not quite so clear-cut as that. Dana also says: 'We had no idea that these defendants were being tortured, that the charges were made up – all the things we know about today.' This may be true, too. But I think it is also true that, then as now, many people will have known as much or as little as they chose to know. Even in Western democracies, most of us have some vague sense that certain things done by our governments – or perhaps by the corporations we work for – might be morally hard to defend. Most of us deal with such perceptions by keeping them vague. The less we know, the less we have to worry about, the less reason to disturb our otherwise comfortable lives. Respectable Germans did this in their millions during the Nazi era, but they were not unique. And if a little, nagging voice was whispering to Emil that perhaps the state's case against Horáková was a monstrous travesty – well, he would not have been the first person to ignore such a voice.

In Czechoslovakia there was an additional incentive not to inquire too deeply: fear. To allow the full obscenity of the situation to come to the front of one's mind would have been to invite catastrophe – to risk becoming a victim rather than a bystander. Six years of Nazi occupation had given the Czechoslovak people a brutal crash course on how to survive under a fanatical tyranny. Many were once again putting that lesson into practice.

'We did not live at that time,' a Czech archivist told me when I was beginning my research into Emil's life. 'So we cannot judge it.' She is right. But we can speculate – and in Emil's case the riddle is particularly perplexing. Just a few months earlier, an internal report in Emil's personal military service file had painted a picture of an officer of unusually independent spirit. Written in March 1950, it stated that, the previous March, Emil had refused point-blank to inform against his room-mate, Miloslav Ladýř. He told his superior officer directly that even if he knew that someone was speaking against the state, he would not report it – although he might intervene by 'explaining certain things' to him. He also stated that he was disillusioned with Communism, because of the violence the Party was now using, and because of the way it divided the country into two opposing groups, positive and negative. 'His honesty and directness, at times childish, are quite surprising,' wrote the scandalised reporting officer. 'He stated that he was himself aware that he could be locked up for many of his statements, but he thought it preferable to state them all rather than give the impression that he was pretending.'

That had been March 1949. Two months later, an education officer, Warrant Officer Vejvoda, had been entrusted with the political education of First Lieutenant Zátopek. In November, Emil had been sent on a six-week training course in Marxism at the Central Political School (ČSM), in Klecany, near Prague. We do not know what he learnt there, but we do know he developed a habit of cutting off his anti-Party grumblings with the words: 'I keep quiet, or else they would lock me up.'

In December 1949, Emil was reported to the military authorities for making 'adverse statements about the system of People's Democracy'; in May 1950, he was investigated for refusing to join the Federation of Czechoslovak Soviet Friendship; the same month, an informer accused him of being less enthusiastic about the USSR in private than he was in public. He was also under suspicion because, unusually for an officer (and unlike his father, brothers and father-in-law), he was not yet a member of the Communist Party: he claimed that his application had been held up. One informer's report in 1950 mentioned the notebook (possibly his training diary) that Emil kept in his tracksuit pocket and suggested that, if this could be stolen, it might reveal 'his true political opinions'. The fact that all this is preserved in his records (along with some pointed comments about Dana's reported lack of enthusiasm for the regime) reminds us how fanatically the army cared about conformity – and how much danger Emil was placing himself in by refusing to conform. Political attitudes were monitored, assessed, recorded and, if necessary, acted upon. In the words of the influential General Karel Procházka: 'He who does not have a positive attitude cannot serve as a commander.'

We can only guess how these circumstances affected Emil when the Horáková storm broke. Had his spirit been crushed by then? Was it put to him that, if he didn't co-operate, he could expect a similar fate himself? Was Dana mentioned? All we can say with certainty is that the letter appeared, with his name at the bottom.

Dr Libor Svoboda of the Institute for the Study of Totalitarian Regimes in Prague – an institution not known for its reluctance to condemn the crimes of Communism – was surprisingly sympathetic to Emil when I asked him about this. Dr Svoboda's aunt was at school when her head teacher and other functionaries came into class and told the pupils they had to sign a form requesting the death penalty for Horáková. No one volunteered, so the officials pointed to some students and told them to sign first. Such scenes were common throughout Czechoslovakia; and, Dr Svoboda argues, 'if inconsequential students had to sign, it wouldn't have been possible for an officer of the Czechoslovak Army to refuse.

'I imagine that they summoned him and political operatives "introduced him to the situation" and invited him to sign, as he had to be an example . . . I can't imagine what would have happened to him in that tense and hysterical atmosphere had he not signed. What would have awaited him was the fate of working in the mines or in agriculture and the end of any kind of career, not only in terms of athletics.

'I don't want to be an apologist for Zátopek – it was a failure on his part. An ideal hero would have refused and left the army. But Zátopek wasn't an ideal hero in this regard; he wanted to run and he sacrificed very much to achieve this end.'

In fact, Emil had found the backbone to defy his superiors more than once, not least in connection with marrying Dana. But perhaps he felt that he had used up his credit. Nine months later, in the more militantly Communist environments of ATK Praha and the Ministry of Defence, a doomed, heroic stand on behalf of Milada Horáková would have required an altogether more suicidal form of courage. Perhaps, in June 1950, Emil simply didn't have the stomach for a fight that would have ended his career and sporting dreams and risked his life and liberty as well.

So he signed – probably – whatever was put in front of him, with or without reading it; and then, presumably, put the whole matter to the back of his mind.

It would remain for ever a shadow on his past. But perhaps it also cast a shadow over his future, colouring his resolve to make nobler choices were similar situations to arise.

8

The Czech locomotive

Whatever Emil really felt about the purges, we can assume that he kept any dissenting thoughts largely to himself. Alexej Čepička, the new Minister of Defence, was a leading instigator of the persecution, and the army was expected to be beyond reproach in its orthodoxy. Yet it must have been around this time, or not long afterwards, that Emil admitted to his friend and fellow athlete Ivan Ullsperger that he 'had problems' with some of the things the Communists were doing.

He felt – according to Dana – that the movement he believed in had been hijacked by what he called 'quick brew Communists' who saw the ideology as a route to personal advancement rather than a recipe for universal happiness. But he avoided direct revolt, once saying that, rather than run in fear all the time, he preferred to 'bend' – without actually breaking. Sent for further political training later in the year, he veered between seeming 'politically mature' and making 'basic errors in Marxism-Leninism'; his supervisor was unable to decide if he was was 'cunning' or 'childish'. According to Ullsperger, Emil took the view that the world was divided into people who had 'the will to power', and made others conform to their views; and those who didn't. Emil considered himself to be in the latter camp and allowed himself – up to a point – to be pushed around. Perhaps this kind of outlook was inevitable for a soldier whose primary duty was obedience to his superiors; but it also tells us something about Emil's approach to life at the time. Another friend quoted him, later on, as saying that the key to happiness was to learn to behave as a domesticated animal rather than a wild one. Meanwhile, he did not allow the unpleasantness of the Terror to distract him from his relentless self-improvement as a runner. Perhaps it even encouraged it, in the same way that running had offered a form of escape from the Nazi occupation. On the running track, no one could tell him what to say or think.

On the day his letter appeared, Emil ran and won a 5,000m in Prague. His time, 14:17.2, was his best of the year so far. There was another 5,000m the following week, then a two-week break – during which he must have heard reports of Milada Horáková's execution, although perhaps not the ghastly details of her slow, cruel strangulation.

Five days later Emil was in Warsaw to win another 5,000m; the following weekend he was in Bratislava to win both a 5,000 and a 10,000m. Afterwards, there was a dinner in the nearby town of Modrá, where the wine flowed freely. 'Local people kept saying to him: "Drink a toast with me!", "Drink a toast with me!",' recalls Milan Švajgr. 'At the end of the evening, he couldn't stand up.' You can understand why someone might enjoy the release of alcohol in such tense, dangerous times. But it was perhaps not ideal preparation for his next big target: a crack at the Czechoslovak national record for 5,000m.

The plan was to make his bid in Ostrava, in the Army Championships at the beginning of August. His results in the preceding months – eight victories in eight races, seven of them at 5,000m – were almost incidental to his heavy, record-focused training, which he built up to a peak of thirty-two kilometres per day in early July. At the last minute, however, he was told that there had been a change of plan: an invitation had been accepted on his behalf to take part in a series of events in Finland, organised by the Finnish Workers' Sports Federation (TUL).

He could hardly object, given his publicly expressed enthusiasm for the centrally directed, politically guided state management of sport that the Communist regime had imposed on Czechoslovakia, but he cannot have been happy to have his athletics ambitions sacrificed so casually in the interest of diplomacy. Yet the trip offered chances to race as well as to meet and greet. The first of these came on 2 August, in Helsinki. The competition was minimal – his opponents were all TUL members – but the crowd was world-class. They already recognised Emil as a worthy visitor to the home of distance running, and they appreciated the fact that, despite effectively running alone, he appeared to be pushing himself to his limit from the start. With mounting enthusiasm, they urged him on – and he finished in 14:06.2. It was exactly two seconds faster than his previous Czechoslovak record, and the second fastest 5,000m time ever.

From there he went straight to Turku, Paavo Nurmi's birthplace, where he was due to race at 10,000m two days later. One of the first people he saw there was the Czechoslovak ambassador, who warned him that people in the town had hopes of a world record. Emil, notwithstanding his public speaking duties, was in the mood to oblige.

Once again, he had to all intents and purposes to run alone. Once again, he flung himself into the challenge; and, once again, the Finns were stirred by the sight. There is a nobility to running against the clock. For some aficionados, the truly great distance runner is the one who – as *Sports Illustrated*'s Kenny Moore later wrote of another giant of the discipline, Ron Clarke – accepts 'each of his races as a complete test, an obligation to run himself blind'. And Finnish athletics fans are nothing if not aficionados of distance running. They understood what Emil was trying to do, were excited by the thought that they were witnessing a historic piece of running, and cheered accordingly.

Emil was aiming for 29:15 – just over six seconds faster than his existing record – but in the second half of the race he began to step up the pace. The Finns roared him on. He ran the final lap flat out and finished in a scarcely believable 29:02.6 – nearly twenty seconds faster than his world record from the previous year. Afterwards, he warmed down outside the stadium, then returned to the centre of the track to retrieve his tracksuit. The spectators spotted him, and gave him a standing ovation that still brought tears to his eyes when he recalled it more than forty years later.

By the time he got back to Czechoslovakia, another victory parade had been organised for him in the streets of Prague. If monster trials were the stick with which the Communist regime beat its citizens into obedience, sporting glory was a carrot with which life in the new Czechoslovakia could be made to feel palatable. The fuss about Emil's achievements may seem excessive from today's perspective, but in those grim days a little triumphalism could go a long way. The message was simple. As František Kožík wrote, the record showed that: 'we have a supreme sportsman who is capable of anything if it is a question of winning the recognition of the whole world for his country.'

The acclaim for Emil was certainly becoming increasingly international. A Finnish newspaper hailed him as 'more than just a runner'. *The Times* of London, known for its sobriety, called him 'the fabulous Zátopek'. A few weeks later, a Belgian paper would call him 'a super-runner who enchants the whole world'.

There was additional justification for this last accolade, although the journalist who wrote it may not have known it. Emil's next major sporting engagement after returning from Finland was in Brussels, where he was due to be racing in the European Championships on 23–26 August. In the 5,000m he would get a chance to avenge his Olympic defeat by Gaston Reiff, who was back to his best form, so he stepped up his training to forty fast 400m laps a day. Then disaster struck.

Just over a week before the championships, Emil ate some cold Moravian duck that had been left for a little too long. The resulting acute food poisoning put him in hospital, where he had to have his stomach pumped. By Monday, 21 August he had stabilised but had lost five kilograms in weight. He would have lost more had he not taken advantage of the lack of medical staff at the weekend to sneak into the hospital kitchen and cook himself some sausages – washed down, he claimed, with beer – to give himself strength for a few desperate jogs around the hospital garden. On the morning of Tuesday 22nd the doctors finally gave way to his pleas to be discharged, which gave him just enough time to catch a plane to Belgium an hour later. Common sense suggested that it would be folly even to attempt to run, let alone try to win.

Even so, he ran – and it was as if he had winged feet. On the Wednesday, on a waterlogged track, scarcely twenty-four hours after leaving hospital, Emil ran the second-fastest 10,000m of all time, in 29:12.0. Alain Mimoun, who won the silver medal, was seventy-nine seconds behind.

On the Thursday, he won an easy 5,000m heat. Then, on Saturday, 26 August, came the showdown with Reiff, the local hero. There was a time when he would have been intimidated by the sound of 60,000 spectators chanting 'Gaston! Gaston!', but Emil was no more intimidated by the partisan atmosphere than he was by Reiff's coach telling him, shortly before the race, that Reiff would win in 14:03 – a time bettered only by Gunder Hägg's extraordinary 1942 record of 13:58.2. Reiff did indeed set off at something like world-record pace, but Emil was determined that, this time, he would not allow his rival to open up a lead.

This was easier resolved than achieved, but Emil stuck to his rule of keeping the gap between them to an absolute maximum of twenty metres and, where possible, less, no matter what the effort cost him. For the third and fourth laps he actually led; then Reiff overtook and, from that point on, led until the bell. Reiff was hoping that, as in London, he could simply burn Emil off, and it is possible that he assumed that he had opened up a decent lead. The loud support prevented him from hearing if anyone was close behind, and he did not want to offer the encouragement of a backward look. Then, as the last lap began, he did finally glance over his shoulder. Emil was right on his heels. The sight visibly punctured his morale – especially since Emil chose that very moment to launch his signature 400m finishing sprint. Reiff's stamina leaked away with his self-belief. Emil opened up a lead of more than 100m and won in 14:03. (Reiff's coach had been right about the winning time.) Reiff lost so much impetus that he finished twenty-three seconds behind, and Alain Mimoun just managed to overtake him for the silver – which the world was coming to regard as his customary position behind Emil.

It is hard to overstate the immensity of Emil's achievement in Brussels. For the second time in four days, fresh from hospital, he had run the second-fastest time ever for a distance, and had not just beaten but trounced the best endurance runners in Europe. His 10,000m victory had been another largely solo effort against the clock; for the 5,000m he had soaked up lap after lap of high-speed punishment from an Olympic champion before counter-punching with a devastating final lap. It was a dazzling display of the runner's art, and one can only assume that 'fresh from hospital' is the apposite phrase. Whatever the rest of his body had been going through, Emil's legs had had an unaccustomed rest.

But the truth was that, rest or no rest, Emil was now in a different league. He ended the year undefeated, after (by my count) thirty-two races – excluding relays. He had run the world's seven fastest times of the year at both 5,000 and 10,000m. The next fastest 10,000m-runner of the year, the Soviet Union's Ivan Semyonov, had a season's best more than a minute slower than Emil's.

It was around this time that the nickname 'the Czech locomotive' became popular, to convey the image of Emil leading every race, with the other runners stretched out behind him like a line of carriages – then dropping off one by one. (The nickname had appeared in *Rudé právo* as early as 31 July 1948, but took a couple of years to catch on in the West.) Other reporters deployed the idea of there being two races: one for Emil and one for everyone else. It was hard to disagree, when Emil was so far ahead. He won races by one lap, sometimes getting on for two laps – and no matter how far ahead he was, he would always finish with a flat-out final lap.

There had never been a runner like him.

Inevitably, people asked themselves how he did it. Was he a freak? Did he cheat? Or did he have some secret formula?

The answers are surprisingly mundane. Emil was not a freak: in most respects, he was a rather average physical specimen. He was 174.3cm tall, weighed just under 68kg and had well-developed thighs and calves – as one would expect, given his training regime. He had relatively long legs for his size, and his left thigh (circumference 52cm) was slightly smaller than his right (54.3cm), which might have had something to do with his ungraceful gait, either as cause or as effect. His resting pulse rate was at different times reported to be 68 beats per minute (which seems implausibly high), 56 and 52 (both more plausible, but still barely less than average – and high by the standards of today's elite endurance athletes). His VO2 max was estimated (later) at 76.2ml/min/kg – good, but, again, not as good as many modern athletes. He could hold his breath, after inhaling, for 127.6 seconds; after exhaling, for 11.4 seconds. His blood pressure was high when first measured, in 1944; but by 1945, after he set his first record, it had come down to 136/70mm Hg – that is, a little below 'normal'.

What made Emil exceptional physiologically were his powers of recovery: his heart rate would return to normal very rapidly, even after extreme exertion. In a test requiring him to get up and down off a chair fifty centimetres high 150 times in the space of five minutes, his pulse rate rose from a resting fifty-six beats per minute to a high of seventy-six beats per minute – but was back to fifty-six within a minute of finishing.

His muscles, too, seemed quick to revert to their relaxed state. One slow-motion analysis suggests that his fellow Olympic finalists' thigh muscles remained contracted in mid-stride for four times as long as Emil's did. But these are qualities that one might expect to result from years of intense training.

He had a relatively short, quick stride, averaging 170cm in length – although the physician who made that measurement, Dr Zdeněk Hornof, admitted that Emil had complicated the study in question by deliberately varying his stride length as a joke. He ran with a full ankle movement, landing on the balls of his feet but with the heel relatively low. As for the rest of his running style, there were those (notably the great Australian coach Percy Cerutty) who hypothesised that his agonised upper body movements were part of his secret, but there was never much evidence to support that theory: otherwise all elite runners would now run as though wrestling with an octopus. If Emil had a technical secret, it was that he ran with the utmost economy of effort below the waist.

But his real secret was less complicated than that. It was simply that, for five years now, he had been training harder, longer and more ferociously than anyone had ever trained before. He was not in the least secretive about his methods, and was happy to discuss them with anyone who asked. Ultimately, it could all be expressed in a simple equation: volume x intensity. Eventually, other athletes began to imitate him, and their times improved, too.

What nearly everyone agreed on was that Emil's success had nothing to do with tactical cunning. Ron Clarke, the future 10,000m world record holder, described his tactics in races as 'poor – or non-existent'. He tended to start slowly, partly because he had less basic speed than 5,000m rivals such as Gaston Reiff. (Reiff's best time over 1,500m was seven seconds faster than Emil's.) He tended to finish strongly for much the same reason: it was the only other option available.

If he had a tactical speciality, apart from his flat-out final laps, it was a tendency to put on surges, especially on bends. Generally, though, to revert to Ron Clarke's assessment, 'he ran too eagerly. He grabbed the lead and kept swopping it. He threatened his own resources.'

It was almost as if Emil saw tactics as unchivalrous. 'I am not particularly interested in beating my opponents,' he said. 'Above all I am interested in improving on my own performance. Why should I profit from my opponents' weaknesses?'

'A lot of journalists found that impossible to comprehend,' Clarke told me. 'For him it was competition for competition's sake, rather than the end result. He took the view that you're far better competing against someone at their best. It was the competition that was the exciting part, not the standing on the rostrum.'

Rather than try to outwit his fellow athletes, Emil liked to take advantage of their company, not just after the race but during it. He would chat away in mid-race as if he was in a pub. His growing command of languages allowed him to do this with most of his competitors, even in international meetings. Some welcomed it; others felt that he was trying to mess with their heads. I don't think he was, though: he was just a talker.

It could be argued – and a few in the West did argue – that Emil's role in the army was not a real job and thus, at a time when athletics was supposed to be strictly amateur, gave him an unfair advantage over those who had to fit their training in the small gaps around 'proper' work. It is hard to answer this definitively. The nature of Emil's military duties varied – in 1950 he was transferred to the Ministry of Defence, where he was made responsible for the physical training of troops – but all his jobs seem to have involved some combination of red tape, direct supervision of fitness training and testing, and absence from his post because of racing requirements. J. Armour Milne, the Prague-based British journalist and Communist who wrote for the *Morning Star* and *Athletics Weekly*, claimed that 'Zátopek is always to be found in his office or visiting an Army unit'; while Emil told his friend Jaromír Konůpka – who visited him at the track around this time and found him unavailable because he was at work – that he had to fit in his training around eight hours of other work each day. His service records suggest that he sometimes struggled to strike a suitable balance between his military duties with his running commitments. And the work must certainly have presented some kind of obstacle to his athletic training or the Ministry of Defence would not have decided, on certain specific occasions, to reduce his duties. In addition, Emil's status as a propaganda figurehead placed extra demands on his time that no Western runner had to worry about; and the regime expected him to perform social duties, too, such as providing fitness instruction at a hostel for miners' apprentices. (Not all of this was strictly compulsory, but Emil didn't like to refuse requests. 'If the decision is left to Captain Zátopek,' noted one superior officer wearily, 'he would say yes to everything.')

Having his workload reduced occasionally to allow him to train harder arguably constituted an advantage. Perhaps it was an unfair one. But he was not the only runner to receive such help. As Christopher Chataway, the British 5,000m runner (and future Conservative MP), admitted: 'There are certainly few top-class athletes in this country who would have difficulty in finding a firm to "carry" them for a few years.' Different societies support their athletes in different ways.

In any case, it was not just lack of time that prevented Emil's rivals from training as hard as he did. A lot of them simply didn't believe in it.

In Britain, for example, the prevailing orthodoxy was that athletes should train sparingly, resting several times a week and saving themselves for races. According to Gordon Pirie, one of the few Western runners to see Zátopek as a challenge rather than a freak, 'his training methods seemed quite fantastic. They were . . . derided by the take-it-easy British school.' Jimmy Green, editor of *Athletics Weekly*, spoke for many when he wrote: 'No athlete would be wise to emulate his colossal amount of severe work.' And Chataway, a runner with huge natural talent but a limited appetite for training, said, 'For me and many others, it is simply more than we could stand.' (Chataway, who like his friend Roger Bannister was Oxford-educated, admitted many years later that this was 'misplaced intellectual arrogance. I suspect that Zátopek, who was doing all this training that we disdained so much, was a great deal more intelligent than we were.')

The most important part of Emil's formula, in other words, was simply the effort he put in. Anyone could do interval sessions. The difficult thing was doing them as Emil did them: not just churning out the laps but doing each one to the genuine limits of one's endurance, without surrendering (as most runners do) to the instinct to keep a little bit in reserve. Sometimes, looking at the details of Emil's ruthless, obsessive self-punishment – the same drills again and again and again and again – you don't just wonder at his discipline: you wonder if there wasn't some kind of personality disorder that allowed him to tolerate it. Yet everything else we know about his character suggests the opposite. It wasn't his hard-won victories that made him a legend. It was his generosity of spirit. That was the special 'something' that made him unique.

How exactly? It is hard to pin it down. But countless friends and loved ones remembered him as, simply, a joy to be with. J. Armour Milne put it like this: 'His tremendous daily training has built him into a human powerhouse, power which he expends not only in breaking records but in making life agreeable for those around him.' More than sixty years later, Emil's nephew Jiří said something similar: 'He lightened people's lives.'

He was startlingly clever, in a slightly unworldly way, with a near-photographic memory. Years after they had taken place, he would discuss incidents and conversations in minute detail. His brain was full of poetry and songs.

He spoke many languages – eight, ultimately – but in childhood had learnt only Czech and a little German. The rest he taught himself from dictionaries. 'Learn enough words,' he said, 'and the grammar looks after itself.'

He was good-looking: not as a film star is but in the more intimate way of a man whose energy and good humour shine through his face. People remarked on his clear blue eyes and his engaging smile, while his receding hair and creased forehead gave him an air of thoughtful, confident maturity that women, especially, found attractive.

He was witty and playful; some would say incorrigibly immature. He made mundane tasks into games, and loved to make people laugh.

He was a gifted mimic. 'He used to imitate the way different people ran,' says the British steeplechaser John Disley, who raced against Emil a few times and also knew him in later life. 'It's hard to explain, but he was terribly funny. It was the way he used his hands.' Another long-term friend, Olga Lišková, almost weeps with laughter as she tries to describe how 'he did this thing when we were having dinner once where he demonstrated how you clean a rifle – and we were laughing so much we were actually rolling on the floor. I wish someone could have filmed him.' Years later, someone did film him telling a story about a trip to Paris where a teammate tried to buy a bra for his girlfriend without knowing a word of French. The humour is indeed in the hand gestures, but the delight is in seeing Emil's listeners, initially stony-faced, creasing up in spite of themselves. His comic timing is perfect.

He had beautiful manners: not the grand kind, but the profound politeness that places great value on obligations of hospitality and courtesy. Nothing was too much effort for them. If there was a problem, Emil would make light of it and try to solve it himself.

A character assessment in his military service files for 1951 identified his defining characteristics as 'doggedness and humility' – but forgot to mention his frivolity. 'He would turn everything into fun,' said one friend; or, as Dana put it, 'He solved problems with jokes.'

If someone needed warmth or reassurance, he would offer it, unstintingly. Children and animals warmed to him. He made everyone feel special.

Neighbours and friends of many ages and nationalities have recalled the Zátopek home in U Půjčovny as a place of fun and friendship. Gordon Pirie called it 'the gayest and merriest home I ever visited'. 'His vitality shone,' said Ron Clarke, many years later. 'The man was pure joy.' Everything got caught up in the whirlwind of his cheerful energy. Jarmila Jamnická recalled Emil's habit of clowning around on the balcony, and the parties with wine and singing; another neighbour, Marie Hainová, would remember Emil's wonderful anecdotes, and the fact that he was always running, even when he went to the shop to buy milk.

Emil and Dana both believed that hospitality was one of the most important virtues. They enjoyed cooking, especially traditional Moravian dishes – although Emil had a tendency to insist that only he knew how to prepare them correctly. And they both loved to tell stories, during and after dinner, often interrupting and correcting one another as they burnished their anecdotes to new levels of hilarity.

They loved nature, and would escape to the countryside when they could. Emil enjoyed hunting for mushrooms, and cooking meals over campfires. Above all, both he and Dana seem to have had an insatiable appetite for mucking around. 'For the world's greatest runner,' wrote J. Armour Milne, 'he takes the craziest risks with his precious limbs. He seems to have no respect for them whatsoever.'

He was impulsive and restlessly energetic. Many people noticed something childlike about him. J. Armour Milne called him 'a boy in spirit and behaviour'. 'Physically he was more machine than man,' wrote Ron Clarke; 'in spirit, more boy than man.'

Claims in officially approved interviews that Emil never touched alcohol are contradicted by numerous accounts of celebrations at which wine and beer were drunk. Emil himself later joked that Dana came from south Moravia, where there were vineyards and wine, whereas he came from the rougher region to the east, where there was only beer. Dana, he said, believed that wine makes you sing, whereas beer merely makes you stupid. But Emil believed that beer was not only noble – the drink of the old Moravians – but positively beneficial for running. 'This gives me power,' he once said to Jaromír Konůpka, quaffing from the bottle on the day of a race.

Music played an important part in the Zátopeks' shared life. Both played the guitar, and both loved folk songs. Dana had the better ear but was less inclined to show it off. Emil's musical gifts were his memory, confidence and enthusiasm: 'I sing out of key, but I sing. Dana is a good singer, but she doesn't sing.' Dana insists today that she did like to sing, but didn't like songs that involved harmonising with Emil, because of his strange sense of pitch. On a less discordant note, Emil would often recite poetry as well. It helped that 'Král Lávra', which Emil had memorised as a child, was one of Dana's favourites.

Their mutual affection was palpable. Dana called Emil by the nickname 'Ťopek'. Emil used to call her Danuška, or 'Dušinko' ('my little soul') or, occasionally, 'Macku', roughly the same as 'sweetie'.

But the romance in their relationship was tempered by a playfulness that often spilled over into simple silliness. Emil, for example, encouraged Dana to think of household objects as living creatures – so that she would be less careless with them. 'It started when he saw me pull a plug out the wrong way, by its wire,' says Dana. 'He said: "You wouldn't pull a cat by its tail." He thought that if I felt an emotional connection with appliances, I would be more likely to look after them. He was right.' Soon all their devices had names, from Terka-Perka, the noisy washing machine, to Dáša, the bulky refrigerator, named after a big-bosomed friend. And then there was the concept of the Day of Complete Bliss, which either one of them was allowed to declare unilaterally. On such a day, no one was allowed to do any chores (especially washing) or anything else they didn't truly want to do. Such days happened very rarely, but their occasional occurrence – and constant potential occurrence – was one more thing to keep a smile on the young couple's faces.

They did argue, quite often. But when they did, according to Dana, they often ended up making one another laugh. Emil had two preferred techniques. 'Sometimes he would go quiet for a long time, and then, later on, he would say in a pathetic voice: "But you still love your Ťopek a little bit, don't you?"' On other occasions he would end the silence by adopting a mock military demeanour, calling Dana to attention and demanding to know her name ('Dana') and rank ('wife'), which they both found highly amusing – and which Dana, from the warmth of her laughter as she describes it, clearly still does.

Emil must have been maddening to live with at times; on the plus side, though, he was practical and happy to do his share of household duties. He had a cupboard that he called 'Paradise', in which he kept every possible kind of tool, nut and bolt, all carefully graded and organised. He was competent at DIY but not infallible. The kitchen table (a wedding present from the national sports federation) was unusually high in the early days of their marriage but ended up unusually low: Emil shortened the legs several times before he succeeded in getting rid of the wobble. Such mishaps were all part of the fun of living with Emil.

What do you miss about him most, I asked Dana, fifteen years after his death.

'The laughter,' she said.

In those early years of their marriage, it must have helped that they were both equally committed to the overwhelming importance of training. Their shared obsession may have seemed odd to Majda Štěrbová, a schoolfriend of Dana's who lived in their second bedroom for a while. It didn't seem odd to Emil and Dana. It helped, too, that they were both orderly: a career soldier married to a colonel's daughter. Gossip in military circles suggesting that Captain Zátopek paid too much attention to his training and not enough to his wife may tell us more about military circles than about the Zátopeks. They rarely quarrelled about misplaced priorities. Their main dissatisfaction was with the drudgery of endlessly washing sports clothes.

Sometimes, Emil and Dana used to train together, with Emil occasionally shouting advice about a javelin-throwing technique that Dana dismissed as 'pathetic'. In the flat, they would round off their own training sessions by playing catch with a heavy medicine ball; the caretaker, who lived underneath, would bang on the ceiling furiously when they dropped it. And sometimes, too, at the track, they would play a game of high-risk catch with a javelin. According to Gordon Pirie, who witnessed it, this involved throwing it 'full tilt' and catching it, far across the stadium, above the head. The aim was to throw it back as quickly as possible.

Pirie believed that part of the secret of Emil's training was that he would never let himself get bored. His home-made gym included not only wooden wall bars (which he would use for endless leg raises) but, later, a system of weights and pulleys that allowed him to exercise his legs when work and weather prevented him from training outdoors. On at least one occasion he trained by running on the spot on the family washing in the bath, pounding the clothes with his feet ('soft and squishy, easy rhythm, thinking of other things') for two hours. Given Dana's reported horror at the resultant flood, it seems unlikely that he repeated this.

Sometimes he would alleviate the boredom of such indoor improvisations by reading a book or listening to the radio as he exercised. Usually, though, at least when running outdoors, he was too focused on doing his utmost to have need of (or be capable of enjoying) distraction.

Like many great athletes, he was keen on sleeping: he liked to sleep eight or nine hours a night. But he was not fussy about diet, his only rule being 'I eat when I am hungry'. Sometimes he would buy rolls, butter and a litre of milk on the way to work, and eat and drink his way through them in the course of the day. Yet he was always looking for ways to innovate, too. One friend, the pentathlete Karel Bártů, recalled seeing Emil emerge from the woods where he had been training near Stará Boleslav with dried salt on his tracksuit trousers (from sweat) and green stains around his mouth. Emil revealed that he had been eating the leaves of a young birch tree, on the grounds that deer are good at running and these were the deer's favourite food. This seems, however, to have been a short-lived fad – as were similar experiments involving dandelions and, on a separate occasion, vast quantities of garlic.

Another friend, Ludvík Liška, was among a group of athletes who, with Emil, contracted diarrhoea while at the Stará Boleslav training camp. Emil cured himself several days before the others by self-medicating with vodka, which he claimed helped him to sweat the illness out. It's probably best not to try this at home.

None of this squares remotely with the idea, popular among Western journalists of a certain kind, that Emil was some kind of robotic Marxist-Leninist machine, cranking out his victories as remorselessly and unfeelingly as a railway engine. Those who knew him testify to something far more mysterious: a paradoxical mixture of scientist, artist and dreamer. On the one hand, he would approach his running empirically, calculating lap-by-lap schedules, monitoring his speed and endurance, guarding against self-deception by keeping a training diary and modifiying his training according to his objective needs. On the other, he often ran his laps on the grass outside the track, to avoid hogging a lane that other athletes might want to use. He believed that training was a science, but he brought to it an intense subjectivity – focusing not on the stopwatch but on what it felt like at the limits of endurance, and learning how to manipulate those limits. (As he put it: 'You must listen to your body. You must feel hard, and you must feel easy.') And holding together those two contrasting sides of his character was a supercharged power of personality: dynamic, eccentric, intense and life-affirming.

Christopher Brasher, future founder of the London Marathon, interviewed Emil at length with the help of his fellow Olympic gold medallist Herb Elliott. Their conclusion is as good a summary of Emil's special spirit as I have read. He was, they wrote, 'not mad . . . just utterly absorbed, with every fibre of his explosive body, in what he is doing, and damn what the rest of the world thinks.

'It makes him the most refreshing, and the most exhausting, person to be with.'

9

Mission: invincible

He may have been made of tougher stuff than other athletes, but Emil was still human. Early in 1951, he crashed into a fir tree while skiing, tearing a ligament. He spent several weeks in plaster and could not train until April. Even then, he struggled with speed-work, and found himself focusing, by default, on endurance.

That summer, he raced less than usual, and, by his standards, less successfully. Between mid-May and mid-September, he ran nine races at 5,000 and three at 10,000m, mostly in Czechoslovakia. He won them all, but slowly. At 10,000m, he broke thirty minutes only once. At 5,000m, he was more often outside 14:30 than inside (and on two occasions he didn't even break fifteen minutes).

Emil also ran four 3,000m races, one of which, in Prague on 11 July, saw him beaten by Václav Čevona, the national champion at 1,500m.

It would be hard to interpret such results as a loss of form, yet the fact remained that Emil's rivals were closing in. Gaston Reiff looked suddenly dangerous again, recording a 5,000m time of 14:10.8. Herbert Schade, a German, had done 14:15.4 and was beginning to make an impression at 10,000m as well; as were Bertil Albertsson, of Sweden, and Alain Mimoun. It wasn't that Emil was past his peak: he had yet to reach his twenty-ninth birthday, and was much the same age as Reiff and Schade. But his best times over shorter distances were many years behind him, and, in the meantime, others had been raising their game. Perhaps it was premature to speculate – but could an end to Emil's period of invincibility already be approaching?

There were obvious explanations: the injury, the demands of work and the fact that Emil was giving up a lot of his time to the making of a propaganda film, which showed him meeting groups of workers and young people all over Czechoslovakia. None the less, Emil's superiors were worried – especially by the defeat to Čevona. Emil had pledged, at a meeting of the country's leading athletes at the end of 1950, that he would break a world record in the coming year. What if he was no longer capable of meeting that pledge?

Orders were given to suspend the filming, and Emil's military duties were rearranged again, so that he could train more easily – by day rather than at night. Emil was happy to take advantage. It is unlikely, however, that he was especially worried. He had already decided that he would adjust his aim this season.

By the end of the summer, his times were picking up. He ran 14:11.6 for the 5,000m in Berlin on 18 August and 29:29.8 for the 10,000m in Třebíč on 1 September. But those were just warm-ups, giving him the confidence that he was once again in good shape.

On 15 September, the world discovered just how good.

The scene was the Strahov stadium in Prague, where the annual Army Championships were being held. Emil felt that this would be a good occasion to attack the world record for 20,000m, which had been set by Viljo Heino in 1949. The distance was so rarely run that it was hard to be certain how impressive Heino's time of 1:2:40 really was, but Emil reckoned that he could cut at least a minute off it, and set himself a schedule of seventy-five-second laps – fifty of them.

He ran the first twelve and a half with competitors in the army 5,000m event, whose start he shared; but he was a good 100m ahead of all of them by the 5,000m mark. The pace seemed slow to him, but he forced himself to stick to it, and passed 10,000m in 31:05.6. Then, bored of 'dawdling', he decided to run as fast as he could. He polished off the second 10,000m in 30:10.4 – giving him a 20,000m time nearly a minute and a half faster than the old record.

But Emil was dissatisfied. He had set his promised world record – two, in fact, for he had also beaten Heino's 1945 record for The Hour (that is, the greatest distance run in sixty minutes) by 219m. But he knew that he had been running within himself, and he wanted to know what he could have done if he had gone all out from the start. His time – one hour, one minute and sixteen seconds – was tantalisingly close to a nice round hour, while the distance he had run within sixty minutes – 19,558m – was tantalisingly close to a nice round twenty kilometres. And the thought that gnawed at him now was the same thought expressed by Heino when Finnish journalists asked him for his thoughts on Emil's achievement. 'Believe me,' said Heino, after passing on his congratulations, 'Zátopek could run 20 kilometres in one hour.'

Two weeks later, on the afternoon of 29 September 1951, Emil put that theory to the test. The scene was Houštka Spa, an idyllic track on the edge of the woods just outside Stará Boleslav, which – according to a helpful map in *Svět v obrazech* magazine showing how far Emil's Strahov stadium effort would have got him had he been running in a straight line – is twenty kilometres north-east of Prague. The roads were lined with people on the long walk from Stará Boleslav, and the little stadium itself was packed. Emil would eventually set eight world records here, but no attempt caused such excitement as this one.

Emil had set himself a schedule that would take him to twenty kilometres in one hour and twenty-four seconds; but it had certainly occurred to him that it might be possible to break the sixty-minute barrier, and he joked beforehand about which would be considered the 'real' record – the time or the distance – if he ran exactly twenty kilometres in exactly an hour. It was a still, warm afternoon, and the cinder track had been brushed smooth. As in Prague, there were other runners with him at the start: sixteen of them. But from the moment the gun was fired, at 4.23 p.m., there was only one runner who mattered.

Or perhaps there were two. In the words of František Kožík: 'The Emil Zátopek of 29 September was fighting the Emil Zátopek of 15 September.' The latter had shown what could be done comfortably. The former had to discover what could be achieved at the furthest extremes of pain and exhaustion.

The Emil Zátopek of 29 September didn't spare himself. After 1,000m, he was 6.7 seconds ahead of his previous pace; after 2,000m, 11.5 seconds. He passed 5,000m in 14:56 and 10,000m in 29:54 – faster than his winning time in the London Olympics. He was one minute and twelve seconds ahead of his time two weeks earlier, and a sub-sixty-minute twenty kilometres now seemed a distinct possibility.

But running for a whole hour at your fastest possible speed, round and round a track, can never be easy, even for a supreme athlete. It involves, almost by definition, sixty minutes of uninterrupted pain – or, at least, as much pain as you're prepared to go looking for. That's the agony of it. You have to keep asking yourself, can I keep this up? If the answer is no, you've blown it. If the answer is yes, you're not going fast enough. And while getting it just right may bring you glory, it won't bring you any less pain. Sir Bradley Wiggins, after setting a new world record for cycling's equivalent, The Hour, in June 2015, described it as 'the closest I'll ever come to knowing what it's like to have a baby'.

But an athlete whose training revolved around the mastery of pain was as well equipped as anyone to have a go. For more than three-quarters of an hour, Emil maintained the delicate balance, keeping the fatigue just within manageable levels while lapping runners with dizzying regularity. The track at Houštka Spa is unusually small – just 364m – and the spectators, around 6,000 of them, were exceptionally close to the runners. So Emil had plenty of encouragement, even without the timekeeper's regular announcements. He passed 16,090m, or ten miles, in 48:12 – more than a minute faster than the fifteen-year-old world record for that distance.

His work was not yet done, though. He still had another 4,000m to run, fast, and only a little more than ten minutes in which to cover the distance. He needed to be accelerating to the very limits of his ability. And now, just at that critical moment, he felt the agonising pangs of a stitch in his side.

If he gave any sign of it, it would have been difficult for the spectators to tell. Emil always looked agonised. As far as they were concerned, the locomotive was powering away at full steam, unstoppable as ever, as they roared their deafening support. But these grimaces were real. Emil – who had had a huge lunch barely three hours earlier – hardly felt able to continue. All he could do was grit his teeth and hang on, hoping the agony would subside.

It didn't. 'The continuous pain increased with every lap,' Emil recalled. 'It reached such a level that I lost track of things . . . I gritted my teeth, grimaced as I had never done before, and tried not to let up.' It was hardest when, having lost a few seconds, he no longer knew if he was on target for the record or not. He told himself to ignore everything he could feel above the waist. All that mattered were his legs.

Even they hardly bore thinking about. That's the trouble with The Hour: the mounting muscle fatigue resolves itself eventually into a continuous groan of distress. Jens Voigt, an earlier record holder for cycling's equivalent, had a simple formula for dealing with it: 'Shut up, legs!' But Emil was almost delirious by now: so overwhelmed that he could no longer keep track of his laps or his schedule. 'I really didn't know whether at that pace I would break the record or myself.'

The torture continued for four or five laps. Then, 'when I was feeling the very worst . . . something that I had never before experienced happened to me: that constant pain which grew with every lap reached such a limit that I stopped noticing it. The pain became duller.' He focused on the laps ahead – only four or five more now – and on the importance of keeping his legs, which he could now barely feel, moving at the same metronomic speed. The spectators kept urging him, with mounting excitement – and at Houštka, as Emil observed, it was a bit like having them screaming in your face. Eventually he was within a lap of the 20,000m mark – and the gunshot that would announce the final minute of his hour had not yet sounded. When it did so, he was well into the lap. He launched himself into a final semblance of a sprint with renewed hope. Or perhaps desperation would be a better word: the thought of failure was terrifying. To run all that way, through all that pain, without breaking sixty minutes would be too much to bear.

Listening at every stride for the second shot, which would mark the end of the hour, he sprinted towards the line – where the man with the gun crouched dramatically, pointing it skywards while a timekeeper, inches away, squinted at his stopwatch. Emil passed them before the gun had sounded. His surge had meant that his final kilometre was the fastest of the twenty (2:51.8). It also meant that he had to keep running, knowing that he ought to be hoping for the gunshot to be delayed as long as possible – but actually longing for it to come. 'What's going on?' he shouted to the timekeeper, when nothing came. 'Run! Run!' screamed the spectators. By the time the shot fired he had gone another fifty-two metres.

The acclaim was overwhelming: one report described the post-race ovation as 'indescribably cordial and enthusiastic'. Once again, Emil had redrawn the boundaries of the possible. His first thought, though, was: 'Today I really had more than enough.'

Having first had his pulse rate checked by Dr Zdeněk Hornof (it measured 168), he was carried on his fellow athletes' shoulders from the back-straight finish to the grandstand, where he made a short speech, broadcast on the PA system and on national radio, thanking the spectators and urging them to support youth athletics. Four minutes after the finish, his pulse rate was down to 108. Four minutes after that, the first of the runners who had started with him – remember them? – passed the 20,000m mark.

Three hours later, Emil's pulse was down to fifty-two beats per minute. The rest of the world found it harder to calm down. Only five other men had ever run 10,000m in less than thirty minutes. Emil had just done it twice, back-to-back, without a break. One newspaper hailed his performance as 'unique in the history of athletics'. *Rudé právo* took the exceptional step of reporting the record on its front page, hailing Emil's achievement as another success for the regime's centralised administration of sport.

But Emil knew that, already, that triumph was in the past; and it was not in his nature to dwell on achievements that were behind him. 'To boast of a performance which I cannot beat is merely stupid vanity,' he once said. 'And if I can beat it, that means it lies in my power to beat it, and therefore again there is nothing special about it. What has passed is already finished with. What I find more interesting is what is still to come.'

What was to come now was a more conventional challenge – but also a far more daunting one. The XVth

Olympic Games were due to begin in Helsinki in July 1952. Emil was expected to win at least two medals – both of them gold. Anything less would be considered a failure, or perhaps even a dereliction of duty. And the fact that he had, in the words of J. Armour Milne, just 'belted the living daylight out of two tremendous world records' did little to alter the fact that, at the less obscure distances of 5,000 and 10,000m, rivals – some of them starting to imitate Emil's training methods – were closing in. That gave him just over nine months in which, on the one hand, to work himself to still greater heights of fitness while, on the other, avoiding setbacks such as food poisoning and skiing accidents. It was, in its way, as hard a balancing act as The Hour. Yet Emil knew that he would never get a better chance to claim a place among the immortals of sport. Somehow, over the next nine months, he had to get it right. He needed to make himself invincible.

At Christmas, he and Dana took another winter holiday in the mountains. Emil avoided skiing this time, training instead by dabbling in speed skating and, more often, running through deep snowdrifts. Dana sometimes added a bombardment of snowballs, which Emil tried to dodge, adding to the intensity of the workout. There was also a notorious incident when, having agreed that they should give themselves a day off, Emil took them on a seemingly endless jog through the hills instead. Dana eventually rebelled and refused to go any further, flinging herself down in the snow. 'So he got an old washing-line out of his pocket and tied it around my waist,' she remembers. 'He said: "I thought this might happen." Then he dragged me all the way back like a sledge. I didn't move a muscle the whole way.'

In January 1952, at a meeting of Czechoslovakia's elite athletes, Emil renewed his commitment to win two golds. This was supposed to be a private commitment, but word of it leaked out. He might as well have been signing a contract. The imminent release of *One of the Relay*, an hour-long propaganda film devoted to his achievements and training methods, would soon add to the weight of public expectation on his shoulders. It was beautifully shot, as Czech propaganda films tended to be, and many of the iconic images of Emil that subsequently caught the world's imagination (training in the snow; running in his army boots, torch in hand; or striding through the sand of the indoor riding school) can be traced back to it. It would all look a bit silly, though, if Emil stopped winning. Somehow, he had to turn all that weight into a positive.

To do so, he retreated to Stará Boleslav, where he could combine the monastic existence of a military training camp with endless hours training alone in the birch forest that hid the Houštka Spa track from the outside world. This was one of his favourite places: an old wood with tall, well-spaced trees and mossy undergrowth; broad clearings in which to practise his repetitions; wide, silent plains to be glimpsed occasionally through gaps in the foliage; and, not least, a growing stock of memories of triumphs on the track. The sandy, yielding soil – a vestige of the days when this was a riverbed – was kinder to his legs than a cinder track or road; and when the light began to fail his army boots protected him from hidden mishaps. The uncomplicated asceticism can only have strengthened his conviction that, by sheer self-discipline, he could control his fate.

In mid-April, fate struck back.

Emil later blamed it on the fact that he had been persuaded to submit to a post-training massage, followed by an unplanned cold shower. Whatever the cause, he woke up the next day with a severe chill that became tonsillitis. The obvious solution was a few days in bed, but Emil was reluctant to follow the doctor's advice: partly because he had an athlete's aversion to missing a single training session but also because he was due to be racing in the national cross-country championships in Prešov that weekend. He was told to pull out, but he insisted. He had promised the organisers he would be there, and they had already printed the posters.

So he went, and, on a windy day, he ran, having fought his way through the usual crowds to get to the start; and he managed – just – to win. Afterwards, he was close to collapse – yet he still somehow managed to drag himself a few days later to Hradec Králové, where he won a slow 3,000m. Then he really did collapse.

It is hard to say with certainty what the problem was: the word 'angina' is ambiguous in Czech. But he seems to have entered that dangerous territory that is sometimes reached when a stubborn runner attempts to 'run off' a serious infection, viral or otherwise, and chest pains and fever result. He was confined to his bed and could not train for two weeks.

On 9 May he tried some tentative exercise, marching about four kilometres in full uniform from his workplace near Letná to the Strahov stadium. This is harder than it sounds: it is steeply uphill all the way. None the less, a would-be multiple Olympic champion would have hoped to be doing infinitely more, just two months before flying to the Games. Over the next few days he increased his workload: jogging, then running, wearing two tracksuits. The result, he claimed, was that he 'sweated' the illness out of himself – just as he had with vodka on a previous occasion.

Whatever the medical truth of the matter, by late May Emil reckoned that he was back to full health, which was something. But he had lost six problem-free weeks of super-intense training. He began to race again, and immediately resumed his winning habit, but his times were not impressive: 14:46.4 for a 5,000m in Prague on 21 May, 30:08.8 for a 10,000m in Leipzig in June; 14:33.6 for a 5,000m at the same venue the following day.

His rivals, meanwhile, were gathering in strength. Athletes with their eyes on the same Olympic medals as Emil included Herbert Schade, who had reduced his 5,000m time to 14:06.6, while Soviet runners such as Vladimir Kazantsev, Aleksandr Anufriev and Nikifor Popov (who had run 14:08.8, 14:12.2 and 14:16.0 respectively) also looked dangerously fast, as did the Englishmen Christopher Chataway and Gordon Pirie. At 10,000m, Anufriev, Mimoun, Pirie and Albertsson were all improving.

In mid-June, Emil, Dana and other members of the Czechoslovak Olympic team went to Kiev, where they competed and fraternised with other Soviet bloc athletes and underwent various measurements and tests. Emil's performances were unimpressive: on 11 June he came third in the 5,000m, behind Kazantsev and Popov; two days later, he just held off Anufriev to win the 10,000m. According to one report, he also did worse than any other athlete involved in a test to measure the force of runners' strides. His position wasn't quite hopeless, but, with a month to go, 'it was worth asking if I should even start the 5,000 metres in Helsinki at all'.

He didn't really have a choice. He had made a public vow: 'I will focus my training and performance for the Olympic Games in Helsinki to win two gold medals for our People's Democratic Republic.' Such undertakings were not to be made lightly: it was part of the Stalinist philosophy of sport that underachievers should face dire consequences. A few years later, for example, the celebrated Czechoslovak cyclist Jan Veselý would be accused of betraying the working class after giving up during the Karlovy Vary to Karl-Marx-Stadt stage of the Peace Race – and would be made to become a truck driver as a punishment. Emil had thrown away the chance of 5,000m gold in 1948; if he simply threw in the towel four years later, he risked bringing shame on himself and, worse, on his nation.

But what if he wasn't fast enough?

If the pressure didn't get to him, it might have been because, in the back of his mind, there was an escape clause: if he messed up one race, there might still be an opportunity to put things right. All he had to do was enter the marathon as well. This was an idea that had first come up the previous summer: his superior officer, Colonel Sábl, had suggested it, concerned at Emil's apparent loss of speed in the first half of 1951. Emil had never run a marathon, but, as Colonel Sábl pointed out, he was frequently running more than thirty kilometres a day, so it shouldn't be too great a shock to the system to do a race of 42.195km. Emil was non-committal, and they had left it as a tentative thought. But his successes with the twenty-kilometre and one-hour records had reassured them both that the idea of trying to win Olympic gold with his first attempt at the race was not quite as absurd as it sounded. Indeed, the idea had also been floated by Harold Abrahams, the British former Olympic 100m champion, who light-heartedly suggested in *World Sports* in September 1951 that 'that phenomenal runner, Zátopek' was 'quite capable of having another crack at both the 5,000 and 10,000 metres and then throwing in the Marathon on the last Sunday just for the fun of the thing'.

That's not to say that the idea wasn't far-fetched. A certain amount of pre-Games practice is generally considered essential for Olympic events; and a certain amount of rest – as opposed to two fiercely contested Olympic finals – is generally considered desirable in the days leading up to a marathon. But now – when the time came to send off the entry forms – it seemed to make sense to put Emil's name down for all three races, just in case. With a bit of luck he would have no need of his marathon entry, but it would be nice to have that little bit of insurance in his back pocket.

All that remained now was to survive the last few weeks before the Games without any further mishaps. In early July, the entire Czechoslovak Olympic team were summoned to Prague, where they were subjected to a series of last-minute checks, training sessions, political pep talks, lectures about Finland and, not least, a ceremonial parade, at Tyršův palace. Emil was chosen to make another public vow, this time on behalf of the whole team: 'We are aware of how greatly we are honoured by the confidence that the centralised sports department of the democratic people's republic of Czechoslovakia has placed in us. We solemnly promise our people, who have sent us to the Games, that we shall fulfil every task with which we will be faced . . . for the honour and glory of our beloved republic . . . This is our pledge.'

He was filmed as he spoke these words, for use in one of the weekly propaganda newsreels which usually preceded feature films in cinemas. (Television broadcasting would not begin in Czechoslovakia until 1953.) It all added to the burden of expectation. To many of Emil's fellow countrymen, it must have seemed as though his medals were already won.

He made the pledge on 8 July. The Games opened on the 19th. The first Czech athletes, including Emil, were due to fly to Finland on the 10th. After four long years, Emil's appointment with destiny had arrived: a chance to put right his lapse of concentration in London, and to put beyond all possible doubt his status as the greatest distance runner of his generation.

10

Fairy-tale Pete

And so we return to that curious incident in July 1952 with which we began, when Emil gambled everything he had worked for on the wildly optimistic hunch that, if he challenged the exclusion of Stanislav Jungwirth from the Czechoslovak Olympic team, the authorities would back down.

The more one thinks about this episode, the stranger it seems. What made Emil imagine that a regime implacable enough to destroy both its greatest sports stars (its world-beating ice hockey team, for example) and its own most senior officials (such as Rudolf Slánský) would make an exception in his case? What drove a man whose every waking moment for the past decade had been dominated by a yearning for athletics greatness to jeopardise his entire future as a runner? And what gave a man who two years earlier had allowed his name to be used against Milada Horáková the courage now to risk everything for the sake of a friend?

We can only speculate. The prospect of being sent to a concentration camp was both real and terrible, but it may have seemed less significant to Emil than the equally real danger of never being allowed to run competitively again. And that prospect was so obviously intolerable for him that, in an odd way, the Party officials may have been wrongfooted by it. Perhaps they simply did not believe that Emil would stick to his guns, and thus didn't bother to take further steps to intimidate or coerce him. When it began to seem that he really wouldn't back down, they panicked. (Imagine what would have happened to the official who had had to explain to his superiors that, actually, Emil Zátopek wasn't going to be at the Olympics after all.) As for Emil's lack of courage in the Horáková case, it seems entirely plausible that, if he felt ashamed of his behaviour then, that would have encouraged him to show more backbone this time.

He stood his ground. The authorities blinked first. Two officers found Emil at the Strahov stadium and drove him to the Ministry of Defence, where, to his surprise, he was not arrested but presented with his travel papers and a reinstated Jungwirth. The pair then flew to Helsinki on a later plane.

The precise timings are confused. Most accounts – including at least one of Emil's – have the stand-off lasting three days; some say that Emil and Standa flew in a third plane. But the official record shows them arriving in Finland just one day late, on Friday, 11 July, in a second aeroplane. It is by no means certain, however, that the official record is trustworthy; some say that he didn't arrive until Sunday 13th; and Dana, for whom it was a matter of life and death, insists that she cried for at least two days.

What can be stated confidently is that now, more than ever, Emil needed to return from Helsinki laden with gold and glory. As his friend Zdeněk Fator, the future manager of Sparta Praha athletics club, starkly expressed it to me: 'If Emil had sprained his ankle training, he would have been sent to the uranium mines.'

So it would have been understandable if the twenty-nine-year-old army officer and athlete who belatedly made his way to his quarters in the Olympic village had been a little preoccupied; perhaps even irritable and tense.

In fact, from the moment he set foot in Finland, Emil conducted himself with a good-humoured charm that was, in the circumstances, almost miraculous. Somehow, while engaged in the most soul-consuming physical struggles of his life, he found the time and energy to charm the world, with a generosity of spirit that shamed the distrustful orthodoxies of Cold War politics. If greatness is defined as showing grace under pressure, this was the eighteen-day period in which Emil most clearly demonstrated his greatness.

The world was glad of it. The Helsinki Games were perhaps the most politicised in Olympic history, dramatically embodying the frightening divisions of the post-war world. Nations competing for the first time included the Soviet Union, the People's Republic of China and Israel. Japan, barred in 1948, had just been re-admitted to the Olympic fold, as had Germany (although it would be another decade before the German Democratic Republic – East Germany – was recognised by the International Olympic Committee). The scope for ill feeling was considerable and obvious: the nation now known as Taiwan pulled out in protest at China's presence two days before the opening ceremony. And it did not bode well for international harmony that the Soviet Union had insisted on separate accommodation for athletes from Communist nations.

The main Olympic village was at Käpylä, on the western edge of Helsinki. But 1,360 athletes from the Eastern bloc nations (plus forty from China) were housed in a hastily constructed complex with a barbed-wire perimeter in the pine woods at Otaniemi, a couple of miles west, near the Soviet-owned naval base of Porkkala. The Soviet barracks there had a giant photograph of Stalin affixed to an outside wall. There was also a scoreboard to show how the Soviets were outstripping the Americans in the medals table – a new invention. (This was quietly removed when it became clear that they weren't.) If this was an international festival of friendship, it had a strained feel to it.

Emil was still in Prague when Erik von Franckell, president of the Finnish Olympic Committee, proclaimed 'Ekekheira' – the traditional Olympic truce between nations – on 10 July. By the time Emil arrived, however, there was an armed guard stationed at the entrance to Otaniemi.

But no one has ever succeeded in entirely suppressing the instinct of young people to make friends. Almost immediately, some US shot-putters struck up a cordial relationship with their counterparts from the USSR. Then Les Perry, the Australian 10,000m runner, made a tentative trip to Otaniemi, 'waltzed' past the guards, and was rewarded by seeing his idol, Emil Zátopek, training on a track by the woods on the edge of the site. He plucked up the courage to introduce himself. 'You come from the other village to see me?' said Emil. 'You honour me. Join me. We will run together.'

So they did, for twenty laps, chatting all the way (in English) about their lives at home. Afterwards, Emil invited Perry back to the Czechoslovakian accommodation in Otaniemi's Building No. 2. They ate with the Czechoslovak team, and then watched the entertainment that had been laid on for them: a performance by the Bolshoi Ballet. By the time Perry had jogged back to Käpylä, it was around midnight.

After that, the floodgates opened. Every Western runner wanted to meet Emil, or at least to see him train. The Otaniemi track that Emil used was on the edge of the village, and those who watched him running on it included the British journalist Norman Banks, who reported seeing Emil's tongue 'hanging out like a dog's' as he ran his fast laps, while his head 'rolled from side to side with every stride he took'.

There were plenty of laps to watch. Emil ran thirty fast 400m laps on his first day and forty a day thereafter, although he eased off as the competition drew near. But he still found time to seek out Bill Nankeville, who was unwell, and express his condolences; and to share his training secrets with everyone from John Disley, who found him 'a real gentleman' who was 'open and honest and willing to share his training ideas with anyone', to Australia's John Landy, the future world record holder for the mile, who quizzed Emil extensively and by one account went home with 'his notebooks crammed' with details of Emil's methods.

We can infer from this that Emil was now speaking English relatively fluently (or perhaps that John Landy had quite small notebooks). Nor was this the only example of Emil's proficiency as a linguist. The French writer Bénigno Cacérès enthused about the excellence with which Emil spoke to him in French, adding that Emil (whose second language was German) seemed equally confident in English, Russian and Polish. Even more impressively, he had taught himself Finnish (of sorts), and the accomplishment did wonders for the special relationship between the host nation and the Games' most celebrated distance runner – who had never lost a race in Finland. According to the relay runner František Brož, who was on the first Czechoslovak plane to touch down in Finland, thousands of Finnish fans had turned out in the hope of seeing Emil arrive on 10 July. As Emil told one American reporter (in English): 'I get a bigger welcome here than on Czech tracks.'

It is possible that Emil was grateful for the constant interruptions, which may have calmed his nerves. He was clearly pleased to see Gordon Pirie, inviting him to join him in training and, on noticing that (for some reason) he had no socks, insisting on giving him one of the pairs that he was wearing. (Emil often wore several, to keep his Achilles tendons warm.) He will have been touched, too, by a visit from Herbert Schade, his most dangerous rival in the 5,000m, who presented him with a gift of Solingen cutlery.

But it is hard to believe that Emil particularly appreciated the behaviour of Percy Cerutty, the eccentric Australian who coached Les Perry and John Landy. Hearing how his charges had been welcomed by Emil, Cerutty invited himself to Otaniemi, picked Emil's brains for hours and eventually stayed so late that it was no longer practical to return to Käpylä. Emil insisted on giving Cerutty his own bed, before retreating to the woods with a sleeping bag. Later still, an official came looking for Emil, found Cerutty instead, and made a scene. Cerutty was ejected, and Emil, recalled from the woods, was reprimanded for allowing a potential 'spy' into the camp. Cerutty was so taken with Emil's courtesy that he described the encounter in an effusive letter to a friend in Melbourne. The friend, in turn, was so impressed that he sent the letter to the Melbourne *Guardian*, whose readers thus learnt about Emil's desire to (in Cerutty's words): 'bring a cooperative understanding of the brotherhood of man, through sport, to peoples'. Cerutty summed up the meaning of Emil's chivalry thus: 'The willingness of athletes from all countries to meet on friendly terms makes it seem preposterous that we should ever be required to hate each other.' Emil's message had already reached the other side of the world – and he hadn't even started racing yet.

On Saturday, 19 July, the Games were opened. Heavy rain did not detract from the drama of seeing the great Paavo Nurmi bring the Olympic flame into the stadium and light the cauldron there, after which another immortal of Finnish distance running, Hannes Kolehmainen, lit the flame in the stadium tower. There were no arguments about Emil needing to keep out of the sun this time, but the 10,000m was, as in 1948, scheduled for the next day, and it is probable that, like most people present, Emil was too preoccupied to notice the scantily clad intruder (arguably sport's first ever streaker) who completed an unscripted lap of the track before she was hustled away by officials. His main concern was keeping dry – and hoping that he would not have to run the next day in the kind of deluge that had helped ruin his last Olympic race.

He didn't. By Sunday morning the rain had gone and the consensus was that, whatever his difficulties at

5,000m, Emil was the favourite for the 10,000m. He had a personal best nearly half a minute faster than Anufriev, the next fastest man in the race, while Schade, who at least one expert had tipped as an alternative winner, had decided to withdraw three days before the race to save himself for the 5,000m.

The thirty-three remaining runners gathered at the starting line for a race that would eventually begin at 6.13 p.m. Gordon Pirie had wished Emil luck as they were warming up, to which Emil deadpanned: 'I wish Anufriev to win.' But no one really expected such an upset. As the American competitor Fred Wilt had put it a few weeks earlier, 'The only thing we can hope for is that Zátopek breaks a leg.'

Emil later claimed that, even before the gun, people 'respectfully backed away' and 'gave me precedence' because of his reputation and his world record. But when the gun signalled the beginning of the first track final of the Games, Perry started off at an extravagant pace and led for a lap. Then Anufriev took the front and led for four. Emil coasted comfortably, mostly in tenth place, keeping an eye on the times on the giant electronic scoreboard that was the technological highlight of the Games. His time for the first lap was 68.9, and his time for the first kilometre was 2:52 – the second fastest of the ten. So it was not Emil who was running too slowly but the others who were going too fast.

After six laps, Emil moved smoothly into the lead. Gordon Pirie tried briefly to contest it with him, but Emil asserted himself, and from that point on he never looked back. Instead, with supreme self-confidence, he continued to churn out laps of around seventy-one seconds – knowing that none of the others could live with such a pace indefinitely.

The field was soon strung out: a line of carriages pulled along by the Czech locomotive and, one by one, falling off. One British commentator saw this as a reason to dismiss Emil, snootily, as a 'robot runner', and the race as one of 'inexorable monotony'. It wouldn't have felt like that to the athletes who were desperately struggling to keep in touch, and the 70,000 spectators showed no signs of being bored. Instead, the familiar rhythmic cries of 'Zá-to-pek! Zá-to-pek!' began to ring out; except that his Finnish admirers – thousands of them – had modified his name to 'Satu Peka', which sounds very similar but in Finnish means something like 'Fairy-tale Pete'.

Emil continued to justify their enthusiasm. He passed the halfway point in 14:43.4 – and then, mercilessly, turned the pace up a notch. If you looked at their faces, Emil was the only one who seemed to be suffering. The reality was quite different. Perry actually retired; the others merely gave up trying to keep in touch. Soon there were only Zátopek, Mimoun and Pirie in contention; and then, with about 3,500m to go, Pirie slipped back. The future 3,000m world record holder eventually finished seventh, forty-seven seconds behind Emil, in 'an oblivion of fatigue'.

Alain Mimoun, who had been imitating Emil's training methods for some time and was not afraid of pain, hung on grimly in his slipstream for several laps more. For a while it even looked as though he might pose a threat. But Emil kept injecting little bursts of acceleration, which he liked to apply on the bends. Once a lap, when the sun was behind them, he could see Mimoun's shadow, which allowed him to note that, gradually, Mimoun was becoming slower to respond to these bursts. A fast eighteenth lap may have been the killer blow. By the twenty-first lap Emil had opened up a big lead, and from then on he drew steadily away.

If the thought occurred to Emil that he could perhaps ease off, to save himself for the 5,000m, he dismissed it. Instead, he scorched round the final lap in sixty-four seconds, finishing in a new Olympic record of 29:17.0. Barely had he crossed the line than a Czechoslovak trainer came rushing to hug him and trod on his foot; but Emil had time to regain his composure before welcoming Mimoun, getting on for a hundred metres behind, as he came in second in 29:32.8. Anufriev was third in 29:48.2.

It had, despite the predictability of the result, been a remarkable race. Emil had run 42.6 seconds faster than the Olympic record he had set in London four years earlier. Mimoun had set a new French record, and Fred Sando, who came fifth, had set a new British one – an amazing achievement given that he had lost a shoe after barely a lap. Six men had run sub-thirty-minute times – still unusual – and sixteen had run times that would have won them silver in London four years earlier.

For those who knew what they were watching, it had been a compelling spectacle. One French journalist, Gaston Meyer, described it as 'a pitiless race of elimination', while another, Jacques Goddet, wrote of a 'battle conducted by Zátopekian fury'. *Rudé právo* (which seemed disproportionately excited by the bronze medal won for the Soviets by Anufriev) called it a 'dramatic fight'. *The Times* of London called it a 'rout'. But it was a front-page headline in *L'Équipe*, the French sports paper, that captured best the impression of total, ruthless dominance, dubbing Emil '*La brute magnifique*'.

After Emil had collected his medal – and the Czechoslovak anthem had once again been the first of the Games to be heard in the Olympic stadium – crowds of jubilant Finns accompanied him back to Otaniemi, where some of them had prepared a celebration dinner for him. He was presented with flowers and regaled with Finnish songs, while the Hungarian team gave him an enormous chocolate cake. He also received a morale-boosting visit from the great Gunder Hägg, the Swedish runner whose sub-fourteen-minute world record for 5,000m would soon be ten years old.

Later, Emil and Dana 'retreated into the Finnish solitude'. Emil had learnt his lesson from London and was determined to celebrate sparingly. Instead, they explored the woods around Otaniemi. The combination of pines, meadows, a lake and the long 'white nights' of the summer were profoundly calming to a couple who remained at heart mostly rural creatures. But even the peace of the forest was not quite enough to dispel the restless impatience that came from knowing that, for both of them, the biggest challenge was yet to come.

The 5,000m heats were held on Tuesday, 22 July, two days after the 10,000m final. They confirmed Emil's fears that his rivals were in the form of their lives. In the first heat, Alain Mimoun set a new French record of 14:19.0. Herbert Schade won the second in 14:15.4 – a new Olympic record – while Ernö Béres set a new Hungarian record of 14:19.66. Seventeen competitors finished in less than 14:30.

Yet Emil's own heat was a relaxed affair. He spent much of the early part of the race on the shoulder of the leader, Anufriev, whom he appeared to urge not to set too demanding a pace. Then, after about 2,000m, he spoke to Anufriev in Russian ('Sasha, come on, we must get a move on') to initiate a two-lap surge that left the five leaders – Emil, Anufriev, Albertsson, Chataway and Perry – with a fairly unassailable lead, whereupon they slowed down again, and Emil devoted the rest of the race to extravagant displays of friendly behaviour. He chatted away, in English, with Chataway. Then he dropped back to encourage the struggling American runner, Curtis Stone, with the words 'Come along, Stone, if you want to qualify', before speeding ahead to rejoin the leading group – whom he reminded, with five fingers, that all five of them would qualify and that there was thus no need for unnecessary effort. Anufriev – a big, long-sideburned young man who was reputed to hunt bears – none the less accelerated for the final lap, whereupon Emil waved him politely ahead. At least, that was what most people saw; Perry thought it was a wave of encouragement to him, and responded by kicking on to achieve fourth place, a personal best and a precious place in the final. Whatever the truth – and whether this behaviour constituted sportsmanship, showmanship or gamesmanship – the crowd loved it. Emil, meanwhile, could congratulate himself on having managed his resources infinitely better than in 1948, when he had exhausted himself with that unnecessary battle with Ahlden. Only three of the fifteen qualifiers were slower than him. (Emil came third in 14:26.) What mattered was Thursday's final.

The next day, Wednesday, was marred by the discovery that the women's javelin final was due to start just five minutes after the beginning of the men's 5,000m final.

Emil comforted Dana. 'We have been training together,' he reasoned, 'so we will compete together.' But Dana was concerned that she would not be able to concentrate if the stadium was echoing with screams that reminded her that Emil was in mid-race.

There was nothing to be done, though; and even if there had been it wouldn't have altered the size of the challenges they faced. Dana was up against three powerful Soviets, Aleksandra Chudina, Galina Zybina and Yelena Gorchakova, two of whom – Chudina and Zybina – had beaten her in Kiev barely a month earlier. She had set her heart on winning, but she would have to be at her best to get a medal of any kind.

As for Emil, the 5,000m was clearly going to be a far tougher challenge than the 10,000m. Talk of 'the race of the century' was perhaps an exaggeration – none of the contenders had seriously threatened Hägg's world record – but there was something about the balance of the field that suggested that something special might happen. On the one hand, you had Emil, the toughest endurance runner the world had ever seen. There was Mimoun, too, growing stronger with every race; not to mention Pirie, Perry, Albertsson and Anufriev, all of whom had run in the 10,000m final but might be better suited to the shorter distance. And then, from the other end of the spectrum, there were people like Reiff, the reigning champion; Schade, the new Olympic record holder; and the young Englishman Chataway, a future world record holder with a devastating final kick. All three of these speed specialists had fresh legs and might, on their day, simply burn the endurance runners away. The heats and the 10,000m final had confirmed that all fifteen finalists were in good shape. All that remained was the showdown.

Reiff had told *L'Équipe* that the final would be 'the atomic bomb of the Games', and the Finnish public seemed to agree. By late afternoon on Thursday, 24 July, 66,100 spectators were packed into the stadium. There were reports that people had been hanging on to the outsides of heaving trams in order to get there. Emil, who had spent the morning at Otaniemi fretting, uncharacteristically, that he might forget something crucial such as his shoes, was alarmed when the car from the Czechoslovak Embassy that was taking him to the stadium became stuck in a road blocked by crowds. The driver had to lean out of the window and shout 'Zátopek!' in order to clear the way.

Yet when the runners began to gather near the starting line at around 4.30 p.m., Emil seemed calmer than most. The afternoon was sunny and the stadium was buzzing. Emil spoke in German to Schade, who was clearly nervous, reassuring him that he was the favourite and advising him not to set off too fast; although it may not have helped Schade's nerves that, when he asked Emil who he was most worried about, Emil replied 'Reiff'. In fact, the consensus among commentators seemed to give Schade the best chance, marginally ahead of Reiff. Emil, remarkable as it seems now, was a relative outsider. The 10,000m/5,000m double had been accomplished only once before in Olympic history, by Hannes Kolehmainen in 1912. It would take a stupendous performance to replicate that feat, forty years later, against a field as competitive as this.

The starting gun sounded on time, at 4.40 p.m. The auburn-haired Chataway was the first leader, but the bespectacled Schade, who often forced the pace from the front, soon took over. Emil remained near the back, ignoring the cries of 'Zá-to-pek! Zá-to-pek!' (or, possibly, 'Satu Peka! Satu Peka!') that urged him on from, in particular, an area beneath the stadium tower. The first five laps passed quickly, with splits of 65.8, 67.6, 67.8, 68 and 68 seconds; Schade had completed the first kilometre in sub-world record pace. Then Emil moved forward, and led the field through another sixty-eight-second lap.

By Emil's account, he was concerned that Schade was being forced to do all the pacemaking and had taken the lead purely out of sportsmanship; Les Perry, who was close enough to see, was convinced that this was the case. Schade wasn't so sure and fought his way back into the lead. Emil then moved on to Schade's shoulder and shouted (in German): 'Herbert, come with me for two laps.' This time Schade allowed himself to be led, and the spectators, somehow managing to decipher what was going on, applauded warmly.

They passed 3,000m in 8:30.4 – fast but not blistering – at which point Schade, Chataway and Reiff moved smoothly into the lead. Emil began to wonder if this wasn't going to be his day; although Mimoun, who was once again in Emil's slipstream, clearly thought otherwise. Pirie made a brief attempt to take hold of the race, but his lead was short-lived and he lost touch with the leading five. Half a lap later, Schade took the lead again, and then, at 3,500m, Reiff detonated an explosive attack – 'like lightning', said Emil – much like the one that had won him gold in London four years earlier.

Emil responded immediately. There was an assertiveness to the way that he immediately took back the lead each time Reiff accelerated that Reiff found deeply disheartening.

With two laps to go Reiff had been neutralised as a threat – and with 600m to go he dropped out of the race altogether. But Schade, Mimoun and Chataway were looking as strong as ever, and it was clear that, unlike his rivals in the 10,000m, they were not prepared to step back politely and let the great Zátopek win. They wanted gold for themselves.

With so many people in contention, Emil – who one observer described as appearing to be 'on the verge of strangulation' – felt tempted to make his attack there and then. He resisted, however. He had a plan, one that he had been nurturing in his heart for four years: he would kick from the bell and break his rivals' will with one of those flat-out 400m bursts that were a staple of his daily training. Since the London Olympics he must have done at least 40,000 fast laps: each one had been fuelled by the thought that he would never again allow gold to slip from his grasp by mistiming his finishing sprint.

Now all he had to do was one more: one more flat-out lap to justify four years of self-torture. No matter what his rivals had to offer in terms of freshness, youth or raw speed, none of them would be able to match him when it came to soaking up the pain and maintaining the intensity to the very last stride. He had a fight on his hands, but he was ready to fight.

The bell tolled. The minute of his destiny had begun. He kicked. For a moment the whole stadium seemed to thrill to the prospect of another crushing Zátopek victory. Then, just as Emil was powering into the bend and wondering how big his lead was, Schade darted past him, followed closely by Chataway and, barely a pace behind, Mimoun. Coming out of the bend, Emil was fourth.

Despair overwhelmed him. He felt himself slipping backwards; a gap of several metres opened up between him and the third-placed Mimoun. 'You've messed it up,' he said to himself. 'You're going to come fourth.' And, as he often reminded people when he relived the race afterwards, 'There is no medal for fourth.' One journalist described him as looking like 'a tortured wreck' at this point. Yet he refused to succumb. That, in a nutshell, is what makes a champion a champion – that strange, irreducible lust for victory that dispels everything from fear to fatigue. It's the same instinct that allowed Muhammad Ali to walk into a storm of unexpectedly murderous punches from George Foreman in 1974 and think not of survival but of winning. The greatness lies in the split-second decision to fight back. The rest of us would be starting to think of excuses, of damage limitation; perhaps even of coming to terms with defeat. The champion seeks a new route to victory.

So it was with Emil. His plans in ruins, he was still thinking about gold. In the space of a few strides he considered the situation rationally and concluded that, in overtaking him so early, the other three must have been responding instinctively to the threat they perceived from him. They had, in other words, panicked, and sprinted earlier than they intended. Did it not follow, then, that they were likely to tire? In that case all was not lost.

Halfway down the back straight, Chataway, auburn hair flapping, sped past Schade, who responded by accelerating himself, as did Mimoun. With each flowing stride, Chataway looked more like a winner. But Emil, still in fourth, had persuaded himself that victory was, after all, in his grasp. The others were tiring. The others didn't have those 40,000 fast laps in their legs. The others could be beaten.

Going into the final bend, he had closed down the gap. Halfway round it, he launched a fresh attack, running wide past all three of his rivals in an agonised blur of flailing arms and pounding legs. Mimoun and Schade responded, pulling out to pass the tiring Chataway at the same time as Emil. For a tantalising fraction of a second, all four were abreast – and then . . .

What goes through a runner's mind at such a moment? Emil retold the story of this race many times, but at this point the narrative tended to peter out into generalities ('I ran like the wind') sometimes spiced with an expressive 'Grrrrrr'. Yet watch the footage today and you see beyond doubt that this – the final 150m – is the white-hot core of the race. Four men – three, if you exclude Chataway, who had run himself to exhaustion and tripped and fell shortly after being passed – each at his physical peak, each focused with every fibre of mind and body on the same prize, each giving the last possible drop of effort he can summon . . . and yet still it isn't over. Still there is another notch to be turned up. This is where words fail and all that remains is to imagine the boiling intensity of their struggle, in which the roar of the crowd and the roar of the bloodstream cease to be distinguishable. This is the lost zone, a place on the edge of death, in which only a handful of champions have ever set foot, and from which none has yet brought back a coherent account.

If you watch the footage, I urge you to find a version with a soundtrack that captures a little of the frenzied, spine-tingling excitement of the moment. The English newsreel commentary is cold and insular. ('Chataway falls. Oh dear, what a pity. Zátopek wins it.') The Czech version (actually a radio commentary) is barely comprehensible even to Czechs, but captures superbly the dizzying, table-thumping excitement as Schade fades and Emil and Mimoun match one another stride for stride on the bend, only for Emil – rejuvenated by the knowledge that victory is indeed still there for the taking – to find new reserves of strength and power madly forward. Somehow he thrashes his arms and legs with even more passion and conviction than before: not clinging on but driving, desperately seeking more intensity, more pain. His body seems to take on the shape and movements of a deranged insect: it is just like that crazy last-lap sprint in London four years ago – except that this time will be different. He believes now that he can win; that no one can endure this. ('The track seemed to be flying beneath me,' he said later. 'I could already see the gold medal.') Seventy thousand spectators are screaming with disbelieving excitement: it feels like an electrical storm. The commentator's inarticulacy (compounded by the yelling of a second Czech commentator right next to him) adds to the sense that something sensational and unprecedented is happening: '. . . Mimoun [*leads*] . . . But Zátopek finishes wonderfully . . . With a great burst he overtakes all three . . . Zátopek, you have four metres . . . five metres . . .'

Emil's winning time was 14:06.6 – a new Olympic record and his best time for two years. He had run the final lap in 58.1 seconds (within two seconds of his lifetime best for a single, one-lap 400m race); the final 200 took 28.3 seconds. It was, Emil thought, the fastest home straight he had ever run.

But times are just numbers. Afterwards, Emil and Mimoun embraced with the kind of warmth that you only see in sportsmen who know they have just taken part in something that no one who was not involved could ever fully understand. Schade, who understood well enough, was none the less distraught, and Emil spent some time comforting him, even going so far – according to one account – as to offer to give him his medal; an offer which, if it was made, was certainly not accepted. There could, in any case, be no question as to who had earned the glory.

The world was unanimous. *L'Équipe* hailed Emil's victory in 'the most terrific 5,000 of all'; *The Times* declared that Emil had 'established himself, beyond all argument, as the greatest long-distance runner of his period'; *Rudé právo* said that he had 'proved himself to be the best athlete in the world'. Australian readers could reflect on Percy Cerutty's verdict – 'Surely the deeds of the greatest generals pale before the deeds of athletes of the superhuman calibre of Zátopek' – while a Czechoslovak writer, the publisher Otakar Mašek, would go further still: 'The name Zátopek has become synonymous with the idea of speed, endurance, efficiency, reliability, fighting spirit and will-power. It would not surprise me if one day we should find his name in the dictionary as a common expression for all these terms.'

It was arguably the most extraordinary athletic achievement of Emil's extraordinary life. Yet others would say that it wasn't even the highlight of his week. And Emil claimed at the time that it wasn't even the highlight of his day.

One of the few people in the stadium unaware of the outcome was Dana. The women's javelin final had been delayed, apparently because of safety concerns.

(An English journalist, Guy Butler, had almost been hit by a javelin during qualifying that morning.) So Dana was waiting by the changing rooms in the bowels of the stadium, trying to stay warmed up and focused as she waited to be called for her own event. She could hear the roars and, later, saw officials rushing excitedly backwards and forwards. Eventually she managed to get a passing Soviet trainer to explain what had happened. He told her, and Dana squealed with delight. It was obvious from his face that he was thinking: 'What kind of wife doesn't watch her husband win a gold medal?' to which Dana thought in reply: 'The kind of wife who wants to win a gold medal of her own.'

Dana headed for the javelin ring immediately after the medal ceremony and met Emil just as she was emerging into the arena. They embraced quickly. Dana said: 'Ťopek, quick, give me the medal, for luck.' Before he could answer she had snatched it, put it into her bag and raced off to compete.

Emil, meanwhile, was hurried back to the changing rooms to shower. He was just emerging when he met the Czechoslovakian coach, Karel Kněnický, who told him excitedly: 'Dana just threw fifty metres.'

Emil refused to believe it. Fifty metres would mean not just beating her personal best (49.9m) but smashing the Olympic record. Kněnický was insistent: that was precisely what she had done. Stunned, Emil emerged into the stadium to watch the rest of the drama; but he had missed the highlight. Four other athletes threw further than the old Olympic record of 45.57m, but no one could match Dana's first, elated throw of 50.47m. Less than an hour after Emil's triumph, she had a gold medal of her own. She celebrated with a cartwheel – and earned a mention in the official report of the Helsinki Organising Committee as the 'happiest gold medallist' of the Games.

Emil later claimed that Dana's gold medal 'pleases me more than all the others', which was probably true. The couple finally caught up with one another by the team bus. 'I will never forget the way he looked at me,' Dana said many years later. 'It was as if he had never seen me before – as if I were a revelation.'

But Emil still had enough mischief in him to put into words, later, a thought that must have occurred to many people: that Dana's excitement at his 5,000m victory had 'inspired' her to make her best-ever throw. Dana memorably retorted: 'All right then, go and inspire some other girl to throw 50 metres.' As with much of the Zátopeks' banter, one could never be entirely sure how much of this was in jest.

Back in Otaniemi, the Czechoslovaks gathered for their daily team assessment. The political officer taking the session, Emanuel Bosák, congratulated Emil on his second gold medal but could not resist a reference to his insubordination in Prague: 'Comrade Zátopek runs well. If he could improve his behaviour, he could be a good example to our youth . . .' His teammates, few of whom yet knew of the Jungwirth incident, were baffled; some were later told that Emil was being too friendly with Westerners. The boxer Jula Torma, who had won a gold medal in London and thus had more liberty than many to speak his mind, made a pithy response that I'm told is best translated as: 'Ignore him, Emil. He's a prick.'

Late that night, in the women's quarters, Dana was too excited to sleep. Tiptoeing out of the room that she was sharing with a gymnast, she walked out of Building No. 8 – which the Czechoslovaks shared with six other Communist nations – and wandered through the silent woods to the lakeside. There she sat for two hours with her medal, marvelling at the midnight sun on the still water, and the wonder of her winning throw, and the sheer ridiculous beauty of everything.

But Emil was sleeping soundly, with the quiet confidence of a man with a hunch that his finest hour was yet to come.

11

The longest day

There were those in the Czechoslovak camp who felt that Emil should skip the marathon. He had reached his target. Why risk the loss of face that would come from a defeat? Emil later justified his insistence on going ahead with another famous piece of Zátopekian half-jest: 'I decided that the ratio of medals in the Zátopek household was insufficiently weighted in my favour.'

But there were other, more obvious motives. He had conquered the mountain that he had feared: the one that threatened to expose his weakness. Now he had a chance to make history: to show the world that what others considered impossible could in fact be done. This was the kind of challenge he lived for.

Even so, when the final day of the Games dawned on Sunday, 27 July 1952, it would have been odd if he hadn't been a little on edge. His body had enough experience of running very long distances to suspect that it was about to be put through the wringer. As for his mind: by defying those who urged him to avoid this final test he had once again stuck his neck out. If he was going to be in it, he needed to win it.

He spent much of the morning trying to learn to run slowly. He had calculated that the Olympic record for the marathon was equivalent to eighty-five-second laps of a 400m track. Assuming the record was likely to be improved a bit, he decided to aim for eighty-three-second-lap pace. But when his teammate Jaroslav Šourek (the Czechoslovak marathon champion) timed him, he kept running too fast. Even keeping over eighty seconds seemed beyond him.

Finally, he came up with a different strategy. The Englishman Jim Peters was the strong favourite. He had set a new world record, 2:20:42.2, just weeks earlier, and, said the newspapers, he would be wearing the number 187. If Emil stuck with him, he would be unlikely to go far wrong.

When the athletes assembled that afternoon at the starting line, Emil approached the tall, dour, pale-skinned man wearing 187. He did not want to discover later on that the papers had made a mistake.

'How do you do?' he said. 'Are you Peters?' Peters confirmed it. 'I am Zátopek,' said Emil. It barely needed saying. Half the world now knew that Zátopek wore 903 on his red shirt. In any case, Peters had raced against Emil before. Four years earlier, in London, he had been so demoralised by being lapped by Emil in the 10,000m final that he had given up running altogether for a while, before returning at the longer distance. It is unlikely that he relished the prospect of having a talkative, world-beating Czechoslovak for company for the next two hours or so.

None the less, polite words were exchanged. Then, at 3.28 p.m., the race began. The sixty-six runners, who had lined up in four rows, began by running three and a half laps of the track. Aslam, the barefooted Pakistani, was first to show in front, but Peters soon forced his way to the front, and by the time the first runners emerged from the stadium he was over a hundred metres ahead of a group that included the Englishman Stan Cox; the Swede Gustaf Jansson; and Emil.

Emil was unsure how to respond to Peters's aggressive start. He was wary of burning himself out: those laps felt much faster than eighty-three seconds. Behind him, all sorts of dangerous, experienced runners were lurking: notably the Argentinians Delfo Cabrera and Reinaldo Gorno, the Korean Choi Yun-chil, and a third Englishman, Geoff Iden. But what if Peters just kept on drawing ahead? Emil discussed the problem with Jansson – which was strange, since they had no language in common – and they concluded that Peters must at all costs be prevented from increasing his lead to 200m.

As they made their way northwards and eastwards through Helsinki's tree-lined streets, with a slight breeze behind them and thousands of spectators on either side, Emil, Jansson and Cox established themselves as the second-placed group. It was a straightforward out-and-back course: 41.95km in non-imperial reckoning. The weather was pleasant – 18°C – and the pace, though exceptionally fast by marathon standards, was still nothing special by Emil's. The difficulty was to run sensibly while keeping Peters in sight.

By the time they had passed the main Olympic village at Käpylä, Peters had a nineteen-second lead. He had run the first five kilometres in 15:43, equivalent to a track pace of seventy-five seconds a lap. After Emil's group, the nearest challengers, a further eighteen seconds behind, were Gorno, Yakov Moskachenkov (of the

Soviet Union), and Doroteo Flores (of Guatemala). As they headed out into the countryside on highway number 137, the field was strung out. Anyone with aspirations to a medal already had a fight on his hands.

The roadside was still lined with Finns, often two deep. Many had bicycles and picnics. They clapped politely as each runner passed. A bus just behind the leaders carried selected journalists, with a separate open car for photographers; sometimes one or other drew alongside, and Emil was seen to exchange pleasantries with those on board. Everyone agreed that he looked relaxed and strong.

The landmarks rolled by: Pakinkylä, Tuomarinkylä, the Vantaa river and its bridge. By ten kilometres (Malmi), Peters had slowed very slightly. Jansson was sixteen seconds behind him, with Emil just a second back in third.

The city suburbs thinned; buildings gave way to green fields of newly mown hay; but still the road was lined with applauding Finns. By the time runners were approaching Helsinki parish church (fourteen kilometres), Emil and Jansson had made significant inroads on Peters's lead; by fifteen kilometres Jansson had caught up. Soon afterwards Emil, too, was running alongside him. Emil, inevitably, started talking. His exchange with Peters is one of the most famous in sporting history, but it has been repeated in so many variations that it is hard to say authoritatively precisely what was said. Peters gave one version, which he admitted might have been clouded by exhaustion; Emil, characteristically, gave several. Jansson, the only other witness, did not speak English.

The most plausible sequence is this:

Emil: 'The pace, Jim – is it too fast?'

Peters (irritably): 'No, it has to be like this.'

(Pause.)

Emil: 'Are you sure it is not too fast?'

Peters (with what he later described as Cockney defiance): 'Actually, it's too slow.'

Soon afterwards, Peters moved to the other side of the road, the implication being that he would not welcome further questioning. Emil took this as a sign of weakness; he had noticed, in any case, that Peters looked more haggard than he had at the start ('like a boxer after the third round'), and he sensed, correctly, that he was struggling.

Emil did not – as legend suggests – immediately go speeding into the lead, but he did feel emboldened to keep pushing the pace. Just as Peters was ready to ease off, Emil made sure that he couldn't. The next five kilometres offered a classic demonstration of a distance runner being tortured by a pace that is just a tiny bit too fast for him.

By the twenty-kilometre mark, at Ruotskylä, Peters was ten seconds behind, although he had made back three by the time they turned at Mätäkivi. Emil and Jansson began the homeward journey side by side. No one was talking now. Even the wide-eyed Finns who watched them from the roadside seemed to do so largely in silence. There is something dreamlike about the black and white footage that survives, with pale skies, still pine forests and a straight, featureless, seemingly endless road. Perhaps it seemed dreamlike to Emil, too; he was, at the very least, in unknown territory. He had been running for longer than he had ever run in a competitive race before, and he was barely past the halfway mark. He had no real idea of what the rest would feel like; no idea what ordeal awaited him; no idea how best to manage his failing strength.

He later claimed that, around this point, he felt an almost irresistible urge to give up, and was deterred only by the thought that he had no money in his pocket with which to get back to Helsinki. If that seems unconvincing, it is almost certainly true that he was in pain. The easy chatting of the early kilometres had given way to dogged endurance (although he still exchanged the odd word with the accompanying press pack). Like every marathon runner, he found himself appreciating, from the gut, what a monstrous, unnatural distance 26.2 miles really is for running. His mouth was dry. His feet felt sore. He had bought some new shoes specially for the race – some say Karhu (a Finnish brand), others Adidas (disguised for political reasons) – and although he had followed the advice of the American 10,000m runner Fred Wilt to soften them in advance with cooking grease, they were still basically just track shoes with the spikes removed. There was none of the cushioning that modern road runners take for granted. To make matters worse, Emil had made a marathon runner's rookie mistake – of checking his socks for irregularities with insufficient paranoia. First one foot, then the other, developed a blister. He was still running within himself in terms of aerobic exertion, yet his body was taking a beating.

As they passed the refreshment station at twenty-five kilometres, Emil and Jansson were offered half a lemon each. They had ignored all the previous refreshment stations, not wishing to lose precious time, but Jansson's supporters seemed to feel that their man could do with a boost. Jansson took the proffered fruit, but Emil, who had no experience of eating while racing, felt it would be too much of a risk to try it for the first time now. Instead (he claimed later), he decided to see what happened to Jansson. If the lemon appeared to help him, at the next station Emil would take one, or perhaps several.

The self-denial hurt. Shortly afterwards, however, they came to an uphill stretch (one of several on the middle part of the course). By the time he reached the top Emil realised that Jansson had slipped behind – and appeared to have a stitch. Emil kicked on, his thirst to some extent offset by the satisfaction of having made the right decision. And then . . . well, after that, all that remained was to keep going.

To the sportswriters on the bus – none of whom, as far as I am aware, had ever run a marathon – perhaps it looked easy. It wasn't. No marathon is easy. Those final seven or eight miles are an ordeal – a test of pain management. No matter what your speed, your preparation or your talent, one screamingly obvious fact never goes away: you would feel better if you stopped. But Emil faced an additional trial: he was alone.

By thirty kilometres he was twenty-six seconds in front of Jansson, and more than a minute ahead of Peters. Cox had dropped out by now, collapsing at around twenty-five kilometres and having to be taken to hospital. But Emil had no way of knowing this, or of knowing what other threats – Gorno, Cabrera, Choi – might be gaining in strength and speed. An experienced marathon runner might have felt confident enough to coast. Emil had no experience, but he did know that at the previous

Olympics the eventual winner, Cabrera, had not taken the lead until he entered the stadium for the final lap. He dared not do anything but run as fast as he could, fighting the urge to take it easy, telling himself that each step taken meant one step less to go; and perhaps also reminding himself that, as Tomáš Baťa had taught, 'There are 86,400 seconds in a day' – from which it must follow that there are 8,700 seconds in a 2:25 marathon and, no less certainly, that running the final ten kilometres of a marathon at that pace would take 2,062 seconds.

Just over 2,000 seconds: that was all that stood between him and sporting immortality.

In fact, for all his efforts, he was losing speed – lots of it. His ten-kilometre split times for the race were 32:12, 32:15, 34:15 and 36:38. He admitted later that he had felt 'terribly tired' from around thirty kilometres. 'The finish line was a long way off. I was alone, and my strength had gone.' But his spirit hadn't – not quite.

As he passed back through Pakinkylä at thirty-five kilometres, Emil was still only sixty-five seconds ahead – a significant lead, but not unassailable. There were still nearly five miles to go. This was where he needed to find his unbreakable core of champion's stubbornness. If you look at his face in the brief, surviving footage of this stage of the race, you see a man who is no longer enjoying himself. There is something trance-like about him. His eyes are glazed; his face has settled into a fixed, almost peaceful mask, like a man close to death. He has rolled up his vest, bikini-like, to expose his dehydrated body to the breeze. His hands claw the air feebly. If he were wrestling an octopus, the octopus would win. 'If you want to enjoy something,' he said later, 'run 100 metres. If you want to experience something, run a marathon.' These are the words of a man who knows what it really costs to keep going for 26.2 miles.

But the price was worth paying. The fast early pace had taken even more out of Emil's rivals than out of him. Peters had dropped out at thirty-two kilometres, slumping to the pavement in an agony of cramp and heat exhaustion. As for Jansson, he was struggling desperately to keep in touch. Gorno was gaining on him, while Emil, without realising it, was now increasing his lead.

By forty kilometres Emil led by more than two minutes. The tower of the Olympic stadium was visible by now, with the Olympic flame blazing from it. The roadside support was growing denser and louder. He must have known that victory was within his grasp, yet the pain never stopped. The bounce had been hammered out of his calves and thighs: the next day, he had to hobble downstairs backwards, and it would be a week before he could walk normally. 'My legs were hurting up to my neck,' he said later. Yet still he kept pounding on, fixing his eyes on the flame, refusing to yield.

Not far from the stadium, he heard a 'Bravo, Emil!' among the Finnish cries of '*Hyvä,* Satu Peka!', and was boosted by the sight of several of the athletes who had been battling with him for medals earlier in the week – Mimoun, Reiff, Pirie – cheering him on from the roadside.

The final uphill slope before the stadium seemed, as such stretches do, to go on for ever. Somehow he reached the top. He was in the stadium tunnel. He could see the track. He later claimed that, even now, he was afraid that he might collapse before the line, but he cannot seriously have doubted that the 'impossible' third gold was now his.

A trumpet fanfare greeted his entry. Nearly 70,000 people rose to their feet and erupted into ecstatic applause. According to the official report of the Games' organising committee, he arrived at the stadium 'in extremely good condition', with 'no sign now of that look of agony to which the public had become used in the 5,000 and 10,000 metres'. According to Emil, this was the first moment in the race when he felt happy.

The final 300m could hardly have been more different from that dramatic last half-minute of his battle with Mimoun, Schade and Chataway three days earlier. Yet they were equally unforgettable. The acclamation was deafening: 'Zá-to-pek! Zá-to-pek! Zá-to-pek!' – a pulsating, spine-tingling thunderclap of celebration and goodwill. The Czechoslovak radio commentator struggled to make himself heard as he proclaimed: 'We declare to the republic, at these, the fifteenth Summer Olympics in Helsinki, Staff Captain Emil Zátopek is approaching the finishing line in first place . . .'

The applause prompted Emil to think about a final sprint on the home straight, to please the crowd, 'but my legs would not listen.' Instead, 'I tried to balance my steps and started to smile, so that no one would see how tired I was.' At last, his wet chest touched the longed-for tape. The attempted smile finally became visible, weak but radiant, the smile of a man who knows, blissfully, that he has just taken the last step of a 26.2-mile race; and that, as a bonus, his wildest dream has just come true.

He limped off the track. As soon as he could, he sat. He took off his shoes. His feet were bleeding. Someone offered him a blanket. He refused, but asked for a fresh vest instead. He ate an apple. Then he looked for Dana, and jogged happily over for the most famous kiss in Olympic history.

Gradually, over the next thirty-six minutes, the other fifty-two finishers struggled over the line. Emil greeted several, offering Gorno, who had overtaken Jansson towards the end, an orange and a consolatory hug. To Jansson he gave a blanket. It was striking how wrecked the runners-up looked – a reminder that, simply in physical terms, this had been no ordinary race. It was the first time that every finisher in an Olympic marathon had broken the three-hour barrier. The first fifteen finishers had run personal bests; the first nine had broken the old Olympic record; the first twenty had run fast enough to have won gold at the previous Games. Cabrera, who finished sixth, was more than eight minutes faster than he had been when winning gold in London in 1948. Emil, the novice in the field, had spurred everyone else to surpass themselves. That was one of the things his fellow athletes loved him for.

You know the rest. There was the chairing by the Jamaican relay team, the lap of honour, the third medal ceremony in the space of eight days, broadcast to well over a hundred nations on radio and, in a few cases, television. The young man who just eleven years earlier had feigned injury to avoid running less than a mile through the streets of Zlín had, in the words of the *New York Times*, forced 'the once-peerless Paavo Nurmi . . . to yield his pedestal as the greatest distance runner in history'. In the space of eight days he had done thirty-eight and a half miles of racing, in 3 hours 20 minutes 52.8

seconds (less time than it takes many good recreational runners to do just a marathon), at an average speed of 11.5mph; and, in the process, he had rewritten sporting history. All over the world, people who a month before had never heard of Czechoslovakia listened to its anthem with a growing sense of familiarity, and chattered excitedly about 'Zátopek'. This latest triumph meant that only twenty of the sixty-nine nations competing at Helsinki had won more gold medals than Emil and Dana; if you limited the medals table to athletics, they had come second, behind the United States but ahead of all the other great powers of East and West.

In Czechoslovakia itself, Emil's parents were among the millions who listened to his achievements live (although the much reproduced photograph of them stooped anxiously by the wireless in Kopřivnice was taken some time before the Games). Word even reached the men-to-be-eliminated in the concentration camps in Jáchymov. Ladislav Kořán, Emil's old training partner, was given the news as an example of what a 'decent socialist' could achieve. Jan Haluza, Emil's old trainer, was told by a non-political prisoner – a common criminal – who came swaggering across the yard shouting: 'Emil Zátopek won three gold medals! Emil Zátopek won three gold medals!' Seeing Haluza, he upbraided him for appearing insufficiently delighted. Haluza told him: 'If you knew the relationship between me and him, you would not talk to me like that.' He rejoiced at his protégé's triumph; yet the joy was inseparable from sharp grief at being prevented from sharing it with him.

But the moment was a bittersweet one for Emil, too. As he embarked on his final slow lap of honour, and the cries of 'Farewell, Fairy-tale Pete' echoed around him, the sheer perfection of the moment made him feel suddenly sad. 'I was sorry that, already, it belonged to the past – like when a man is reading a book and turns the last page. It has happened, and now it cannot happen again.'

Strictly speaking, he was right. But if he imagined that this marked the end – or even the high point – of the drama of his life, he could not have been more mistaken.

12

The people's champion

If Emil was not the most famous person on the planet at the end of July 1952, he would certainly have been in most people's top ten. In Czechoslovakia, he was beyond famous. He returned to a blitz of parades, presentations and fawning dignitaries that might have left even a twenty-first-century celebrity dizzy.

The adulation seemed endless. An event in honour of the returning athletes in the giant Strahov stadium, with Emil as the star attraction, was packed out. Politicians and senior military officers rushed to congratulate him. Two leading poets, Miloslav Bureš and František Branislav, wrote epics in his praise. Two senior figures in the world of sport, Emanuel Bosák and Josef Pondělík, embarked on a new, hagiographic mini-biography. There were fresh editions of František Kožík's biography, too, rebranded as *Zátopek: The Marathon Victor* and, in one case, lavishly illustrated with photographs. Many of these images were stills from the filming of *One of the Relay*, which itself acquired a new momentum; some were almost certainly staged rather than genuine. But the image of Emil and Dana kissing after his marathon victory was not just authentic but, for a while, the most famous news photograph in the world.

Emil was on the covers of magazines everywhere; his achievements were front-page news in serious as well as popular newspapers. In the Czechoslovak press he was hailed as an example of a new 'unique breed of conscientious athlete, tireless in training and able to fight for the honour and glory of our people's democratic republic'. Even *Rudé právo*, not given to the hero-worship of anyone but Stalin, joined in the excited chorus: 'Staff Captain Emil Zátopek's name flew around the world, and with it the name of our country . . . In capitalist countries, where workers still live under the yoke of the exploiters, the workers, peasants and other labourers rejoice at the success of our athlete . . .'

Scarcely less dizzying, from Emil's point of view, was the fact that the caretaker at 8 U Půjcovny, who had been hostile to Emil for years because of his habit of treating the apartment as a gym, organised a party to celebrate his homecoming. Emil later cited this startling volte face as his greatest achievement.

There were other, more tangible rewards. Emil was promoted again, this time to the rank of major. Alexej Čepička, the defence minister, personally announced the promotion, saying that it was 'for services to sport'. He also announced that Emil had been given the Order of Work (Řád práce). What he didn't say was that while the Olympics were still going on and he was on holiday, a document proposing 'the exemplary punishment of Staff Captain Emil Zátopek' had found its way to his in-tray. General Jan Kratochvíl, the chief of staff standing in for him, looked at the plan, then at the headlines in that day's newspapers, celebrating the extraordinary achievements of Emil Zátopek, hero of Helsinki. He called in his secretary and asked: 'Tell me – I'm not very well up on sport – are there two Emil Zátopeks?' The secretary (who Emil claimed later told him about this) assured him that there were not; whereupon General Kratochvíl looked again at the recommendation for punishment, dismissed it as 'nonsense' and tore it up.

There is (obviously) no documentary evidence to corroborate this story. But Emil repeatedly told it, once it was safe to do so; numerous friends, fellow athletes and family members have assured me that it is true; and although it has been widely published in Czech I have never heard it disputed. Meanwhile, it certainly seems fair to say that, a month after his outrageous insubordination over Stanislav Jungwirth, Emil showed no sign of being out of favour with the regime.

No doubt it helped that he was finally in the process of becoming a member of the Communist Party. It was remarkable for such a senior army officer not to be one already. But what really assured him of official favour was the fact that, thanks to his fame and achievements, he was an irresistible instrument of Party propaganda: a one-man solution to the problem of national morale.

Emil had been doing his bit for the regime – making speeches, visiting factories, encouraging grass-roots sport – ever since his first gold medal, but his triumphs at Helsinki took this aspect of his life to a new level. Proclaiming the Party line – often in speeches that had been written for him – became as crucial a part of his duties as winning races. Mostly he was supposed to proselytise about the virtues of sporting participation, but sometimes he was expected to deliver more specific messages. The Olympics were still technically in progress when, on 3 August (the morning of the closing ceremony), Emil addressed an audience of 2,500 at a peace rally, organised by the Finnish Communist Party, at Alppilava in one of the parks outside Helsinki's Olympic stadium. Emil spoke – rapidly rather than passionately, according to one witness – about the evils of American foreign policy. He would address a similar theme later in the year at the World Peace Congress in Vienna.

Where possible, however, Emil spoke about matters closer to his heart: the rewards of working systematically towards a sporting (or other) objective; the pleasures of forming friendships with athletes from foreign countries; and the endlessly re-told tale of his hard road to Olympic glory, fuelled by self-belief, self-discipline and unlimited hard work.

From the Party's point of view, this was useful enough, allowing them to present Emil's values as Communist values, and to promote the narrative that Emil's triumphs represented a triumph for the entire Communist system. Large parts of the Czechoslovak public still seemed perplexingly unenthusiastic about Stalinism. Emil's popularity could be exploited to rectify this. Some senior figures also saw it as an opportunity to boost the productivity of the workforce. According to apologists for the regime, workers all over Czechoslovakia were inspired by Emil's achievements to increase their output. As František Kožík put it, 'The workers followed his example and set a higher pace for their work, in order to hasten the building of socialism in their country.'

It hardly needs saying that reports of a surge of spontaneous mass enthusiasm for hard, Zátopek-style work should be taken with fistfuls of salt. It may well be true that the miners at the General Yeremenko mine in Ostrava achieved their highest rate of coal extraction since 1945 in the aftermath of Emil's Helsinki triumphs, or that a tinplate-making factory in Prague increased its output by 218 per cent. What is open to question is the degree to which this 'Zátopkovite' movement (consciously modelled on the Russian Stakhanovite movement) was spontaneous. In later life, Emil met workers who reproached him for having caused unwanted increases in their compulsory workload.

Emil's own, supposedly voluntary workload was not exactly light. Public appearances became as regular a feature of his life as racing – often more regular. Ota Pavel claimed that he had up to twenty-five public engagements a week; whatever the truth, it was heavy enough for Emil to find it tiresome – and, indeed, his exploitation for these purposes became so notorious that Věra Čáslavská, the gymnast, would speak half a century later of Emil being 'chased like a bloated goat . . . from one forum to another'. At one point, in the course of yet another excursion to address a 'forum', Emil made his Party minder laugh with a joke to the effect that he would probably be addressing a forum on the day he died. He was later reprimanded for his disrespectful words, which the minder had reported. Meanwhile, no matter how much he grumbled, he had little choice but to comply. As his friend Jaromír Konůpka points out: 'He was a soldier. He had to obey orders.'

There is footage of Emil engaged in this kind of work in *One of the Relay*. In one sequence, in a factory, he listens with a glazed grin that will be familiar to British royal-watchers, while a spokesman for the workers tells him: 'I promise you that, taking your performances as an example, we at the factory will work with the same zeal and enthusiasm with which you win your races.'

Unspontaneous as such encounters feel, it is clear that Emil had a talent for them. He was smart enough to know what was required of him, and what he needed to say to keep out of trouble. But he was also charming and humorous and enjoyed engaging with ordinary people – who, in turn, were genuinely excited to have any kind of contact with the greatest sporting hero the world had ever seen. His life-lessons-drawn-from-sport felt (and still feel) relevant to ordinary people: 'You cannot jump to the second floor from the pavement – step by step, though, a man will come to the fifth floor'; 'What a man wants, he can achieve'; 'One's willpower increases with every task fulfilled'. Compared with some of the politically edifying addresses that Czechoslovaks were expected to listen to, an event involving Emil must have seemed thrilling.

It is also likely that Emil believed at least some of the messages he was delivering. He had clearly begun to have his doubts about the fanaticism, cruelty and stupidity of the Communist regime. But it is unlikely that much arm-twisting was required to persuade Emil to assert that, at Helsinki, the friendship that developed between athletes of most of the world's nations 'was so beautiful that it could only arise among people who want to live in peace'. As for the regime's wider political message, Emil had been brought up as a Communist, had been bombarded with Communist ideology since joining the army in 1945, and had experienced both the evils of fascism and the poverty of the 'have-nots' under capitalism. He once said (much later in life) that he would prefer to live on bread and water under Communism than in luxury under capitalism, and this was probably true. He had his reservations about the Party's authoritarianism, but the system had improved his own life immeasurably, while rescuing his family from the gnawing insecurities it had known before 1948. He knew, too, what life had been like for Czechoslovak athletes before the Communist era: Koščák, Emil liked to point out, had laid paving stones in Wenceslas Square in between his records, while Černý had slept rough during a period of unemployment. If Communism offered something better than this, he was in favour.

Emil cannot have been unaffected, either, by constant exposure to crowds of adoring members of the public, or to the idealistic messages he was expected to share with them. If people were inspired by his preaching of Communism's nobler ideals, how could he scorn them? Dana, who experienced similar adulation but to a lesser extent, was at first uncomfortable with the attention, until Emil told her: 'The people love us, Dana. We have to love them back.' For the cult of Zátopek to thrive, Emil had to believe in it, too.

There were believers in the West, as well: not just among the ideologues who – like the Communist *L'Humanité* newspaper in France – saw him as 'the new man: Socialist Man', but also among the wider, non-Communist public. Wonder at his achievements fed an appetite for his back story, which Party propagandists had been polishing for years. In a world still scarred by the Second World War and chilled by fears of a Third, there was something compelling about this socialist with a human face – this working-class hero who, no matter how dubious the regime he lived under, seemed to embody universal values of human decency. He was a soldier – an occupation with which millions could identify – but there seemed to be no hint of brutality about him. Instead, he was courteous, charming, humorous, with an extravagant sense of sportsmanship that recalled the noblest ideals of chivalry. He owed his achievements not to privilege but to unremitting hard work which was evident both from his agonised style and, no less memorably, from the photographs and film footage that were now becoming more widely available, showing a lone, indomitable soldier bounding uncomplainingly through the snow at night.

'As a good soldier, he must obey. As a true champion, he must surpass himself. And, behind him, the youth of the nation follows . . .' You didn't have to share the pro-Soviet sympathies of J. Armour Milne to find the message stirring. Friends who sang Emil's praises in the West, such as Les Perry (who had left Helsinki with Emil's red vest and white shorts) and Gordon Pirie were anything but pro-Soviet. They loved Emil for his human qualities, not his politics. 'I am sure that for very many years yet he will be an inspiration to new generations,' wrote Pirie. 'Above all he is . . . the greatest sportsman I have ever met.'

Meanwhile, ideology or no ideology, Emil still had to find time to perform at least a semblance of his military duties. These would become easier in November 1952, when Emil was made a desk officer at ATK – a simple, unexciting role that, without affecting his seniority, allowed him to train without the stress of worrying about how to get his job done. The racing, however, must sometimes have felt more like performing in a circus. On 17 September 1952, for example, more than 20,000 fans crowded into the little stadium in Ústí nad Labem, to watch Emil run the 5,000m in a club match. Many workers were reported to have refused to work their afternoon shifts, so that they could be sure of seeing him, and reports of forged tickets led to a police investigation.

Two weeks earlier, in the little Moravian town of Znojmo, Emil had won a fiercely contested 5,000m against Milan Švajgr – the local runner who had trained with Emil for a while in Hranice. The ferocity may have had something to do with the fact that Švajgr had been dropped from the Olympic team for Helsinki at the last minute, despite having the world's fastest time of the year for 3,000m. According to Švajgr, who had been selected to run 5,000 and 10,000m, this was because of something Emil said to one of the personnel commissars in charge of vetting the team for political reliability. Švajgr claims to have been in the room with Emil and the commissar when Emil said that he considered Švajgr a defection risk – or, at least, refused to guarantee that he was not. When Švajgr protested, Emil withdrew the remark. None the less, this supposed risk was cited as the reason for Švajgr's sudden omission from the team, despite protests from his home town of Opava. If this is true, it may tell us something about Emil's ambiguous relationship with the regime. He was, after all, a major: it would have been difficult to hold down such a job without buying into the Party's programme to some degree. Perhaps he felt that Švajgr was dispensable; there was no great bond between them. Or perhaps he really did have doubts about Švajgr's loyalty. Under the 'knew, but didn't tell' law, standing up for the wrong person could have disastrous consequences. With Jungwirth, by contrast, Emil's efforts to keep him in the team included an undertaking that he would vouch for his loyalty – one he would have been foolish to give had he mistrusted Jungwirth. One reason for his success in that battle may have been that he appeared to accept in principle the Party's right to enforce ideological conformity. He engaged with the idea that defection had to be guarded against – and evidence from his later life suggests that he genuinely felt it was a form of treason.

None of that was of any comfort to Švajgr, who may have felt that Emil had been trying to safeguard his own medal chances at his expense. But the contest in Znojmo made a nonsense of that imputation. Emil ended up a convincing winner, while Švajgr, for all his motivation, was twenty-five seconds outside Herbert Schade's bronze medal-winning time in Helsinki. Afterwards, there was a dinner at some wine cellars in Jaroslavice, where they all got drunk. Švajgr berated Emil, who held out his hands and said: 'OK, so beat me! Beat me!' The two men later resumed a friendship, of sorts; but when I met Švajgr more than six decades later it was clear that he had not forgiven him.

Emil, meanwhile, whatever his true beliefs, continued to add to his credentials as a Party loyalist. He joined the Central Committee of the Czechoslovak Union of Youth – a kind of Young Communists organisation – and when Stalin died, in March 1953, Emil was among those who put their names to tributes in the daily newspaper *Mladá fronta*, mourning, in his case, 'a great teacher of Soviet sport'. Did he really believe that? It seems unlikely, but it is impossible to tell. Part of the tragedy of Czechoslovakia's decades of Communist tyranny is that all but the most simplistically fanatical learnt to keep their real motives to themselves. Dissimulation became the norm.

But one thing that remained unambiguous was Emil's passion for running. On the track, if nowhere else, he could be himself. And if he carried on torturing himself in training as obsessively as if he had never won a medal in his life, well, perhaps it didn't always feel like torture. Perhaps it felt like release.

If further incentive was needed, it probably came from the knowledge that most other leading distance runners were now imitating Emil's methods. This was particularly noticeable among his fellow athletes in Prague and in Stará Boleslav, where young men such as Ivan Ullsperger and Stanislav Jungwirth were beginning to get impressive results by attempting to do their own versions of Emil's training sessions. Even beyond the specific discipline of endurance running, the general Zátopkovite principles of hard work and systematic progress towards supposedly unthinkable goals were gaining currency among athletes generally. No doubt Emil found all this flattering. It also served to remind him that, where he had pushed back the frontiers, others, including rivals, could now follow.

On 4 October, in Opava, Emil made an unsuccessful attempt on Gunder Haäg's 5,000m world record; he failed by more than eight seconds, but even that produced a time – 14:06.4 – that suggested that he was still in excellent shape. Three weeks later, at Houštka Spa, he set a world record for thirty kilometres (1:35:23.8) and, in the process, world records for twenty-five and fifteen miles as well. The next finisher was fifteen minutes behind.

The following year started badly, however. Emil began to be troubled by sciatica, which occasionally caused him agonies in his legs. He had to have his tonsils removed, and some teeth. And there was an unfortunate incident in the spring when, messing about, he wrecked Dana's hopes for the season.

Dana had been in brilliant form – so much so that her coach rewarded her with a Sunday off. Emil suggested an excursion to the countryside, with a swim in the River Sázava as a highlight. 'So in the morning we ran up to this place where Emil knew there was a pool,' says Dana, apparently relishing the memory. 'When we got there, there was a young man lying there, reading a newspaper. We never even found out his name. Emil said, "OK, let's go for a swim." But the man said: "There's not enough water here."

'So Emil said, "OK, we'll throw her a little bit further, into the deep bit." So he and the young man grabbed me by the hands and legs, swung me, and threw me into the water, as far as they could. The riverbed was sandy, but when I fell in I got my foot stuck under a rock.' She broke her right leg – the one that matters most for javelin throwing – just above the ankle.

All things considered, Dana took this well – at least, she laughs as she describes it now. Emil's punishment was to carry her on his shoulders all the way back to the cottage they were staying at: a journey of just a few miles that gave birth to the enduring legend, which Dana denies, that Emil regularly ran while carrying her. Meanwhile, the accident was a salutary reminder to Emil that things wouldn't automatically work out perfectly just because he was Emil Zátopek.

This was no time for complacency. Rivals were rising in the east who threatened his dominance. In early June, Aleksandr Anufriev achieved an impressive double, running 13:58.8 for 5,000m in Moscow and then 29:23.2 for 10,000m the following day. In July, Vladimir Kuts, a young Russian who had been developing his own version of Emil's methods and would soon become a byword for implacable dominance on the track, ran 14:14.6 for 5,000m; while József Kovács, of Hungary, ran 14:07.4. The higher echelons of distance running were starting to feel a bit crowded.

In August, Emil confronted Kuts and Kovács over 5,000m at the International World Youth Games in Bucharest and was forced to produce a stunning final kick of fully 800m to hold them off. The 10,000m, four days later, yielded a rather easier victory for Emil. The races were also memorable for Emil's visible gestures of sportsmanship: carefully guiding Dave Stephens, during the 10,000m, to the best ever 5,000m time by an Australian, or stooping to tie Kovács's loose shoelace for him just before they began to race. You would never have guessed, from Emil's manner, that he was under any pressure. Stephens, who collapsed in the second half of the 10,000m, joined the growing band of overseas athletes who considered Emil a lifelong friend. He later spent two weeks training with Emil, studying his methods; Emil, in return, received a boomerang and lessons in how to use it.

In the course of the next six weeks, however, Kuts, Pirie and Kovács all produced sub-14:03 5,000m

Zátopek in action:
he lack of challengers
does nothing to
soften the agonised
body language.

:mil leads the Olympic
eld in a rain-drenched
10,000 metres in
London 1948; Gaston
Reiff is second.

His finest hour

Emil on the point of breaking the world records for both 20,000km and The Hour at Houštka Spa, 29 September 1951.

His finest moment?

Emil takes the lead coming out of the final bend in the Olympic 5,000 metres final in Helsinki, 1952. Alain Mimoun is second, Herbert Schade third; Christopher Chataway is on the ground behind them.

Crossing the line at the end of his first marathon, Emil claims his third gold medal at the Helsinki Olympics.

Bounding through the snow in the woods at Stará Boleslav.

Above left: Dana throws for gold at the Helsinki Olympics in 1952 and, right, celebrates her victory.

Below: the most famous kiss in Olympic history, moments after Emil had finished the Helsinki marathon.

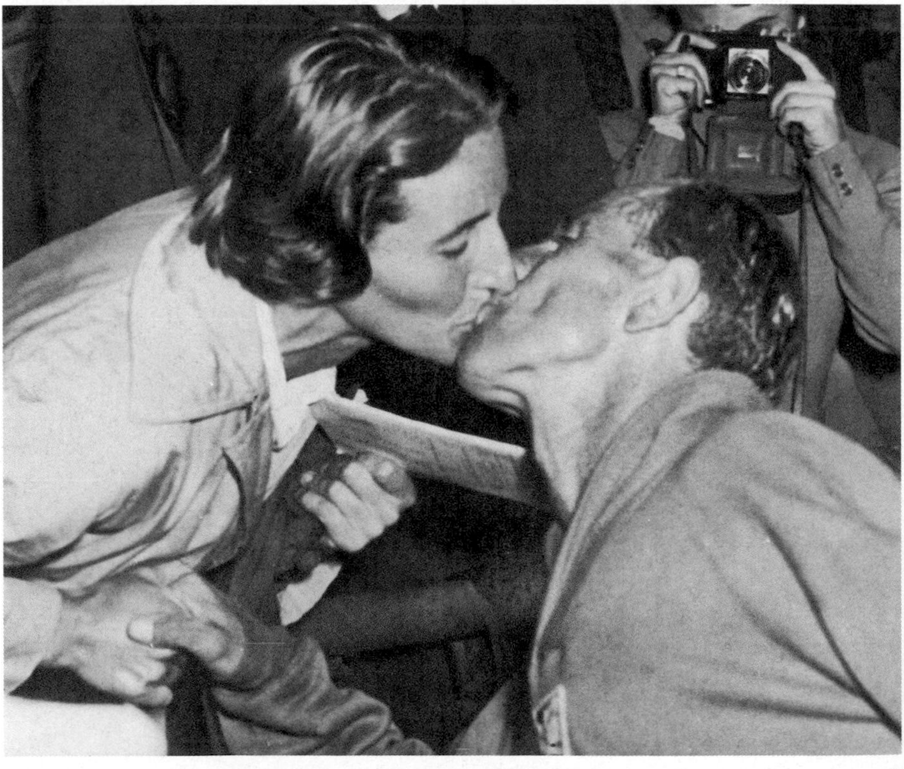

Above left: Uherské Hradiště, 24 October 1948: fellow athletes pay their respects at Emil and Dana's wedding.

Above right: Emil and Dana in their hillside garden in Troja.

Below: towards the end of Emil's life, sharing a glass of wine in the house they built there.

Emil, in and around Wenceslas Square, denouncing the Warsaw Pact invasion that crushed the Prague Spring in August 1968.

'Great is the victory, but greater still is the friendship.'

Emil congratulates Alain Mimoun after the 1956 Olympic marathon in Melbourne, and the two friends relive their old rivalry in 1988.

'Because you deserve it...'

Ron Clarke with the Olympic gold medal that Emil gave him in 1966.

performances. Emil was now fifth in the all-time list of 5,000m runners. He managed to put Kovács in his place by beating him in a head-to-head at the Strahov stadium in October, but even that was a struggle – Emil had to overcome a twenty-metre deficit in the final lap before sprinting away to win by a similar distance. Was he starting to rely more on desperate willpower and less on superior fitness and talent? It was hard to tell. Meanwhile, it had not escaped the attention of the management of ATK that Emil ranked no better than fourth – behind Pirie, Kovács and Anufriev – in the list of the best times of the year for 10,000m.

This prompted a late attempt to put things right. On 1 November, on a damp, windy day at Houštka Spa, Emil knocked a second off his 10,000m world record, which he reduced to 29:01.6. In the process, he also beat Gordon Pirie's world record for six miles; a congratulatory telegram from Pirie arrived shortly afterwards.

The result was also gratifying for the Melichar family, who lived next door to the athletes' retreat on the edge of Stará Boleslav, and who were among the spectators for Emil's record-breaking run. They had first encountered Emil when one of his shoes, left outside the athletes' villa to dry, was snaffled by their dog, Arko. Emil eventually tracked it down, only lightly chewed, and, in the process, met and made friends with the family.

Over the next few months, he dropped in regularly, sometimes with fellow athletes in tow; and on one visit the conversation turned to Emil's growing interest in using resistance training to build up strength. Various examples were discussed: running in army boots, or wearing a heavy rucksack. All you needed was a worthwhile amount of extra weight, arranged in such a way that you could run with it. Someone asked if it was feasible to run with a person on your back. There was only one way to find out, and the Melichars' six-year-old daughter, Iva, was produced as a guinea pig. Emil put her on his shoulders, and off they went.

The details are a bit of blur today, but Iva – now called Iva Kazda and living in the USA – remembers that 'he went very fast. It was cool. We ran down the hill to the woods, and then ran around the woods for a long time.' She doesn't know if he was doing his usual repetitions, or just messing around; she remembers only the speed, and the fact that he was funny and kind and didn't seem bothered by the load. Iva became a keen marathon runner. Now nearly seventy, she still loves running in the woods – and still marvels at the fact that, once, she saw with eyes just a few inches above Emil's what the woods of Stará Boleslav looked like to the great Zátopek as he bounded tirelessly through them.

The new world records at 10,000m and six miles were pleasing proof that this exercise had done Emil no harm, and that his shoes had not been too badly damaged by Arko's attentions. But if reports of Emil's decline were premature, the problem of his ever-more dangerous rivals remained; as did the inconvenient truth that, no matter what he did to boost his strength, his basic speed was – at the age of thirty-one – unlikely to improve. In an interview with J. Armour Milne for *Athletics Weekly* at the end of the year, Emil warned: 'You must not expect too much from me in the future . . . I shall be able to compete in the shorter of the long distances only as a sort of 'guest artist'. I feel that my true distances are from 10,000 metres upwards.'

To most of the world, Zátopek remained simply Zátopek: a man of unique sporting genius and charisma whose powers verged on the supernatural. At the end of the year Emil was allowed to travel to Brazil, where he had been invited to take part in the famous Saint Sylvester New Year's Eve road race in São Paulo. Between 800,000 and a million spectators turned out to watch the event, which began shortly before midnight. Shrugging off the humid conditions, Emil easily defeated 2,139 rivals over the 7,300m course. He remained in the city for nearly a week and, despite catching a chill and having to be treated with penicillin, rounded off his visit with an impressive 10,000m victory.

Overseas visits by Czechoslovak athletes were frowned upon by the Communist authorities, who feared defections and the corrupting effect of contact with the West. But Emil was becoming a special case. He had already travelled widely and had, on the whole, proved himself reliable. Each visit had to be cleared in advance with the security services and observed by an accompanying representative of the 'sharp eyes'. Travellers would then be expected to report back on what they had seen: whom they had spoken to; what they had noticed about the customs and condition of the host country; and, if relevant, the behaviour of those who had travelled with them. Emil, whose gifts as a linguist far outstripped those of most professional spies, seems to have reported back regularly, although not necessarily reliably. No transcripts of his debriefings survive in the archives of the security services, but indirect evidence implies that, initially at least, his brief was to bring back something comparable to travel journalism: general impressions, not without telling detail, gathered by looking around and talking to people. I am not aware of his ever having commented on the behaviour of a fellow athlete.

What made Emil valuable to the regime was not the information he provided but his gifts as a diplomat. His track triumphs had done wonders for Czechoslovakia's international profile, but one day those triumphs would dry up. His charm, on the other hand, was capable of being exploited for years. An age of Zátopek diplomacy beckoned.

But Emil had other priorities. He was still bubbling with energy, still hooked on the buzz of competition ('To stand on the starting line, to look my rivals over, and tell myself: "Well, boys, let's get going and see who's best . . ."'). And his appetite for sporting glory remained unsated.

The winter of 1953–4 saw him subjecting himself to his toughest workload yet, much of it away from home at the camp in Stará Boleslav. His training diary recorded that, in a twelve-day period in mid-February, training in the woods twice a day, he accumulated the following daily totals (with 150m recovery jogs in between each approximate lap):

Monday 15th: 70 x 400m
Tuesday 16th: 40 x 400m
Wednesday 17th: 40 x 400m
Thursday 18th: 80 x 400m
Friday 19th: 80 x 400m
Saturday 20th: 70 x 400m
Sunday 21st: 40 x 400m
Monday 22nd: 80 x 400m

Tuesday 23rd: 80 x 400m
Wednesday 24th: 80 x 400m
Thursday 25th: 80 x 400m
Friday 26th: 50 x 400m

By the end of the month (from 29 February to 2 March), he was doing 100 laps a day. The speed varied. A giant session might be done largely at racing speed, or as near as Emil could get to it. But somewhere in the middle would be a sequence of fifteen or more flat-out, frenzied, catch-Reiff-or-die sprints. Given the volumes involved, the will-power required was superhuman.

To help his focus, he took the radical step of shaving his head – temporarily dampening the interest of the photographers, film-makers and sculptors who were constantly asking him to pose for them. The fact that his hairline was continuing to recede may have played a part in this, but it is also a characteristic expression of his belief in the empowering effects of asceticism. He ran 1,845km in February and March alone – getting on for three-quarters of it flat-out; and that's not counting the hours of extra exercising he did indoors (back at home), jogging on the spot on a rubber mat for up to two hours at a time when the weather was so severe that even he couldn't train outdoors.

His clear priority for the year was to defend his two titles at the European Championships, to be held in Berne in July. But he was also committed to improving his world record for 10,000m and his national record for 5,000m, and to achieving a classification of 'outstanding' in 'party political education'. We know this because by early 1954 the 'Zátopek movement' had been more or less formally enshrined in the administration of Czechoslovak sport. Leading athletes were expected to make specific, public pledges about their goals for the year. The Ministerial Council for Physical Education and Sport announced the most prominent in a poster displayed in a shop window in Wenceslas Square. (Dana was committed to a new national record in javelin throwing and 'active participation in sport education of youth'; others had targets including 'mastery of the Russian language' and a 'thorough study of the history of the Bolshevik party'.)

The 1954 season began with Emil in scintillating athletic form; as a diplomat, however, he was initially not at his best. His first event was a cross-country race in Paris organised by *L'Humanité*. Several top athletes from Soviet bloc countries had been invited, but Emil was the star attraction. The French athletics federation (FFA) disapproved of the event – partly for bureaucratic reasons and partly for ideological ones – and had forbidden French athletes to take part. The race that Emil won in the Bois de Vincennes on 21 March – the first day of spring – was therefore an unofficial one.

This minor irritation may have had something to do with some uncharacteristically blunt comments that Emil gave to the journalists who welcomed him on his return to Prague – some of which were published in *Svobodné slovo*. Asked about the impression that Paris had made on him, Emil replied that he had been disappointed. Apart from the notorious Pigalle district, there wasn't much to see, and he saw little to enthuse about in 'the Paris of junk literature, the Paris of pornographic revues and magazines', in which everything seemed to be subservient to a hunger for commercial gain. The journalists may have polished his quotes a little. None the less, they were enough to form the combustible raw material for '*l'affaire de Colombes*'.

It took time to ignite. For a few weeks more, Emil simply trained and raced. The training was merciless: at times he was doing 100 x 400m, sometimes seven days a week; 'horse dosage, every day' was how he described it. Then, as a race approached, he would reduce the quantity – to 30, 20, even 10 – and increase the speed accordingly. The combination was irresistible. On 25 April he won an eleven-kilometre cross-country race in Nové Město na Moravě, in the scarcely credible time of 31:12. On 14 May he won a 5,000m at Houštka Spa, in 14:04.0; two days later he won another one, in Kladno, in 14:19.2. He was, in short, ferociously fit: so much so that his weight had dropped to sixty-two kilograms – five or six kilograms less than normal. The last time he had weighed so little was when he left hospital on the eve of the last European Championships, in August 1950, following that famous bout of food poisoning. Given his stupendous performances on that occasion, he and Dana joked that perhaps another world record was on the cards; and the conversation somehow ended with Dana vowing to bow down to him, literally and publicly, if he succeeded in breaking Gunder Hägg's seemingly unbreakable record for 5,000m.

There was an obvious opportunity to do so. On 30 May Emil was due to return to Paris, to race in an international match in the northern suburb of Colombes. But that was when the trouble began. The exact chain of cause and effect remains confused, but there is no dispute about the component parts. The French athletics authorities may have been ruffled by reports that Emil, having committed to the match, might race in Hungary instead. There were elements in the French establishment who objected to a Communist figurehead such as Emil being an honoured guest in their country. And then, shortly before he was due to arrive, Emil's comments about his earlier visit found their way back to France.

This was the final straw. The Czechoslovak team arrived in Brussels on 26 May. From there they were due to travel to France – but the journalists who greeted them had already heard the news: Emil was not going to be granted a visa. A three-day diplomatic storm followed. The Czechoslovaks were outraged; the French stood upon their dignity; others weighed in according to politics and prejudice. French commentators were divided between those who found their foreign office's stance embarrassing and those who suggested that Emil was a 'Communist fanatic' who should make a public apology. Even in the era of McCarthyism, it was a bizarre spat – and a bizarre stance for a Western government to take in relation to the world's most famous sportsman.

Emil tried to focus on his training, while frantic phone calls were exchanged in the background. Finally, late on Saturday, 29 May, the French foreign office authorised its consulate in Brussels to grant Emil a visa. Emil rushed to the consulate shortly before midnight, and just had time to catch a flight that arrived in Paris at 6 a.m. on Sunday, 30 May. The race was to take place that evening.

The Stade Olympique Yves-du-Manoir was filled to overflowing. Emil, tired and grumpy, lined up for the 5,000m against a weak field of just four others – and proceed to run one of the most astonishing races of his life. There was no one to pace him; nothing to pull or push him on apart from several days' worth of accumulated frustration and a desire to provide something special for the ordinary French athletics fans who had turned out to see him. But that was enough. Running alone for all but the first half-lap, he pushed himself as even he had rarely pushed himself before, simultaneously driven and liberated, upping the tempo as the fans responded to what they could sense was a historic effort.

His final kilometre was sensational. Encouraged by rhythmic applause, Emil ran it in 2:43.8, overturning a four-second deficit on the world record schedule to finish in 13:57.2 – an improvement of an entire second on Gunder Hägg's twelve-year-old time. The second finisher, Yugoslavia's Drago Štritof, was forty-six seconds behind. Afterwards, Emil was mobbed by autograph hunters, and eventually had to be escorted from the track by gendarmes – whose own requests for autographs confirmed to Emil that he had made his peace with the French people. The next day's headlines confirmed this: Emil was praised for his '*admirable réponse*' to the rudeness of the French government, which, in turn, was condemned for its '*incroyable stupidité*'. Emil had won the diplomatic battle as resoundingly as he had won the race.

The day after that, Emil was back in Brussels, where he raced at 10,000m in the Stade Trois Tillauts. Despite forty-eight hours of rain and little serious opposition, Emil once again ran as if his life depended on it – and was rewarded with a time of 28:54.2. Less than a month after Roger Bannister had made global headlines by running the first sub-four-minute mile, Emil had reclaimed his position as the most noteworthy athlete in the world by becoming not only the world record holder at 5,000m but also the first man to run 10,000m in less than twenty-nine minutes.

The fact that the diplomatic stakes had been so high gave extra weight to Emil's triumphs when he returned to Prague. His immediate reward was to be greeted at the airport by Dana, who presented him with a bouquet and, at Emil's insistence, made a low(ish) bow to him. But the Czechoslovak state was even more enthusiastic, seizing hungrily on this fresh propaganda fodder. A new wave of Zátopkovism was reported: some miners in Příbram were said to have broken a world record for fast coal cutting. The message was simple. As Otakar Mašek wrote: 'The delight in work, the conscientiousness, the courage, the feeling of responsibility of a Zátopek should run throughout our whole lives.'

Emil, meanwhile, was promoted yet again, this time to lieutenant colonel, which in military terms was farcical. Emil had barely more experience now than he did when he graduated from military academy. None the less, it was a relatively decorous way of bestowing on Emil some arguably legitimate material reward. In addition to a generous salary, there were perks: a car, for example (Klára the Saab – although technically this belonged to the Ministry of Defence and some of Emil's colleagues had access to it, too). Athletes also received a 'nutrition allowance', which was not supposed to be spent on items other than food but often was. Even if rumours of cash bonuses for Olympic medallists weren't true (and Dana insists that they weren't, in those days), the Zátopeks were becoming steadily more entrenched in Communism's elite: the new ruling class, whose privileges – however justifiable they seemed from within – insulated them from the hardships and frustrations the system inflicted upon ordinary people.

Somehow, though, the privilege didn't stick to Emil. When people saw him driving Klára, they forgave him the (relative) ostentation. They knew how hard he worked, and they knew that he always had time for ordinary people and cared about their welfare. When Emil saw that Ivan Ullsperger didn't have a watch, for example, he not only asked him why but took note of the answer – Ullsperger had been been planning to buy a watch but had, like many Czechoslovaks, lost all his savings in the great currency reform of 1953. A few days after explaining this, Ullsperger was stunned to receive a watch from Emil as a gift. Much later, he learnt that it was the watch awarded to participants in the Helsinki Olympics.

To say that Emil was entirely indifferent to material things would be an exaggeration. No one who has known poverty ever is. But apart from good food and drink, which he relished, and freedom from financial anxiety, which he appreciated, he does not seem to have been interested in luxury. Rather, he cared about people, and about running. Running was not a means to an end: it was an end in itself. And his accumulated medals and glory counted for little compared with that gnawing anxiety that every runner knows – the fear that the slightest loss of willpower and focus will see the accumulated fitness of the years haemorrhaging away, irrecoverably.

13

'Today we die a little'

On 3 July 1954 there was a sporting earthquake in Hungary. In an international match in Budapest, Emil was beaten over 10,000m. It was his thirty-ninth race at the distance, and the first he had ever lost.

He took the end of his six-year winning streak in his stride. There was only an eighth of a second in it; he had not been well that day; his conqueror, József Kovács, was an athlete he admired; and the winning time, 29:09, was respectable. It would have been silly to overreact.

Even so, he must have worried. No champion likes losing, or, worse, feeling his powers ebb away. Emil responded, inevitably, by training harder. In August, he got his revenge, beating Kovács by nearly twenty-eight seconds to win in 28:58 in the European Championships in Berne. But third place in the 5,000m at the same meeting, behind Kuts and Chataway, spelled out the dispiriting underlying message: there were runners out there who were faster than him. And speed, as Jan Haluza had taught, is the foundation of everything.

Nothing Emil could do would rectify this shortfall. He could redouble his efforts, but only with respect to those areas that were within his control: endurance; strength; resilience; and, not least, the ability to function and thrive on the borderline between tolerable and intolerable agony. But with his thirty-second birthday approaching there was no more raw speed lying latent in his body, waiting to be unlocked by training.

The clock was ticking. He had nine successive victories at 10,000m before losing again: to Kovács in Bratislava in September 1955 and to Pirie in London three weeks later. But his times were worsening, while at 5,000m he was losing almost as often as he won. In fifteen races between the 1954 European Championships and the end of 1955, he won eight and lost seven, and ran faster than 14:10 only four times. Even Ivan Ullsperger, Emil's protégé at ATK Praha, managed to beat him twice.

As far as the general public was concerned, Emil's pre-eminence remained beyond doubt. When the first Spartakiáda mass gymnastic display was held in Prague in July 1955 – the Communist alternative to the now suppressed Sokol *slets* – nothing could have been more natural than that Emil should address the packed Strahov stadium, urging everyone to join him in contributing to 'the glory of our physical education'. That autumn, at Čelákovice on 29 October, he added some extra glory of his own, setting new world records – his seventeenth and eighteenth – for fifteen miles and twenty-five kilometres. But these would be his last, and, meanwhile, the world's athletics journalists had been following a different narrative. In the words of *Athletics Weekly*'s Jimmy Green, 'the great Czech master has reached the point where he is capable of being beaten by younger, speedier runners.'

In October, Emil conceded the obvious. 'I am not fast enough for the 5,000 metres,' he said in a television interview in London. He would not, he announced, be defending his Olympic title at the distance.

That Christmas saw Emil, Dana and other athletes from ATK (soon to be renamed Dukla) sent to India, where they visited Bombay, Delhi and Calcutta. Emil made such an impact that he was later said to have single-handedly started an Indian running boom. Emil beat the Indian champion, Gulzara Singh, over 5,000m in Calcutta. Singh was so overwhelmed that he touched Emil's shoes and sprinkled dust from them on to his head. Emil responded by giving Singh his shoes.

The trip was also notable for the heat, for the welcoming crowds, and for at least one spectacular marital row between Emil and Dana, which was written up with ill-concealed relish for the Czechoslovak secret service by an agent who appears to have been eavesdropping. They seem, however, to have been on relatively good terms on returning to Czechoslovakia, and according to some reports early 1956 saw Emil incorporating wife-carrying into his training regime as a regular feature. If true, this would be consistent both with Emil's character and with his preoccupations at the time – and with the fact that, around the same time, he suffered a painful hernia in his groin.

There is, however, a difficulty. Dana insists that the only time she remembers Emil carrying her was after he broke her leg, in 1953. This is the problem with writing about Emil: myths and legends swirl around his name, and many evaporate when you try to grasp them. In this case, as in many, the legend seems to originate with him. He told at least two writers that his problems in 1956 began when he went running in the woods carrying Dana on his shoulders. Others have recorded that it took place in the snow; that Dana complained about Emil's bony shoulders; and that at one point Emil tripped on a tree root. J. Armour Milne, in a book published in 1956, described Emil attempting 'to jog trot for several hundred yards along a forest path' with Dana 'astride his shoulders'. Does any of this make it true? Not necessarily. Emil liked few things better than to entertain people with anecdotes that would become more amusing each time he retold them; and he seems to have adopted a similar approach when it came to those who sought to set his own story down in words. He knew a good tale when he saw one, knew how to improve it, and wasn't too fussed if journalists – or publishers, or Party officials – did a bit of extra polishing of their own, just so long as they got what they wanted and stopped bothering him. 'Do anything they ask of you,' was his media strategy, 'because there's no other way of getting rid of them.' So he helped package his story into anecdotes – the medal in the swimming pool, the running in the bath tub, the sausages and beer from the hospital kitchens – and the anecdotes crop up again and again, with variations, in contemporary and subsequent writings about him, without necessarily becoming any truer as they mature.

And the wife-carrying? We can only guess. Perhaps Emil was exaggerating; perhaps Dana has forgotten; perhaps he had a different passenger (a child?), and the journalists misunderstood. But at some point in early 1956 Emil became aware that, probably as a result of some kind of running with a heavy load, he had injured himself.

Like countless lesser athletes after him, he had tried too hard to halt time's depredations. Like them, too, he responded at first by trying to shrug off the injury. By June, however, after coming a dispirited fifth in the Rošický memorial 5,000m in Prague, he faced facts. He had surgery in early July, and he spent a fretful summer reading reports about his world records being broken: by Pirie (13:36.8 for 5,000m); by Hungary's Sándor Iharos (28:42.8 for 10,000m); and by Kuts (28:30.4 for 10,000m).

A short spell in Moscow, advising Soviet marathon runners such as Ivan Filin and Albert Ivanov, did little to restore his equanimity. He made a tentative comeback on 26 August, winning a low-grade 5,000m in Kladno in a spectacularly slow 15:18.6 – his worst time since 1944. In late September, less than two months before the Olympics, he was forced to take a break from heavy training. He returned to run 10,000m, at a military meeting in Prague on 7 October, and won, against modest opposition, in 29:33.4. Then he ran out of time.

The Czechoslovak team touched down in Australia on 9 November. Emil, desperate for fitness, had trained incessantly during the four stopovers; he had even tried training in mid-flight, but the rest of the team forced him to stop, terrified that he would cause the plane to crash.

They reached Melbourne on the 10th. Six days earlier, Soviet tanks had rolled into Budapest to crush the Hungarian uprising – Eastern Europe's first significant revolt against the Kremlin's dominion. Tens of thousands would die by the time the rebellion was extinguished. Emil admitted to journalists that the events cast a shadow over the Games. 'It's a pity . . . To have this sudden shadow of strife and misery cast over the whole affair so late in the day is a great disappointment. Many of us feel it has spoilt the Games before they have begun.' He stopped short, however, of apportioning blame for the events; or of invoking the 'Olympic truce'. Instead, he announced that he would compete only in the 10,000m, adding: 'And I've no chance of winning that because I'm too old.' Asked who was likely to beat him, he said, 'Probably the whole field.'

In the Olympic village, however, he seemed to be in good shape, and in good spirits. He had brought a case of Pilsner Urquell beer with him, for 'medicinal' purposes – he believed that nothing replaced a runner's lost body fluids so well. But he found himself sharing rather more of it with his teammates than he had intended. Despite the shadow of Hungary, and the ubiquitous 'sharp eyes', it was impossible not to feel thrilled at being at the Olympics, in such a strange, distant land.

Athletes from all nations were housed in the same complex this time, and Emil was once again the focal point for fraternisation between athletes from East and West. One hour-long track session saw him giving encouragement and advice in a variety of languages to athletes from several nations, with barely an interruption or a pause for breath. This prompted the *Melbourne Argus* to observe that 'the true Olympic spirit burned brighter than ever at the Village yesterday. And – fittingly – it was the "grand old man" of modern Olympiads, Emil Zátopek, who gave the lead.'

One of the runners who took advantage of Emil's generosity was a young American marathon runner called John J. Kelley. The US distance runners were initially nervous about approaching Emil: they felt that it would be presumptuous. But Nick Costes, the eldest of their party, eventually went over to say hello, and before long Kelley had been introduced, too. He ended up training with Emil most afternoons. He noticed that his hero was now running with a very slight limp. His main recollection, however, was that: 'He was a wonderful, affable fellow. He put me at ease instantly, and I marvelled at all the languages he spoke.' They remained friends for years afterwards, and would send one another cards. Kelley thought so highly of Emil that he named his first daughter Emily in his honour. Emil marked her birth by sending the Kelleys 'a beautiful cut glass bowl'.

But no number of friendly laps could alter the fact that Emil was way short of the kind of fitness he would need to be a medal contender for any of the track events. He tried to avoid journalists, and claimed that there was a special cupboard in the Czechoslovak team's quarters where he would hide whenever he heard unfamiliar footsteps in the corridor. By the time of the opening ceremony – where Emil raised eyebrows by high-spiritedly throwing his hat in the air as he passed the Duke of Edinburgh's box – he had conceded that he would not defend his 10,000m title either. He would save himself for the marathon instead, just over a week later.

On the first day of competition (23 November), he watched the 10,000m final from the stands, using a towel and a stick to signal to his Australian friend Dave Stephens whether or not he was on schedule for his target time of twenty-nine minutes. The ruse proved futile. Stephen couldn't keep the pace up, while Vladimir Kuts stormed irresistibly to gold in 28:45.6; all three medallists beat Emil's Olympic record from Helsinki. Five days later, Kuts knocked forty-seven seconds off Emil's Olympic record to win the 5,000m as well, destroying Gordon Pirie in the process, and causing several commentators to make observations to the effect that (as the *Canberra Times* put it): 'Kuts has proved conclusively that he has taken over the mantle of the great Zátopek as the outstanding stayer of world athletes.'

Emil hardly needed to read these reports: the observation made itself. He will not have welcomed it, no matter how sincere his congratulations to Kuts, with whom he was on friendly if not especially intimate terms. (Kuts was a more abrasive character than Emil, and was never likely to take over his mantle in terms of charm.) The fact that Dana managed only fourth place in the javelin final that same afternoon cannot have improved spirits in the Zátopek household. The marathon was three days later. It would be gratifying if Emil could win it.

But it was a palpably less confident Emil Zátopek who stood at the Olympic marathon starting line shortly after 3 p.m. on 1 December than the effortlessly invincible superman who had introduced himself to Jim Peters in Helsinki four years earlier.

True, he was among friends rather than strangers this time: Alain Mimoun, for example, who had belatedly decided to try the marathon after finishing a disappointing twelfth in the 10,000m; Les Perry; John J. Kelley; or the Soviets, Ivan Filin and Albert Ivanov, whom he had been advising in Moscow. But he must have sensed that, for all the reverence and affection in which he was held, he no longer instilled fear. He was a hero, but he was beatable.

To spectators who were close enough, it was obvious that Emil had aged. He wore a cap to protect his increasingly bald head from the sun, but the face beneath had the tired, stretched look of an athlete in the twilight of his career. There were even those who felt that he had 'allowed himself to be persuaded against his better judgement to run'.

Emil also had the disadvantage from which all but first-time marathon runners suffer: he knew what it would be like. He knew what he had been through the last time. The conscious mind forgets; deep down, though, the body remembers the ordeal, and dreads repeating it.

This time it would be worse. The temperature was officially reported at 30°C – 12° hotter than in Helsinki – and some measured it at nearer 35°C. Several runners had coated their shoulders in Vaseline to protect them against the sun; many wore hats. Few could doubt that, as the race headed out into the open road and the afternoon's heat accumulated, the torture would come from the conditions as much as the pace. This was the kind of weather that did for Pheidippides.

This must have been what Emil had in mind when he – allegedly – uttered the famous words: 'Men, today we die a little.' I say 'allegedly' because, despite the large number of reputable works in which this remark is quoted, I have not been able to identify a primary source in which it is reported in this precise form. Even if the accepted phrasing is apocryphal, however, I make no apology for celebrating it. Emil certainly said something along those lines; and it is hard to think of a neater encapsulation of his spirit: his cheerful camaraderie; his dry humour; and his slightly bonkers bravado in the face of the agonies of his sport. It was also, in context, a starkly accurate prognosis.

The race began oddly, with the Olympic marathon's only ever false start. They set off correctly at the second attempt, at 3.13 p.m.; circled the track two and a half times; and headed off into the hot afternoon. There were forty-six runners from twenty-three nations. A broken green line – an Olympic first – had been painted on to the tarmac to guide them. Paavo Kotila of Finland and Arap Sum Kanuti of Kenya were the early leaders. Emil was content to hang back, conserving his energy and hoping that the fast starters would eventually come back to him. But when Mimoun hung back with him, Emil revealed what he really felt about his chances: 'Alain,' he told him, 'I am not good. Don't stay with me.' Mimoun hesitated: sticking with Emil, or trying to, had for so long proved the best way of making sure he was in with a chance of a medal at the end of a big race. But Emil insisted – and, in so doing, proved beyond doubt that friendship in sport mattered more to him than stealing a march over a rival.

They ran past palm trees and parked cars, along wide, prosperous streets. Some runners varied the side of the road they ran on to take advantage of the occasional scraps of shelter; others stuck to the shortest route. The crowds were perhaps a little thinner than in Helsinki; no doubt the heat deterred a few. But Emil was as warmly applauded as anyone.

After 8.6km they passed a railway bridge and joined Dandenong Road. It was a thoroughfare that few of them were ever likely to forget.

The first 1,500m or so were uphill. By then, Kotila was leading by two seconds from Mimoun, Filin and Ivanov. Emil was seventeen seconds back in eleventh place. One television commentator was already describing him as 'in trouble', but he was in contention.

After 12.2km they left Dandenong Road – but not for long. A mile and a half later they were back on it, once again heading uphill. The straight single-carriageway road seemed to go on for ever, bare and largely featureless. The only shadow came from the sporadic groups of spectators on the roadside. The sun beat down viciously, the heat rebounding from the hot tarmac, and still the slope continued upwards.

At fifteen kilometres, Mimoun was just ahead; Emil was still eleventh but now only five seconds behind. He could see that others were struggling with the heat, pausing to douse themselves with water at the drinks stations, and the sight may have encouraged him. But he, too, was struggling – with, among other things, his shoes. The heat of the asphalt was melting the glue that stuck the crêpe soles to the leather uppers, causing the crêpe to disintegrate into little pellets. The agony, stretched out over the best part of two hours, must have been unspeakable: Emil's room-mate, the triple-jumper Martin Řehák, was horrified when he saw Emil's raw, bloodied feet afterwards. For Emil, the memory of gluing so many thousands of soles and uppers together himself can only have made the experience more frustrating.

There was nothing for it but to continue, rolling and slipping slightly with every step. It was too hot to go much faster anyway. This was a contest of resilience rather than speed. But Alain Mimoun, the veteran war hero who had won so many silver medals as Emil's 'shadow', was resilient, too, and around the halfway point he sensed his chance. First to reach the short downhill stretch before the turnaround, he put on a sudden spurt, turned, powered back up to the crest of the hill and then strode out confidently on the long downhill return journey while his rivals were still negotiating the turn. His lead was soon unassailable: by twenty-five kilometres he was fifty seconds ahead.

Emil had nothing to keep him going but pride, and perhaps the odd scrap of hope. He had seen the demoralising sight of Mimoun speeding homewards while he was still heading outwards, but he could not be sure that the Frenchman was keeping it up. Meanwhile, he was moving up the field: to sixth place at twenty-five kilometres and fifth at thirty. Nine runners had already dropped out, while others were going backwards. But as for the kind of sustained attack that he would need to make a dent in Mimoun's lead – you had only to look at him to see that the strength was not there.

Marathon runners can imagine for themselves the remainder of the ordeal: an hour or so of constant struggle, teetering on the edge of despair without ever quite succumbing, that niggling hint of old injury becoming steadily harder to ignore. From the outside there is nothing to see but a glassy-eyed runner, banging out the same monotonous pattern of largely identical strides. Inside it is an epic drama of suffering, courage and endurance; even if, from a competitive point of view, it is a failure. At thirty kilometres, Emil was two minutes twenty-two seconds behind Mimoun; by the end, that gap had almost doubled. The lowest point, from Emil's perspective, was being overtaken with a couple of kilometres to go. He tried to respond as Korea's Lee Chang-hoon passed him, but he was no longer able to accelerate even a little bit.

By the time Emil reached the stadium, at 5.41 p.m., Mimoun had been waiting at the finish for several minutes, applauding each new arrival in turn: Mihalič, Karvonen, Lee, Kawashima. But everyone could see that he was still looking for someone. Then Emil appeared on the track – and was cheered as deafeningly as if he had won. Stubbornly keeping up his rhythm, he completed his final Olympic lap, perhaps more dead than alive; then crossed the line, stepped off the track, gratefully accepted the officials' proferred blanket, took off his cap and sank heavily to the ground. The fact that, at the age of thirty-four, he had beaten all but five of the world's forty-five top marathon runners (thirteen of whom failed to finish) – or that his Olympic record for this event, at least, remained intact – meant nothing. This was a man who had had enough.

Mimoun rushed over to him. 'Emil, congratulate me,' he said. 'I am an Olympic champion.' After all those years as Emil's shadow, he was now the hero in his own right. 'Emil turned and looked at me,' Mimoun recalled in later life, 'as if he were waking from a dream.' He got to his feet, took two steps backward, 'snapped to attention', took off his cap and saluted him. Then he embraced him. 'For me,' said Mimoun, 'that was better than a medal.'

If you like Olympic moments that make your eyes prick with tears, seek this one out. You will see from the brief footage that Emil really does look as delighted as if he had won himself. 'Great is the victory,' he is supposed to have said, 'but the friendship of all is greater.' I'm not sure that he really did. But if you see the two old warriors smiling and embracing, suffused with joy in Mimoun's triumph and in their long bond of respect, love and shared suffering, you will understand what that old Olympic saying means.

Later on there were questions from journalists. Emil's face was etched with weariness and defeat; it was hard to believe that he had crossed the Helsinki finishing line with that radiant, boyish smile only four years earlier. When he told journalists, 'It was too much for an old man,' he said what many were thinking.

Later still, he was more specific: 'I realised I was licked at the halfway point. I started confident that I could make a good race of it, but I suddenly realised about all that was left was to go out like a champion. That was when I decided it was no use breaking my neck with any more speed and risk collapse . . .

'This was my last race.'

14

The ambassador

It wasn't, of course. No champion surrenders his greatness so lightly. But it was the beginning of the end.

In the short term there was plenty of time for Emil to reconsider his position: not just in the final days of the Games, when Percy Cerutty enjoyed showing him round the local zoological and botanical gardens, but on the journey home. A bizarre outburst of Cold War paranoia meant that, instead of flying home as planned on a French aeroplane, the Czechoslovak team, supposedly fearing sabotage, travelled instead by sea. They shared the ship, the *Gruzia*, with the Soviet team and a large cargo of live sheep. The extra mouths to feed were bad news for the sheep – lamb dominated the menu – and the overcrowding caused ill feeling among both Czechoslovaks and Soviets. An angry Vladimir Kuts got drunk three days in a row and, when reprimanded for his behaviour by a political officer, suggested that they resolve the matter with their fists. Emil took a more placid approach. He spent an hour a day running around the deck, and suggested to Dana that they treat the voyage as a second honeymoon.

It was hardly idyllic. The toilet paper ran out halfway through the three-week journey: everyone was made to contribute diaries and notebooks to meet the common need. There were typhoons when they passed Japan, and when they landed at Vladivostok the temperature was -32°C. By the time they got home, via the Trans-Siberian Express and Moscow, Prague was in the grip of a severe winter as well, and Emil, several pounds heavier, could certainly be said to have cooled off.

He announced in March that in future he would compete only domestically. In fact, in the course of 1957 he ran nine times at 5,000m and ten at 10,000m, with a couple of cross-country races thrown in for good measure; the venues included Oslo, Stockholm, Athens, Krakow, Moscow and Berlin. But these appearances were very much a coda to Emil's career. There were no big international meetings, no showdowns with the new giants of his disciplines. He won just over half his races, in times that were respectable rather than world-beating. It kept him in shape, though, and the cross-countries, in November, helped set him up for his final famous victory.

This took place just over a year after his agonies in Melbourne. Patxi Alcorta, a Spanish journalist, race organiser and bar owner, persuaded the Czechoslovak sports federation (now called the Československý svaz tělesné výchovy and referred to from now on as the ČSTV) to send a couple of athletes to Spain for the prestigious cross-country race in San Sebastián, in the Basque region close to the French border. Emil was sent with the young Miroslav Jurek, escorted by an official called Jan Jirka, an old friend. They flew to Paris, then caught a train. From the moment they crossed the Spanish border, they were mobbed by fans; even the customs officials were interested only in securing Emil's autograph. The fact that the visiting Czechoslovaks were Communists, while Spain was still ruled by the Fascist General Franco, does not seem to have bothered anyone. The Basques felt that Emil was one of them.

When the party reached San Sebastián, the rocky coastal town was in the grip of Zátopek-mania. An estimated 50,000 spectators – getting on for half the population – turned out to see the race, over a hilly twelve-kilometre course on a cold, windy day.

It was a world-class field. Britain's George Knight – the fastest man in the world over 10,000m in 1957 – was favourite, with France's Hahmoud Ameur also fancied, along with the promising Jurek. Emil responded to the threat by running aggressively from the start, as if he were still in his prime. There were five big laps to run, and for part of each one the wind gusted directly into the runners' faces. Emil, whose preparations had included hundreds of 200m uphill repetitions in heavy boots, chose those sections to crank up the pace mercilessly, turning the race into a test of physical and mental toughness. One by one, his rivals dropped off, until only Ameur and Jurek were still in contention. With 2,000m to go Ameur took the lead, but Emil responded imperiously. In the words of the next day's report in *The Times*: 'The old master produced a relentless burst of speed in the final straight.'

His emphatic victory was met with celebrations that even Emil may have found disconcerting. The rejoicing Basques chaired him on their shoulders, threw him gourds of wine, kitted him out with a beret and took him to Alcorta's bar, the Iru Txuli, where, in keeping with tradition, he was made to do a stint as a barman before being invited to celebrate long into the night.

At some point – the accounts are a little confused – someone tried to present Emil with a puppy. (Alcorta was also a dog breeder.) Emil demurred, partly because it would have been illegal to transport a dog into France. But when, the next day, the train carrying the exhausted Czechoslovaks crossed back over the Pyrenees, there at Hendaye station on the French side of the border was an old Basque woman with a basket which she presented to Emil. Inside was the little white puppy.

Emil didn't have the heart to refuse a second time, and so his new companion, whom he christened Pedro, accompanied him for the rest of the journey, hidden in his kitbag. Jirka, who was supposed to be keeping a sharp eye on the athletes' behaviour, turned a blind eye instead, even during the awkward moment when they were approaching Czechoslovak customs and Emil kept whispering to Pedro to keep quiet. 'But,' Jirka objected later, 'the dog didn't even speak Czech.'

He soon learnt what it sounded like, though, becoming a valued if anarchic member of the Zátopek household who was particularly devoted to Dana. An Andalusian terrier, he was bred to hunt waterfowl, and would often leap in uninvited when he saw someone taking a bath. Years later, travel commitments forced Emil and Dana to give Pedro away to friends, the Rašíns, but by then they were firm dog-lovers, and they subsequently obtained several other puppies from Alcorta, for themselves and their friends.

The gift of Pedro may have had more significance than the Basques realised. The visit to Spain seems to have coincided with – or been preceded by – another rocky patch in the Zátopek marriage, and Emil was reported to be reluctant to go back to Czechoslovakia: not for political reasons but because Spain somehow felt less complicated. Talked out of this, he was said to have asked if, on their return, he could be taken straight to the training retreat at Stará Boleslav instead of going home. But Pedro, of course, made such a plan impossible; and, like many a puppy before and since, he seems to have been a healing influence.

The fact that such an influence was needed may come as a surprise to some. Emil and Dana's relationship is generally presented as an idyllic love story. In fact, it had more ups and downs than is usually suggested; and the decade that followed Emil's last Olympic race may have been one of the more troubled periods. One obvious source of tension was the fact that, while Emil's competitive career was all but over, Dana's emphatically wasn't. She felt stronger than ever, had her eye on the 1960 Olympics in Rome, and was living and training – and travelling – accordingly.

Another issue, which would manifest itself more clearly as the next decade unfolded, was the couple's inability to have children. The problem may have originated with a bout of peritonitis suffered by Dana during a trip to Poland in 1945. They both adored children, and would have loved to have had their own; and Dana, in particular, was distraught to find that they could not. Emil tried to comfort her, telling her: 'Do you think that the human race will die out, just because we do not have children?' But such sorrows are not so easily dispelled, and it seems likely that the issue contributed for a long time to a niggling sense of dissatisfaction with their lives. In the long run, perhaps the shared pain brought them together; in the short term it may have done the opposite.

Eventually, according to Dana, their relationship became 'more like a friendship'; I suspect that this long transition was more painful for Emil than for Dana. There were intimate outside relationships, and distressing jealousies, on both sides. Dana is reluctant to discuss the details – and it would be wrong for me to invade her privacy further. But she concedes that 'of course there were incidents. It happens in life, once in a while, that someone finds themselves liking somebody. Things like that happen.'

Yet the special bond between them – that peculiar shared outlook based on playfulness, warmth and a sense of infinite possibility – always brought them back together. And, 'as time went on, our relationship grew. We went through hard moments as well as good moments, and the experience made us stronger.'

Meanwhile, there was nothing that either Dana or Pedro could do to alter the fact that, as a competitive runner, Emil had nowhere left to go. Five weeks after his San Sebastián triumph, on 6 March, he announced his retirement. 'I can't run until my death,' he said. 'I want to stop racing and devote myself entirely to the Army.' The world believed him this time, and marked his departure from the competitive stage with a fanfare of praise. In the words of the *Manchester Guardian*, 'He departs once more a winner and can rest as one of the immortals of his sport.' There would be no better time to go; and if he had any sense at all there would be no coming back.

You have only to think for a moment about the enormity of Emil's commitment to his sport – the years of demented, all-consuming dedication – to see what a gap this must have left in his life. In eighteen years he had run more than 50,000 miles – the equivalent of twice round the earth – and at least half of that had been at fast racing speed. His life had been a blur of championships, records, medals – and now all that was over. His fellow athletes, including his wife, were making plans for the European Championships in Stockholm that summer, but he could only look back, not forward. In fact, there had been voices in the ČSTV suggesting that he should make one final appearance in Stockholm, but he was wise enough to resist. To symbolise the finality of his decision, he hung a pair of his running shoes from a nail in the wall of his living room. He knew that his body could not cope with the required degree of intensity of training any more. The question was, could his mind cope without it?

It is hard to believe that he really relished the prospect of focusing on his military career; at one point shortly after his retirement he talked about becoming an adventurer instead, joining the celebrated writers Jiří Hanzelka and Miroslav Zikmund on their travels around the world. Following a brief spell after the Olympics as a trainer at the Miroslav Tyrš military school, Emil was moved in 1958 to the Ministry of Defence, where, once again, he was supposed to oversee the promotion of physical fitness in the army. This was a pleasant and comfortable place to work, in Prague's prestigious Dejvice district and within jogging distance of the Strahov stadium, with regular excursions to pursue his brief in military installations across the country. It was hardly an adventure, though, and sometimes Emil's continuing public duties as a propaganda icon must have felt like a welcome diversion.

He seems to have been well-liked by his colleagues, and he clearly enjoyed the physical disciplines of a soldier's life: he once said that 'to be in the military in peacetime is heaven on earth'. From now on, however, he would be largely desk-bound. His San Sebastián victory had earned him yet another promotion: this time to full colonel. He does not seem to have taken naturally to the dignity of the role. He once went swimming in the Vltava in Prague, in defiance of regulations, and was ordered out at gunpoint by some soldiers. He retrieved his uniform from behind a bush, dressed hastily, and was amused to see the expression on the soldiers' faces when they realised that they had threatened a senior officer.

On another occasion, in 1959, arriving for a spell overseeing army athletes in Lipník nad Bečvou, he was escorted into a room full of conscripts who were watching one of their number demonstrate his ability to walk on his hands. The escorting officer called them sharply to attention, and the hand-stander responded by standing to attention upside down. Then he realised the seniority of the visitor and hastily righted himself. Emil put him at his ease by saying: 'I can do that too' – and proceeded to demonstrate.

Some years later, on a similar assignment at the Higher Training Institution of Artillery in Martin (in what is now Slovakia), Colonel Zátopek allowed himself to be diverted from his fitness inspection duties into a trip to the shops, a mile and a half away. A liaison officer, Václav Bednář, escorted him. Emil insisted that they go on foot – but soon said: 'I can't walk this slowly. Let's jog.' They bought a huge, eighty-litre jar for Dana to make jam in. Bednář, already sweating heavily in his uniform, tried to summon an official car; but, he recalls: 'Emil flatly refused: "Don't call any car – we'll walk." I took one handle of the pot, but that was a serious mistake. Zátopek immediately ordered: "Captain, at the double, jog." I had no choice but to obey.' When they were close enough to the artillery school for soldiers to be watching, the order was revised. 'He said: "Come on, we will show these gawkers how we can sprint." I had to use the last part of my strength and join him. My colleagues teased me about it for years.'

Generally, Emil seemed more comfortable as a doer than as a giver of orders. Coaching athletes, he liked to jog along the track with them. Supervising marches, he was known to ask someone else to take over so that he could enjoy marching himself; supervising artillery exercises, he insisted at least once on having a go at firing a gun. Such eccentricities were harmless. But it seems reasonable to infer from them that, had it not been for his genius on the track, he might not have progressed so far in his military career. As one (early) internal report on his exercise of command observed: 'He is kind-hearted, has a soft nature, and is humble, talkative, sometimes childish, which is perhaps what makes him popular with his subordinates. But his command authority suffers as a result.'

There was also the question of politics. The armed forces were a stronghold of Communist orthodoxy. Most commanders had sworn oaths of loyalty to socialism and the Soviet Union, and officers were regularly assessed for ideological soundness. The annual reports on Emil preserved in his military service record painstakingly log his supposed views. He tends to score better on Marxist philosophy than on the workings of the Communist Party – but it is the tone of scrutiny that is most revealing: 'In political terms he is quite mature, applies his theoretical knowledge in practice, and can discuss his opinions. He is capable of being directed by and promoting the policy of the Party and government . . .' You half expect them to add that Emil has been learning to cut out basic shapes with scissors.

In such an environment Emil had no choice but to go through the motions of being an enthusiast for the regime. His tireless public speaking helped bolster that impression. Yet he unquestionably had doubts by now – and it is striking that, as the 1960s unfold, those official assessments of him take on a more critical tone: 'Sometimes he discusses questions which he has not yet understood completely. Sometimes he adopts the wrong opinion on a certain matter, which he finds difficult to drop . . .' Years of travelling had opened his eyes to the fact that life beyond the Iron Curtain was not all bad, while life in the Soviet empire was not all good; he could see, as he put it later, 'the progress in the world – and return home to a country where time has stopped'. He knew better than to express dissent openly, but like many young men who had felt passionate about Communism at the outset he was no longer an uncritical admirer. He had learnt, however, like most Czechoslovaks, to adjust his expansiveness according to the company he was in.

What he couldn't adjust was his individualism. He watched his words, and avoided direct challenges to authority, but he was still a maverick – a one-off. He had, in the words of one StB informer's report, 'peculiar' views on a range of subjects. And for all his efforts to conform, the fact remained that he thought – knew – that he was special. How could he have felt otherwise? Everywhere he went, people clamoured to see him, to talk to him, to touch him. It was like being a one-man forerunner to

The Beatles; and, as he had grown used to it, so he had developed a sense that, where he was concerned, otherwise inflexible rules could be bent.

One famous example of this took place in the aftermath of the Melbourne Olympics. Olga Fikotová, who had won gold for Czechoslovakia in the discus, had begun a romance at the Games with the US hammer thrower Harold Connolly, also a gold medallist. There were those in the Party, and perhaps even in the Olympic team, who saw this as little short of treason. Others, including Emil and Dana, saw it as a charming expression of the Olympic ideal.

After the Games, Connolly came to Prague to seek Fikotová's hand in marriage. He stayed at a hotel but Emil and Dana lent Fikotová the keys to their flat, so that they had a safe place to meet. The obstacles to this unprecedented cross-Curtain union seemed insuperable, even when Connolly wrote personally to Antonín Zápotocký (Klement Gottwald's successor as president). Then Emil interceded. He saw the president at a conference on sports administration in the Smetana Concert Hall in Prague's Municipal House and took the opportunity to ask him to give the marriage his blessing. President Zápotocký insisted that it was not his business; none the less, it seemed to make a difference. The next day Fikotová was invited to an audience at which the president agreed to 'put in a kind word', and shortly afterwards a licence was issued. Tens of thousands of people turned out to see the couple married in Prague in March 1957. There were three separate ceremonies, in the Old Town Hall, in a Catholic church and in a Protestant church; Emil and Dana were witnesses at all three.

A more daring example of this independent spirit took place in 1962. Two years earlier, Ladislav Kořán, Emil's old training partner, had been released from concentration camp under a general amnesty. Unable to find work, and shunned by many former friends and associates, he continued to work at Jáchymov in a private capacity, as an electrical engineer. Sometimes, though, he visited Prague, and on this occasion, in early August, he went to see the European Rowing Championships taking place on the Vltava. He noticed Emil among the spectators on the starting line but stood well away for fear of embarrassing him. (Just a few weeks earlier, an old friend had run away from him at an athletics meeting in Brno.) 'I was maybe thirty, forty metres away. But Emil saw me, and he ran over. He embraced me and said: "Láďa, I am so pleased to see you. We were all afraid you wouldn't make it." It was not very smart of him – there were StB people everywhere.' It seems hard to believe that such small actions can once have had such large significance, but they did; and when Kořán told me about it more than fifty years later, there was still a catch in his voice.

It is possible that Emil was bolder than most because he missed the thrills of competition – including the satisfaction of taking those risks under pressure that separate the champions from the also-rans. His legs might be worn out, but his spirit was not. He was not yet ready to sink into obscurity.

Yet that is the role that life seemed to have lined up for him. In 1960, for example, the Zátopeks travelled again to the Olympic Games, this time in Rome. Dana, three weeks short of her thirty-eighth birthday, threw magnificently to win an unexpected silver. Emil – despite training in the Olympic village with Western athletes such as Bruce Tulloh, Ron Laird and Colin Young – was only a spectator. A few weeks later, the Zátopeks were guests of honour at a reception in Zlín, where Dana had many friends. When the master of ceremonies presented them, he raised a big laugh with an introduction that reversed the order of priorities that Dana had grown all too used to over the years. He began: 'Welcome, Merited Master of Sport Dana Zátopková, world record holder, winner of two Olympic medals' – and continued, slowly and at great length, to list all of Dana's achievements. Emil, meanwhile, sat smiling in his chair, fidgeting and looking increasingly awkward as the list continued. Finally, as if as an afterthought, the speaker added: 'And I welcome her husband too.'

It was the kind of leg-pulling that was bread and butter to the Zátopeks' bantering relationship, but I doubt that Emil enjoyed it quite as much as Dana. He knew that it would be many years before his existing fame really began to subside – but how would he ever earn fresh renown? After rising to so many impossible challenges, he needed fresh worlds to conquer.

He found one, of sorts, in an unlikely place. On a sunny Saturday afternoon early in 1961, he and Dana decided to go for a walk. The area they chose was what is now the wealthy Prague suburb of Troja. In those days it was countryside, beyond the final tram stop at Pelc-Tyrolka, with little in the way of development apart from a zoo and a grand estate (the Kazanka). They walked for a while along the riverside, then turned northwards until they found themselves on a lane that was little more than a track. It was called Nad Kazankou. There were a few houses on the southern side; the steep slopes on the northern side were divided into plots and gardens but were largely overgrown.

The sun was shining, and the hill was bright with bloom; the yellow forsythias were particularly brilliant. Emil stopped suddenly and said: 'It would be great to have a plot like this here. I can see a fire, sausages, and a group of friends . . .' Then they carried on walking.

But the thought wouldn't go away. By Monday, it had become a plan. Emil went to the municipal council office in Holešovice and made tentative enquiries. Some time later, news came back of someone – a Mr Brejcha from Břevnov – who had inherited a plot at Nad Kazankou from his grandmother and was so fed up with the resulting red tape that he wanted to sell it. Emil and Dana went to see him – and in due course they found themselves the owners of an acre or so of impenetrable wasteland on a steep slope five miles from the centre of Prague.

They were soon doubting the wisdom of their purchase. But they were not short of strength and stamina, and for Emil, in particular, hacking and digging away at their patch of sloping jungle became as all-consuming a passion as his interval training had once been.

They had no plans at first beyond making a nice garden for themselves, but a week or so of frenetic excavation produced an interesting discovery: a tiny garden house or shed, buried beneath the bushes; it even had a small cellar. Emil attached a board to the door, with the words 'Santa Puelo Pub' painted on it in red. Clearing the wilderness became a social as well as a physical activity. Friends from near and far were quick to lend a hand, and to bring gifts for the garden. Half a century later you could still see a blue spruce smuggled from her homeland by the Austrian athlete Erika Strasser; and the pines brought from Wallachia by the Tempír brothers (then leading athletics coaches); and the walnut planted by Jarda Kovář, the high-jumper; and, biggest of all, the cedar of Lebanon given by Herbert Schade.

It would be more than a decade before the project was finished, partly because the mission expanded, and partly because there were regular interruptions. Dana continued to travel to sporting events even after retiring from international competition in 1962. (She had left her magazine job after the Helsinki Olympics and was now employed by the ČSTV, training young athletes at the Strahov stadium. Unlike Emil, she turned out to have a talent as a coach.) As for Emil, the fact that he was no longer competing had done little to diminish his perceived value as a diplomatic pawn.

His later years as a competitor had been increasingly marked by what could almost be described as state visits, and these continued after his retirement: sometimes initiated by the nation in question or, sometimes, set up by the Czechoslovak government. Emil and Dana spent the last three months of 1958 on a Far Eastern tour that took them, via Moscow, to China (where Emil ran a post-retirement 10,000m), Korea and Vietnam (where he ran a 5,000m). Other such trips would follow: to Egypt, Tunisia, Syria, Cuba – seemingly any part of the world with which the regime wished to establish or maintain good relations. Some people joked that Emil's hosts confused him with President Zápotocký. It is not inconceivable that this was true.

The most disruptive of all these missions began in October 1963, when Emil and Dana were dispatched to Indonesia for a whole year. It was a pleasant enough experience, with light coaching duties and a comfortable expatriate lifestyle, and Emil, characteristically, learnt the language. He would get up at 4 a.m. to learn words from a dictionary. But neither Emil nor Dana seems to have been particularly inspired by the adventure, and Emil was later scathing about the folly of Czechoslovakia giving aid to such regimes. Emil, tormented by mosquitoes when he sat out on the balcony in the evenings, even tried taking up smoking, briefly, to deter them. The experiment was not a success; but the fact that he even thought of it suggests a certain mental restlessness.

No one could accuse Emil – or Dana – of being incurious about foreign cultures. But the place that enthused them most was that patch of hillside in Troja. On returning to Czechoslovakia, they set about improving it with renewed enthusiasm. Not only that: they expanded their mission. Rather than contenting themselves with a garden and a shed, they decided, they would build themselves a house – just as Emil's father had done forty years earlier.

This was an enormous undertaking: a huge amount of clearance and levelling was required before they could begin; and they intended to do it all without professional help. But there was no hurry, and the difficulty of the challenge was what made it enjoyable. Emil held the record for shifting forty barrel-loads of earth in a day, whereas Dana could manage only twenty-eight. Later on, Dana would come into her own, with an unmatchable performance throwing pebbledash on to the walls. 'Now, at last, Dana's javelin training is paying off,' joked Emil.

The author Ota Pavel, one of many friends who were persuaded to lend a hand, wrote a memorable account of running to the plot with Emil from his workplace in Dejvice, before struggling to keep up with Emil's astonishing work rate. 'After two hours,' he reported, 'I had flickering in front of my eyes . . .' Emil was way past his physical best by now. An army test in 1963, shortly before his forty-first birthday, recorded surprisingly ordinary figures: he could run 100m in 13.9 seconds, throw a grenade forty metres, and run a 3,000m cross-country course in eleven minutes thirty seconds. But he could still bring a breathtaking intensity to everyday tasks – and, no less characteristically, a slightly crazed creativity. Many uproarious evenings were spent arguing over their plans around the campfire with friends. As it grew, the building acquired, like most of Emil and Dana's possessions, a name: 'Domeček' ('little house'); and, in due course, its own distinctive character. When the time came to think about insulation, the Zátopeks opted for a new material of their own invention. They called it *Warmflaschenizolation*; a more prosaic description would be empty wine bottles set in concrete. Later still, Emil took great pride in a particularly complicated (and temperamental) stove that he had installed; other oddities included an old ship's bell, attached to the side of the house as a doorbell, which was a gift from František Šťastný, the motorcycling champion.

Of course, this was just one facet of the Zátopeks' life. They still had their jobs; and, not least, their busy social lives, being in demand not just among old friends but also, increasingly, in the fashionable Prague circles of intellectuals, artists, journalists and politicians. There were regular visits from former rivals from abroad, too; on one memorable occasion, in 1966, Herbert Schade, Gaston Reiff and Alain Mimoun all arrived simultaneously. Emil also kept in touch by letter with sporting friends around the world. There was something special about the friendship of athletes, he thought: 'You honour opponents in a different way than the friends in the street,' he explained once. The shared experience of 'a fight about who was better' remained 'deeper in the soul' than the everyday friendship of those 'who have not been through anything together'.

Emil and Dana had families and friends to keep in touch with in Moravia, too, although Emil's parents were both dead by now. Anežka had died in 1962 and František a year later. He was, according to one granddaughter, 'too sad to live without her'. But Emil continued to make regular visits to Kopřivnice, for school reunions and get-togethers with his surviving siblings. There were always excited crowds when he did so. 'People would come out on to their balconies,' says Jiří, Emil's nephew. 'He used to come down by train, all the way from Prague,' says Marie Vlachová, a former neighbour who was in the ninth grade with Emil, 'and he would be so tired, because everyone on the train wanted to talk to him, and he would find time for them all.' And then, in Kopřivnice, it would start all over again.

The globally celebrated superstar must have seemed a slightly unreal figure to the brothers and sister who had stayed behind. But Jiří (the brother), who had done a spell in the air force before returning to Kopřivnice to join Bohuš and Franta at Tatra, was certainly devoted to Emil, and the siblings' reunions appear to have been warm, usually culminating with all the brothers singing folk songs. 'They stayed close,' remembers Jiří's daughter, Dana. 'And they sang from the heart.'

Often, on such visits, Emil would stay with his old schoolfriend Jaromír Konůpka. Occasionally they would even retreat into the countryside together, with no more comforts than they had had when they were two hard-up schoolboys three decades earlier. It was a far cry from chatting with the president in Prague, but I think we can guess which Emil preferred. 'He always thought of himself as a Kopřivnice person,' says Konůpka. 'He remembered how we used to play in the woods together as children.' Such moments were the exception, though, and not the rule. No matter how much he might sometimes yearn for a simple, down-to-earth life, Emil could not erase his celebrity. He was a member of the privileged elite, and – it seemed – would always remain one.

His public speaking duties tailed off only slightly as the memory of his golden moments faded and younger athletes from far-off lands began to chip away at his dominance of the record books. His nephew remembers an address to the young people of Kopřivnice, in which Emil hammed up his Olympic adventures for their amusement. 'When he talked about the marathon,' says Jiří, 'he made it sound funny: "The Swede, Jansson, he was a giant, two heads taller than me, with legs as long as a toilet spider. I had to take three steps for each one of his . . ."' Jiří rocks with laughter as he imitates Emil's mock-scary voice.

Emil also had a regular but not-too-onerous slot as a speaker at the ROH Leningrad, a luxury hotel owned by the national trade union federation (Revoluční odborové hnutí) in Mariánské Lázně – Europe's most luxurious spa town. It was here that, in 1966, Emil heard that a local athlete, Hana Trejbalová, was seriously ill. Not yet nineteen, she was the national junior hurdling champion, but had suddenly developed cancer in her neck. (It has recently been suggested that she was a victim of early, reckless experiments by the Czechoslovak sporting establishment with anabolic steroids.) Emil and Dana repeatedly visited her in hospital in Plzeň; and attempted to ensure that she received the best possible specialist treatment. Emil left her a gift, a teddy bear, which she kept in her bed until her death later that year.

It is hard not to sense, somewhere below the surface of this period of relative calm in Emil's life, a faint but persistent throb of longing. 'It was my dream to give a good example to children and get them started,' Emil told an American journalist shortly before his seventieth birthday, 'but it was only a dream.' In the mid-1960s, that dream was still fresh, and it is possible that, while Dana came to terms with their lack of children, Emil began to feel it more keenly. 'He loved children very much,' said his friend Zdeněk Fator. 'He loved my son, and Jiří loved seeing him.' 'Our boys used to ask: "When is Mr Zátopek coming? We have so much fun with him,"' said another friend, Olga Lišková. Jaromír Konůpka said much the same about his children, and both he and his son (also Jaromír) reminisced delightedly about the time when they visited Emil in Prague, and Emil spent half the afternoon racing young Jaromír and his sister up Prague's first escalator, off Wenceslas Square. They used the up escalator while Emil used the downward one, and Emil in any case let them win; so, naturally, they insisted on repeating it again and again, until a large crowd had gathered to watch.

Others spoke of Emil exasperating his relatives, and countless Kopřivnice mothers, by disrupting his visits to the town with endless games of street football with the children who followed him around; and of his strange habit, when driving with children on board, of using his feet to steer – just to entertain them. 'It made the boys crazy with happiness,' said Olga Lišková. Emil's nephew Jiří has a comparable memory of being taken for a drive in Emil's smart Saab when he was six or seven years old. Emil let Jiří sit on his lap as he drove and then, to make things more fun, let Jiří drive. Half a century later, Jiří's jaw still drops at the memory of executing a left turn across a street full of traffic, with Emil apparently exercising no control at all.

'Perhaps it was just as well that we never had children,' Dana laughed, when we talked about such matters once. 'We would have argued all the time about how to bring them up. I would have wanted to give them rules about how to behave, while Emil would have wanted them to have no rules at all.'

She was speaking in the tone that she often uses about Emil: that kind of affectionate exasperation that develops through the decades of a long, mostly happy marriage. For a spouse, the habitual flouting of convention that the rest of us find so charming in Emil could be maddening – and yet still be charming. One day, for example, Dana decided to sweep the floor and noticed something odd – and familiar. Closer investigation revealed that Emil had been using his DIY skills. The old broom handle had broken; so, rather than buy a new broom, he had improvised a new handle by using the wooden javelin with which Dana had won her Olympic gold medal in 1952. She still has it today, and brings it out proudly, surprisingly small and light compared with a modern javelin: a permanent memento of her greatest sporting moment, and of her husband's restless, slightly deranged ingenuity.

Ota Pavel, the writer who knew Emil best, thought his great gift was his ability 'to think how to do it differently. He uses the word "if" . . .' There were some rules he respected: those of hospitality, for example, or fair play. But the limiting rules of unthinking convention were, as he saw it, there to be challenged and, if appropriate, ignored.

There are obvious drawbacks to such an outlook if you are, say, an army officer, or if you live in a society where ideological conformity is rigidly enforced. But Emil – who since January 1967 had been deputy to the head of the physical educational unit of the Defence Ministry's Operative and Combat Readiness department – had convinced himself that, where he was concerned, the drawbacks could be overcome. He was right, for now; and the habit of doing things as he saw fit became an ingrained feature of his life. In March 1967, the British sports journalist Neil Allen met Emil at a reception at the British Embassy in Prague, while Emil reminisced happily (in English) about times gone by. The encounter resulted in a much-quoted article by Allen in *The Times*, including Emil's famous remark about the 1948 Olympics being 'as if the sun had come out'. Emil also talked about how stupid he had been in the 5,000m at that Games, and about how much more competitive distance running had since become; and about how he would still try to be a champion if he were young again. 'You have something inside you which makes you always try, however hard it may seem.' Strictly speaking, Emil should have given a report of this encounter to the secret police; but I can find no record of his having done so. Luckily, Allen was not so negligent, and wrote it up for *Times* readers.

Let us end this chapter, and this phase of Emil's life, with perhaps the most revealing snapshot of all, in which the restless nobility of his spirit finally found the gesture that it craved. It was the summer of 1966. At the request of the ČSTV, Emil wrote to the great Australian runner Ron Clarke, inviting him to compete in a meeting in Prague. Clarke had by then redrawn the boundaries of distance running scarcely less dramatically than Emil had in his prime. He had set fifteen of his eventual total of seventeen world records – twelve of them in a forty-four-day period the previous summer – and had obliterated most of Emil's in the process. He had just lowered his 5,000m time to 13:16.6 – more than forty seconds faster than Emil's best. As for his 10,000m record, set the previous summer, it was 27:39.4 – a minute and a quarter faster than Emil's supposedly superhuman 28:54.2 in 1954. Clarke had, however, never won a gold medal, either at the Olympics or at the Commonwealth Games. For an athlete who towered so spectacularly over his sport, it was a startling and rankling omission.

Clarke cancelled some engagements to come to Prague – 'I wasn't going to miss that opportunity' – and from the moment he landed Emil was the perfect host. 'He met me on the steps of the plane,' said Clarke, still enthusing about the experience when I spoke to him a few months before his death in 2015. 'He just waved us straight through customs and drove me to his home rather than the hotel. We had a great chat, then he took me to the hotel, by the track.' Clarke won his race, over 3,000m, cheered on by Emil. Then, at six o'clock the next morning, Emil picked him up from his hotel and drove him to Stará Boleslav.

'It was a beautiful forest, and we did a huge workout, talking and chatting, and he showed me all the training things he did.' There was a television cameraman there to record the event, but he left his lens cap on: the few images that survive were taken on a camera borrowed from Ludvík Liška, caretaker of the athletes' villa. But Clarke wasn't interested in the visual record: he was absorbed in the moment, and the thrill of running with Emil Zátopek. 'We just clicked – I felt very comfortable with him.' Emil was eight years into his retirement, but Clarke later wrote that it had been one of the most demanding sessions he had done for a long time.

Later on, Emil took him shopping, to buy a souvenir of Prague crystal for his wife. 'It was the middle of the day by then, and in the centre of town it was very busy. Emil drove to this big store and just parked right outside it. This traffic policeman stormed over – and as soon as he got within recognition distance his face transformed: "Emil! Emil!" Emil signed his book for him, and we left the car and went in.'

They couldn't find what they wanted, so they came out – to where the policeman was guarding the car. Emil did a highly improper U-turn, and they repeated the process at another store – complete with another traffic policeman, initially angry and then starstruck. This time, when they came out, the car had gone – but Emil just whistled and the policeman brought it back. 'Any sportsman who can do that,' said Clarke, 'anywhere in the world, has made it.'

Finally, it was time to leave. Emil drove Clarke to the airport, shepherded him through customs and passport control and accompanied him all the way up the steps to the plane. As he said goodbye, he pressed a small package, roughly wrapped in brown paper and string, into Clarke's hand, and said words to the effect of: 'Look after this, because you deserve it.'

Clarke said nothing, thinking that perhaps he was being asked to smuggle something out to the West. He kept a close grip on the package until they were well outside Czech airspace. Even then, he wasn't sure what to do. Should he declare it at customs in London, where he was changing flights? He resolved not to open it. Then, at last, with the plane taxiing on the runway just after landing at Heathrow, 'curiosity overcame me'.

At this point, the accounts get blurred. The way Clarke told it to me, forty-eight years later, he was sitting in the front of the plane. In an account given much nearer the event, he retreated to the toilet. Either way, he was sitting alone and unobserved as he unwrapped a small box. Inside was an Olympic gold medal – one of the three that Emil had won in Helsinki. Emil had signed the inside of the lid, adding (in the limited space available): 'To Ron Clarke, Prag. 19-7-1966'.

For a moment, realising what it was, he felt 'overwhelming excitement'. And then (reverting here to the earlier account) he understood what it meant – and: 'I sat on that lavatory seat and wept.'

Like all the best Zátopek stories, this one has been endlessly retold and 'improved'. The most widely repeated revision places the story two years later, in late 1968. This is impossible, for all sorts of reasons, and, as it happens, not true. But you can see the attraction. The 1968 version finds Clarke – who almost killed himself making one last desperate bid to win a gold of his own, at altitude, at the Mexico City Olympics – at the lowest point in his life, and Emil (as we will see) at his own moment of desperate crisis; and the gift thus becomes an act of magnificent selflessness and compassion. It is a neater story this way.

Yet the true story carries its own, stranger message. By 1966, Clarke had missed out on an Olympic medal only once. He was not in desperate need of Emil's generosity. If there was such a need, it must have been Emil's. Perhaps he felt his spirit smothered by middle-aged normality; perhaps he craved a gesture with which he could once again express his generosity of soul, and affirm that, if he chose, he was still capable of greatness. Or perhaps – in keeping with a world view that his nephew Jiří summarised with the sentence 'If you are happy, I am happy' – he just wanted to lighten Clarke's life. The gesture was no less great for that.

Clarke became a permanent convert to the Zátopekian ideal of sporting friendship, and spent the best part of a half-century thereafter 'trying to tell people what a good man Emil Zátopek was'. He rarely did so more eloquently than in an article he wrote for *Athletics Weekly* in 1987. Describing the moment when he opened Emil's gift, Clarke wrote: 'I thought back to the words he said as he passed it across to me, which at the time I did not understand. "Because you deserved it," he said. I wish I had.'

Then he added: 'I do know that no one cherishes any gift more than I do, my only Olympic gold medal, and not because of what it is but because of the man whose spirit it represents.'

After a brief spell in a museum on Australia's Gold Coast, the medal is now back in the hands of Clarke's family. Contrary to popular belief, there is no identifying inscription on the medal itself. You cannot even tell which race Emil won it for.

None the less, it is the noblest Olympic medal of them all.

15

Spring fever

Unlike the Arab Spring of 2011, which spread like a series of summer wildfires, the Prague Spring of 1968 really was spring-like in its dynamics. It began imperceptibly, as a thaw does. By the time most people realised that it was happening, it had been in progress for ages.

Some historians trace its beginnings to the adoption, in 1960, of a new constitution, which declared the 'building of socialism' complete and proclaimed a new mission to create an 'advanced socialist society'. Others point to the final abolition of the concentration camp network, in 1961; or to the destruction, in 1962, of that giant statue of Stalin, five-and-a-half years in the making, that had towered over central Prague from Letná since 1955. Antonín Novotný, who succeeded Antonín Zápotocký as president in 1957, was a hardliner in most respects, but he lacked the almost comically slavish pro-Soviet tendencies of President Gottwald. And then there was the intervention of Professor Ota Šik, the economist, who in 1966 persuaded the Party leadership that, without some kind of radical decentralisation, economic catastrophe loomed. His reforms were introduced in 1967, and green shoots of private enterprise began to appear.

That same year, a group of writers led by the novelist Ludvík Vaculík called for a relaxation of censorship. Vaculík's address to the Fourth Congress of the Union of Writers, in July 1967, was one of the bravest and most inflammatory acts of defiance of the Communist age. His audience that day included such prominent figures as Milan Kundera, Pavel Kohout and Václav Havel. The fact that he escaped jail shows how far the thaw had already progressed.

One underlying theme of the 'spring' was that, in purely economic terms, the existing system clearly wasn't working. Another was that the generation who had risen to prominence as young, enthusiastic Party members in the early days of Communism – including Kundera, Kohout, Vaculík and, not least, Emil – had come of age and, at around the same time, acquired both perspective and influence. The idea that things could be different, and better, ceased to be totally heretical. And when Alexander Dubček replaced President Novotný as First Secretary of the Communist Party in January 1968, the advocates of reform acquired a political figurehead who was actually in a position to instigate change. Dubček was initially a compromise candidate, acceptable to conservatives as well as reformers. Once he took charge, however, it was clear that the reformers were taking over. A new kind of Communism seemed possible. Dubček called it 'socialism with a human face'.

For those who had spent the previous two decades buttoning their lips, the spring and summer of 1968 were a glorious time to be alive. Students, intellectuals, artists, celebrities – everyone seemed to be excited, talkative, optimistic; almost anything seemed possible. 'A time of sunshine, great music, great theatre, beautiful women' was how one Prague-dweller evoked it for me. It can't really have been that good, but there was no denying the excitement. Reformers, including those who had fallen from favour in the 1950s, were appointed to other key positions: General Ludvík Svoboda became president in March, while Josef Smrkovský became chairman of parliament. Hundreds of victims of Stalinist persecution – even Milada Horáková – were partially (though often posthumously) rehabilitated. In June, censorship was abolished. Programmes made by Radio Prague began to discuss what was going on – and were suddenly deemed unsuitable for retransmission in the Soviet Union; the circulation of the Writers' Union's journal, *Literární listy*, soared to 300,000 copies.

Around the same time, a young woman called Marta Kubišová recorded a song – based on a prayer by the seventeenth-century Moravian philosopher Comenius and initially broadcast in a children's television series about the defeat of a cruel tyrant – which became the accidental soundtrack of Czechoslovakia's awakening. 'May peace settle across all of this land,' it began. 'Anger, envy and resentment, fear and strife, may they all be banished . . .' And then, in a spine-tingling but almost untranslatable final line: 'Now your rule over the things that are yours, which was taken from you, is coming back to you – people, it is coming back to you!' By the time the remaining hardliners had realised how subversive it was, the song that became known as 'A Prayer for Marta' had gone viral, and the Prague Spring had long since turned into a Czechoslovak Summer of Love.

It was not all sunshine, of course; partly because of the menacing rumbles that kept emerging from the Soviet

Union about 'threatening the foundations of socialism'. But the taste of freedom was too intoxicating to be surrendered lightly. To stiffen the reformers' resolve, Vaculík wrote a manifesto, called 'Two Thousand Words that Belong to Workers, Farmers, Officials, Scientists, Artists, and Everybody' but more generally known as 'The Two Thousand Words'. With remarkable frankness, it spelled out the failings of the old system: 'Most of the nation welcomed the socialist programme with high hopes. But it fell into the hands of the wrong people . . .' It praised the 'regenerative process of democratisation' that had been taking place since the beginning of the year and called on the public to take direct action – from public criticism of discredited officials to demonstrations and strikes – to keep the momentum going. Published simultaneously in three national newspapers on 27 June, it enraged the hardliners and their Soviet backers, but was endorsed by nearly seventy public figures: authors, journalists, scientists, academics – and, not least, Czechoslovakia's most famous sporting couple, Emil and Dana Zátopek. In the weeks that followed, thousands of ordinary people spontaneously added their signatures.

A month and a half later, in the third week of August, two young American students, George Fenigsohn and Roy Kephart, found themselves in Prague at the tail-end of a backpacking tour of Europe. Being keen runners, and being young, and it being 1968, they decided to see if they could find Emil Zátopek. They looked him up in the phone book and called. Kephart, who knew a few words of Russian, tried to explain who they were and what they wanted. 'Let's talk in English,' said the voice at the other end of the phone. The next thing they knew, Fenigsohn and Kephart had been invited to 8 U Půjčovny, and were being fed, entertained, shown memorabilia and regaled with Olympic reminiscences.

'He was just so kind,' remembers Fenigsohn, nearly fifty years on. 'We just showed up, these American *studenti,* and he looked after us for a day and a half. He showed us round Prague, and people kept stopping him, because they all recognised him. He was incredibly gracious. We had meals with him. Then he drove us to the woods where he used to train [i.e. Stará Boleslav], and the three of us jogged around together on the paths there. It was beautiful.'

They were not the first strangers to be welcomed so warmly to 8 U Půjčovny, or the last. But the timing of their visit was poignant. The picture of Emil preserved in their memories – and in Fenigsohn's photo album – is a snapshot of his life as it was in the final, deceptively idyllic moments before everything changed utterly. Straight afterwards, the students took a train to the West. Disembarking in Amsterdam, they bought a newspaper, and realised that, unwittingly, they had visited at a historic time.

On the evening of 20 August, Emil and Dana were asked to a party in Prague but decided not to go. Dana went to bed early. Then the hosts rang up and Emil was persuaded to run over and join them. He was still there at 2 a.m., when someone turned on the radio – to hear a breathless newscaster trying to explain that a huge Soviet-led army of Warsaw Pact forces (including twelve tank divisions, thirteen motorised rifle divisions and two parachute divisions) had begun to invade Czechoslovakia twenty minutes before midnight. Czechoslovakia's army was confined to barracks, just as it had been in 1938 and 1948.

Emil's first thought – oddly – was of the house at Troja: nearing completion, unguarded and, in his view, irresistibly tempting to invading soldiers. He drove straight there, turned on the lights, locked the doors and windows and generally tried to make it secure and inhabited-looking. Then he attempted to drive home through roads that by then were blocked with tanks. He asked them politely in Russian to get out of his way, but it didn't always achieve the desired effect. He ended up abandoning the car in a backstreet and completing the journey on foot.

By the time he got home, Dana had been awake for some time. A friend had phoned with the shocking news. 'I realised that Emil was gone. I looked out of the window and saw that Klára was gone. Where was he? Had he been arrested already? Would I be next? I was so frightened. It was the worst hour of my life; or two hours – I don't know how long it was. Then I heard footsteps coming up the stairs . . .' When they stopped outside the door of the flat, she could hardly breathe: 'I was so wound up.' Then the door opened. When she saw Emil's face, she slapped it.

They calmed down. Dana apologised. Emil justified his actions with the assertion that 'Domeček was there all alone, crying.' ('I understood what he meant,' says Dana.) Then they decided to go out and see what was happening.

There were tanks and people everywhere. A low growling sound, mechanical and human, filled the air. Slowly, Emil and Dana made their way to Wenceslas Square, where the crowds were thickest. Some people were shouting, some hitting the tanks with their fists. 'Then people started to notice Emil,' says Dana. 'They asked him what he thought. He was quite mad. He said the Russians should not be allowed to go to the Olympics.'

Some people were speaking directly to the soldiers, asking them in Russian what they were doing; Emil joined in. A few soldiers replied to the effect that they had come to help the Czechoslovaks to deal with the counter-revolution that was threatening them; others said that they didn't know. 'Some of them didn't even know what country they were in,' says Dana.

It is difficult to imagine the sense of shock and violation that Czechoslovaks must have felt at the invasion. Europe had been at peace for more than twenty years. The Soviets were supposed to be their best friends. Yet here were Soviet tanks on the streets, soldiers with machine guns and live ammunition. Was this mere political theatre? Or was it all-out war? Were people actually going to get killed? The answer, tragically, was yes: at least nineteen people were killed in Prague alone on the first day; by the end of the year, the civilian death toll had reached at least 108.

For the most part, the invaders tried to avoid violence, firing machine guns in the air or driving vehicles towards crowds at high speeds only to halt at the last second. But the angry thousands who poured out on to the streets refused to be intimidated. Much of the resistance was passive: road signs were vandalised with remarkable speed, to make it harder for the invaders to find their way around. But there were also young men who not only threw stones at tanks but found ingenious ways to set fire to them.

The invaders moved ruthlessly to assert themselves, seizing Dubček and key supporters from Party headquarters and attempting to take control of the media. The staff at Radio Prague, which had been broadcasting protests against the invasion since the small hours of the morning, were driven out at gunpoint. The national news agency, ČTK, was among the last to fall, releasing its last bulletins at eight minutes before midnight: 'Russian troops are entering the ČTK building' and – before a KGB man in civilian clothes ripped off the ticker tape – 'This is the last item of the free ČTK news agency. All further statements will not be issued by—'

But the reformers were quick, too. As one Western news report put it: 'No sooner had the great mailed fist clanged down on the land than the Czechs everywhere were scrambling out from underneath it, standing on top of it in voluble and hostile crowds.' Many gathered outside the national public radio headquarters in Vinohradská Street, trying to defend their precious uncensored radio. When that battle was lost, they massed around the corner in Wenceslas Square. It was a remarkable display of popular unity and defiance. And the most visible symbol of that defiance was a balding man in a rumpled jacket, standing on a pedestal by the statue of St Wenceslas, furiously denouncing the invasion.

It was Emil.

According to his fellow reformer Luděk Pachman, the chess grandmaster, on that first evening, 'Emil was clearly the dominant figure'. With his champion's instinct for recognising the moment that really mattered and seizing it, he was throwing every ounce of his energy into the battle. He had already been on the radio, with Dana, calling for the invading nations to be barred from the Olympic Games, which were due to begin in Mexico City on 3 October.

Now Emil was making the same point in person – and from time to time expanding it by addressing the invaders directly, invoking the idea of the Olympic truce.

Given the chaos, anger and fear, it is hard to set down with absolute confidence what was said when and to whom. According to Pachman, however, at one point Emil 'quite literally rushed towards a group of Soviet soldiers, he announced his name and sporting titles, and then straight away said (in Russian), "Come on, let's talk."' Other accounts spoke of Emil moving from tank to tank, talking to individual soldiers in turn.

'They didn't want to listen,' he told *Sports Illustrated*'s Leigh Montville two decades later, 'but the people kept saying, "Hear him out. Do you know your Olympic champions? He is our Olympic champion."' Eventually an officer came over, and Emil told him how upset everyone was by the invasion, and how harmful it was to the Communist movement. 'He said nothing, but at the end, he shook my hand. That told me that maybe he felt not right about what he was doing.'

Over the next few days, Emil would talk to many more Russian soldiers. Most were given the same two-fold message. First: the Czechoslovak people didn't ask for this invasion, no matter what you may have been told at home about our requests for 'help' against counter-revolutionaries. And, secondly: speaking as an Olympic champion, I tell you that you should be ashamed of taking part in this military operation, and invading a friendly neighbour, at a time when the Olympic Games are imminent, and all nations are supposed to observe a truce.

There is no evidence that Emil persuaded anyone with this argument, although he may have sown seeds of doubt. Nor, of course, was he the only figure around whom protesters rallied. But his presence and active involvement were hugely encouraging. Even after a decade of retirement, Emil remained his country's most instantly recognisable hero. It was like seeing the barricades manned by David Beckham.

It was also astonishingly brave of him. Not only was there a very real risk of being shot; there was also a secondary danger – and motivation – that had been eloquently spelled out in 'The Two Thousand Words': 'We have spoken out and come so far out into the open that we can only complete our intention of humanising this regime. Otherwise the revenge of the old guard would be cruel . . .' Large parts of the military establishment had been bitterly opposed to reform, and many actively supported the Soviet invasion. For Emil to oppose it so publicly and passionately was to risk a major disciplinary backlash.

The first six days of the occupation were later described by Milan Kundera as 'the most beautiful week that we have ever lived through'. At a political level, the reformist leaders, several of whom were now in Moscow, haggled with the Soviets in search of a compromise. On the streets, what one historian later called 'the most dramatic case of non-violent action against foreign aggressors that the world has ever known' continued.

On Thursday, 22 August, the second day, Emil – wearing military uniform this time – could once again be seen haranguing the crowds in Wenceslas Square, and round the corner in Na Příkopě as well. According to one report, he 'addressed the crowd under the muzzles of Soviet cannon and called for Russia to be banned from the Olympic

Games'; according to another, he 'called on the Russians to leave and accused them of violating the sovereignty of a friendly socialist state'. In snatches of sound recording, he mentions 'the internment of our representatives' and 'the raid on radio and television'.

Employees of Radio Prague, meanwhile, had continued to broadcast, calling themselves Free Radio and using a network of underground studios that had been set up in case of war. Some (unconfirmed) accounts suggested that Emil, perhaps exploiting his professional knowledge of Operational and Combat Readiness, might have been involved in the distribution around the capital of small parabolic FM transmitters to facilitate this.

Czechoslovak television, broadcasting in sound only, appealed for caution: 'We must develop a new citizen tactic, continuing normal life peacefully, completely ignoring the invaders.' Emil, who may have been involved in facilitating this form of pirate broadcasting as well, echoed its message: 'Do not give them a provocation,' he implored. The 20,000 people protesting in Prague appeared unconvinced.

Friday saw the first of a series of general strikes. In the morning, Emil was seen outside the offices of *Mladá fronta*, once again addressing a large crowd; his words were broadcast shortly afterwards on Free Radio. Emil's public speaking skills had been developed through years of involuntary practice at the Party's behest, and now he had found a fitting use for them. It is unlikely that many in the Party enjoyed the irony. Later that day, Free Radio broadcast an urgent warning, telling Emil and Dana not to go home, because 'our good friends' – that is, the Russians – were waiting for them. They spent three days with friends in the suburb of Spořilov, but eventually decided that the danger had been exaggerated.

Emil, in any case, had been out on the streets again the next day. According to Pachman, Emil was seen putting up a poster 'without even noticing that just a couple of steps away from him was a soldier with an assault rifle'. When the soldier approached and poked his gun into Emil's back, Emil just turned round, offered his hand and said (in Russian): 'Everything is OK, comrade.' Then he went round the corner and stuck up the poster there instead.

Each day, Emil struck another blow in the PR battle against the invader. On the 24th a statement from him appeared in *Svobodný svět*, spelling out his demand that the Soviet Union be barred from the Olympics. On the 25th, speaking on Free Radio, he went further: 'We made a big mistake, collaborating with the Russians these past 20 years. This collaboration has cost us dearly.' On the 26th he made a similar point (in French) in the television interview with France's INA channel, adding: 'The young, the old, workers, intellectuals, students – the whole nation shares the view that we have the right to live according to our dreams and our sovereignty . . . The Russian people desire the same liberty.'

By then, however, the politics had moved on. Seeking to salvage something from a hopeless situation, President Svoboda and his fellow delegates had given in to overwhelming Soviet pressure and signed the Moscow Protocol – a compromise agreement that they hoped might offer a way out of the emergency. Censorship was to be reintroduced, and the 'leading role' of the Communist Party was to be reinforced; but Dubček would be allowed to continue as First Secretary, and the occupying forces would, with some exceptions, be gradually withdrawn from cities and confined to (Czechoslovak) barracks.

Some saw this as a betrayal: all that risk and loss of life, only for the 'spring' to be smothered on the Soviets' say-so. Others saw it as the least bad option: a compromise that offered some hope for the future, with many of the good guys still in place. Emil, speaking from the branches of one of the large lime trees that used to line Wenceslas Square, urged protesters to contain their anger, 'because anger leads to bloodshed. We must be united in the future,' he added, 'for that is our only salvation'.

He was right, but it was a futile hope. A crack had appeared in the reform movement that could never be entirely mended; the hardliners would have ample opportunity to exploit it in the months ahead. The next day, Dubček, Svoboda and Smrkovský attempted to justify their compromise to the nation in a series of emotional and occasionally tearful addresses. Some believed them, and many more sympathised. But the fact remained that, in Emil's words: 'It's over.'

All that remained was to defy the inevitable as bravely as possible – and wait for the backlash.

In the West, Emil's friends feared the worst – and tried to do what they could to help. On 31 August, athletes competing in a meeting at White City signed a petition, organised by Gordon Pirie, expressing their 'grave concern' for Emil and Dana's personal safety and calling on the Soviet authorities to 'guarantee the safety of this great and courageous athlete and his wife'.

Prudence suggested that Emil should quieten down a bit. He struggled to do so – despite an anonymous note pushed through the door at 8 U Půjčovny, denouncing him as a CIA agent bent on counter-revolution and warning that punishment would follow. Journalists from many nations remained keen to hear his views, and he still had plenty to say. Sometimes he said it discreetly. An interview with Jaroslav Dietl for *Stadion* magazine, ostensibly about the role of fear in sport, discussed the need to keep going in a long, hard marathon – in terms that could easily have referred to a different kind of struggle. 'Every race has its finish line,' said Emil pointedly. But an article in the Swedish newspaper *Arbetet* included some less guarded comments about, among other things, the way that Emil and Dana's overseas travels had turned them into reformers: 'In West Germany we saw new homes and free people. In East Germany, we saw mostly desolation, decay and poverty.' This was not the kind of remark that was calculated to keep him out of trouble; and trouble was closing in.

The second week of September saw Emil at the spa of Teplice, presumably for a pre-arranged visit. Instead of his usual talk, he spoke out against the Soviet Union. Then, on the night of 12–13 September, he caused the watching 'sharp eyes' great concern by disappearing. Subsequent investigation – including a four-hour interrogation by the security services in Prague on 20 September – suggested that he thought he was being watched by the Soviet KGB as well as the Czechoslovak StB, and was afraid for his own safety. He had spent the night at the apartment of the spa manager, before taking a car back to Prague. The StB were not sure whether to believe this; one of their three different reports on the incident concluded that, if Emil could not learn to respect the law, some action might have to be taken – action relating to his personal freedom.

It's possible that a demonstration on 23 September outside the Soviet Embassy in London by athletes bearing 'Zátopek in danger' banners may have helped to persuade Emil's enemies to exercise restraint. It seems more likely that, for the time being, Emil was still considered 'too big to jail'. The Olympic Games were just three weeks away, and he and Dana had been invited as honoured guests. As Emil later put it: 'If they punish me, they will discredit themselves in the eyes of the world.'

The Czechoslovak security services agonised about the possibility of the trip backfiring, but it was felt unlikely that Emil would defect – he had had plenty of opportunities to do so in the past – while Dana promised that they would not discuss politics with Westerners. Meanwhile, colleagues at Dukla and athletes in the Olympic team undertook to try to influence Emil 'positively'. The couple flew to Mexico City with the rest of the Czechoslovakian team, and the politicians in Prague kept their fingers crossed that they would not do anything provocative.

In fact, the Games passed quietly as far as the Zátopeks were concerned. The eyes of the world were upon them, but they kept their heads down and confined themselves to watching the sport and meeting up with old friends. There was a brief, warm reunion with Ron Clarke – before he collapsed at the finish of the 10,000m on the first day of athletics competition, his heart permanently damaged by the effects of the altitude. Emil was also seen jogging with Gaston Reiff, and had lunch with the Swiss middle-distance runner Paul Martin, who may have made veiled enquiries about Emil and Dana's interest in defection. Emil reportedly responded, 'We love our country too much to live anywhere else.'

There were also discreet offers of overseas coaching work in Sweden and Finland – but, as Emil later explained: 'If I had left my country at that time, our people would have thought the situation was hopeless for all of us . . . I did not want to leave my country like a rat abandoning a sinking ship.'

No amount of discretion on Emil's part could disguise the warmth of the world's concern for his and his country's wellbeing. Applause and encouragement followed him, just as they had when he was electrifying earlier Olympics with his running. This time, though, Emil responded with diplomatic diffidence. There were others who could make patriotic gestures – notably the gymnast Věra Čáslavská, another signatory of 'The Two Thousand Words', who won four golds and two silvers and, on the two occasions when she was on the medallists' rostrum while the Soviet anthem was being played, made plain her displeasure by pointedly looking downwards and away. Her homeland would reward her with years of persecution.

But three weeks was a long time for Emil to keep quiet. Eventually, he got into an animated discussion about the invasion with Will Grimsley of the Associated Press. 'The Russians . . . were acting out of fear,' he told him. 'They were afraid their political system might fall under the weight of freedom and social progress.' As he talked, Dana could be seen walking past repeatedly, gesturing with her hands. It wasn't that she disagreed: it was just that she could see where such comments might lead. Emil laughed. 'Dana wants me to shut up,' he said. 'She thinks I talk too much.' Christopher Brasher had a similar experience, chatting with Emil in a café while Dana said: 'Hush, Emil. They'll hear you, and then it will be bad.' In both cases, she was right.

The most difficult moment was the encounter with Vladimir Kuts. Emil bumped into him in the hotel they were both staying at, and their angry discussion grew into a shouting match in which Dana, too, became involved. Kuts, now a hard-drinking trainer, considered Emil a traitor to the Communist cause, and said so; Emil and Dana were appalled by Kuts's unapologetic support for the killing of Czechoslovak civilians. By the end of the confrontation, Dana was in tears. They would never exchange a friendly word again.

Shortly afterwards, the Games came to an end. The Olympic flame was extinguished, and the athletes began to return to their 112 different nations. There was a brief last hurrah, in the form of a flamboyant, chaotically crowded wedding in Mexico City Cathedral between Věra Čáslavská and the runner Josef Odložil. Then the Czechoslovaks, too, headed for the airport, and Emil and Dana returned to Prague to face the music.

16

Disgrace

The hardliners took their revenge slowly. There was no hurry. In the short term, the reformers could be left to calm things down. So when students occupied Charles University in November 1968 to protest against the compromises of the Moscow Protocol, it was Emil who went to the campus to talk to them, sympathising with their anger yet urging restraint.

But not everyone wanted to be restrained. Notwithstanding Dubček's undertaking in October that attacks on the Soviet Union in the Czechoslovak press would now stop, the weekly magazines *Politika* and *Reportér* continued to criticise both the Soviets and the undertaking. In November, both were banned (*Reportér* temporarily). For many reformers, including Emil, this was too much to bear. Emil, Dana and Luděk Pachman put their names to a 300-word 'proclamation to defend press freedom', copies of which ended up in, among other places, the Dukla sports club. It was hard-hitting stuff, denouncing 'foreign despotism' and warning of 'a new dark age' in which 'insincerity will become a virtue, lies will become truth and silence will become an existential necessity'.

Emil also read this out publicly, at a rowdy meeting at the Alcron hotel on 13 November. An agent of the secret services attempted, with limited success, to eavesdrop on this gathering, which seems to have been organised by the Belgian journalist Hugo Claes. There was much drinking and singing of patriotic songs – and little doubt that Emil, who arrived late, was the star attraction. It seems inconceivable that he could have imagined that such behaviour would go unnoticed or unpunished. If he did, he was wrong. Two days later, he was called into the Ministry of Defence, told to restrain himself and warned that there would be consequences if he failed to comply strictly with the army's rules and regulations. But that was just a faint foreshadowing of what was to come. The approaching new year would be as bleak as the old one had been full of hope.

First came the personal attacks. An editorial in *Sovietsky sport* on 1 January 1969 was devoted to denouncing Emil as a 'traitor'. A few days later, Friedrich Janke, the East German distance runner, observed acidly that 'Zátopek changes his convictions the way he changes his shirts'. But that was just mood music. What followed was real. On the morning of 16 January, Jan Palach, a twenty-year-old student at Charles University, doused himself in petrol in Wenceslas Square and set fire to himself. He died of his injuries three days later. A letter found in his briefcase indicated that his self-immolation had been a political protest: not so much against the Soviet invasion as against the reformers' subsequent 'demoralisation'. Alarmingly, it suggested that, unless the reformers reasserted their independence, if necessary encouraged by a general strike, then other 'human torches' would follow.

Much controversy surrounds the details of Palach's death and motivation, and of the authorities' response. Other self-immolations did follow; some may have been copy-cat acts by disturbed young people unconnected with Palach; it is possible that the clandestine movement implied by his letter never existed. It can be said with confidence, however, that most Czechoslovaks, reformers and hardliners alike, were horrified – not least by the fear that other young lives, perhaps closer to home, would be thrown away, terribly, in the same cause.

Emil's reaction was mixed. He was overheard speaking animatedly about Palach's suicide, praising the moral qualities of his action. Yet he spent a day in Wenceslas Square a few days later, talking to students and, once again, urging calm. It was an awkward position for reformers to find themselves in, caught between the threats of Soviet retribution and student self-harm. Even Luděk Pachman, one of the most reckless champions of reform, agreed to appear on television to discourage other young people from following Palach's example.

But Emil had other things on his mind as well. On 19 January he was summoned to the Ministry of Defence, reprimanded for his behaviour – and dismissed from his post as the army's Director of Sport. He was given a revised role at Dukla instead: as youth coach and deputy to the chief coach.

Emil and Dana were still digesting this news – which Dana, in particular, took badly – when a new cloud appeared. On 20 February, at a public meeting in the Merkur hotel in Česká Lípa, Vilém Nový, a hardline member of the Central Committee of the Communist Party, made an astonishing claim about Jan Palach's death. Palach, he said, had not intended to kill himself: he had been tricked into it by a group of liberal conspirators who had persuaded him that he would be using a conjuror's substance called 'cold fire' that would not actually burn him. Then Nový named the five alleged conspirators: the authors. Vladimír Škutina and Pavel Kohout; Lubomír Holeček, the student leader; Luděk Pachman; and Emil Zátopek.

The claim was so preposterous that it was barely worth responding to. (You can hear the audience's hoots of disgust in the recording of Nový's address that has, remarkably, survived.) Yet there was something chilling about being singled out and named. Nový's main aim was, presumably, to undermine the 'human torch' movement by spreading doubt as to Palach's motives, while simultaneously smearing some leading liberals. But there may have been another message: we're coming for you.

Four weeks later, the five named men lodged a defamation suit against Nový. It is not clear who instigated this; what is clear is that it was rash. It would, however, be well over a year before the case came to court.

Meanwhile, the hopes of the Prague Spring continued to recede. Those who had supported liberalisation were steadily disempowered – and, in some cases, eased out of their jobs. Emil, talking to fellow reformers in the offices of *Svobodné slovo* at the beginning of April, said that it felt like a 'time of darkness'. Ten days later, at a district conference of the ČSTV in Tachov, he gave a slightly rambling address in which, having said that he would not discuss politics, he talked about little else.

He made derogatory jokes about the Soviet Union and East Germany and talked, among other things, about the billions of crowns' worth of aid – including tanks smuggled in oil tankers – that the Czechoslovaks had given, on Soviet instructions, to North Korea and Hungary. The message seemed to be that this was wasteful, or possibly corrupt; it certainly wasn't the sort of thing that his military superiors would have wanted him to talk about. Answering questions afterwards, Emil said that the army was 'a pile of shit' and that officers just took money for doing nothing.

He returned to the theme of the army's deficiencies two days later, on 14 April, in a discussion with students at the law school at Charles University. The theme was 'post-January politics'. Speaking dressed in uniform, Emil was again in loose-cannon mode. He suggested that the money spent on the army might more usefully be spent on education. He discussed gossip he had heard about alleged plans for a military coup – presumably before the invasion – and implicated, among others, the defence minister, Martin Dzúr. And he revealed that he had been ordered to report on the morale and attitude to the Soviet Union of the athletes under his charge at Dukla – but had resolved the matter in a characteristically maverick fashion, telling the commander that 'everything was all right' without having asked the athletes to do anything more than indicate a broad sympathy for socialism and democracy. With hindsight, it seems astonishing that Emil could have expected to get away with such behaviour. But he had, over the years, grown used to the idea that he could be a law unto himself. Those days were coming to an end.

Disorder following demonstrations that celebrated Czechoslovakia's victory over the USSR in the world ice-hockey championships at the end of March had provided the Soviets with the excuse they needed for piling on the pressure, and the reformers in the higher echelons of the Czechoslovak Communist Party could hold on no longer. On 17 April, Dubček was forced to resign as First Secretary of the Party. He was a broken man, and the movement he had led was as good as broken, too. He was replaced by Gustáv Husák, a former political prisoner who was now thoroughly committed to a pro-Soviet agenda that he called 'normalisation'. Dubček's supporters knew what to expect.

On 21 April, Emil was suspended from his coaching role at Dukla, pending investigation of 'reasonable suspicion' that he had spread 'false news' and for 'conduct at variance with the relevant orders of the Minister of Defence'. He was questioned by military investigators about some of his public statements, and there was talk that he would soon appear before a military tribunal. The official transcript of the interrogation shows Emil in typically baffling mood, alternately submissive, evasive and insolent. ('Question: "As an officer, you should not talk about certain things, and yet you do talk about them. Why?" Answer: "It's mostly like this: people ask me, and I answer them . . ."') At the end he says helpfully that he will 'happily accept any solution' to the conflict between his need to speak freely and the army's need for him to conform. If he is bluffing, he will soon regret it.

In public, meanwhile, he remained cheerfully defiant. He told an Associated Press reporter that he didn't care if he went to prison: 'It would be quiet, and I could write without being disturbed.' The Ministry of Defence, which received a large number of concerned letters from Emil's friends and supporters abroad, felt it necessary to reassure the world that his case would be 'dealt with entirely in harmony with the prevailing legal provisions' and that 'his merits will be taken fully into account'.

Later that week, an article appeared in the Swedish publication *Aftonbladet*, in which Emil admitted that he and Dana had been offered coaching jobs in Sweden and would like to take them up – if the ČSTV would give them permission to do so. Emil revealed that the offer had first been made in Mexico, but he had not wanted to admit defeat at that point. 'It is better to be beaten in a fair game than to win an unfair one.'

The following week, Emil announced that he was unable to take up the Swedish offer. 'Under normal conditions I would accept, but when people are leaving the country I do not want to leave . . . I belong here.' The implication now was that, if he did leave, he would not be allowed back.

He was, however, in need of new employment. The news would not be made public until December – but on 22 April Emil had effectively been dismissed from the army as well. In an interview published in *L'Express* in Austria on 18 August, he explained that he had 'received a letter firing me from the Army. After 1 October 1969, I will no longer belong to the military.' The extended notice period may reflect the friendly feelings that many of Emil's colleagues still had towards him, and their regret that twenty-two years of military service should end like this. It also meant that he could be summoned to account for his behaviour in giving the interview, in which he had also expressed the view that, following Dubček's resignation, 'people came to power in our country again who think of nothing else but a good job and a good salary for themselves but don't care about the people.' Emil's excuse was that two young Austrians had visited him at his flat, and he had thought they were just talking about sport. 'I am not a politician,' he told the head of Dukla, 'and I don't know why so many people visit me day in day out, and everyone wants to hear my opinion.' Dana, he added, was now sending all visitors away.

Emil was still physically spending much of his time at Dukla, despite his earlier suspension. Presumably it was felt that he could do less damage here than inside the Ministry of Defence – or out on the streets. A secret service report on 19 August noted approvingly that he had not been saying anything provocative while at work; but six days later a different Dukla informer reported a conversation in which Emil had said that the 1950s were making a comeback in Czechoslovakia, and that the best outcome might be for him to be sent to prison, where he would work honestly and at least have a break from everything.

Prison was looking increasingly likely. On 21 August, Emil and others marked the anniversary of the invasion by signing the 'Ten Points', an uncompromising condemnation of foreign interference, censorship and the one-party state. Unlike 'The Two Thousand Words', which struck fear into the Soviet empire and temporarily rallied a nation, the 'Ten Points' seems to have had little impact beyond getting its signatories into trouble. Pachman, one of its main instigators, was arrested the next day; Emil spent a long time comforting his wife, Evženka, on the phone.

But these were not the 1950s. The hardliners imposing 'normalisation' were not war-hardened fanatics but the Eastern bloc equivalent of baby-boomers – led, in Husák, by a former victim of totalitarian repression who hoped to achieve his ends with rather less brutality than he had suffered. In any case, it had been agreed at the highest level that celebrity martyrs should not be created. The notorious Law 99, which came into effect in December, gave the state more or less unlimited powers to jail people for political offences; but its victims could be counted in hundreds, not thousands. Normalisation deployed a different weapon: freezing out.

All over Czechoslovakia, the purge was enforced. People were asked to renounce reform or lose their jobs; the most active reformers often lost their jobs anyway. By the mid-1970s, more than 300,000 people would have lost their employment for ideological reasons; they included around 11,000 army officers and 30,000 NCOs judged to be politically unsound.

Many, especially the more vociferous liberals, found it all but impossible to get alternative work – they had to all intents and purposes been blacklisted. Those who had signed 'The Two Thousand Words' were particularly visible among the victims. The academic Milan Hübl, formerly Dubček's chief ideologist, spent a year unemployed before getting work on a building site; Jan Kladiva, former dean of the Charles University philosophy department, became an undertaker's apprentice; Karel Pecka, the author, became a sewer-worker; Miloslav Vlk, a future cardinal, became a window-cleaner. Others were unable to get their work published or performed. Some writers, such as Stanislav Neuman, Jiří Pistora and Jan Alda, committed suicide. Marta Kubišová, whose only crime had been to become Czechoslovakia's most popular singer, was hounded out of the music business and ended up (after a divorce, a miscarriage, a physical breakdown and a court case involving faked pornographic photographs of her) doing menial work for a doll-making co-operative, attaching the legs to plastic bears.

It was an almost invisible form of persecution, and horribly effective. As the film director Pavel Juráček put it, the normalisers were 'counting on starving us out so that finally we come to them and humbly do whatever they want of us'. Most people, of course, had no desire to starve, and preferred to go through the motions of obedience to Husák's regime – even if this meant dissociating themselves from the dissenters. Being a troublemaker began to be a lonely business.

Even Emil found that – in Dana's words – 'people who had been friends became less than friends', with some literally crossing the street to avoid him. There was also the worry that those who didn't avoid him might get into trouble on his account. Václav Bednář, Emil's liaison officer in Martin, remembers bumping into him in Prague around this time. He greeted him warmly; but Emil, who was wearing a tracksuit, backed away. 'He didn't want to talk to me. He said, "Vašek, don't stop, so you won't get into trouble because of me. I am being watched by the counter guys [i.e. military counter-intelligence]." I said I didn't give a damn, but he ran off. I never saw him again.'

Emil was used to being spied on. A less familiar but increasingly pressing issue was the need to find a job.

He was not poor: the royalties from his books provided some income, and he was getting a military pension of sorts, although almost certainly reduced. In the short term, Dana could support him – assuming that she did not lose her job, too. (She didn't. Her fellow javelin trainers closed ranks around her – a kindness she never forgot.) But they had ploughed their accumulated savings into Troja: Emil later reckoned that, by the time it was finished, it had cost them 180,000 crowns.

In any case, Emil was only forty-six, and to be jobless was a criminal offence. He had to find something – but one option after another melted away. In August, he had talked of joining a sporting goods firm near Prague – or perhaps (in a rhetorical flourish) becoming a garbage collector. That came to nothing, as did another prospective job in Vlašim, where the town committee of the Communist Party did not agree with his being taken on. By September he was talking of finding a job in chemistry in Karvína, or as a storeman for the state railway company. But those came to nothing, too. By October he was simply on holiday, working on the house at Troja, having promised to inform Dukla if he left Prague. Even if he wasn't formally blacklisted, no one who knew what was good for them would have anything to do with Emil Zátopek.

At the end of October, he finally left the army. When he went to collect his belongings from Dukla, he was devastated to find that no one came to say goodbye to him.

Meanwhile, a threatening new mood music had been building in the freshly tamed media. In September, an article in *Květy*, the Party central committee's weekly magazine, raised the prospect of trials for Dubček,

Smrkovský, Pachman, Šik and Zátopek. 'I heard the word treason used in connection with their activities,' wrote Bořivoj Horák. 'One cannot avoid using it.'

In October, an article in *Rudé právo* both revealed and justified the fact that Emil had been expelled from the Communist Party. (The expulsion had actually taken place the previous month.) Emil had committed 'a number of acts at variance not only with the duties of a Communist but also with the law and the statutes of our state,' wrote Jiří Hečko, a member of the army's military administration. Among other things, Emil had 'betrayed a number of internal measures of the Czechoslovak Army contained in secret documents of the Ministry of National Defence. Every young lieutenant knows how to deal with secret documents. It would not seem to be asking too much if one demands the same from a colonel with more than twenty years of service.'

On 30 October, the governments of Czechoslovakia and the Soviet Union issued a joint declaration confirming that the invasion of August 1968 had been a welcome act of solidarity to block the progress of counter-revolutionary forces. A month later, on 28 November, the Czechoslovak Olympic Committee formally withdrew its request, made with Emil's encouragement a year earlier, that the invading nations be barred from the Olympics. It also confirmed that Emil had resigned from the Committee. Dr František Kroutil, its secretary general, told reporters that Emil was fine, working on his house in Troja, drawing a full pension and receiving royalties from his books. 'He can,' he added, 'do everything – except controlling himself in press interviews.'

The same day, *Obrana lidu* published a justification of Emil's expulsion – hitherto unreported – from the army. It was, wrote the army weekly, 'naturally unprecedented that a colonel, worker of the defence ministry, was speaking in such a way . . . No wonder the army eventually had to part company with Emil Zátopek in spite of all his merits.'

Finally, in early December, a Ministry of Defence statement applied the final seal of disapproval. Emil had been dismissed from the army, it confirmed: for 'violating legal norms', according to General Dzúr, by 'making serious revelations' about Czechoslovak leaders.

There was no avoiding the message. Emil had fallen, spectacularly, from grace. He was no longer a national hero – and if he knew what was good for him he would keep his head down for a very long time.

But while that was clear enough, there was one question that was exercising a growing number of people: where *was* Emil?

He had been seen at the annual *Rudé právo* run on 28 September, where he had acted as official starter. (The race organiser was Emil's close friend, Zdeněk Fator, the athletics manager of Dukla's civilian rival, Sparta Prague; this small act of defiance deserves acknowledgement.) For a few weeks after that, he was occasionally glimpsed by passers-by in Troja, working on his house and garden. Since late October, however, even those sightings had stopped.

There had been rumours. Some said that he had been working as a garbage collector, only for the process to be disrupted by members of the public insisting on doing his work for him. This rumour has been widely repeated, but I have never heard of anyone who actually saw it, while Dana and others insist that it was not true. Other reports had him driving a water-sprinkler lorry for Prague's sanitation department, provoking demonstrations by passers-by that were deemed a 'threat to public order'. But that, too, was almost certainly mere rumour.

But the fact remained that Emil appeared to have vanished – in which case, where was he?

17

Exile

It depended on who you asked – and when. Some said that Emil had been seen in the Slavkov Forest region, in the remote north-west, or in the grand spa town of Mariánské Lázně. Others spoke of sightings in the Bohemian–Moravian highlands, in the south. There were even suggestions, later on, that he was working in the mines of Jáchymov, up by the German border. Each of these reports was, in its own way, accurate. Emil was on the move, usually in obscure, sparsely inhabited areas. He was not, however, on the run.

This was his new life: yet another re-imagining of what it meant to be Emil Zátopek. With the help of Zdeněk Fator and other friends, he had been found a menial job with one of the few companies that was not discouraged from employing out-of-favour citizens. It was called Stavební geologie ('Structural Geology') and prospected for underground resources, mainly on behalf of the state, throughout the region of Bohemia (roughly the western two-thirds of what is now the Czech Republic). Its 1,200-odd employees included a dozen or so other dissidents, mostly intellectuals; they were generally assigned the least demanding work, measuring water-surface levels with the pumping crews. Jaromír Malák, the regional manager who was made responsible for Emil when he arrived in November 1969, initially assigned Emil to this. But Emil kept demanding a 'real job'. Within a few weeks he got one, as part of a small drilling team.

The team's work ranged from boring new wells to maintaining existing ones and could take place pretty much anywhere where there was or might be water. There were usually just three or four in a drilling team, including the foreman. Being itinerant, they all lived together in a *maringotka* – a traditional caravan not unlike an old wheeled shepherd's hut – where they shared their leisure hours just as they shared the working hours in between. The same three or four might live in this kind of proximity for months at a time – and one was usually an StB informer. Every two or three weeks, they were allowed a couple of days off to visit their families.

The work, from dawn to dusk, could be hard. Much of it involved digging – making ditches, or excavating ground for drilling – and much of the rest involved carrying. According to Emil, his fellow workers 'could have made things quite nasty for me, as I had been a "brass hat". But they were OK.' Some of his friends weren't convinced. 'I fear that they humiliated him,' Zdeněk Fator told me. There certainly seems to have been an early incident when Emil hurt his arm trying to lift a 50kg bag of cement – and was mocked by a foreman who said, in effect, 'What's the point of being an Olympic champion if you can't even lift a bag of cement?' There is little doubt that Emil, who for as long as he could remember had been fitter and stronger than anyone, felt the frustration deeply. 'He had worked so hard for his achievements, and he was used to being among people who appreciated them,' says Dana. 'Now they counted for nothing. It was very hard for him.'

But he buckled down without complaint, and he seems to have won a tolerable amount of respect. His workmates welcomed his willingness to run and fetch items of kit; and he could also be persuaded to run to the nearest pub with a backpack to fetch supplies of beer. He enjoyed the escape and the exercise – which was all the more beneficial because it had to be done in heavy rubber work-boots – and the team, one imagines, enjoyed sending him. But Zdeněk Fator's assessment, that Emil spent his time being bullied by 'drunkards', seems pessimistic. Emil insisted that his workmates 'taught me to drink beer from the bottle and I taught them Moravian folk songs', and claimed that he won their special respect when he showed them his training diaries and they realised how hard he had worked for his glory. Some refused to believe that anyone could have worked so hard.

If there was friction, it may have related to the way that Emil's celebrity sometimes attracted intolerable amounts of public attention. One early assignment, in Mariánské Lázně itself, seems to have been brought to an early conclusion because unacceptable numbers of visitors to the spa, including foreigners, were recognising Emil and taking photographs of him. There was also the problem of women. According to one former Stavební geologie employee, Richard Händl, 'Emil could be a little bit crazy. Often in the morning he would come out of the *maringotka*, naked, and pour two buckets of freezing cold water over himself. But of course he was very famous, and he was attractive, so women from all the local farms would come and watch him doing it. And because word travels quickly, within a few days women from neighbouring villages would want to watch as well.'

But none of this seems to have caused serious resentment. Emil was never the kind to give himself airs, and it is hard to believe that even the most enviously disposed could have envied him for long. Unlike some public figures who had been forced to become menial workers, he was at home among the working classes; and, of course, he had no fear of hard physical work. When friends expressed concern he said: 'I have already got to know the world from on high. Now I am getting to know it from down below.'

For a while this was literally true. One relatively early job during Emil's time with the team took them to Jáchymov, to repair a well deep in the Svornost mine shaft. This gave rise to the much repeated rumour that Emil had been 'sent to the uranium mines' like Jan Haluza and Ladislav Kořán. In fact, the concentration camps had been long closed, as had the mines, the last of which ceased operating in 1964. Svornost remained open so that radioactive water could be pumped down to the Radon Palace in Jáchymov itself. (The 'palace' had begun life as a general health spa – one of many in north-west Bohemia. When the lethal effects on clients' health became apparent, it was rebranded as a source of specialist treatment for clients who actually needed radiotherapy. But the well still needed to work.)

Emil spent most of his time in Jáchymov 150m underground, moving barrowloads of earth. According to Petr Loukota, a mining electrician who still works at

Svornost today: 'He was a good worker. He didn't complain. He just got on with it. We all used to sit in the same hut for our breaks, and he used to entertain people with tales about his experiences in life.' Sometimes these tales were punctuated by complaints about Luděk Pachman, although the details of the gripe went over Loukota's head. Emil also spent many evenings in a Jáchymov pub – drinking not with his co-workers but with a local policeman. Perhaps a proper policeman felt more comfortable as company than a bunch of colleagues who probably included a secret informer.

The team also spent a long time based in the desolate, depopulated Slavkov Forest area, near the tiny village of Nová Ves, where many key springs were drilled. Even today, it feels like a godforsaken area, on the western edge of the Sudetenland. Hundreds of thousands of ethnic Germans were deported from these parts after the Second World War. (Czechoslovakia expelled three million altogether.) They left behind a highland wilderness of ungrazed pastures, untamed woods, derelict houses and, in places, abandoned villages. If you wanted to make a public figure disappear, it would be hard to think of a better place to send him.

Emil passed many months here. He was in a more congenial crew by now, with a sympathetic foreman who had at least some sense of what Emil had achieved in life, and what he had sacrificed to achieve it. But sympathy couldn't alter the loneliness of exile, and the knowledge that the familiar comforts of Mariánské Lázně were down in the valley below can only have served to remind Emil how overwhelmingly the world he had once conquered had now turned against him.

The physical demands of the work here were exacerbated by the environment – bitter cold in winter, tormenting midges the rest of the year – and by the lifestyle: beer, slivovice, more beer, and little else. It must have taken its toll, but Emil bore it with the same stoicism with which he had endured all the other hardships of his life.

According to Alžběta Vlasáková, a Slovakian-born former farm-worker who says that she is the last remaining inhabitant of Nová Ves to remember those days, Emil fitted in well with what was then a reasonably close-knit rural community. 'No one had a problem with him. There was nothing grand about him. He worked hard, and would talk to anybody. There was no "*I'm Zátopek*" about him' – which she accompanies with a gesture indicating a turned-up nose.

Sometimes Alžběta would see Emil on a bicycle, but more often he would be running. 'He used to run to Bečov [Bečov nad Teplou, more than seven hilly miles there and back] or Mnichov [nearly ten], just by himself, on the roads. He wasn't racing then. But he kept running – because if you're running, you're alive.'

There was a pub in the village, and the drilling team were familiar faces there. There was a dance floor on the first floor, and Saturday nights involved marathon sessions of ground-floor drinking and first-floor dancing. Emil was an enthusiastic participant.

It is hard to know if he was happy, but it is clear that he had found a way of adapting to his exile. He was earning good money (more than he earned in the army, he later claimed); he was keeping fit; and at least there was a point to the work. In some ways it was like making the garden in Troja. You put in the physical effort, and the land obeyed. Emil certainly felt he was doing something useful, and took pride in working hard with his hands. By the time the team left Nová Ves for the last time (probably in 1972) there were several new well-heads in the area. One was named the '*Zátopkův vrt*', or Zátopek spring – although when I looked for it in 2015 it appeared to have vanished under a small lake.

But even Emil had to concede that working on the drills 'was not seventh heaven'. It was not the life he had won for himself with all those years of effort and sacrifice. For most of the past two decades he had been courted by presidents, sports stars, intellectuals – the great and good of the land. Now he was a nobody, in the middle of nowhere. He must have felt the difference. And if he didn't, others did.

Once, on a team working near Jihlava – about eighty miles south-east of Prague – Emil received a surprise visit. Dana had driven down with Patxi Alcorta, the Spanish sports official who organised the San Sebastián cross-country race. Alcorta was a colourful character who could charm his way anywhere; he was visiting Prague en route to Moscow. The old friends embraced – Emil still in the overalls in which he often slept as well as worked. On the journey back to Prague, Alcorta wept. 'Is this how they treat their hero?'

Perhaps he was overreacting. It was not as if Emil couldn't cope – with the work or the lifestyle. Yet I suspect that there was something heartbreaking about the sight of him. According to the Czech author Pavel Kosatík, there was one occasion when a boy from a village near Litomyšl knocked on the *maringotka* door to offer Emil a present – a piece of smoked meat – from his mother. The shambling figure who greeted him looked tired and had a bottle in his hand. He thanked the boy, but added: 'I am not the Zátopek who you used to know.' I got much the same impression from a fleeting clip of film footage that I have seen of Emil during this phase. He looks tired and, for the first time in his life, defensive. He does not appear to be suffering, but the relaxed confidence has gone. He seems to be holding himself in check. It is like seeing a lion in a circus.

Forced dislocations such as Emil's did not occur in isolation, and it was often the context, not the discomfort, that hurt. It is easy to imagine how Emil, with his physical energy and natural grace and empathy, found ways to bond with his new companions. It is much harder to imagine how he reconciled this new life with his old, lost life with Dana in Prague. This – even more than the long winter nights in the crowded *maringotka* when even the slivovice wasn't enough to keep out the cold – must have gnawed away at him, just as family memories have always gnawed at those kept away from home by war, prison, education or work. You can adapt yourself: humans always adapt. But what do you do with the part of you that you have left, unchanged, behind?

Every few weeks, Emil would return to Prague for a day or two. It was not enough, for either of them. 'Emil changed during that time,' Dana recalls sadly. It hardly matters how. The visits were largely taken up by doing his washing. There was no time to get to know one another again. She, like him, was adapting, keeping herself going through her work as a coach, through other friends, and through feverish needlework, to which she applied herself with the same discipline she had brought to her athletics training. 'People thought I must be doing a lot of shopping,' she says, 'because I kept appearing in new clothes. But I was just making them.'

For Emil, meanwhile, there was no guarantee that his punishments were at an end. One evening, visiting Troja on his way back from the *maringotka*, he was beaten up by a group of men who appeared to be soldiers. He shrugged off the injuries with difficulty – several of his ribs were damaged – and took home the message that this was 'a warning'.

Harder to shake off was the pain of his distance from Dana, and the growing divergence in their experiences and outlooks. Emil, in Dana's view, had become 'wild'; while Emil, as far as we can tell, felt misunderstood. This, I suspect, was what bothered him most: not the discomfort or the humiliation, but the sense that he was losing his marriage.

In the spring of 1970, reports given by the informers of eastern Bohemia to the security services paint a picture of a man trying to avoid controversy. In February, in Osík, near Litomyšl, some young people recognised him and asked him to sign autographs, but Emil, uncharacteristically, refused; he also turned down an invitation to speak at a village function. In March, in the villages around Polička, Emil is quoted as saying that he liked the quietness of the place. In Prague there had been too many parties and public events and it hadn't been good for him. In Vendolí, in April, local people kept inviting Emil to their parties, but Emil didn't like this: he would prefer to be alone – and he didn't want to talk about politics. In Svitavy, in May, he declined an opportunity to officiate at a sports event: he knew the security services followed him everywhere and he didn't want to risk doing anything to make the situation worse.

It is possible that Emil expected that what he said and did would be reported, and adapted accordingly. But even that is revealing. The Emil of 1968 or even 1969 had seemed indifferent to what the authorities made of his pronouncements. Now he seemed to be sending a message: that he was going to behave himself.

We cannot be sure why. No doubt loneliness and despair played their part, but there may have been a more pressing reason. Emil's joint defamation lawsuit against Vilém Nový was getting closer to its long-delayed hearing, and it seems likely that pressure was being put on Emil to back down. Much of it was 'soft' pressure: people in high places trying to persuade him that, in bringing the case, he was damaging a cause – socialism – in which he believed. At some point, too, someone seems to have persuaded him that at least one of his co-plaintiffs, Luděk Pachman, had double-crossed him and was about to flee the country. But there were probably 'bad cops' on his case as well as 'good' ones. One informer's report, from Agent 'Saša', said that Emil was 'afraid of being sent to jail for 20 years' – and some of Emil's closest friends are convinced that he was being explicitly threatened with prison (although Dana doubts this). At the very least, Emil's resolve was cracking. And when, on 30 July 1970, the case was finally heard, it – or he – broke.

The hearing took place at the ward court for Prague 7. Emil sat with his co-plaintiffs, Lubomír Holeček, Pavel Kohout, Luděk Pachman and Vladimír Škutina. The judge read the indictment. Emil got up, approached the judge and asked if he could apologise to Nový and withdraw from the action. He said that he did not want to be perceived as an enemy of socialism, having always supported socialism, and that he regretted that the court case had happened. The judge gave her consent, whereupon Emil approached Nový and asked his forgiveness.

According to Pachman, who later dismissed the hearing as 'a farce', Emil 'went over to Nový, his hand extended – it looked as if they were about to hug each other in a "double Khrushchev", but they merely shook hands'. Pavel Kohout compared it to seeing 'a grown man collapse like a house hit by a bomb'. Emil spent the rest of the case sitting in the public gallery.

On a practical level, Emil's U-turn made little difference. The judge, after a peremptory hearing, threw out the case anyway, claiming (preposterously) that Nový had not said the words complained of and, in any case, had been acting within his rights. Kohout later claimed that Emil's climbdown was 'an example of surrender which meant the end to the solidarity of Czech society'. That seems an overstatement: the solidarity of 1968 had dissipated long ago. On a personal level, however, for Emil, the difference was huge. He had avoided the threat of further punishment by the regime – but at what price? No one could read the report of the proceedings in *Rudé právo* without a degree of sympathy for various witnesses who had clearly been bullied into undermining the case. (For example, the sound engineer who had recorded Nový's speech testified that the recording might not have been an accurate representation of what Nový had said.) But sympathy is a vague and shifting thing. The solid fact was that Emil had failed conspicuously to live up to his image as a hero of the liberal cause.

That was not all. It would emerge much later (although few people noticed) that, at some point, Emil had withdrawn his signature from the 'Ten Points' manifesto that he, Pachman and others had signed the previous August. It is not clear how or when this happened, let alone why, but there is no shortage of possible reasons. Signatories faced trial and imprisonment: Pachman was already in jail; others would follow. Backing down got Emil off the hook (although he would later be called as a witness), and he was not the only signatory to withdraw. But he may also have been motivated by a desire to dissociate himself from Pachman. He seems to have felt that he had been hustled into getting into more trouble, and adopting a more anti-Communist position, than he had intended. There were probably more personal issues, too. Pachman was a difficult personality – a womaniser with a huge ego – and it was easy to fall out with him.

Emil later told friends, referring to the Nový trial: 'I was prepared to go to the edge of the abyss but not to jump into it.' It is unlikely that he was left undamaged by the choice. For two decades his identity had been bound up with his heroism: he was the man with the strength and willpower to hang on while others succumbed to despair. Now he too had succumbed – and presumably learnt the great drawback of such shame-faced surrenders. It's like quitting in mid-race. The longed-for relief soon fades; the regret doesn't.

Just a few months earlier, Christopher Brasher had written of Emil in the *Observer*: 'He is as great a human being as he was an athlete . . . Those who have dismissed him have demeaned themselves. Zátopek himself will never be demeaned; he will never be defeated.' Now his greatness seemed to have deserted him.

It got worse. In May 1971, a British journalist named Brian Freemantle tracked Emil down during one of his breaks from drilling. Their conversation resulted in an article in the *Daily Mail*. 'Zátopek . . . The will to win is crushed' said the headline. Emil was portrayed as a broken man, who described himself as 'reconciled' to the state of his nation and yet plainly wasn't: 'Once I was unhappy, but not now. There seems little point. I exist.' Emil added that he had been stripped of his army rank and pension, and was quoted as confirming the rumour that he had been working as a dustman. This may have been a misunderstanding, or a mistranslation, or perhaps just Emil getting carried away – but the Czechoslovak authorities were furious. This was precisely the kind of bad publicity that the Husák regime was trying to avoid. It was also the kind of loose-cannon behaviour that Emil was supposed to have had bullied out of him.

A month or so later, Emil came back from his drilling shift to Prague. He was exhausted and a little frightened: he was being harassed by the police about a small car accident in which he had been involved and a problem with a stolen tractor at work for which he seemed to be being made the scapegoat. It was hard to know if he was becoming paranoid or if, as was common security service practice, a deliberate effort was being made to soften him up. Either way, he was vulnerable. Dana was away for the weekend. He had not been home long when the phone rang. A friend with close connections to the Party was inviting him to dinner. Emil knew that she wished him well, despite their recent political differences, so he went over – and found that his fellow guests were two *Rudé právo* journalists, Zdeněk Hoření and Václav Švadlena. 'Perhaps Emil's friend was trying to help,' says Dana today. 'But these things were "organised" . . .'

There was a lot of talking and plenty of wine; there appears to have been a tape-recorder; and by the time Emil left, Hoření and Švadlena had a scoop. According to Dana, Emil realised that he had got carried away. He rang Hoření later that weekend and asked him not to publish anything without showing him the article first; he also sent the paper a short letter, clarifying a particular point about his *Daily Mail* interview. Then he went back to his drilling.

On 20 July 1971 *Rudé právo* published precisely what the Party had been hoping for: a 3,000-word interview under the heading 'Emil Zátopek answers the *Rudé právo* editorial board concerning matters of the past and the present', in which Emil recanted pretty much everything he had fought for in 1968.

Among other things, Emil was quoted as saying that he was still a reserve colonel and still receiving a military pension of 1,160 Czech crowns (just over half of the average male wage). He denied that he had been persecuted for his opinions and distanced himself from 'The Two Thousand Words' and its authors, expressing regret that 'I was one of the wild ones who poured fuel on the fire that might have grown into an inferno which could truly endanger the socialist world.' Far from being an enemy of the regime, he added, he would 'consider it shameful to be an enemy of the socialist regime'. The article ended by quoting in full Emil's short letter of clarification.

The interview took up most of a broadsheet page, and the main illustration was a giant reproduction of Emil's signature. Close inspection of the image reveals that the signature is taken from Emil's letter of clarification, but the average reader will have assumed that it referred to the article as a whole. There could be no doubt about the message: this was a signed, public retraction – one of the most prominent since Galileo's.

According to Dana, Emil 'got what for' when she found out. 'Emil did not talk to me before . . . If he had, I don't think he would have done it.' Perhaps this was a little unfair. Remembering her father being dragged off in the night to Buchenwald by the Gestapo, and fearing that something similar would happen to Emil, Dana had told him many times not to be a hero. Well, now he hadn't been.

He could reasonably have argued that he hadn't been especially cowardly, either. He had just been manipulated – as he had been in the Nový case. Such protestations were useless. You can't uneat your words. Word of the 'retraction' soon reached the West (in contrast to the Nový case), and Emil's admirers on both sides of the Iron Curtain struggled to reconcile the news with their long-cherished ideas of Emil. Had his heroism been an illusion?

Emil was not the first or the last famous dissident to retract in the face of normalisation. Most people who came across such statements gave them little thought, knowing the circumstances in which they must have been extracted. But Zátopek – Zátopek, who could endure everything . . . could they really have got to him, too? For anyone who had ever been inspired by Emil's character and achievements, it was a bitter disappointment.

It must have been bitter for Emil, too. He had built his life around the idea that pain could be endured – and now, publicly and irrevocably, he had capitulated in the middle of his biggest test of all. It is understandable that he did so: what choice did he have, with the entire might of the Czechoslovak state against him and, behind that, the might of the Soviet Union? No one who has not lived and behaved heroically in a totalitarian society has a right to judge him. That will not have made Emil feel any better about it. Waking up on the morning after he first saw the *Rudé právo* article in print, Emil must have felt what Robert Browning expressed with the line: 'Never glad confident morning again . . .'

What must have made it even harder was Emil's awareness that he had already been cast off by many of his former friends: the Party hardliners at home and abroad who felt that he had betrayed the Communist cause; and less committed types who none the less felt that it was no longer wise to be associated with him. Now he was scorned by the other camp, too: the reformers – henceforth to be known as dissidents – who had briefly seen him as an ally and a figurehead.

In practice, the general public seem to have judged him less harshly than he may have feared. They had loved him for so long; it was hard to get over the habit just like that. But Emil's self-esteem may be assumed to have taken a battering, and at times he seems to have sought refuge in, among other things, the bottle. It was not an unusual response. A popular joke of the period suggested that the Marxist-Leninist theory of historical development had been revised, with a new intermediate stage now appearing in the progression from socialism to Communism: alcoholism.

I don't think Emil was an alcoholic, but it is clear that, with no thoughts of heroism to sustain him, he drank heavily and often. With the drilling team, it was hard not to – Emil is supposed to have complained to friends that, in addition to struggling with those 50kg bags of cement, he couldn't keep up with his workmates in the pub either. Now he began to spend more of his Prague evenings out drinking as well – in wine bars where everyone who saw him either cut him dead or insisted on buying him a drink. This, of course, was part of the problem: Emil's glory followed him wherever he went. But he must have realised that, no matter what people said to his face, they knew as well as he did that he was running away – from the fact that he had let both himself and his admirers down.

One kindred spirit he found in this period was a young actor called Ladislav Županič, who would later become director of the Karlín Musical Theatre but was then struggling to make progress in his career because of his refusal to declare to his superiors at the National Theatre that he approved of the Soviet invasion in 1968. (Such declarations were becoming an increasingly widespread workplace requirement.) Županič and Emil drowned their sorrows together several times, often in a wine bar called Malokarpatská, where they could talk uninterrupted. Sometimes Emil talked about his frustrations. 'He used to say how he envied the Czechoslovak pilots who went abroad to fight Hitler during the Second World War. "At least they could fight," he'd say. "I just sleep in a *maringotka* and look at the forest."' At other times, conversation would turn to 'the sort of matters that men discuss only when they're drunk'. From the context of our discussion, I took this to include Emil's marriage – but the details are lost in drink and discretion.

One evening, Županič invited Emil to the opening night of a production of *The Vagabond King* at the National Theatre. Afterwards, they went backstage, and Emil, predictably, stole the show. No one wanted to talk about the production; everyone wanted to talk to Emil, and be seen with him – and, not least, buy him a drink. As the cast headed for the bar, the departing audience noticed Emil too – and they, too, wanted to join in the adulation. The theatre's director, a hardline Communist, glowered impotently. Emil was the star of the evening, and there was nothing he could do about it without risking a public order incident.

Such moments must have been exhilarating for Emil: fleeting reminders of the charmed life he once led. 'But it ended badly,' Županič added, 'because we didn't get home until six in the morning.'

Županič smiles at the memory, yet there is something sad about it, too: a life forged in the unsparing realism of the running track, melting away in a blur of greasepaint and wine-drenched self-pity.

But Emil was not wholly broken. Nor had he lost his lifelong habit of believing that he could, through his own efforts, improve things. He sought comfort not just in alcohol but also, more helpfully, in his marriage. The home at Troja was almost finished. He and Dana resolved to complete the work. The shared objective helped bring them back together. Breeze-block by breeze-block and fitting by fitting, the slightly ramshackle structure edged closer to completion.

Progress was slow. Materials and skilled assistance were harder to obtain than they had once been. Those who knew what was good for them kept their distance. But by mid-1972, Emil and Dana were making serious plans for moving in – and, as a result, for moving out of 8 U Půjčovny. Emil took advantage of this impending change to attempt another wild act of kindness. His friends the Fators had been struggling to fit into their cramped one-bedroom flat since the birth of their son. So Emil proposed they swap homes. The Fators would get a nice, centrally located two-bedroom flat in 8 U Půjčovny with plenty of space for a young family; while the flat that the Zátopeks eventually vacated would be somewhat smaller than the one they had been living in.

The scheme came to nothing, but Emil and Zdeněk Fator did get as far as signing a formal application (dated 2 August 1972) and delivering it to Prague's City Hall. Whatever else had happened to crush his spirit, Emil had retained his taste for extravagant generosity.

Afterwards, he and Fator went to the restaurant at the Zoological Gardens in Troja, but decided that they didn't like the look of the food. 'Emil took one look at it and went: "*Jesus!*"' remembers Fator. 'So we simply got drunk. And much later, we went from the restaurant to their place [at Nad Kazankou]. It was about five hundred metres, and we were singing "Communists, go fuck yourselves" at the top of our voices. Dana was furious.'

The curious thing about this is that it took place only a few weeks after Emil had appeared in court (on

5 May 1972) for the trial of Luděk Pachman. The proceedings were closed to the public, but the charges were thought to include subversion, slandering the Republic, incitement and preparing a felony. Emil is assumed to have been called as a witness. Pachman later claimed that Emil's evidence related to a conversation in which Pachman and the Soviet chess player Paul Keres jokingly discussed emigration. As with the Nový case, what Emil did made little practical difference. Pachman was found guilty – that had never been in doubt – but was immediately released: the two years he had spent in prison on remand cancelled out his sentence. He emigrated to the West soon afterwards.

Was Emil just saving his own skin? Was he motivated by malice? Or did he genuinely consider it his duty (as one informer's report in the StB archives suggests) to give evidence against a 'reactionary' who wanted to undermine Communism? I suspect it was the latter, at least in part: he never stopped believing in the core ideology. Yet it is hard to reconcile this with the attitude he drunkenly expressed in Fator's company. No doubt he was confused; or, more accurately, conflicted. His attempts to behave as a dutiful Communist citizen were forcing him into stances and actions that he must have known were unheroic. I cannot believe that he felt comfortable about this. Maybe his discomfort occasionally expressed itself in alcohol-fuelled fury at what the Communists had done to him.

Luckily for Emil, the Communists didn't hear his song – because this was almost exactly the time that they were deciding a delicate question about his future. The Olympic Games were due to begin in Munich on 26

August and the West Germans had put the Czechoslovak authorities on the spot by inviting Emil to be guest of honour at the Olympic Games in Munich, daring them to embarrass themselves by saying that he was unavailable – their usual approach to enquiries about Emil from overseas – or, worse, that they did not even know where he was.

They did not dare: apart from anything else, a diplomatic push for better relations with West Germany was in progress. Emil had to be made available, and made to behave. An invitation arrived in west Bohemia, via the Sports Ministry in Prague. Emil requested leave of absence to go to the Olympic Games. 'No way,' said the foreman. 'Where am I going to get someone to replace you for three weeks?' So Emil wrote back, politely declining.

Frantic behind-the-scenes activity followed. Eventually, in mid-August, it was announced that Emil was available to go to the Games after all. There could, however, be no question of Dana going as well. 'Normalised' Czechoslovakia was a land that only one half of a married couple could leave at once – just in case anyone felt tempted not to return.

Emil arrived back from the drills the night before departure. 'Quick,' he said to Dana, 'mobilise!' They dug out some respectable clothes, and spent hours frantically trying to scrub the black ingrained dirt from Emil's fingers. Twenty-four hours later he was being escorted into Munich's most luxurious hotel, with a brief that could not have been clearer: to look happy and keep his mouth shut.

There were plenty of old friends to catch up with. One of the first people he met there was the former 1,500m world record holder, László Tábori, a Hungarian who had defected to the US after failing to return from the Melbourne Olympics. Later, Emil sat near Jesse Owens in the VIP section of the stands during the opening ceremony, and spoke briefly to the West German Chancellor, Willie Brandt. He generally avoided journalists, but he did give one interview to *Spiegel.* He talked mainly about sport, discussing the increasing prominence of Third World athletes. Asked about what he was doing now, he said: 'I am a simple worker and drill outside Prague for mineral water. But, please, I am very reluctant to talk about politics.'

But the eyes of the world weren't really on Emil, or on Czechoslovakia – and especially not after 5 September, when members of the Black September Palestinian terrorists broke into the Olympic village and took eleven Israelis hostage – all of whom were subsequently killed. Controversially, the Games then resumed, but no one was taking much pleasure from them after that. At the ceremony for the victims, held in the stadium on 6 September, Emil was seen wiping away tears. For a man who believed so warmly in the power of the Olympic ideal to heal divisions between nations and ideologies, the tragedy must have felt heartbreakingly grotesque.

A week later, Emil was at the airport waiting to go home, at the same time as a party of *Runner's World* readers. One of them, Joe Henderson, plucked up the courage to approach him. He was rewarded with twenty minutes of Emil's time and autographs for most of his party. Emil was happy to talk about running – in English – but avoided politics. He did say, however, that it was odd to receive so much attention. 'In my country I am just a common man – a nobody.'

Then he flew home, to assume the workman's clothes in which he would work and sleep for the next two weeks – or, for all he knew, the next ten years. He was still a decade short of retirement age, and had no reason to believe that the rest of his working life would be any different. Very slowly, however, an end to his exile was approaching.

18

In the drawer

On 24 August 1973, Arthur I. Wortzel, chargé d'affaires at the US Embassy in Prague, sent a cable to the US State Department assessing the state of Czechoslovakia five years after the Soviet-led invasion. The anniversary itself, he reported, had passed 'almost without notice', although there had been extra police on the streets and special fencing had prevented access to Jan Palach's grave. 'Normalcy', he concluded, had been restored to such a degree that it was almost as if 'this upheaval had never occurred'.

Not everyone had forgotten, though. 'Former Olympic champion Emil Zátopek,' reported Wortzel, 'was seen August 20 muttering into beer "Five years, five years . . ."'

Five years is a long time to spend in limbo, half living as a kind of outlaw, watched and warned, cut off from your dreams and from the love of your life. Emil was far from the only Czechoslovak to endure such frustrations in the Husák era. But few can have experienced such a soul-sapping contrast. Once, his refusal to accept limits had thrilled the world; now, almost nothing was possible.

He was comfortable on the drilling team – comfortable enough to annoy his colleagues, sometimes, with his incessant talking; or by challenging them, once, to race him to the work site they were heading for, with them going forwards while he ran backwards. And they, too, had accepted him for who he was. Once, seeing Emil struggle with a heavy load, his foreman said to him: 'Emil, relax. You've already earned your oats.' But acceptance, and endurance, are not the same as happiness. Emil was still caged.

Yet that visit to Munich had loosened the lock. Enquiries from the outside world about his availability – to present the prizes, to be guest of honour – kept coming in, and the ČSTV grew weary of lying in response to each one. In October 1973, Paavo Nurmi died. The Finns organised a race to honour the memory of their greatest distance runner. Emil was invited to be starter. Once again, he was given permission.

The visit passed quietly, and the authorities decided that Emil no longer posed a threat to the re-established order. It was time to end the awkwardness of having to track Emil down in the wilderness. All that remained was to find him a job where he couldn't do any damage.

Wheels were set in motion. While they turned, Emil and Dana continued their strange, disjointed existence. Dana developed her gift for coaching. The work became both fulfilling and demanding of her time; sometimes, when Emil came home, she was away. Any positive feelings Emil had developed towards his itinerant, outdoor existence were offset by the thought that, unless he could return to Prague permanently, he would barely see Dana at all – when what they really needed most was time together.

But at least, when they were both at home, they could, if they chose, be left to themselves. Being out of favour politically meant being less in demand socially. This left space in which to rediscover one another. Dana says that she took to heart her mother's advice: to 'hold each other's hands while you still have one another'. She knew what the regime required. 'They wanted,' she says, illustrating the point with an opening and closing gesture, 'to put us in a drawer.' She and Emil decided to turn this into a positive, saying to themselves (as Dana puts it): 'Life is the most precious thing we have, and even though it just treated us badly, we live on; and we can find a corner where we will feel comfortable even in a table drawer.'

You could think of it as a kind of twilight: a grey no-man's-land somewhere between celebrity, notoriety and anonymity that was, in their case, the price of peace. Other heroes of the Prague Spring ended up in prison, in exile or, in a few cases, in suspiciously premature graves. Emil and Dana still had enough friends in high places for an exception to be made in their case – if they would just refrain from making a nuisance of themselves.

It wasn't always easy. Emil was troubled, in a way that he never had been before. 'What happened after 1968 wounded his soul,' says Dana, without quite being able to put her finger on how. 'It was hard for him. He had been a star, and all of a sudden he was unknown. Books about him disappeared. He stopped being invited to schools to talk. There was an emptiness. Most people didn't see it, but it left a scar.' Sometimes he would be his old self, urging Dana not to be hurt by the friends who had deserted them – because 'at least we know that those who stayed are really worth something'. At other times a shadow would fall on him: a new pessimism that could manifest itself in anything from drinking to uncharacteristic grumpiness.

Yet life 'in the drawer' was less alien to his temperament than some might have imagined. Even with a smaller audience than he was used to, Emil never lost his instinct to brighten the lives around him. He would still make everyday matters into jokes, still exercise his restless mind; occasionally, he would indulge his romantic side. Some of Dana's happier memories of this period are of sitting under the walnut tree at Troja, drinking wine while Emil recited poetry to her from memory. Happiest of all were his performances of 'Král Lávra', which often degenerated into wild hilarity as he got carried away with the characters' different voices.

At other times, they focused their still considerable energies on caring for their home and garden. Dana grew flowers but left the vegetables to Emil. And, as she points out: 'One good thing about the invitations for public speaking drying up was that it left us with a lot of time.' Between them, she says: 'We made an environment of our own.'

Yet it was not always a particularly private environment, especially when Emil began to indulge his lifelong taste for offering hospitality to strangers on the spur of the moment. He had always liked the idea that he had a sacred duty to put his home comforts at other people's disposal: Les Perry and Percy Cerutty were among the beneficiaries in Helsinki, just as Olga Fikotová and Harold Connolly were in Prague when seeking permission to marry. If a friend needed somewhere to live, as Ivan Ullsperger did for a while, Emil and Dana would be quick to offer their spare room. As Dana put it: 'Our door was never really closed.' Sometimes there were strangers-in-need, too, such as the German tourists, lost in Prague late one rainy night in the mid-1960s, whom Emil invited back to U Půjčovny. 'When they saw Emil's colonel's uniform hanging up inside, they were terrified,' laughs Dana.

Now, however, in Troja, Emil began to invite so many strangers to dine and to stay, so regularly, that Dana – who usually ended up doing the catering – found herself dreading coming home from work. She would scan the windows for signs of unexpected guests before deciding whether to come in or not.

You can see her point of view; yet you can see Emil's, too. Maybe he was motivated by loneliness. Maybe he wanted an excuse for the familiar comforts of wine, anecdotes and song. Or maybe he just felt a restless desire for something – anything – beyond his new tamed normality. Whatever the truth, it is hard not see something noble in his compulsion to share what he had with strangers. When the world fell in love with the idea of Zátopek in the days of his athletic prime, it was partly because, in contrast to other athletes who competed only for themselves, Emil seemed to see himself as part of a wider human family, and behaved accordingly. Now he was doing the same, in the privacy of his own drawer.

Some of the guests turned into lifelong friends. But the sheer volume of visitors drove Dana nuts, especially when she discovered, in 1975 or 1976, that many of these guests were coming from a campsite down the road whose owners would direct them to the Zátopeks' house when their site was full. 'At that point,' she says, 'I declared the Tourist Hotel closed.' Even then, there were quite a few who slipped through security over the next couple of decades, as dozens of grateful admirers from around the world will testify.

Back in the early 1970s, however, perhaps there was one additional attraction to the company of strangers: there was no risk that they would get into trouble from being seen to associate with the Zátopeks. Emil took this concern seriously, and for that reason was relatively relaxed about those who chose to keep their distance. But a few friends insisted on standing by them. Their loyalty meant a lot. One example was Emil's former teammate Ludvík Liška, who since leaving the army had been caretaker at the Stará Boleslav training retreat, and his wife Olga. Emil and Dana were regularly guests of the Liškas for Saturday night village dances in Slapy, just outside Prague. It was a modest form of entertainment for such a fêted couple, and quite a big risk for the Liškas. But it formed an important part of what Dana calls a 'process of renewal'.

It must have been around this time that Emil first raised the question, which he and Dana discussed many times, of whether there were more good people in the world than bad – or vice versa. Dana felt that the good were in the majority; Emil disagreed. They also talked about the possibility of starting a club – perhaps even a worldwide organisation – whose members would all be good people. 'The trouble was, we couldn't agree on the criteria for membership,' says Dana. They had fun discussing it, though: sometimes at dinners where other loyal friends – Jan Veselý, the cyclist; František Šťastný, the motorcyclist; Zdeněk Ujčík, the ice hockey player; and their spouses – would gather with the Zátopeks and the Liškas and, instead of trying to change the world, quietly celebrate their shared humanity. They drank wine, told jokes and stories, sometimes sang songs: did, in short, the things that people who love life have always enjoyed doing, in tyrannies as in democracies. After a while, they began to talk of themselves as the Old Guard. They carried on meeting for decades, until (quite recently) the gang became too depleted by ill health and death to be viable.

'This table has so many memories,' says Dana, reliving some of them for me over slivovice on a cold winter's morning in Prague. Seeing how her face brightens as she dips into that pool of remembered friendship, I begin to sense what Emil must have meant by his observation, mentioned earlier, that the key to happiness is to learn to behave as a domesticated animal rather than a wild one. Luděk Pachman, who reported it, clearly felt that it was discreditable to his erstwhile friend. I am not so sure. Learning to live well, irrespective of who controls the levers of worldly power, has much to be said for it; the Christian injunction to 'render unto Caesar the things that are Caesar's' expresses much the same view. Not everyone who lives under a tyranny can fight it head-on, all of the time; someone has to keep the flame of ordinary humanity alive as well.

Emil was an atheist. But he was also a humanist, and there was something almost sacramental about his insistence on the basic human virtues of courtesy, consideration and hospitality. If this part of his life now became more important to him than his public profile, that does not seem inappropriate.

Even then, however, Emil's life was not yet permanently settled. In 1974 he was told that a job had been found for him with the ČSTV. There was probably little option other than to accept, and at least it meant working in Prague. The job involved monitoring foreign publications for the latest developments in sports science and training techniques, taking advantage of Emil's proficiency as a linguist. 'I became a sports spy' was how he described it.

He handed in his notice at Stavební geologie in June and began work in July, in the ČSTV's documentation centre, in a little office underneath the Strahov stadium. It was a pretty lowly job, shuffling papers in a way that seemed significantly less worthwhile – and perhaps even more humiliating – than what he had been doing before. He endured it because there was no alternative. To speak of it as a liberation would be overstating it. None the less, that was how it appeared in the West, and perhaps how it was intended by the Czechoslovak regime. As Neil Allen wrote in *The Times* on hearing the news: 'Emil Zatopek has been welcomed back into the fold of Czechoslovak sport.'

In fact, he was on the outermost edge of the fold. The 'sports spy' label made the job sound more interesting than it was. Emil was just providing a not particularly important cuttings service. He could use his language skills but little else. It was tolerable but dull.

His old friend Jaromír Konůpka visited Emil one day at work and found him delighted with the distraction – and apparently indifferent to his employers' approval. 'After we had been chatting for a while,' recalls Konůpka, 'his manager came in and summoned him to the daily "ten-minute meeting", which was about to start.' (Such collective political pep-talks were a daily occurrence in

Czechoslovak workplaces.) 'Emil said he'd be along in a minute, then carried on chatting. Five minutes later, the manager came back: "Come on, Emil, it will look bad if you're not there." "Yes, yes," said Emil, and waved him away. Then, after he'd gone, he turned to me and said: "I'm glad you're here today. It means I don't have to go."'

In some ways, the documentation centre was more soul-destroying than the *maringotka*. At least with drilling wells he had been outside, exerting himself and doing productive work. 'Emil always wanted to be useful,' says Dana, 'and he didn't feel that this work was useful.'

But his half-rehabilitation brought one big benefit: he could travel again. The invitations took time to start coming in, but he appreciated them all. In 1975, for example, he was allowed to travel to Paris, to receive a UNESCO Pierre de Coubertin Fair Play medal. This may have been the trip from which he returned by train, laden with gifts, including a signed, limited edition print by Pablo Picasso. Emil pronounced this 'sort of OK' before giving it away to the photographer with whom he was sharing a compartment.

But the freebies weren't what mattered. Emil was the first Czechoslovak sportsperson to receive such a prestigious international award. Even the most hardline normaliser could see that there was a diplomatic benefit to such honours. Bit by bit, the shackles loosened.

There was still a price to be paid, though. On 6 and 7 January 1977, a group of Czechoslovakia's most stubborn remaining dissidents (including Václav Havel, Pavel Kohout and Ludvík Vaculík) published the 'Manifesto of Charter 1977', urging the government to allow its citizens the basic human rights to which it had supposedly committed itself in the 1975 Helsinki Accords. The manifesto was instantly suppressed, but was widely published abroad, and many of the 242 signatories were in due course arrested. Meanwhile, the regime launched a ferocious counter-attack of propaganda-based intimidation that recalled the hate campaign against Milada Horáková in the 1950s, though without the threat of death. *Rudé právo* kicked it off on 12 January, with an issue denouncing the charter as Goebbels-esque anti-socialist propaganda and its authors as 'remnants of bourgeois reaction'. Then came the supposedly spontaneous attacks from ordinary people; and then public figures were 'invited' to join in. Singers, writers, actors, artists and musicians were encouraged to sign an 'anti-charter' promising 'new creative acts in the name of socialism and peace', on the unstated but clear understanding that, if they didn't, they would find it impossible to get work in future. There was little resistance; most Czechoslovaks had long since succumbed to what Pavel Kohout called 'the great surrender' (which he blamed Emil for starting). For two weeks, *Rudé právo* printed the names of compliant celebrities, filling page after page with well over seven thousand signatories.

Emil was not among them. He did, however, take part in television's precursor to the campaign, appearing on ČST on 15 January to express his condemnation of 'political adventurers who with this Charter have tried to stick a knife into our collective work'. I don't suppose he gave it much thought; nor would he have read the manifesto that he had been told to denounce (it was impossible to get hold of). He had made enough speeches in defence of socialism in the past: what difference did one more soundbite make, when his reputation as a liberal was ruined anyway?

No one's life was at stake, in contrast to 1950; while in contrast to 1968 the prospect of regime change seemed infinitesimal. Why risk wrecking his life again? In any case, he really was opposed to the undermining of socialism – and *Rudé právo*'s description of the Charter, which he probably had read, made it sound like a blueprint for precisely that.

None the less, it was one more gesture of submission to the Stalinist forces that Emil had once defied. A few more former admirers found themselves thinking a little bit less of him; and no doubt Emil did, too. Once he had preached that 'one's willpower increases with every task fulfilled'. Now he was discovering the dispiriting opposite: that each surrender makes it easier to surrender again in future.

From this point on, however, the burden of official disapproval lightened. That autumn, Emil was allowed to attend the dinner following the annual *Rudé právo* road race. The Finnish runner Lasse Viren – double gold medallist at the previous year's Montreal Olympics – was the star guest, and Emil, Viren and Zdeněk Fator drank many toasts together (one of which was 'Death to all Bolsheviks'). Emil 'sang English songs extremely loudly', by one account.

The following year, Emil attended a ceremony to mark the fiftieth anniversary of the stadium at Mikkeli, in Finland. Dana was allowed to travel with him. The world would hardly have noticed had they not been there, so it seems fair to see this as an act of trust – or perhaps a test – on the regime's part. Huge numbers of Finns turned out to see Emil, and were rewarded by hearing him give a seven-minute speech in what his (superfluous) interpreter called 'beautiful' Finnish.

That year also saw the European athletics championships held in Prague. Emil kept a low profile, but one British journalist bumped into him at the stadium and was delighted to obtain his autograph, which he then showed proudly to a nineteen-year-old member of the British team. 'Who's Emil Zátopek?' was the response.

Some people remembered, though. The following year, George A. Hirsch, chairman of the New York Road Runners and founder of *The Runner* magazine, invited him to the USA to serve as grand marshal for the New York City Marathon. Emil spent several happy days being shown around the city, where, according to Hirsch, 'he captivated everyone with his engaging manner, bubbling storytelling, and absolutely unassuming demeanour'. At one point, he was taken to a meal in a Chinese restaurant, and impressed both waiters and guests by ordering in Chinese.

The race itself, Emil later said, 'was like a miracle for me – all those people jogging'. But a scarcely less memorable moment occurred the day before, when Hirsch took Emil to Central Park for some photographs, along with Bill Rodgers, the leading US marathon runner of the day. The photographer asked the driver of a passing parks department cart if he could stand on the cart's back step to photograph the three men as they jogged. The driver turned out to be from Prague, and, on realising who Emil was, rushed to embrace him. 'Zátopek!' he shouted, and was overcome by tears.

The subsequent photograph, of Hirsch, Rodgers and Emil jogging, sticks in the mind for three reasons. Emil, in shorts and T-shirt, looks strikingly fit. Rodgers and Hirsch, no underachievers themselves, are visibly thrilled to be running with him. Most memorably of all, Emil looks radiantly joyful, with an ear-to-ear grin and laughing eyes. This was him in his element: making people happy by sprinkling a bit of Zátopek magic into their lives.

The air miles began to accumulate. In June 1980, Emil and Dana spent two days in Zurich, where Emil had been invited to present the prizes at the West-athletic Cup by the Indian spiritual leader and running enthusiast Sri Chinmoy. At the airport, Chinmoy made to shake hands with him, but Emil folded his hands in the Indian way and said 'Namaskar' and continued to talk in Hindi until he ran out of remembered phrases (which related largely to drinking tea).

Then there were trips to Japan, to meet Kohei Murakoso, the great Japanese marathon champion; to Germany, to be official starter of the 1982 Frankfurt Marathon; and to Finland, in 1981 and 1983. For the latter trip, Emil was supposed to help promote sales of Czechoslovak tractors. He found himself having to demonstrate the alleged manoeuvrability of an enormous tractor and trailer combination, and credited his tank-driving experience for the fact that he did not make a mess of it.

Emil had retired by then. He and Dana both had, on the first day they were eligible to do so: 19 September 1982. Emil was not sorry to leave the documentation centre behind, although his final year had been enlivened by sharing the office with another sports star who had vanished under normalisation: Věra Čáslavská. She, too, was being grudgingly edged towards rehabilitation, and although she was even less enthusiastic about the work than Emil, their shared sense of humour helped pass the time. Sometimes, she told her biographer, 'work with him didn't even feel like working'.

Dana found that her annual pension was just 1,427 crowns: barely half what she had been expecting. When she enquired, she was told that it was because of 1968. She complained, pointing to her lifetime of service to her country as athlete, trainer and ambassador. She was told: 'Yes, but you signed the "Two Thousand Words". You will get no more.'

In fact, they were not too badly off. Emil had a pension, too, and they had saved enough over the years. Later on, a retainer to Emil from Adidas would add financial security – while further still into the future the house and garden in Troja would become a valuable piece of real estate. Yet it must have been dispiriting to realise that, getting on for quarter of a century later, and despite having lost all credibility as liberal reformers, they had still not been forgiven for their support for socialism with a human face.

Dana shrugged off her disappointment and continued to mentor young athletes in a less formal capacity for many years more. Emil responded, characteristically, by setting himself a new challenge, creating a large wine cellar, in the Moravian style, beneath a walnut tree in the garden. He put a considerable amount of effort into this, and in due course filled it with a considerable amount of wine, which might not have been a brilliant idea for a man who now had so much time on his hands but did help keep alive the Zátopeks' reputation for warm hospitality.

Around the same time, Ludvík and Olga Lišková invited Emil and Dana to a special celebration at Houštka Spa. Their friends wore Moravian costumes and welcomed them, in the traditional way, with bread and salt. It was a brave, poignant, heartfelt tribute – only slightly marred by the fact that the coaches who were using the track at the time hurriedly ushered their young athletes from the track, forbidding them even to go near the clubhouse window while the Zátopeks were present. It is possible that they would not have recognised him anyway: his name had long since been removed from school textbooks – just as it had been removed from the sports stadium in Kopřivnice, which had been renamed (and remains) the Summer stadium.

Yet the message must have sunk in eventually that Emil and Dana were no longer as toxic as they had once been. In 1983, the first World Athletics Championships were held in Helsinki. Emil was an honoured guest – and saw Grete Waitz win the women's marathon in a time only five minutes slower than his own victory on the same course in 1952. Back in Prague, there were enquiries from Juan Antonio Samaranch, president of the International Olympic Committee, about the possibility of meeting both Emil and Věra Čáslavská, so that he could honour them on behalf of the IOC. He was told that Emil was ill and Věra was unable to meet him because of family problems. He persisted, and eventually, in November 1984, he came to Prague and presented them both with the golden insignias of the IOC's Olympic Order.

By then, another Olympic Games had taken place: in Los Angeles. Emil did not go; nor did anyone from Czechoslovakia. Like the rest of the Warsaw Pact countries, they were boycotting the Games, in retaliation for the US boycott of the Moscow Olympics four years earlier. Asked for his views on the matter, Emil had been diplomatic but lukewarm. He gave his broad backing to the boycott but also expressed his sorrow for 'all athletes who have conscientiously trained for the Games and can't go now'. He said nothing about his own sorrow – although US sources suggested that, a few months earlier, he had been invited to be the torch-bearer at the Games. But he did observe pointedly that 'our [Czechoslovak] functionaries see their role model in the Soviet Union and follow every counsel the Soviets give them'.

He had learnt his lesson, though. Pressed to say more, he talked instead about his sincere distaste for the creeping commercialisation of the sport he loved. 'The modern Olympics should not be subject to commercial exploitation, but should glorify the ideals of the Olympics.'

Emil was reminded of what those ideals had once meant to him when, the following year, Les Perry arranged to fly him to Australia for the Jubilee running of the Zátopek race, which he, Percy Cerutty and Reg Prentice had set up in Melbourne in Emil's honour in 1961. According to the *Sydney Morning Herald*, 'The generosity, charm and charisma that so impressed John Landy, Les Perry and the other Australians who met him at the 1952 Helsinki Olympics were on display throughout his stay.' Emil not only attended the main race but also insisted on supporting all the lesser events, cheering, helping to officiate and presenting prizes. 'He had a word for each of the hundreds who met him,' the *SMH* continued. 'His presence transformed an otherwise mundane occasion into one to remember.'

It was an occasion to remember for Emil, too. 'I think he was genuinely touched to see a far-off country had recognised his achievements,' said Les Perry. But, of course, it was not just his achievements that were being honoured. All those years of kindness and charm, all those small courtesies and words of encouragement – that was what people were really trying to repay.

Whether they succeeded in soothing the scars on Emil's soul is a different matter. He still tended, sometimes, to drink too much – to such an extent that, if Dana was away, the Liškas would ring him up every now and then to see if he was all right. Olga used to challenge him to recite a tongue-twister, 'and if he couldn't say it we'd know that things were bad'. Sometimes, if they sounded really bad, or if there was no answer, they would drive over and check. On one such visit, in 1986, they found him on the floor. He had had a heart seizure.

Emil was out of hospital soon enough, but the episode brought a temporary halt to his travels. It also brought an end to his running. He had not been doing much anyway, despite regular encouragement from Dana, who seemed untouched by age, to go jogging with her. But it was still a huge, unwelcome landmark in a life that had been defined by running.

Age had not treated him kindly. Perhaps it was the years of self-torture on the track; or perhaps the more recent years of unhealthy living. More probably it was coming from a family with a history of cardiovascular problems. It was no less cruel for that. There would be other invitations, and other visits: for example, to London in September 1987 to be starter for the *Sunday Times* National Fun Run in Hyde Park, where, according to John Disley (who arranged it), 'He was a delight. He didn't need entertaining. He just disappeared into the crowd and started talking to people. He didn't hold himself aloof at all.'

There was, however, a difference. There could be no question of Emil joining in the running, as he had originally intended to do. And no matter how many other races he started in future, that single, crushing reality would not change. From now on the guest of honour would not be Emil the tamed but unbroken hero.

Instead, it would be Zátopek: the old man.

19

'Say it ain't so, Emil'

In the autumn of 1989, following months of unrest across Eastern Europe, the Berlin Wall came down. Czechoslovakia's Communist tyranny evaporated soon afterwards, abruptly as morning mist.

It was over in weeks. The Wall fell on 9 November. On 17 November, a student demonstration in Prague was broken up violently by police; days of wider protests followed, swelling in numbers until the crowds could be counted in hundreds of thousands; the police abandoned the streets. A wave of strikes began, culminating in the first general strike since 'victorious February' in 1948. A new pro-democracy movement, Civic Forum, came to the fore, and half-forgotten icons of the dissident movement began to be seen in public. More than 200,000 people packed Wenceslas Square on 24 November to cheer Václav Havel, the dissident playwright who had spent five of the past twelve years in jail, as he waved and spoke briefly from the balcony of the Melantrich building; then they listened in dumbstruck silence, hands raised in V-for-victory signs and tears streaming down careworn cheeks, as Marta Kubišová emerged from two decades of obscurity to sing 'A Prayer for Marta' from the same balcony.

The popular unity was irresistible. The despised First Secretary of the Communist Party, Miloš Jakeš, recognised that the game was up and resigned. The rest of the Party leadership followed suit. On 30 November, the Communist Party relinquished its monopoly on power. Free elections – the first since 1946 – were announced. By the end of the year, unthinkably, Václav Havel would be president and Alexandr Dubček would be speaker of the federal parliament.

Emil and Dana spent that first crucial fortnight of protest at home.

Then, on the day after the Party leadership's resignation, between 800,000 and a million people gathered on Letná plain – the park overlooking the city from which Stalin's statue had once loomed. It was a miraculous, haunting occasion; as if an entire people had emerged blinking into the daylight, still scarcely able to believe that now, perhaps, the land that had been theirs truly was coming back to them.

Emil and Dana joined them. Songs were sung and speeches were made and solidarity was expressed. Someone spotted Emil and suggested that he say something, too. He shook his head. 'This revolution belongs to other people,' he said. 'It is their world now.'

But Emil and Dana had to live in it, too, and they soon noticed the difference. There was no more fear of arbitrary disgrace and exile; no more looking over the shoulder for eavesdroppers. Censorship was abolished; borders were opened. On 11 March 1990, Emil was formally rehabilitated. Just ten weeks into Václav Havel's presidency, the new defence minister, Miroslav Vacek, publicly apologised for Emil's dismissal from the army.

In Troja, the phone began to ring. For a long time, it rarely stopped. Friends, admirers and curious journalists from around the world all wanted to know what their lost hero had been up to. One of the first to call was the Australian journalist Hedley Thomas, to whom Emil spoke with unaccustomed frankness about politics. He had not, he explained, been against the old regime: 'They gave me the chance to compete in the Olympic Games . . . Maybe on the one hand I was very keen to protest, but as Olympic champion I had more than other people.' The telephone interview was punctuated by angry shouts from Dana, trying to get him to shut up, but Emil would not be silenced. 'I am a Communist,' he insisted. 'But the problem with Communism is that people at the top become egotists . . . They had to have two or three houses, an account in a Swiss bank. This is not real Communism.'

There had, Emil admitted, been other drawbacks with the old regime. 'It was not possible to protest . . . This telephone was controlled . . . I was very careful not to say anything bad.'

Now, by contrast, the only control came from Dana, shouting in the background each time he said something positive about the old regime. 'In our house there is democracy,' Emil continued. 'We have different views.' To him, 'Communist ideology means to work and to give to society so nobody will die of hunger.'

Shortly afterwards, the call was cut off, possibly by Dana. The hard-learnt lesson that careless talk about politics can land you in bad trouble was not easily forgotten. For more than a decade, the Zátopeks had found a tolerable existence by disciplining themselves to live 'in the drawer'. Why risk coming out?

'Our hope is that all will be quiet and that we can live the last years of our life in a democracy,' Dana told another journalist, *Sports Illustrated*'s Leigh Montville, who visited them in Troja. 'We hope for peace and good health.'

For a while, that wish was granted. The quiet currents of their late lives flowed on: the meetings of the Old Guard; the birthdays and reunions; the pottering in the garden. There was much-loved new dog, a spaniel–terrier cross called Kuba (a diminutive of Jakub, not a tribute to the socialist state). Old friendships were rekindled. Ladislav Kořán – who had emigrated in 1968, arrived in the US with $5 in his pocket, started an electronics business and become a millionaire – took the opportunity to start making regular visits to his homeland. The Zátopek home was usually his first stop. Emil's trips abroad continued, too: to Spain, where he received the city of San Sebastián's Tambor de Oro award and met the family of his late friend Patxi Alcorta; to Argentina, where he was reunited with Reynaldo Gorno, runner-up in the 1952 Olympic marathon; even to California, where a group of physicians at Stanford University – who had paid for the trip – tried unsuccessfully to help with the sciatica in his left leg and Olga Fikotová-Connolly and her daughter showed him the opulence of Los Angeles. 'To live in such a place – how is it possible?' marvelled Emil.

The following year he went to Barcelona, for the Olympics, and at one point appeared on the track – to be applauded so warmly that it must have brought back memories of his days as a fairy-tale hero.

At times, it must have seemed reasonable to think in terms of living happily ever after. But no new dawn lasts for ever; or even, usually, for long. As the spectre of Communism receded, recriminations began. In December 1990, the secret service that had underpinned the Communist Party's dominance was dismantled. Inevitably, people began to ask what secrets were stored in its archives. Names of supposedly 'compromised' politicians began to be circulated. The government moved quickly to limit access. It has been estimated that during the Communist period one Czechoslovak in four assisted the secret services to some extent. The potential was obvious for an orgy of destructive finger-pointing – the last thing the country's delicate young democracy needed. In May 1992 the government drafted a law, enacted that summer, to restrict publication of the names of StB agents. Not until 1996 was the public given partial access to the archive. Even then, individuals were allowed to see only their own files, or those of dead family members, or to authorise others to do so; alternatively, they could inspect the general index. That was all. Many people decided not to exercise even that limited right, for fear of what they might find.

It would be several years before stories began to emerge about this or that public figure being mentioned in the archives (as many were) and thus being implicated as – perhaps – an StB informer or agent. And it was not until 1998 that word began to spread that Emil might be compromised. The claims were vague at first. President Havel had decided to award the Order of the White Lion – the country's most senior honour – to around ninety public figures, to mark the eightieth anniversary of Czechoslovakia's founding. Emil was to be one of them. The German newspaper *Süddeutsche Zeitung* complained that another proposed recipient, Helmut Zilk, the formerly Prague-based mayor of Vienna, was named in the archives as an StB informer. During the furore that followed, the right-wing politician Václav Benda, a former dissident who had briefly been head of the Office for the Documentation and Investigation of Crimes of Communism, announced that he had doubts about the integrity of several other of the candidates. It wasn't long before a television channel, Nova, was suggesting that one of those under suspicion was Emil Zátopek.

The charge didn't get much further at the time. Emil wasn't paying attention, and, in any case, had never been that worried about what people said about him. Yet the claim planted a seed of doubt that has been bothering Emil's admirers ever since – especially after it emerged that Emil's name could indeed be found in the general index of the StB archive.

In itself, that information implied little: you could be in the archives as an agent, an informant or a 'person of interest' – or, in many cases, as some combination of the three. That did not prevent gossip that 'Zátopek worked for the StB'. There had always been those who could not forgive Emil for his closeness to the regime; and a few who envied him his years of glory. His public climbdowns in the 1970s had tarnished his reputation further. Why not go all the way and mark him down as a Communist snitch?

What made the whisperings worse was that this was not the first time that suspicion had been attached to Emil. In November 1975, Josef Frolík, a senior StB officer who had defected to the US in 1969, gave evidence to a hearing on 'Communist Bloc Intelligence Activities in the United States' to the Senate's Committee on the Judiciary. His testimony included denunciations of prominent Czechoslovaks in most walks of life: politicians, entertainers, authors, diplomats and sportspeople, all of whom, he claimed, had been in the pay of the Czechoslovak intelligence service.

It included this:

> Emil Zátopek, the multiple Olympic victor in the 5-km, 10-km, marathon and endurance run events, has been an agent from the early fifties. He is one of the most cynical of agents who was even informing on his own wife Dana. During the period of the 'Prague Spring' he was being used as an agent-provocateur who, through his own activities and through participation in other operations, was supposed to help compromise the regime of A. Dubček and his supporters. He comes across like an anticommunist and as being very liberal.

For one reason or another, this sensational claim made no ripple in the media, even when a printed record of the testimony was made publicly available in 1976. Perhaps Emil's fame had faded so much by then that the handful of intelligence wonks who monitored such things didn't recognise his name, buried as it was among a series of sensational claims about the sex lives of famous cultural figures and the allegedly subversive activities of British politicians. In Czechoslovakia, meanwhile, the press was scarcely going to report the fact that a senior spy had defected and was pouring out secrets to the West.

But it was only a matter of time before Frolík's claim resurfaced – not least via his book, *Špión vypovídá*, which became available in Czechoslovakia in 1990. Emil's enemies were quick to repeat the allegations – although generally in whispers rather than in public. The rumours don't seem to have intruded much on Emil's existence. Today, however, with Emil no longer around to defend himself, you will find plenty of places on the internet where the allegations are repeated as fact.

And are they fact? Was Emil really working for the secret police, as informer, agent or both?

For a long time, even when I had secured Dana Zátopková's authorisation to inspect the security services' files on Emil, I simply didn't want to know the answer. It is one thing discovering, as I have while researching this book, that your hero was a flawed human being who sometimes did things that he should have been and probably was ashamed of. That's life. But Frolík's suggestion is that everything – the whole Zátopek legend of friendship, chivalry and shared humanity – was just one monstrous fraud. Can it possibly be true?

'Say it ain't so, Joe,' a young fan is supposed to have begged baseball hero Joe 'Shoeless' Jackson when Jackson was implicated in the fixing of the 1919 World Series. I feel much the same about Emil. Please, Emil, you have meant too much, for too long, to me and to so many others. Please don't let this be true.

Eventually, I looked. Frustratingly, even that didn't entirely resolve the matter. Once you enter the world of the spooks, it is hard to be 100 per cent sure of anything. Even gut feeling pulls in two directions. Who do you trust? Frolík – a man who lied for a living and was known to be a dirty tricks specialist? Or Emil, a warm, charming, kind, visibly decent man who made friends easily and inspired trust in nearly everyone he met? The question should answer itself – except that, when you think about it, all those qualities of charm and apparent decency would be precisely what a master of deception would need.

It's the same with the papers in the archive. There are, by my count, twenty-two surviving files relating to Emil in the archives of the StB and the ZS GŠ (Zpravodajská správa generálního štábu), its military counterintelligence sub-section. The former refer to him by the code name ATLET and the latter by the code name MACEK. Between them they contain some 320 pages of often abstruse records. Most are typed; some are handwritten; many are hard to decipher. It would be easy to miss something. Yet certain conclusions leap out at me. Emil is in these files as a 'person of interest', not an agent. He does seem to have reported back from some foreign trips, at least early in his career, but the reports have not been preserved – although at least one such report seems to have been considered unacceptably thin. And I can find no reference anywhere to Emil's having been an agent provocateur, or to his having informed on Dana, or, for that matter, to his having informed on anyone else.

Some of the reports are mind-numbingly mundane; many refer to Emil only in passing. As for the rest, the overwhelming impression is of a security service that sees Emil as an object of suspicion. The raw material comes largely from informers – Agent Vaško, Agent Saša, Agent Marie – who may or may not be reliable and who no doubt have agendas of their own. But there is no mistaking the agenda of the officers for whom the reports are written: they want to know what Emil is up to, where he is, who he is talking to, and what he is likely to do next.

Does that prove his innocence? More or less. But what if the day-to-day agents of the StB and the ZS GŠ weren't in on the plot? What if the reality involved some deep, John le Carré-style game of smoke, mirrors and triple-bluff? What if the archives don't tell the full story? There are gaps in the record: big ones. Some files have been destroyed – many, for some reason, in 1980. The Institute for the Study of Totalitarian Regimes assures me that this would probably have been a routine rationalisation of the records. Yet I can't help feeling uncomfortable about the fact that, where Emil is concerned, most of the 1950s and the first half of the 1960s are a complete blank. The fact that tens of thousands of other files in the archive have been destroyed doesn't really reassure me; nor does the fact that all sorts of people other than Emil (informers, for example, or agents) might have benefited from the destruction of his files. Suspicion poisons everything.

At this point, the only sane approach is to fall back on known facts and common sense. These suggest three things. First: if Emil really was a secret agent, he doesn't seem to have been a very successful one. He was active in the anti-invasion protests at a time when agents provocateurs weren't needed (everyone was protesting anyway) and then went quiet just when a bit of stirring up could conceivably have been useful. His anti-Soviet 'act', supposedly performed for their ultimate benefit, projected worldwide the idea that, in his unforgettable words, they 'have been shown up as the gangsters of the world'.

Wouldn't they have been better off without him? His supposed services to the StB and their Soviet overseers did not save him from four and a half years of internal exile – and if he informed on Dana, how come she didn't get into trouble? If it comes to that, what about all those countless kindnesses, large and small, that he showed to so many friends and strangers over so many years? If they were performed with an ulterior motive, why does no trace of those betrayals survive? It just doesn't make sense.

Secondly: other evidence argues against Emil's having been an StB agent. Close friends who lived and worked with him are adamant he was one of 'us' rather than 'them' – Ivan Ullsperger, for example, who actually lived at U Půjčovny for several months; or Ludvík Liška, who insists that 'we knew who they [the informers] all were' and says that Emil used to pull the wool over their eyes on foreign trips by deliberately mistranslating for them. There were clearly doubts in high places about Emil's political reliability. He didn't even become a member of the Communist Party until December 1953, and he was sent on at least one course of political education. In 1956, he and Dana were reportedly reprimanded shortly before leaving for Melbourne, after indiscreetly telling a Swiss journalist how much they hated being followed around by 'sharp eyes'. And Ladislav Kořán, while in Jáchymov, was interrogated more than once about Emil by the secret police, being asked specifically about the possibility that Emil might defect. Emil's military service records show that, throughout the 1950s and 1960s – and especially after 1968 – he was constantly being monitored by his army superiors for signs of ideological unreliability. If he was actually secretly working *for* the security services, there must have been so few people in on the plot that it is hard to see what purpose it could have served. As for his dealings with Westerners, one of the reasons given for his dismissal from the army, in a three-page internal report dated 21 April 1969, was that he 'doesn't report his contacts with foreign agents and citizens'. None of this seems consistent with Emil being a master agent.

Thirdly: there is no evidence of guilt in the archives; just Frolík's assertion and his enemies' suspicions. The fact that Emil is in the archive proves nothing. In the words of Dr Libor Svoboda, 'It would have been more suspicious if he hadn't had a file.' As for the missing files, Emil would hardly have been in a position to order their destruction, especially in 1980. Nor would he have had a motive: everyone assumed, then, that Communism would last for ever. As for Frolík: it is a fact, and not just a suspicion, that the StB were masters of disinformation, including the trick of smearing enemies as their own informers. They had a whole section – Department D – devoted to such practices. It makes more sense to doubt their version of events than Emil's. According to the British espionage expert James Rusbridger, 'It is now generally accepted that Frolík was a plant designed to waste MI5's resources while important spies remained undetected and to sow seeds of distrust between MI5 and the CIA.' I must admit to being both convinced and relieved by Rusbridger's judgement. I cannot categorically prove that Emil was not an agent of some kind – how do you prove a negative? – but in the absence of plausible evidence that he was it seems foolish to consider him anything but innocent. Or, at least, relatively innocent.

These allegations do not come completely out of the blue. Over the years, Emil was repeatedly tainted by his perceived closeness to the Communist tyranny. He may not have been an agent, but his record is far from perfect. He allowed his name to be used in the denunciation of Milada Horáková in 1950; was unsupportive, to put it mildly, towards his fellow runner Milan Švajgr in 1952; turned his back, in 1970 and 1972, on those who had stood beside him in calling for liberty and denouncing the Soviet invasion; condemned Charter 77; and those are just the instances we know about.

A series of critics have excoriated him for this, from Milan Švajgr, who called him a 'snitch', to the historian Stanislav Berton (another Moravian former athlete who failed to achieve lasting glory on the track), who wrote in 2009 that Emil 'sold his soul to the Communist regime'. Luděk Pachman, too, was scathing about him in his autobiographical *Checkmate in Prague* (although others have been equally scathing about Pachman's reliability).

To fail to address such attacks would do Emil an injustice; but I do not think they are fair. Yes, Emil made compromises with one of Communism's nastier regimes. These do him no credit, and one or two were to his lasting shame. But to suggest that his support for the regime was some kind of guilty secret is absurd. It was public: that was the point of it.

As for the StB, Emil clearly spent a lot of time in their company. Most athletes did. 'They tried to keep themselves secret, but we always recognised them,' says Dana. Some kept their distance more successfully than others. There was one, Dana adds, a Mr Lala, with whom 'we all used to discuss what he should put in his reports about us and what he should leave out'; and another who they persuaded to help out with training by retrieving shots and javelins for the throwers – 'because he might as well do something useful'. With Emil, there were certainly some 'sharp eyes' who took pride in being attached to such a great man – just as that American soldier did, escorting his one-man Czechoslovak team around the track in Berlin in 1946. It would have been out of character for Emil not to talk to them at all (although Pavel Kosatík claims that if he ever talked *about* them, 'it was always as about people whom he feared'). No doubt he was sometimes indiscreet.

Dana is dismissive of the darker charges against Emil, including Frolík's. 'People say all sorts of things. Once you're famous, people start saying anything about you. If you let yourself be bothered by it all, you would never do anything.' She reckons that Emil would have been a hopeless spy. 'They wouldn't have wanted him, because he was so talkative. He would have given away every secret.' Indeed, she claims that one of her 'tame' 'sharp eyes' told her that the StB agreed with this diagnosis.

She also argues that some things that might look like 'collaboration' on paper were actually more trivial than they sound – and perhaps were even close to subversion. Once, before going to race in Paris, Emil was instructed to report back on how many aeroplanes he saw there. He shared this mission with his fellow athletes: 'Quick, everyone, help me. How many planes can you see?' It became the running joke of the trip: 'Look, Emil – a plane!' Presumably at some point the StB were presented with a number. It may not have been of much use.

I feel sure that Emil was not working for the security services in or after 1968: the evidence seems overwhelming that he was their target, not their collaborator. I wouldn't be entirely surprised, though, if the StB archives once contained reports of some kind relating to Emil's foreign trips – or even, conceivably, to his visits to military units around Czechoslovakia. (One of the most persistent rumours is that he worked for military counter-intelligence.) That does not make him a monster or a fraud – and not just because there was so much kindness and decency to set against his moments of weakness. Everyone who lived in Czechoslovakia between 1948 and 1989 faced choices that most of us can barely imagine. Zdeněk Fator, for example, was once called in for interrogation by the StB because he had been associating with an unsuitable friend. He was subsequently put under pressure to become an informer. When he refused, he was told: 'You have a very intelligent son, Mr Fator. Do you really want to ruin his life before he even has a chance to go to university?'

Fator was lucky. He escaped from this trap by having a word with a friend in the sporting world who was also a senior member of the security services. The pressure stopped. But that, too, sheds light on Emil's case. Everyone involved in the tragedy of Czechoslovak Communism was a human being. Some were evil; most were just trying to make the best of things. People compromised; threw the security services scraps of information to keep them off their backs; or did what they had to do but tried to do so in a humane way, bending or even breaking rules to minimise suffering.

And Emil? I think he conformed where he felt he had to, filled in the questionnaires he was supposed to fill in for foreign trips, perhaps shared some additional impressions and gossip about the countries he had visited – and then got on with living. I don't think he collaborated with the StB in a cynical or ill-intentioned way. No doubt his fame and his public support for Communism will have earned him an easier ride than many citizens, and it is likely that he escaped harsher retribution after 1968 because there were people in high places who liked him. Does that make him an agent, or an intelligence officer?

It is possible that Emil's garrulous nature may sometimes have got people into trouble. Once, he earned his dear friend Olga Lišková a reprimand by absent-mindedly revealing that she had lent him an ideologically unsound book. She knew it was he who blabbed because he told her – and was surprised to be told that he had done something wrong. 'But why would I not say it,' he asked, 'when it's true?' This reminds us that his working life was spent in the army, in the Ministry of Defence and at Dukla Praha – three of the most dogmatically pro-regime institutions in the country. He did not have to be a secret informer for word of what he said and did to get back to the security services.

I think Emil knew this, and sometimes led the StB on – just as he led most of the Communist establishment on. He probably believed much of what he said in his pro-regime speeches, but he later confessed that at the end of at least one of them, delivered to him in triplicate in advance from the Ministry of Defence, he felt like weeping. Yet I'm not aware of his ever having dug his heels in and refused to deliver them. Perhaps he should have done. Even Ivan Ullsperger, a close friend to whom Emil often confided his political misgivings, concedes that 'only on a few occasions would he step up against it' – 'it' being the regime.

Even in free societies, few of us speak our minds all the time. You can call it dissembling if you like, but it is how we get by, and it is how most people got by under Communism, too – the only difference being that, under Communism, the quality of your dissembling could make the difference between freedom and imprisonment, even life and death. And with Emil, remember, it wasn't just dissembling. He believed in Communism. Unlike some of his subsequent critics (such as Luděk Pachman and Pavel Kohout, before they became liberals), he was never an aggressive Communist. He just believed that Communism was preferable to capitalism. And – who knows? – perhaps, if everyone had been like Emil, Communism might have worked.

Emil was, Ullsperger believes, 'too trusting', and people in the regime 'took advantage of him'; Dana says much the same, as does Ludvík Liška. They all use the same expression: 'took advantage'. People didn't just bully him into supporting 'it': they persuaded and manipulated him, using his socialist beliefs to convince him that giving in to their demands was not just the easy thing to do but the right thing. Emil had a habit, according to Ullsperger, of starting an argument believing one thing but ending it believing the opposite. It is clear from the StB archives that Ullsperger was not the only person to notice this susceptibility.

To paint Emil as the villain in Czechoslovakia's tragedy is to misunderstand both it and him. He was a victim: not a blameless one, but a victim none the less. He spent most of his adult life being bullied and ordered around: by the Baťa management, by the Nazis, by his superiors in the army, by the ČSTV, by the StB, by the Czechoslovak Communist Party; by the Soviet Union (indirectly); and, not least, by some of the more forceful personalities in the reform movement. Amazingly, he preserved his inimitable character largely intact, with all its childlike kindness, eccentricity and spontaneity. Sometimes – in 1952, in 1968 – he took a stand, and in each case showed immense personal courage by doing so. But if he lacked the strength to defy them all head-on, all of the time, that isn't entirely surprising. Ultimately, there was only one sphere in which he had the self-belief to be certain that he was right, even when the clamour of voices telling him he was wrong was deafening, and that was running.

Czech history is littered with the charred remains of heroes who refused to compromise in the face of irresistible force. Czech geography, too: just look at all the streets and squares named after Jan Hus – forefather of European Protestantism – or, more recently, Milada Horáková or Jan Palach. Emil was well aware of the eternal battle in his nation's soul between pragmatism and principle, unpalatable surrender and suicidal defiance. The Czechoslovak army, which played such an important part in his life, could have fought Hitler in 1939 – and been utterly destroyed. It chose instead to survive. By contrast, the 'Orphan' or Taborite army that refused to compromise in the Hussite Wars was annihilated more or less in its entirety at the Battle of Lipany in 1434. I mention this obscure detail because Emil himself raised it, in one of his addresses on Wenceslas Square in 1968, to illustrate the futility of doomed defiance. History mattered to Czechoslovaks. They were caught in the middle of it.

Defiance looks good on paper. In real life, it comes at a price that many cannot bring themselves to pay. As Dana once put it: 'What good is it if someone says five or ten years after you are dead that you are a hero? Maybe don't be such a big hero. Maybe be alive, instead.'

Ivan Ullsperger cites the contrasting examples of Jan Hus and Galileo Galilei. Hus, who had publicly defied the then irresistible Roman Catholic Church, refused repeated opportunities to recant in 1415 – and was burnt at the stake. Two centuries later, Galileo defied the same church over his claim that the Earth moved round the Sun – but then, threatened with the stake, recanted. He lived, and is supposed to have muttered later: 'Yet it does move.' 'Emil,' says Ullsperger, 'was of the same view as Galileo.'

It is a good comparison. Yet perhaps an even more helpful one comes not from history but from literature, in the person of the most famous of all Czech fictional characters: Josef Švejk. Jaroslav Hašek's comic creation – hero of his 1921 masterpiece, *The Good Soldier Švejk* – drinks and shirks his way through the First World War with unfailing cheerfulness thanks to his simple yet subtle tactic of feigning obedience. His superiors have a nagging suspicion that he is taking them for a ride, yet they can never quite put their finger on it. Švejk, meanwhile, gets on with enjoying life as best he can.

Some say that 'Švejking' has become a Czech national characteristic: a technique by which the powerless individual can maintain a degree of independence in the face of irresistible state power. If this is true, then I suspect Emil was a Švejker.

There are worse things to be guilty of; just as there are worse failings than imitating Galileo. Given what I at one point feared, I am happy to leave these faults on the debit side of Emil's life. There is plenty on the other side to balance them.

20

The last lap

On the first day of 1993, Czechoslovakia was dissolved. Its seventy-four-year life story had been almost contemporaneous with Emil's. Like him, it had known peace and war; poverty and prosperity; social democracy, Nazi occupation and Communist tyranny; and now, finally, another attempt at democracy. At this point, it quit while it was ahead, divorcing itself, painlessly but a little sadly, into the Czech Republic and Slovakia.

Emil outlived the land to which he had brought such glory. He was frail now, but he had not given up. As the world remade itself around him, he settled into the quiet endgame of his life: a kind of lap of honour in which the great currents of history were no longer his concern, and his gaze was more likely to be drawn to the familiar horizons of the past than to seek out new, unexplored ones.

That August, Emil and Dana spent a week on holiday in Finland, in Kuopio, in the north. Láďa Kořán and his American wife, Vaneesa, joined them. Once again, the Finnish atmosphere worked its magic: the round-the-clock daylight made the holiday feel like a happy dream. But Emil was conscious that he was just another tourist, heavy-footed and thick-waisted. He was no longer the unmistakable, charismatic hero he had been four decades earlier, and the absence of adoring fans may have troubled him. At one point on the trip, the friends decided that their evening would benefit if they went out and bought a bottle of wine. Emil asked a passer-by for directions. The man complimented Emil on his Finnish, and, noticing his accent, asked him where he was from. Emil told him. 'Ah,' said the stranger, 'the land of Zátopek.'

'I am Zátopek,' said Emil.

The stranger stared incredulously, then flung his arms round him. 'Zátopek! Zátopek!' he exclaimed. Or perhaps it was 'Satu Peka!'

Emil wept.

So it continued: alternate obscurity and acclaim, at home and abroad. As time went by, the foreign trips became rarer; news of the deaths of friends more frequent. But the reunions with long lost figures from the past grew, if anything, warmer. Emil caught up, for example, with Jan Haluza, his first trainer, who, like Láďa Kořán, had somehow survived Jáchymov. They had kept in touch, sporadically, after his release, but had disagreed about the significance of Haluza's contribution to Emil's success. A blurred but vivid photograph of the two old friends hugging, wreathed in smiles, at Haluza's ninetieth birthday party in July 1994 is a vivid reminder that the friendships forged on the athletics track endure better, and perhaps mean more, than the glory won there.

Later that summer, Emil and Dana returned yet again to Finland, this time to Helsinki, for the European athletics championships. At one point, Emil was spotted in the background at a medal ceremony and was warmly applauded. Yet perhaps it was the place itself that meant most to them: 'Our golden town,' Dana called it – the scene of those miraculous days all those decades ago, when everything went right for both of them, and the world shared their joy, and it seemed as though the daylight would never fade.

This time, the midnight sun obscured the fact that, high in the night skies above them, among all those constellations named after the heroes and heroines of Greek myth, a tiny asteroid was glittering, somewhere between Mars and Jupiter, that had just had its name changed from '1989 WH4' to 'Zátopek' – a fitting tribute to a man whose legend must surely have inspired more people in the twentieth century than Perseus and Andromeda combined.

Back on earth, however, time was running out. In 1995 Emil was invited to Athens for an event relating to the impending centenary of the modern Olympic marathon. The morning after he left Prague, Dana was surprised to receive a telephone call from the organisers, asking where Emil was. After several hours of frantic enquiry, it emerged that he had collapsed on arrival at Athens airport – having had a small stroke. He was rushed to hospital, where no one knew who he was. Only when Emil had recovered his senses sufficiently to say (since he knew no Greek) the words 'Olympic Committee' was he tracked down.

By the time he came home, a few days later, 'You wouldn't have noticed there was anything wrong with him,' says Dana. Understandably, though, it shook him badly. It was another grim landmark in a journey whose destination was all too obvious.

He became depressed. All his siblings were dead now, apart from Jiří; most had died from cardiovascular illness. His friends were slipping away, too, with the great rivals of the past seemingly the most susceptible: Gordon Pirie had died in 1991, Gaston Reiff in 1992, Reynaldo Gorno in 1994. Others, such as Alain Mimoun, increasingly kept in touch by telephone rather than in the flesh.

Yet there always seemed to be something that brought him back from despair. Sometimes it was an unexpected visitor; sometimes it was a chat with his next door neighbour; sometimes it was his work as a figurehead for the Foundation of the Czech Sports Representation; sometimes it was another ripple of glory from the past.

In June he was guest starter for the first Prague International Marathon. Then there was a cameo appearance in a high-profile Adidas TV advertisement that linked the brand explicitly to Emil's story. It never quite spelled out the claim that Emil won his medals in Adidas shoes, but few who viewed it will have noticed. For Emil, the association was more important for offering a useful strand of extra income that he might reasonably hope would help keep him secure during a long, contented retirement.

He was not rich, considering all that he had achieved. But he never wanted much. Sport continued to reward him, periodically, with comforts of a certain kind: dinners, hotels, flights. Possessions didn't interest him. Dana kept their remaining medals and trophies locked away in a drawer, so that Emil wouldn't give any more away. She only found out about Ron Clarke's one years after the event.

He would have liked children. That ache never went away, and perhaps in old age it was more noticeable, like the ache in his left leg. But he had Dana, and Kuba, and the house and garden; a steady stream of friends, dignitaries and strangers eager to share his memories; and just enough public duties to reassure him that his achievements had not been entirely forgotten.

But memories were fading. On a trip to Berlin, to be guest of honour at an ISTAF Grand Prix meeting in September 1995, Emil was seen sitting unrecognised and awkward in the stands. The organisers appeared to have forgotten to introduce him to the spectators; one official even seemed to hustle him away from the medal ceremony. The stars of the event, Haile Gebrselassie and Moses Kiptanui, admitted afterwards that they had little or no idea who he was.

The German film-maker Hagen Bossdorf followed Emil on this trip; the resulting documentary is sometimes harrowingly poignant. Emil is just another old man: harmless and perhaps a little afraid; still the person he used to be, but made invisible by ill health and age. It ends with Emil's arrival back in Prague. Dana and Kuba are there to meet him at the station. His tired face lights up when he sees them, and there is something about the way that he and Dana hug each other that make your eyes prick with tears. There is so much tenderness, so much trust – it reminds me of something that Jaromír Konůpka said about Emil and Dana: 'Those two: they had been looking for one another.'

She takes him gently by the hand and leads him home.

By 1996, Emil was finding it difficult to walk and usually did so with a stick. The old energy had gone: left to himself he would sit in a chair, reading newspapers or dozing. It was frustrating for Dana, who remained fit and cheerful. She felt that he had become pessimistic and, by his standards, 'lazy'. Yet in a curious way it was the closest they had been for years; and sometimes, even then, Emil's cheerful, life-affirming self could be goaded back into life. Dana used to urge him to cut wood for the stove – less because they needed it than to keep him active. It probably helped; as it did when friends came round, and the old instincts to entertain and to welcome would kick in.

By 1997, however, there were crueller challenges to deal with. Two photographs of Emil and Dana, one taken on their seventieth birthday and one on their seventy-fifth, tell the story with harsh clarity. Dana has hardly changed from one to the other: still handsome, smiling, animated. Emil is barely recognisable. In 1992 he seems confident and robust. Five years later he looks shrunken, puffy-faced and stooped, with an unaccustomed hint of confusion in his eyes. He could be a decade older than the soulmate who was born within a few hours of him.

His facial expression is particularly haunting. Anyone who has had any kind of contact with dementia will recognise the fixed mask of bewilderment that can seize even the most animated among us. It was never overwhelming, in Emil's case, and it was disguised by the ease with which, once he was in the groove of a much-told story, he could tell it as joyfully as ever. But there was no getting away from the fact that, by the second half of the 1990s, bouts of forgetfulness or confusion were sometimes muddying the flow of his thoughts. For a man whose greatness had so much to do with the burning clarity of his mind, it was a particularly cruel affliction.

In 1997 Emil Zatopek was elected Czech 'Athlete of the Century', which seems an understatement. His world records had long since been broken – the last fell in 1965 – but no one, Czech or otherwise, had come close to challenging his breathtaking dominance as an Olympian and a sporting figurehead. By the time President Havel presented Emil with the Order of the White Lion in 1998 – and the whisperings about being a collaborator began – he may not have known much about it. Perhaps it wouldn't have meant much to him anyway – he had, after all, received so many trophies, medals and honours before; and the award came only four days after an arguably more momentous occasion: his fiftieth wedding anniversary. But attempts to mark that landmark with a special radio celebration were hampered by Emil's health: the programme makers were shocked at how tired and confused he seemed. Still, at least his countrymen – or some of them – were trying to make some kind of amends before it was too late.

They were only just in time. Not long afterwards, Emil had a second stroke, from which he awoke speaking only English. Not until Dana took him home was he persuaded to speak Czech again. 'Me and Kuba nursed him back to health,' she says. But she sensed that he was losing the will to live. 'At this age,' he told Dana, 'there is no shame in dying.'

Yet his spirit had not quite surrendered; nor had he forgotten one of his guiding principles: that 'the people love us, Dana – we have to love them back'. Whatever else happened, he still liked to make people feel special. Vaneesa Kořán remembers a car journey through Moravia, with Dana, Emil and Láďa. Emil, in poor health, seemed largely oblivious to what was going on. Then they slowed down in a small village. 'I know a good restaurant here,' declared Emil. Before they knew it he was out of the car, asking for directions and, once someone had worked out who he was, happily trying to sign autographs – it was no longer easy for him – for the crowd of young people who mobbed him.

In 1999, the British journalist Alasdair Reid visited Emil in Troja in connection with a feature he was writing. Knowing that Emil's health was poor, Reid took an interpreter with him, but Emil insisted on speaking in English. It was clear, however, that he was finding it hard work retrieving the words he wanted, so Reid suggested, several times, that they speak in Czech. Emil raised his hand and said, very firmly: 'You are a guest in my house, so we will speak in your language.' As Reid later wrote in the *Sunday Herald*, following Emil's death: 'The obituaries recorded the victories of one of the greatest sportsmen ever, but the memory I treasured was of the character revealed in that simple moment of courtesy, and of the human decency he still held dear towards the end of a life of towering achievements and adversities overcome.'

But even the greatest champion cannot overcome adversities for ever. A third stroke, towards the end of that year, damaged Emil still further. The doctor overseeing his treatment revealed that, after the immediate crisis, Emil spent a 'tough week full of deep depression, hardly communicating, sometimes delirious, hardly recognising anyone and not wanting to live. Sometimes he refused to open his eyes.' Eventually, Emil started calling for someone, but no one could recognise the name. Then they realised what he was saying: 'Kuba.'

Dana and Kuba nursed him again, but his final months were dominated by medical mishaps. A fall in October 1999 left him with a broken hip from which he never fully recovered; when he did come home from hospital he spent most of his time sleeping. He joked that he was 'practising for eternal sleep – we endurance runners like to practise a lot'. A bout of pneumonia in September 2000 put him in hospital for a week that included his seventy-eighth birthday; and then, finally, on 30 October he had a stroke from which he would not recover.

For three weeks, the nation and the world of sport hung on the daily news bulletins. He was in a 'serious condition'; he was 'tired'; he had a 'high fever'; his condition was 'sad and very critical'; he was 'on artificial ventilation'. Anxious visitors began to appear. When the Liškas visited, Emil seemed vaguely aware of them. Asked who Ludvík was, he said, 'He's a nice man.' When the Kořáns visited, he seemed to recognise that Vaneesa was there and muttered something that might have been English.

As the end approached, Dana telephoned Emil's closest friends and advised them to come and say goodbye. 'When I came out of that room,' recalls Zdeněk Fator, 'I cried for half an hour. When I went home, my eyes were red like a rabbit's. My wife asked me what had happened to me. I said, "I was saying goodbye to the idol of my life."'

On 22 November, Emil died. The greatest of all endurance runners could not hold on for ever; and, indeed, Dana felt that he had chosen not to hold on. He knew his race was run.

The world, which had ignored him for so long, woke up abruptly to what it had lost. Obituarists retold his story in more languages than even he could have understood; his face gazed out of front pages as well as back; not since Helsinki had he had such global acclaim. In Britain he was 'Zatopek the great'; in France an 'Olympic legend'; in China he was 'Champion of the People'. 'As an athlete he is unequalled and never will be equalled,' wrote Chris Brasher in the *Daily Mail*. The *Sydney Morning Herald* mourned 'the passing of his golden ideals' and quoted Ron Clarke's tribute to 'probably the greatest track athlete of all time'. Clarke added the crucial point that: 'It wasn't just what he did but how he did it.'

'This is a sad day not only for sports people, who saw embodied in Zátopek all the virtues of a champion,' said Lamine Diack, president of the International Amateur Athletics Federation, 'but also for the common people who recognised in Zátopek an honest and intransigent defender of the fundamental principles of dignity and freedom of the individual. Emil Zátopek knew the greatest triumphs and the greatest suffering and that is what will keep him as an eternal symbol of athletics . . .'

Milan Jirásek, head of the Czech Olympic Committee, said something similar: 'With his death, the legend does not disappear. Everywhere in the world, even young generations know him and his achievements.' President Havel, who wrote personally to Dana, added a small but obvious point that many of Emil's compatriots had, by then, forgotten: 'His results made our country famous.'

But for Alain Mimoun, and for many others, the loss was more personal. 'I am losing a brother, not an adversary,' he said sadly. 'It was fate that brought me together with such a gentleman.'

The funeral was held on 6 December, at the National Theatre in Prague. There had been talk of a state funeral, but Dana asked for it to be kept simple. It was; but every seat in the large theatre was filled, and thousands of people queued outside as Emil's coffin was carried in, wrapped in the Czech flag and borne by leading athletes of the day. Inside, a small folk orchestra played on a stage radiant with bouquets, to an auditorium packed with statesmen, athletes, diplomats and friends, including Czech Prime Minister Miloš Zeman. President Havel was ill but was represented by his wife. Old friends and rivals who had come from around the world included Alain Mimoun, John Disley and Lasse Viren, and the Portuguese marathon champion Rosa Mota. Jindřich Roudný spoke briefly, in a voice fragile with emotion: 'You always fought with all your heart,' he said to Emil's coffin. 'You never let your fans down.'

'It was a lovely service,' says Olga Lišková – although, as someone pointed out on the day, Emil used to say, 'Better an ugly wedding than a lovely funeral.' 'It was a moving experience,' says John Disley. 'The theatre was packed. And I think Dana was glad that we took the trouble to come.'

Juan Antonio Samaranch took the opportunity to award Emil, posthumously, the Pierre de Coubertin medal, the IOC's highest honour; Lamine Diack awarded him the IAAF's Golden Order of Merit. There was something slightly futile about the gestures: what use did Emil have for two more medals that he would never see and couldn't even give away? But Samaranch spoke words that bear repeating, fifteen years later. 'Emil was a living legend,' he said. 'And a legend never dies.'

Outside, as the coffin was taken away for cremation, members of the army from which Emil had once been summarily dismissed fired a salute in his honour under a cold, grey sky. Traffic halted; onlookers stood silently. Then, quite by chance, the bells of nearby St Ursula's church began to ring. Someone clapped, and a great wave of applause – Emil's last – swept along the pavements. Dana watched, supported by friends on both sides, her face hollowed out by horror and grief. It was as if all that miraculously preserved youth and optimism had leaked out in an instant, leaving only an agonised mask of bereavement – white skin, red mouth, red eyes, like a thin parody of a clown.

They had been born on the same day, married on the same day, won Olympic gold on the same day. It would have been too much to hope to die on the same day as well.

Epilogue

Gold dust

I am sitting on the low doorstep of an old wooden church, running my fingers through dry Moravian earth. I can feel the glow of autumn sun through high, deciduous trees; my skin is sticky with evaporating sweat. Out of sight, some children are squealing. I am thinking about dust and ashes.

There is a line of graves in front of me. One is bright with flowers. It always is at this time of year: 19 September. His birthday. Her birthday.

I am sitting because I am too tired to stand. I have just run, with 184 other people, the half-marathon distance from Kopřivnice, Emil's birthplace, to Rožnov pod Radhoštěm, his last resting place. Dana brought his ashes here six months after the big National Theatre funeral and buried them in a separate ceremony – or most of them, anyway. Shortly after his cremation, unable to bear the thought of being parted from her soulmate for ever, she removed some and took them back to Troja. She keeps them in her apartment there (she sold the house a few years after Emil's death), in a blue and white Moravian jug which she brings down from the windowsill on special occasions, so that old friends can toast him.

The rest of his remains are here, in Rožnov, beneath a pair of big, grey, lichen-smeared boulders. One of them is blank: waiting, according to Dana, 'for me'. On the other, the carved bas-relief of a runner seems to struggle restlessly, like a sleeper caught in a dream of immobility. The plot looks small and bald, despite the flowers. All that life, all that energy, all that world-enhancing human warmth – all reduced to this: to ashes and to dry, Moravian dust.

It seems an apt image for a thought that has recently been preying on my mind: the thought that something similar has happened to my hopes as Emil's biographer. I set out, barely a year ago, to celebrate the life and soul of one of sport's noblest heroes. Somehow I seem to have spent much of my time since then probing his alleged shortcomings.

It has been hard to resist. Czechs have been picking at Emil's faults since the day he died; sometimes mercilessly. Within a month of his death, he had been denounced on the radio as a 'decadent' or 'fallen' character by the director of the National Gallery, while Josef Frolík's allegations had been raised on television, on the *Katovna* talk show. The internet, just getting into its stride then, has been catching up ever since. The exiled poet Jiřina Fuchsová wrote a blog describing Emil as an 'StB colonel' on the day of his funeral. Some time later, someone dug up his letter about Milada Horáková. The narrative of 'Zátopek the Communist stooge' took root: the last time I looked at Emil's Czech Wikipedia page it stated without qualification that he was a secret collaborator of military counter-intelligence.

It is not as if Emil went un-judged in his lifetime, either: by the Communists who thought he had betrayed them and by the anti-Communists who thought he had betrayed *them*. We in the West could afford to ignore such squabbles; but many Czechs, understandably, cared. The glory he brought to his nation and the honour he brought to his sport were often submerged beneath the claims and counter-claims. Perhaps that is what Emil's brother Jiří had in mind when he said, in 2002: 'He travelled around the world and was welcomed everywhere. But in our country they scorned him.'

Sitting in judgement over our fellow human beings is both easy and habit-forming. It's not just a Czech thing. But that's not what keeps the happier parts of the internet abuzz with Zátopek. Go to any runners' website – any blog, forum or chat-room – and before long you will come across a corner where Emil's memory is celebrated. Most are joyous, energising jumbles of truths and half-truths, memories, motifs and myths. So many of us have felt our lives brightened by Emil's story; naturally, we want to spread the good news. Not all the news is 100 per cent accurate, but who has it broadly right? The finger-pointers? Or the running enthusiasts who look at Emil's life and see cause for awe and rejoicing?

Emil may not have been, as Alain Mimoun claimed, 'a saint', but he had saintly qualities: an innocent, great-hearted spirit that prompted another Olympic great, Herb Elliott, to describe him as 'sophisticated because he is so simple'. There is certainly something saintlike about the cult that surrounds him: the way that stories are repeated and embroidered and cherished and enthusiastically passed on. To throw a cold bucket of investigative water over such a cult seems mean-spirited – and risks missing the point. It's as fruitless as worrying about what kind of person the real, historical St Francis was. So what if the flesh and blood man once kicked a cat on a bad day? The St Francis who matters – simple, compassionate and miraculously attuned to his fellow creatures – is the semi-mythical figure of Christian tradition.

Is it stretching my hero-worship too far to suggest that something similar applies to Emil? It matters little how much of the Emil legend was real and how much mere pretence or aspiration – not least because, if an illusion is wonderful enough, even the illusionist can be changed by it. As the journalist Caitlin Moran once observed, albeit in a different context, 'constantly pretending to be a decent person, and actually being one, are basically the same thing.'

Emil wasn't perfect – but he had a pretty good stab at it. Like millions of other Czechoslovaks, he had the misfortune to live under a regime that trapped all who lived under it in the same cruel dilemma: submit to the Party – or be (at best) a second-class citizen. Failing to emerge from such a tragedy with a spotlessly white paper trail isn't just forgivable: it doesn't need forgiving. What Emil did emerge with was decades' worth of evidence that, at every stage of his life, he retained his humanity, his childlike idealism and his belief that, through his own energy and kindness, he could make other people's lives brighter. Officialdom never stopped being exasperated by him. Ordinary people never stopped feeling empowered and inspired by him. It is hard to imagine a less appropriate response to such achievements than finger-pointing.

Emil's magic mattered partly because the times he lived in were so dark and dangerous. It worked because the kind of hero he aspired to be, or to impersonate, was the kind of hero the divided world needed. Like a shining knight in the Dark Ages, he seemed to offer hope simply by virtue of his perceived character: strong, brave, confident, selfless, magnanimous, tireless, light-spirited, chivalrous. How much of this perception was real and how much invented is of secondary importance.

In his 1967 book, *Běží Zátopek* ('Zátopek runs'), Emil describes sitting on a train, travelling from Hulín to Staré Město in south Moravia, and watching a little boy with his nose pressed to the window. The boy suddenly points to a passing runner and shouts: 'Look, Mum! Zátopek!'

'How do you know it was Zátopek?' asks his mother.

'He was running,' says the boy.

His mother explains that not everyone who runs is necessarily Zátopek, but the boy refuses to be persuaded. 'Zátopek can run best of all,' he adds.

Emil, all the time, is sitting opposite, unrecognised in his officer's uniform.

It is possible that this actually happened. It is also possible that Emil 'borrowed' the incident from Ladislav Kořán; or that it was pure invention. Yet the core message is rock-solid truth: Emil inspired people. Young, old, talented, ordinary; Czech, Slovak, foreign; Communist and capitalist. All through my Czech travels, I have been meeting them: from Zdeněk Fator, who was inspired to take up running as a ten-year-old boy after seeing Emil win the Rošický Memorial Race in Prague in 1947 ('We asked him for his autograph and he talked to us, and from that moment I wanted to be like him'), to Miloš Škorpil, the Czech Republic's most famous ultra-runner, who was inspired to take up serious running after Emil paid a visit to his school in 1967 ('After that, I started running in winter, through the snow, in heavy shoes').

Even now, the name of Zátopek casts its spell over countless young lives by introducing them to the great adventure of running. Dana, who fired the starting gun for today's race and will shortly be presenting the prizes, has spent much of the past forty-eight hours visiting schools in and around Kopřivnice. She does this every year, as part of a birthday ritual that also takes in this Emil Zátopek memorial race through the countryside. The Emil Zátopek elementary school and the nearby Milada Horáková elementary school are just two of the places where she has watched children running 'mini-Zátopek' races. They are clearly thrilled by Dana's beaming presence, and scream with excitement as they run – first for victory and then, with scarcely less fervour, for the extra prize of touching Dana or being photographed with her. Lack of enthusiasm among young people for vigorous exercise, as widespread in the Czech Republic as anywhere else, doesn't seem to be a problem in Emil's birthplace. And, who knows, maybe as they run their laps of their small tracks, some of these children feel an awakening sense of the possibilities of the world beyond Kopřivnice, just as Emil did when he was their age. One former pupil of the Emil Zátopek school, Lenka Masná, now competes at World Championship level in the 800m.

Here in Rožnov pod Radhoštěm, I stand up to bring my stiffening legs back to life. As I do so, I notice that other runners are strolling, singly and in pairs, among the graves. Some are already showered and changed. You can still recognise them: the thin frames, the glow of post-race satisfaction; and the way they glance from grave to grave before pausing when they find the one they were looking for. What draws them to the tomb of Emil Zátopek? What draws them, if it comes to that, to this annual race in his memory – from Prague, from Germany, Hungary, France, the UK; even from Africa and America?

It is, of course, the same thing that draws me: the legend of the Good Soldier Zátopek, a man who started with nothing – not even exceptional talent – and through the sheer quality of his spirit became the greatest sportsman of his age; a man who, in the words of J. Armour Milne, 'proved that the ordinary man is capable of feats previously considered impossible'; and who did all this with grace, kindness, warmth and humour that made an even deeper impression on his contemporaries than his unprecedented haul of records and medals.

We have come here to honour him, just as Les Perry came to honour him in Helsinki; and we hope, too, just as Perry did, that, as we do so, a little of Emil's great spirit will somehow seep into ours. I have met one person after another who is still thrilled – fifty, sixty, seventy years later – by that small moment when Emil touched their existence. One individual described an afternoon in the pub with Emil as 'one of the most important days of my life'.

Many people add an extra detail: 'He not only signed his autograph for me – he drew a special cartoon for me. I still have it; I can show it to you if you like . . .' Further enquiry invariably reveals the same cartoon: a stick-man Emil being pursued by a javelin-wielding stick-woman Dana. He and she must have drawn tens of thousands of them, and every single recipient – rightly – feels special.

'The people love us, Dana – we have to love them back' – that was at the heart of it. But there is a flip-side. Emil put real love into creating his legend for us. Perhaps it would be a fitting response for us to love him back a little more, and to judge him a little less harshly.

Somewhere during the race from Kopřivnice to Rožnov, we crossed the Javorník Mountains – perhaps at the very point where Emil and Milan Špaček once urinated on to both sides of the central European watershed at once. I should have stopped to do the same myself, in his honour; but I was too busy thinking other, more pressing Zátopekian thoughts: 'Pain is merciful'; 'Am I tired? That doesn't matter'; 'A runner must run with dreams in his heart, not money in his pocket'; 'When you can't keep going, go faster'; and, not least: 'Today we die a little.' The thoughts gave me strength. I found courage, belief and renewed motivation from contemplating Emil's legendary approach to life and sport; countless thousands of other runners, fast and slow, have done the same – and not just while running. That, surely, is reality: a reality at least as solid as any gap between the man Emil aspired to be and the man he really was. Even if the magic was partly an illusion – and Emil, like the Wizard of Oz, was in fact just an ordinary man hiding behind an elaborate machinery of image-making – so what? Grand illusions have a power of their own. The Wizard of Oz made the Cowardly Lion brave and the brainless Scarecrow clever, simply because they believed in his magic.

Some people will never forgive Emil for not being the flawless hero he aspired to be; some consider it inexcusable that he allowed himself to be used as a poster boy for Communism. Their criticisms should not blind us to the huge weight of love that others felt and feel for him – as a legend and as a human being. It is not only Dana who comes here each September to honour Emil's memory. (The race, the Běh rodným krajem Emila Zátopka, has been run in his memory every year since 2002.) Friends and admirers gather, too, from all over the Czech Republic and beyond. In a hotel in Rožnov, Dana celebrates her shared birthday. This year, a dinner was held the night before the race. Wine and slivovice were drunk; favourite folk songs were sung; old friends relived golden moments from years gone by. It takes a special kind of person – a special kind of couple – to generate this kind of enduring love.

The ranks of those who shared Emil's golden years grow thinner each year. Jindřich Roudný and Ladislav Kořán were both in Moravia to pay their respects in 2014; neither survived to do so again in 2015. One day, like the Old Guard, these reunions will cease to be viable. But something will – or should – live on.

'All that really matter,' Dana once said, 'are the traces you leave after you.' Emil left many. The athletics world tends to focus on his achievements on the track: the records – eighteen world, four Olympic, fifty national – and the medals. But Emil knew as well as anyone that records and medals are there to be broken, lost and forgotten. The first person to run 10,000m in under twenty-nine minutes? Today's champions are inching their way towards twenty-six and a quarter minutes; Emil would not even have qualified for the event in the 2016 Olympics. One day – who knows? – even that three-gold miracle in Helsinki may be matched. As for Emil's training methods, they have been accepted, absorbed and developed so widely that his role as innovator and pioneer barely warrants a footnote in the training manuals.

But some traces that Emil left are more enduring. Rousing myself to do some half-hearted stretching, I realise that fragments from conversations with Emil's friends and family are drifting through my mind, like leaves in a September breeze: 'He was a simple man – a good boy . . .'; 'He was a gentleman – he never stood aloof from anyone . . .'; 'He lightened people's lives . . .'; 'He was too honest for his own good . . .'; 'I cannot imagine Emil ever doing anything to hurt someone . . .'; 'He was a pure being – he saw the human being inside everyone . . .'; 'He was so beloved . . .'; 'He always had compassion for the simple people . . .' 'There was so much love and friendship inside him . . .'

'He used to see the good in people,' said Dana, 'even when it wasn't there. I could never have been so happy with any other man.'

Nothing I have learnt while researching this book alters that special quality of Emil's soul; or, for that matter, the essential contours of his life. There really was a poor boy from Kopřivnice who built himself up through his own efforts and ingenuity, step by painful step, to be the most famous athlete the world had seen. There really was a man who discovered that, by loading himself up with pain (boots, sand, snow, burdens), he could learn to shrug it off. There really was a runner who reached such summits of achievement that he redefined the boundaries of his sport – and yet maintained throughout his journey a lightness of heart and warmth of spirit that brightened the lives of those whose paths crossed his. And there really was a sportsman whose gift for friendship brought a divided world a little closer together; who shared himself and his success with every ordinary person who asked; who shared his home and his medals as gladly as he shared his time and expertise; and whose charisma, for a while, helped to stop a superpower's invasion in its tracks.

In the end, they broke him. There's no point denying that; and broken lives are rarely pretty. Even then, though, enough of Emil's great spirit remained for more or less everyone who came into contact with him to feel privileged to have done so. That was his great strength: he could shrug off his own pain and make others feel stronger – and make them laugh, too. His great weakness, as a potential political hero in a totalitarian age, was that he loved life too much: not just being alive, but love and laughter and friendship and wine and song. He lacked the cold indifference of the unhesitating martyr, bubbling instead with enthusiasm for the warm things that make life worth living.

Those of us who never knew him tend to feel privileged to have come into contact with him indirectly: to have seen footage of his races, to have heard his stories and sayings, to have met the friends and family who loved him. I am sure I am not alone in feeling this. And I am sure that I have rarely felt it so strongly as I do now, walking tentatively from the graveyard and through the old, wooden Wallachian village, towards the prize-giving area.

When I get there, I bump into Dana, ninety-three the previous day and glowing with energy. Hospitable as always, she checks that I am taking advantage of the hot food that is being distributed to finishers. I tell her that I'm not sure my stomach is quite ready for a meal. 'Have beer,' she says. 'Emil always said beer is best, after a race.'

It is tempting, but I will have to drive soon, back to the airport at Ostrava to catch yet another budget flight (Ryanair this time). So I refresh myself instead by immersing myself in the peaceful spirit of the place. It is Emil's spirit: the spirit of friendship through sport. In the clearing nearby, a couple of hundred people from a dozen or more countries – most either badly washed or still caked, like me, in the long run's grime – are sharing the post-race buzz. You don't have to speak their languages to get the gist of many of the conversations. People are enthusiastically exchanging times, targets, positions, mishaps, injuries and embarrassing chafing – all the minutiae of the latest shared adventure in their life as runners. I can think of few places in the world I would rather be.

Much later, washed and changed, I wander back past the chattering runners, trying to shake a little more circulation into my trashed legs. Maybe I did die a little today, I reflect, but now I am feeling more full of joy and life with each passing minute. Why leave now? Common sense prevails, though, and I head, reluctantly, for my hire car.

I glance again into the graveyard as I pass. The flowers on Emil's grave look brighter: lush and fresh with life. Even the runner in the stone doesn't seem to be struggling any more. He is already free, speeding joyfully towards an unseen destination.

I drive northwards towards the airport, but by a roundabout route, via the nearby villages of Zubří, where

Emil's mother came from, and Zašová, his father's birthplace. These, like Rožnov pod Radhoštěm, are at the very heart of the mountainous sub-pocket of Moravia known as Moravian Wallachia. František and Anežka took great pride in their Wallachian roots, as Emil did in his. He was especially fond of songs from these parts.

The autumn afternoon is losing its brightness; and, I imagine, its warmth. In Emil's honour, I listen as I drive to a recently purchased recording of Moravian folk songs. They are easy to like – although nothing will ever make me see the point of the traditional Wallachian costumes that singers of such songs like to wear. A few tracks in, a frisson of recognition makes the hairs on the back of my neck stand up. That song! I realise that I have heard it before: not once but many times. It is what the folk singers were singing last night, at Dana's birthday party, and before that in Zlín, a year ago, at a ceremony to unveil a life-size statue of Emil in the sports stadium by the power station. They sang it at his funeral, too. It is their song: '*V Zarazicách krajní dům*', the one that Emil whistled to her in London in 1948 to signal that he was outside.

Perhaps it is the combination of exhaustion and endorphins, but the song suddenly seems to embody for me the essence of Emil Zátopek.

There is nothing sophisticated about the words. Strip out the repetitions and you're left with this:

V Zarazicách krajní dům,
měl jsem já tam frajárečku, bože můj

Dyby ně ju chceli dat,
vědel bych ju, ach můj bože, milovat.

Ve dně bych ju šanoval,
ale v noci, ach můj bože, miloval.

. . . which translates (roughly) as:

In Zarazice, in the house on the edge,
I had a girlfriend there, my God!

If they wanted to give her to me,
oh my God!, I would know how to love her.

By day I would look after her,
but by night, oh my God!, I would love her.

If the English set such words to music, it would be a drinking song, with sniggers and lewd gestures. In Moravian hands, it is a song of aching romance, with delicate layers of harmony, swaying between sorrow and bliss with a slow, lazy rhythm like a calm sea's slap on shingle. It is the timeless song of the ordinary man yearning for his lover, echoing across borders and across history, melancholy and life-affirming, melting the physical and the spiritual into a pool of deep, elegiac longing.

That was the thing about Emil. He was a romantic: the most romantic of all runners. He looked for romance not just in love, but in friendship; and not just in friendship but in sport. He took something mundane – 'putting one foot in front of the other, as fast as possible, for as long as possible' was how Ron Clarke liked to describe it – and made it into a thrilling adventure, a daring exploration, in which all were welcome to join him, of just how far a human being could reach. He could have just been a runner who won races. Instead, he was a runner who loved life.

A few miles further on, not far from Kopřivnice, I notice some children playing in a rough field. It strikes me that I may have seen them already today. Every village we passed through during the race seemed to have a whole village's worth of children out on the roadside, trying to touch our hands as we ran while their parents clapped encouragement. (For Emil's second funeral, those same roadsides were lined with people in Wallachian costume.) I am not sure if these ones are playing an organised game or just messing around, but there seems to be a lot of running – and one of them is sprinting away from the main group.

He seems smaller than the rest. Two or three set off in half-hearted pursuit, but he is far ahead and, at the edge of the field, turns up a dusty track. He kicks up a cloud of the stuff: it hangs in the air behind him like the contrail of a jet.

As I pass, there is a moment when I can see straight up the path, which slopes up towards a wooded hillside. The sinking sun shines straight back down from the skyline, and I find myself looking into a golden explosion of light. The boy is a silhouette, elbows flailing, running faster and faster as he shrinks into the distance. He trails glory as he does so, in the gold dust that swirls from his shoes.

'Look,' I say to myself. 'Zátopek.'

Sources

Given the passage of time since the main events of Emil Zátopek's life, it has not been possible or even desirable to rely exclusively on the spoken testimony of eyewitnesses. I have also drawn on a variety of printed, recorded and filmed sources – especially when directly quoting Emil himself.

Most of the non-printed sources I have used are cited in the relevant page-by-page notes that begin on p. 387. However, I must make particular acknowledgement of *Pohádkový Péťa*, a superb television documentary by Miroslav Kačor, shown on Česká televize (CT2) in 2002, in which I first heard the voices of many of the eyewitnesses quoted in this book. I have also benefited from watching: *Sláva vítězům: Emil Zátopek*, dir. Simona Oktábcová, Theodor Mojžíš, a Česká televize documentary first broadcast in 2001; *Z televizniho alba Emila Zátopka*, a Česká televize documentary by Karel Hynie, Zdenek Patocka, Vojtech Peták and Pavel Taussig, first broadcast in 2003; *Život atleta Emila Zátopka*, an Inventura Febia TV documentary, dir. M. Mináč and O. Sommerová, broadcast (as part of an *Emil Zátopek a*

Věra Čáslavská programme) on Česká televize in 2011; *Nejen zlaté vzpomínky*, Česká televize, October 2014; *Slavné olympijské osmičky Podruhé v Londýně vstupuje Emil Zátopek* (2008); *Emil Zátopek: Olympic Highlights, 1948–1952*, Phoenix, 1980; and *Emil Zátopek: Die Lauflokomotive*, a documentary by Hagen Bossdorf for ARTE television, first broadcast 3 October 1995. None of these, unfortunately, is available in English.

I have been helped by a number of radio programmes, including *Životopisy: Emil Zátopek*, a radio series directed by Pavel Krejčí for Česky rozhlas and first broadcast on 1 May 2012; *Emil Zátopek Vyprávění o životě a sportování* (probably recorded for Česky rozhlas in *c.*1953–5 – and abbreviated as *EZVžs*); and *Neznámý Emil Zátopek*, by Karel Tejkal (ČRo 2, 2009). And I have made extensive use of online television archives such as those of Pathé News (at britishpathe.com) and Česká televize (at Archiv ČT24: ceskatelevize.cz) – especially the weekly propaganda newsreels known as Československý filmový týdeník.

As far as printed sources are concerned, I have repeatedly referred to, and quoted from, Emil's own writings: *Dana a Emil Zátopkovi vypravují* (first published 1960; my edition is STN, 1962), in which Emil's words alternate with Dana's; *Běží Zátopek* (Olympia, 1967), in which Emil recycles many of the anecdotes from *Dana a Emil Zátopkovi vypravují;* and *Můj Tréning a Závodění* (ČSTV, 1956). The books' titles can be roughly translated as, respectively, 'Dana and Emil Zátopek tell their stories', 'Zátopek runs' and 'My training and races' (and are abbreviated in the Notes as *DEZ*, *BZ* and *MTZ*). None is currently available in English.

I have also made use of two existing biographies. *Zátopek, the Marathon Victor*, by František Kožík, was first published in Czech as *Vítězstvívůle* (NČOS, 1949) but extensively revised to become *Zátopek, vítěz maratónský* (Artia, 1952). Kožík also did a different version of the text for *Zátopek in Photographs* (Artia, 1954). The English translation I have used was published as *Zátopek, the Marathon Victor* by Artia in 1954. Kožík interviewed Emil at length for the book but was not above distorting facts for propaganda purposes, sometimes grotesquely.

Zá-to-pek! Zá-to-pek! Zá-to-pek!, by Bob Phillips (Parrs Wood Press, 2002; revised 2004) is more reliable, but focuses far more on Emil's races and training than on other aspects of his life.

Other useful biographical works – none, so far as I am aware, available in English – include *Emil Běžec*, by Pavel Kosatík (Český olympijský výbor, 2015), a short, rigorous historical biography which covers some of the same ground as this book but with less focus on Emil's running; and *Zátopek: Le Terrassier de Prague*, by Pierre Naudin (Le Légendaire, 1972), a colourful but sometimes highly speculative life which runs into a brick wall after 1968. Some extra details can be found in: *Emil Zátopek: olympijská legenda*, by František Macák, Alexandr Žurman, Milan Jirásek (Olympia, 2002); *Emil Zátopek a sport objektivem Emila Fafka a jiných*, with words by Zdeněk Hrabica and Marie Šusterová-Fafková (Vytiski Akcent, 2001); *Zátopek: la locomotiva umana*, by Marco Franzelli (Biancoenero Edizioni, 2011); and *Emil Zátopek*, by Emanuel Bosák and Josef Pondělík (Orbis, 1953).

Many enjoyable accounts have been written of specific periods or aspects of Emil's life. The best are the

Zátopek chapter in *The Kings of Distance*, by Pete Lovesey (Eyre & Spottiswoode, 1968), and 'Jak to tenkrát běžel Zátopek', by Ota Pavel, in his collection *Plná bedna šampaňského* (Naše vojsko, 1967; the edition I have used is Vydala Olympia, 1977). Both are excellent on the minutiae of Emil's races. Sadly, Lovesey's book has long been out of print, while Pavel's has never been translated into English.

Most of my other printed sources are either self-evident from the text or specifically cited below. However, I should acknowledge a broader debt to (among others): *Stars of Czechoslovak Sport*, by J. Armour Milne (Orbis, Prague, 1956); *Track and Field: The Great Ones*, by Cordner Nelson (Pelham Books, 1970); *Tracking Heroes*, by Robert J. Corrigan (Winston-Derek, 1990); *Fast Tracks: the History of Distance Running*, by Raymond Krise and Bill Squires (The Stephen Greene Press, 1982); *Running Through the Ages*, by Edward S. Sears (McFarland, 2001); *The Ten Greatest Races*, by Derrick Young (Gemini Books, 1972); *The Lore of Running*, by Tim Noakes (Leisure Press, 3rd edition, 1991); *The Complete Book of the Olympics*, by David Wallechinsky and Jaime Loucky (Aurum Press, 2008 edition); *Olympic Marathon: the History and Drama of Sport's Most Challenging Event*, by David E. Martin & Roger W. H. Gynn (Human Kinetics Publishers, 2001); *Olympic Marathon: A Centennial History of the Games' Most Storied Race*, by Charlie Lovett (Praeger, 1997); *The Austerity Olympics: When the Games Came to London in 1948*, by Janie Hampton (Aurum Press, 2008).

I have both enjoyed and gleaned valuable information from: *Running with the Legends*, by Michael Sandrock

(Human Kinetics Publishing, 1996); *How they Train*, by Fred Wilt (Track & Field, 1959); *Trénoval jsem Emila*, by Oldřich Koudelka (written in close collaboration with Jan Haluza; Lanškroun, 2007); *3:59.4*, by John Bryant (Hutchinson, 2004); *The Perfect Mile*, by Neal Bascomb (CollinsWillow, 2004); *Why Die? The Extraordinary Percy Cerutty, Maker of Champions*, by Graem Sims (Lothian, 2003); *Running Wild*, by Gordon Pirie (WH Allen, 1961); *The Unforgiving Minute*, by Ron Clarke (with Alan Trengrove; Pelham Books, 1966); *The Lonely Breed*, by Ron Clarke and Norman Harris (Pelham Books, 1967); *The Rings of Destiny*, by Olga Connolly (David McKay Company, 1968); *The Destiny of Ali Mimoun*, by Pat Butcher (Globe Runner, 2011); *Pitch Invasion: Adidas, Puma and the Making of Modern Sport*, by Barbara Smit (Allen Lane, 2006); and *Marathon-training*, by Manfred Steffny (Schmidt Hermann Verlag, 2001).

Of the countless available printed sources on the broader history of Czechoslovakia, I owe particular acknowledgement to the following: *The Prague Spring and its Aftermath*, by Kieran Williams (Cambridge University Press, 1997); *Nightfrost in Prague*, by Zdeněk Mlynář (Karz, 1980); *Reform Rule in Czechoslovakia: the Dubček Era, 1968–1969*, by Galia Golen (Cambridge University Press, 1973); *Prague Spring*, by Z.A.B. Zeman (Penguin, 1969); *Fools and Heroes: the Changing Role of Communist Intellectuals in Czechoslovakia*, by Peter Hruby (Pergamon Press, 1980); *The Greengrocer and His TV: The Culture of Communism After the 1968 Prague Spring*, by Paulina Bren (Cornell University Press, 2010); *Srpen 1968: Vzpominka Stale Ziva* (Nekolik Osobnich Ohlednuti, Kopřivnice 2006); *The Deception*

Game, by Ladislav Bittman (Ballantine Books, 1972); *The Frolík Defection*, by Josef Frolík (Leo Cooper, 1975); *Spymaster*, by Ted Shackley (Potomac Books, 2006); *The Intelligence Game*, by James Rusbridger (Bodley Head, 1989); *The Soviet Union and the Czechoslovak Army, 1948–1983*, by Condoleezza Rice (Princeton University Press, 1984); *Prague in Black: Nazi Rule and Czech Nationalism*, by Chad Bryant (Harvard University Press, 2007); *The Hitler Kiss: A Memoir of the Czech Resistance*, by Radomír Luža with Christina Vella (Louisiana State University Press, 2002); *World of Dissent: Charter 77, The Plastic People of the Universe and Czech Culture under Communism*, by Jonathan Bolton (Harvard University Press, 2012). I have also made extensive us of more general historical works such as *Iron Curtain: the Crushing of Eastern Europe*, by Anne Applebaum (Allen Lane, 2012); *Savage Continent: Europe in the Aftermath of World War II*, by Keith Lowe (Viking, 2012); *The Establishment of Communist Regimes in Eastern Europe, 1944–1949*, ed. Norman Naimark and Leonid Gibianskii (Westview Press, 1997); and *Revolution and Resistance in Eastern Europe*, ed. Kevin McDermott and Matthew Stibbe (Berg, 2006). And I both acknowledge and enthusiastically recommend Mariusz Szczygiel's wonderfully entertaining *Gottland: Mostly True Stories from Half of Czechoslovakia* (translated by Antonia Lloyd-Jones; Melville House Publishing, 2014).

I have also benefited enormously from the impending publication, expected in 2016, of Dana Zátopková's own memoirs – provisionally entitled *Jak to bylo* ('How It Was'). I have seen no more than a few sentences from Dana's manuscript, but I know that the hard work she has put into marshalling and authenticating her memories has been of great value for my book as well as hers. Once again, I thank her for the generosity with which she has shared her life with me.

Source notes for material that I have taken from closed archives, such as those of the security services and the Army, are indicated only in general terms (e.g., 'Archiv bezpečnostních složek' for the security services, or, for Emil's military service records: 'Ministerstvo národní obrany – Osobní spis, 24503: Zátopek, Emil'). The Zátopek-related archive of the Czechoslovakian Olympic Committee can be found in the Czech National Archives (NAČR, fond ČSVO, č. 625, karton 42, Karty sportovců a funkcionářů S-Ž, Zátopek Emil, list I). Other printed records can be found at the Emil and Dana Zátopek exhibition in the Technical Museum Tatra, and in the Muzeum Fojtství – both in Kopřivnice. Many of the most important contemporary documents relating to the events of 1968 and 1969 can be easily accessed in *The Prague Spring 1968: A National Security Archive Documents Reader*, by Jaromír Navrátil (Central European University Press, 2006).

It would have been perverse not to have made use of the vast quantities of source material available online – although I have tended to treat such material with a degree of scepticism. For Czech-speakers, Dav Schovánek's Zátopek-related blog at www.bezeckaskola.cz is among the most useful resources. I have also made use, gratefully, of the ourCollectiveMemory project.

In the citations that follow, I have acknowledged only those sources which are not evident from the text itself. I apologise in advance for any accidental omissions and will gladly correct any that are brought to my attention. Titles and references that have not been officially translated into English I have left in their original languages: partly to minimise the risk of confusing readers who wish to follow them up – but mainly because I lack the skill to translate them.

Notes

p. vii: **lost only one of his last seventy races at his specialist distances**

A much higher figure is sometimes quoted for Emil's winning streak: for example, that he had won all but one of his past ninety-six races. I can't make those numbers add up. After his two defeats to Reiff in 1948, Emil lost at 3,000m to Čevona on 11 July 1951, and at 5,000m to Kazantsev on 11 June 1952. See *Můj Tréning a Závodění,* by Emil Zátopek, ČSTV, 1956, pp. 87–90.

p. viii: **the entire national ice hockey team was arrested**

For detailed accounts of this bizarre, complex story, see 'A life on ice: Bohumil Modrý and Jáchymov', by Michael Stein, Česká pozice, May 2012; and the interview with Augustin Bubník by Tomáš Bouškam at politicalprisoners.eu. See also *Fifty Years of Czech Sport in Totalitarian Society*, published by The Institute for the Study of Totalitarian Regimes and the Magistrate of the Capital City of Prague in cooperation with the Czech Olympic Committee and the National Museum, 2014. The arrests clearly owed something to the outspoken nature of the team's drunken protests when they were prevented from travelling to London. The longest sentence was 15 years.

p. ix: **the problem with Stanislav Jungwirth**

There have been many accounts of this incident, none official and some contradictory. The story was first told publicly by Ota Pavel, in 'Jak to tenkrát běžel Zátopek' in 1967. Emil subsequently spoke about it many times, as did Dana. In addition to discussing the matter with Dana, with Jiři Zátopek, and with team-mates such as Ludvík Liska and Ivan Ullsperger, I have taken into account versions of events given by Emil in, for example, *Život atleta Emila Zátopka*, *Z televizniho alba Emila Zátopka* (from which the 'If Standa does not go . . .' quote is taken) and *Životopisy: Emil Zátopek*; given by Dana in interviews with Radio Prague, on 19 July 2012, and with *Zátopek* magazine, No 2, April/June 2007, pp. 62–65; and given by former team-mates, now dead, such as František Brož (quoted by Adam B. Ellick in an excellent obituary of Emil in *Running Times*, 1 March 2001). See also notes to pp. 159 and 196.

p. x: **Western journalists are told that Zátopek has tonsillitis**
AP report, 10 July 1952, published in the *Chicago Daily Tribune*, 11 July 1952 (Part 3; p. 2).

p. xi: **not in either of the biographies**
Zátopek the Marathon Victor, by František Kožík (Artia Praha, 1954); *Zá-to-pek! Zá-to-pek! Zá-to-pek!*, by Bob Phillips (The Parrs Wood Press, 2002).

p. xi **One otherwise staid official Olympic Games report**
Official Report of XV Olympiad Helsinki 1952, p. 248.

p. xii: **'Great is the victory, but greater still is the friendship'**
Kožík, p. 8; note, however, that the words are not actually attributed to Emil.

p. xii: **His fellow Olympians worshipped him**
Running Wild, by Gordon Pirie, p. 137; *The Destiny of Ali Mimoun*, by Pat Butcher, p. 26; *How They Train*, by Fred Wilt, p. 87; *The Lonely Breed*, by Ron Clarke with Norman Harris, p. 103.

p. xv: **would have earned him twenty-fourth place**
Zátopek's best, 28:54.2, would have left him well behind the 23rd placed Ayad Lamdessam, who finished in 28:49.85, but would still have put him ahead of six other finalists. In 2016, on the other hand, his career-best times would not even have won him qualification for the Rio Olympics, at either 5,000m or 10,000m.

p. xvi: **'a man who ran like us'**
Unsourced quote from 1948, quoted by Kožík (p. 84), Pavel (p. 31) and Kosatík (p.110). Magnan's many distinctions included being born on the very same day in 1922 as Emil and Dana; but much of his *oeuvre* is now hard to track down.

p. xvi: **'most epoch-shattering athlete of his age'**
Middle Distance Running, by Percy Wells Cerutty, p. 21

p. xvii: **'Men . . . today we die a little'**
See note to p. 226.

p. 4: **some enjoyable phrase-making**
The first of these quotes, much repeated, is reported to come from a European coach whom I have not been able to identify. The other phrases were coined by, respectively: William Johnson; Kenny Moore; Cordner Nelson; and Red Smith. Some post-date the Helsinki marathon.

p. 6: **'At that moment, I understood what the Olympic spirit means'**
Address by Juan Antonio Samaranch at Emil's funeral at the National Theatre, Prague, 6 December 2000.

p. 6: **'the greatest happening in athletics history'**
Cover note written by J. Armour Milne for the English edition of Kožík.

p. 7: **feels suddenly overwhelmingly sad**
See *DEZ* (p. 109); Pavel (p. 49); as well as Emil talking in (among other places): *Pohádkový Péťa*; and in *EZVžs*.

p. 8: **but has since declined**
Tatra seemed likely to be wound up in 2012, and when I first visited Kopřivnice, in 2014, I assumed that it was closed. It has since undergone something of a revival under new ownership, and in 2015 it sold 850 trucks to India. Production is expected to double by 2020.

p. 8: **the nearby village of Zašová**
Some sources identify Valašské Meziříčí – the nearest town to Zašová – as the Zátopeks' former home. However, both Dana Zátopková (with whom I discussed this in January 2016) and Emil's brother Jiří, talking in *Pohádkový Péťa* in 2002, insist that Emil's siblings were born in Zašová.

p. 9: **in the corner of the kitchen that doubled up as František's workshop**
Jiří Zátopek mentions this in *Pohádkový Péťa*, in which the corner in question is shown.

p. 10: **'limitlessly loving'**
The neighbour was Emil's friend and former classmate, Marie Vlachová.

p. 11: **'with more passion than those who were allowed to'**
This and other direct quotes from Emil in this chapter are, unless otherwise indicated, taken from *DEZ*, pp. 19–30.

p. 12: **The family was no less scarred as a result**
According to Dana, Emil would always point out 'the tree where my brother hanged himself' when they passed it on the journey between Kopřivnice and Štramberk.

p. 12: **Politically, he was more of a trade unionist than a revolutionary**
According to Emil's military service files, František joined the Communist Party when it was founded, in 1929, but left in 1932 after a row with a local official, Mr Urx. He then joined the Social Democratic party – only to join the Communists again in 1948. Jaromír Konůpka, whose father was active with František in the trade union, thought of František as a social democrat.

p. 13: **'the biggest fidget in the class'**
The schoolfriend in question, Jaromír Konůpka, in addition to speaking to me at length in Kopřivnice in May and July 2015, was also kind enough to share with me some of his written recollections, published and unpublished, of his and Emil's childhood – including Emil's various acts of defiance at school.

p. 13: **'Emil the cry-baby'**
Pavel (p. 28); Emil describes his screaming policy in *DEZ* (pp. 24–25).

p. 13: **Emil's bare feet**
A copy of this school photograph, from 1928–29, is in Kopřivnice's Folk Museum.

p. 14: **'If it turned out that it was Emil who did it, everything was all right'**
Jiří was talking in *Pohádkový Péťa.*

p. 14: **'He could hold his breath longer . . .'**
Špaček also described Emil's swimming exploits in *Pohádkový Péťa.*

p. 16: **observing how it sucked up his blood . . . stolen a wooden cup**
Pavel, pp. 28–9.

p. 18: **Emil's brothers would all remain in Kopřivnice**
Franta worked for a while as treasurer at the post office but later became test driver at Tatra. Bohouš worked at Tatra, rising to the post of head company inspector. Jiří left for a while to join the air force but then returned to work at Tatra, where he worked his way up to become head planner. Jaroš, as we have seen, struggled to find work during the Great Depression, at one point even attempting to move to the Soviet Union to find a job; he eventually found employment as a labourer and driver in Kopřivnice, only to run over a horse, with tragic consequences. The horse was killed, its owner demanded compensation, and Jaroš, facing ruin, took his own life.

p. 19: **he wasn't stupid enough to repeat a class**
Emil's brother Jiří, talking in *Pohádkový Péťa.*

p. 20: **There was something miraculous about Zlín . . .**
Of the many published studies of the Baťa phenomenon, the most readable is Mariusz Szczygiel's *Gottland,* from which many of the details in this chapter are taken.

p. 21: **'Every penny spent on our schools will pay back many times.'**
Quoted in the official company history at tomasbata.com. Baťa is now based in Canada.

p. 22: **'a totalitarian town'**
Life and Death in the Kingdom of Shoes: Zlín, Baťa, and Czechoslovakia, 1923–1941, by Zachary Austin Doleshal (University of Texas at Austin, 2012).

p. 23: **'I always had to think for a while about where I was . . .'**
DEZ (p. 31). Much of this chapter relies on Emil's own accounts. (Of the eyewitnesses from this period whom I have met, the only one who was actually at Baťa with Emil was Jindřich Roudný, who sadly died in 2015 before I could interview him at greater length.) Direct quotations come from *DEZ* unless otherwise indicated – although many can also be found in *BZ* and in the *EZVžs*.

p. 24: **Emil told his parents how exciting he found it all**
Jiří Zátopek describes this, and Emil's subsequent disillusionment, in *Pohádkový Péťa*; and Jaromír Konůpka confirmed to me that this was the sequence of Emil's reactions. The honeymoon period appears to have been short – while Emil's reflections on the subject in *DEZ* feel very much like homesickness written from the heart.

p. 24: **'he who passes on to his co-worker a piece of work unfit to be continued . . .'**
Knowledge in Action: The Baťa System of Management, by Tomas Baťa, translated by Otilia M. Kabesova (Fordham University, New York, 1992).

p. 26: **Radomír Luža . . . 'wondered why they were so eager to get to work to make boots for German feet . . .'**
See *The Hitler Kiss: A Memoir of the Czech Resistance*, by Radomír Luža & Christina Vella, pp. 46–7.

p. 29: **when 'it was decided that I would stick with athletics permanently'**
Emil speaking in *EZVžs*.

p. 30: **By one account, Emil was close to tears**
See Kožík, p. 20.

p. 31: **No one had to force him to go to training**
Haluza described his training with Emil at some length in *Trénoval jsem Emila*, by Oldřich Koudelka, from which a number of details in this chapter are taken – although I understand from Dana and others that Emil felt that Haluza (who died in 2011) exaggerated his importance in Emil's development.

p. 31: **'his tracksuit transformed him into a boisterous young man'**
See Kožík, pp. 22–3.

p. 31: **Room No. 19 in Hostel No. 2**
Many of the details I have included here were evocatively described by Jindřich Roudný in *Pohádkový Péťa*. But Emil also wrote about it, in *DEZ*, and discussed his eating excesses with Jaromír Konůpka – who even witnessed an encounter between Emil and Jarda the cook towards the end of Emil's life. Jarda felt that he could claim some of the credit for Emil's subsequent success.

p. 32: **'He was always on the lookout for a girl who was from the butcher'**
Jaroslav Přeček, talking in *Pohádkový Péťa.*

p. 32: **a serious-faced young woman called Jarmila Švehláková**
The most detailed interview I have seen with Jarmila Švehláková is in *Pohádkový Péťa.* Milan Švajgr told me that there were those in Zlín who felt that Emil had treated her badly.

p. 33: **'Emil was very inquisitive . . .'**
Haluza's comments are taken from *Trénoval jsem Emila* and *Pohádkový Péťa.*

p. 35: **'Suddenly I realised I'm coming first . . .'**
Emil reflected on this race in *EZVžs.*

p. 35: **Emil had begun to experiment with a different approach**
J. Armour Milne gives a good account of Emil's first tentative forays into interval training in *Czechoslovak Sport 1945–1955* (Orbis, Prague, 1955), p. 47. Writing in *Athletics Weekly* ('Emil Zátopek', 12 May 1951, pp. 8–12), Milne implies that he began doing systematic interval sessions in April 1944.

p. 36: **It is hard to be certain precisely how much of the method the Emil now developed was original**
Lovesey, Bryant and Phillips are all good on the historical precursors of Emil's methods.

p. 36: **an interview published in the *Observer* in Britain twenty years later**
'Zátopek: athlete on the track', by Christopher Brasher and Herb Elliott, *Observer*, 27 September 1964, p. 18.

p. 37: **Speed, in this context, is an elusive concept.**
Sources that estimate Emil's early lap times as 60 seconds include *How They Train*, by Fred Wilt, p. 87; *Fast Tracks: the History of Distance Running*, by Raymond Krise and Bill Squires (The Stephen Greene Press, 1982) and *The Ten Greatest Races*, by Derrick Young (Gemini Books, 1972). Elsewhere, figures as high as 70–75 seconds (with around 34–35 seconds for the fast 200m repetitions) are often cited: for example, in *Running Through the Ages*, by Edward S. Sears (2nd edition), p. 196; *The Lore of Running*, by Tim Noakes, p. 277.

This seems implausibly slow – especially for these first sessions, when the number of repetitions was small. But I assume that the higher figures would have been accurate for the vast sessions that Emil performed later in his career. Fred Wilt, who knew Emil better than the others, quoted 70–75 seconds as the likely range for the last laps of the kind of sessions Emil was doing in 1948. The fact that the laps were slower would not have meant that they were any easier: just that he was testing his body even closer to destruction.

p. 40: **'There was no athlete who was able to keep up with Emil'**
Address at Emil's funeral, National Theatre, Prague, 6 December 2000.

p. 40: **'This method of training . . .'**
Zátopek, Emil – Vyprávění o životě a sportování.

p. 40: **'I will run with perfect style when they start judging races for their beauty . . .'**
Kožík, p. 93.

p. 42: **Franta, Emil's older brother, was among them**
I found this rather startling detail in Emil's personal military service records (Ministerstvo národní obrany, Osobní spis: Zátopek, Emil – 2-29/2008, 1. část). He was sent to Berlin but seems to have returned home unharmed after the war.

p. 43: **more than half a century later, he said he could still remember the taste**
Interview by Christophe Wyrzykowski in *L'Équipe*, 4 August 1998.

p. 44: **three hours after gorging himself on plum dumplings**
Emil mentions this in *DEZ*, p. 44; J. Armour Milne, writing in *Athletics Weekly* (19 May 1951, pp. 8–12) adds that Emil's hosts – presumably the Hron family – begged him not to eat them so soon before the race, but Emil couldn't resist.

p. 46: **The first thing that Jindřich Roudný did**
Roudný describes this episode in *Pohádkový Péťa.*

p. 47: **'like when a horse digs something up . . .'**
See *DEZ*, pp. 44–7 – where Emil's quote about culture can also be found. Emil also discussed this phase of his life in *BZ* and (on radio) in *EZVžs*, and some of his quotes can be found in more than one of these sources.

p. 49: **their deputies put to sweeping the city streets**
Szczygiel, p. 38.

p. 51: **'competed more joyfully'**
EZVžs.

p. 51: **whose inhabitants had been fleeing in thousands**
Szczygiel (p. 38) says that 13,000 fled within two months of liberation.

p. 52: **the academy's 800m-long corridor**
I am grateful to Petr Cimila for demonstrating, during a long tour of Hranice military academy in July 2015, why this would have been impossible.

p. 54: **touching Heino's leg for luck**
The Great Ones, by Cordner Nelson, p. 57.

p. 55: **'I still remember how elated I was'**
Interview with Ladislav Krnáč, 1992, quoted in Phillips, p. 129.

p. 56: **the romance he had been tentatively trying to rekindle**
'Emil Zátopek – porážka je taky škola', by Dav Schovánek, 16 January 2013, at bezeckaskola.cz.

p. 57: **'Who's chasing you?'**
Kožík p. 47. See *MTZ* for Emil's most detailed descriptions of his training in the woods, including his thoughts on 'killing time without a goal'.

p. 58: **'a bathroom hung with icicles'**
Pavel, p. 32; see *DEZ*, p. 9, for Emil's views on washing in icy water.

p. 58: **'There is great advantage in training under unfavourable conditions . . .'**
Kožík p. 48.

p. 60: **a drink consisting of lemon juice, water and the chalk used to mark lanes on the track**
If this anecdote prompts anyone to wonder if Emil ever sought any other assistance from chemistry, this might be a good place to mention that, according Kosatík (p. 162), Emil admitted towards the end of his life that, while still in Zlín, he briefly experimented with the amphetamine benzedrine, but concluded that it was a bad idea, because it 'did not agree with him'. I have not been able to verify this: one of Kosatik's sources is dead, and at the time of going to press he

had not been able to identify for me the Czech magazine interview in which Emil is supposed to have said this. He insists, however, that he is very confident that the story is true. Assuming that it is, should Emil's admirers worry? Is it conceivable that Emil's real significance in the history of athletics might have been as the chemically-trained pioneer of a system of training that could be sustained only with pharmacological assistance (which was not banned in Olympics athletics until 1968)? I don't think they should, and I don't think it is. Kosatik is also confident that Emil's flirtation with benzedrine was no more than that: a fleeting experiment. In any case, if Emil's amazing powers of recovery suggest any kind of drug use, it would surely be steroids – yet anabolic steroids were not even invented until 1958. Systematic doping in Czechoslovakia did not begin until the 1970s, although there have been rumours of early experiments in the 1960s. I am convinced that, had Emil's success been owed to such practices, it would have left both a paper trail and witnesses. Perhaps it did, and I have missed them. But given some of the people I have spoken to, and some of the places I have looked, I would find this very surprising indeed.

p. 61: **'not just applause – it comes from the belly'**
Quoted in Brasher and Elliott, *Observer*, 27 September 1964.

p. 61: **'like two foolish boys'**
Pavel, p. 33.

p. 62: **'I would have said "Isn't it stupid . . ."'**
Brasher and Elliott, *Observer*, 27 September 1964; Pavel, p. 34.

p. 62: **fighting spirit, or '*sisu*'**
Phillips, p. 29.

p. 62: **Heino did not go to the post-race banquet**
Dav Schovánek, 'Emil Zátopek – porážka je taky škola'.

p. 62: **was sick on the beach**
Pavel, p. 34.

p. 62: **one of the races that had marked him most**
Interview by Christophe Wyrzykowski, in *L'Équipe*, 4 August 1998

p. 63: **congratulated Mimoun on his performance, before sharing several glasses of Russian champagne**
The Destiny of Ali Mimoun, by Pat Butcher, p. 12.

p. 64: **his practice of putting on his running shoes in the street**
Marie Vlacháva said he normally did so outside her family's house, a few doors away.

p. 65: **'Do you collect the results of races? . . .'**
DEZ p. 64.

p. 67: **As the Catholic newspaper, *Lidová demokracie* put it**
23 May 1945.

p. 68: **'If he gets disqualified . . . it will make him more famous.'**
Account by Emil quoted in *Running with the Legends*, by Michael Sandrock, p. 27.

p. 69: **he would welcome a bag of oranges**
Pierre Naudin, citing Gaston Meyer and Pierre Lewden as witnesses, in *Zátopek: Le Terrassier de Prague*, pp. 203–4.

p. 69: **introduced him to the delights of seafood**
Butcher, p. 11.

pp. 70–1: **brought the Tatra factory in Kopřivnice to a complete standstill**
Vítězný únor 1948 (Komunistický svaz mládeže, Praha 2008), p. 18.

p. 71: **'simple and primitive'; 'speed and stamina, speed and recovery'; 'Run fast and try to recover . . .'**
Emil gave the first quote to Michael Sandrock (*Running with Legends*, p. 6) and the other two to Julie Cart ('Back Into the Light', interview in the *Los Angeles Times*, 29 April 1991).

p. 72: **more than a decade before the sports scientists first defined the physiological principles**
Reindell and Roskamm (1959) are often cited as the theoretical pioneers; see: 'High-Intensity Intermittent Exercise: Methodological and Physiological Aspects', by Gerhard Tschakert and Peter Hofmann, *International Journal of Sports Physiology and Performance*, 2013, 8, pp. 600–10; *et al.*

p. 72: **Emil was typically doing 5 x 200m . . . etc**
MTZ, p. 21. Emil says that it was 2km to the clearing where he did his 200m repetitions, and a further 2km to the clearing where he did the 400ms; all of which subsequently had to be retraced.

p. 73: **'Pain is a merciful thing . . .'**
Pavel, p. 30.

p. 74: **grasping it instinctively like a pen**
Phillips, p. 131.

p. 76: **'His fame will become your burden . . .'**
Conversation with Dana Zátopková, January 2015; also 'V Emilově Stínu', in *Zátopek a ti druzí*, by Zvonimír Šupich, pp. 70–6.

p. 77: **'We could have our wedding on the same day too'**
DEZ p. 75.

p. 78: **For one ten day period he upped his sessions to 60 x 400m each day**
See 'Emil Zátopek', by J. Armour Milne, *Athletics Weekly*, 12 May 1951, pp. 8–12. The Hungarian coach Klement Kerssenbrock – or possibly František Kožík (see note to p. 101) – also claimed to have 'personally witnessed' these sessions.

p. 80: **athletes selected for the Olympics were, like coal miners, allowed up to 5,467 calories**
'1948 Olympics: We had much more fun and a greater sense of achievement than modern athletes do", by Mike Rowbotham, *Independent*, 7 July 2005.

p. 80: **equivalent . . . to one-seventieth of the budget for London 2012**
Calculation by Larry Elliott, economics editor of the *Guardian*, considering the budget as percentage of GDP; see: 'London's 1948 Olympics: the real austerity Games', by Larry Elliott, *Guardian*, 30 March 2012.

p. 81: **The BBC paid £1,000 for the television rights . . . Sponsorship came from Craven A cigarettes . . . etc.**
These and other minutiae about the organisation of the Games, in this paragraph and elsewhere in this chapter, are largely gleaned from Janie Hampton's delightful *The Austerity Olympics: When the Games Came to London in 1948* (especially chapter 3).

p. 81: **'It was a liberation of spirit to be there in London . . .'**
Interview with Neil Allen in *The Times*, 24 March 1967; this charming, endlessly quoted article, by one of our finest sportswriters, also features in chapter 14.

p. 82: **the defection earlier that month of General Antonín Hasal . . . or an alleged plot to murder General Svoboda**
See *The Times*, 19 July 1948, p. 3; and 22 July 1948, p. 3.

p. 82: **They had toyed with the idea of excluding Dana**
Dana discussed this in an interview with Mark Eben on *Na plovárně*, Česká televize, 5 March 2006.

p. 82: **only Zátopek understood what training really was**
Lovesey p. 119; Kožík p. 72.

p. 83: **'People at home will ask me what the Olympics were like . . .'**
BZ, pp. 40–1.

p. 83: **'The King is looking at us. How can I go off now?'**
Allen, *The Times*, 24 March 1967.

p. 84: **a red vest would be waved**
Countless different versions of this signal have been reported over the years, not least by those involved, including: white vest (or shirt) and red shorts, red vest and white socks, red shorts and white socks, red scarf and white scarf, even red-and-white scarf and yellow scarf. I believe this version is correct – partly on the basis of Emil Zátopek's own writings (e.g., *DEZ*, p. 78, and *BZ*, p. 42) and sayings (e.g., *EZVžs*), and partly on the basis of a long conversation in May 2015 with Dana Zátopková, who was in charge of the red vest. František Kožík (who opts for white socks rather than shorts) adds that the items were Emil's spare clothes. I have also seen film footage (in *Jeden ze štafety*, dir. Jaroslav Mach, Československo, 1952), which may or may not be authentic, which appears to confirm my version.

p. 86: **'He looked . . . as if he might be having a fit'**
Nelson, p. 55.

p. 87: **he had no idea where Heino was. He decided to ask**
Emil mentions trying to remember how to ask the question in *EZVžs*. See also *DEZ*, pp. 78–9.

p. 87: **the race officials became confused**
See *The Olympics' Strangest Moments*, by Geoff Tibballs, p. 100; Phillips p. 36; and Mike Rowbotham's article, '1948 Olympics: "We had much more fun and a greater sense of achievement than modern athletes do"' in the *Independent*, 7 July 2005. Fourth

place was originally awarded to Sweden's Severt Dennolf and fifth to Norway's Martin Stokken, but the runners corrected the error. Belgium's Robert Everaert was awarded sixth place, until he pointed out that he had dropped out five laps before the end.

p. 88: **'Don't worry, not everyone who goes to the Olympics is a phenomenal athlete'**
Dana Zátopková speaking in *Slavné olympijské osmičky: Podruhé v Londýně vstupuje Emil Zátopek* (2008).

p. 90: **'puffed up like a frog'**
DEZ, p. 79.

p. 91: **'No one was wearing the gold medal yet'**
BZ, p. 44.

p. 91: **'possessed by devils'**
Lovesey, p. 130.

p. 92: **'The roar of cheers from the crowd was almost deafening . . .'**
Quoted in Hampton, chapter 11.

p. 92: **someone had stolen them**
The shoes are rumoured to have ended up in a museum in France. The Musée National du Sport in Nice, which has a pair (with Emil's name on) that looks rather like them, has not responded to my request for information about their provenance.

p. 94: **to show her his latest medal**
The medal in this incident is generally assumed to have been the 10,000m gold, but the last time I discussed it with Dana she told me that she thought it was the silver – which would be more logical, given the timing of Emil's visit. Then again, different accounts give different versions of that, too. My interpretation of the timing is taken from Dana, both in person and in *DEZ*, p. 81.

p. 95: **'you should see how quickly our generals can run away'**
Quoted in 'Když utíkali generálové', by Jiří Jakoubek, *Lidové noviny*, 16 February 2007.

p. 97: **a German shoemaker called Adolf Dassler**
See *Pitch Invasion*, by Barbara Smit. My repeated requests to Adidas to clarify the details of the company's relationship with Emil have failed

to elicit a response, but I have discussed the matter with Smit, who is probably the greatest expert on the company's history. Smit is confident that Dassler did make contact with Emil and that, at some point, he began to supply Emil with shoes. She thinks it unlikely, however, that there was any financial aspect to the relationship. It was simply about the shoes – which, she adds, really were very good. Enquiries at the IOC's Olympic Museum confirm that the two Adidas shoes exhibited there – a spiked track shoe and a spikeless 'marathon shoe' – are just shoes once worn by Emil; the information displayed with the shoes makes no further claim than that, and nor do the loan documents from Adidas. Since Emil only ever ran two marathons, however, it seems probable that the marathon shoe, at least, was used in an Olympic race. It is likeliest that this was in 1956 in Melbourne, when Adi Dassler's son, Horst, spent much of the games distributing his company's shoes to athletes. Dana Zátopková thinks that the first time Emil wore Adidas shoes (with the stripes removed) may have been in 1953, in a championship event in Bucharest; before that, he usually ran in shoes made specially for him, out of goat-skin, in Zlín. Later still, Adidas began to supply kit in bulk to the ČSTV and were, I am told, 'very generous'.

p. 97: **spotted visiting Kopřivnice**
Práce, 31 August 1948; see also records in the Kopřivnice Folk Museum of the creation of what used to be the Zátopek Stadium but is now the Summer Stadium.

p. 98: **attempted to prove him wrong by doing a handstand**
I initially found this detail in an interview with Dana Zátopkova by Guillaume Narguet published in *Zátopek* magazine, January 2007.

p. 100: **'This is how the people reward those who are most faithful to them . . .'**
The footage is in the archive of Krátký Film Praha; it also appears in *Jeden ze štafety*. I do not know if that is what it was originally shot for.

p. 100: **around 300,000 people were driven out public life, including thousands of army officers**
The Prague Spring and its Aftermath: Czech Politics 1968–1970, by Kieran Williams, p. 5; *The Soviet Union and the Czechoslovak Army, 1948–1983*, by Condoleezza Rice, pp. 62–76.

p. 100: **'What you do when the stadium is full . . .'**
Quoted in *Stars of Czechoslovak Sport*, p. 15.

p. 101: **'When a person trains once . . .'**
Quoted in *Zátopek in Photographs*, p. 38; and Bryant, p. 210.

p. 101: **Klement Kerssenbrock**
Kerssenbrock's article in *Leichtathletik* was translated for *Athletics* magazine by Jim Alford in October 1949 (and quoted in Phillips, pp. 43–5) – the curious thing being that the article appears to be identical to a chapter in František Kožík's *Zátopek, the Marathon Victor*, where it appears (in my edition) with no reference to Kerssenbrock. I am not sure if Kerssenbrock omitted to credit Kožík or if, more probably, Kožík forgot to credit Kerssenbrock (who translated *Zátopek, the Marathon Victor* into German). But the appearance of Alford's translation can at least be taken as a reliable date marker.

p. 101: **'When you can't keep going, go faster'**
Quoted in Kosatík (p. 1). Readers who can come up with a better translation of *'Když nemůžeš, přidej'* are welcome to have a go.

p. 102: **crawled deep into the back of its kennel**
This incident is also described, more colourfully, in Pavel, p. 26. I assume that Dana's eyewitness account is more reliable.

p. 105: **a word of encouragement there, a joke false start . . . there**
For example, Gordon Pirie, in *Running Wild* (p. 137), describes how Emil entertained the crowd with a mock false start in Prague in 1955; and how, in Manchester later that year, Emil, who was struggling, none the less found the strength to catch up with Pirie halfway through the 5,000m and urge him: 'Faster, faster – it is getting too slow.' To Pirie, both incidents were evidence of Emil's 'magnificent character'.

p. 105: **'For me it was always about more than the victory . . .'**
Quoted in *Životopisy: Emil Zátopek*, a radio series directed by Pavel Krejčí for Česky rozhlas and first broadcast on 1 May 2012, part 4.

p. 106: **'I can't train when I am supposed to be on duty'**
Quoted by Brasher and Elliott, *Observer*, 27 September 1964

p. 106: **Emil and two other athletes in his unit were excused all other duties.**

Interview with Emil Zátopek in *Slovo*, by Jiří Jakoubek ('Slavný vytrvalec splnil rozkaz a vytvořil světový rekord'), 29 May 1997; *et al.*

p. 106: **feared that . . . he would be put in prison**
Informer's report in Emil's military service records (Ministerstvo národní obrany – Osobní spis, 24503: Zátopek Emil, 1. Část).

p. 109: **The discus thrower Jarmila Jamnická**
Jamnická is interviewed in *Pohádkový Péťa.*

p. 111: **twenty-five kilometres' worth of fast 400m repetitions every day**
See: Phillips, p. 48.

p. 111: **'I have yet to hear of any athlete . . .'**
Jimmy Green, *Athletics Weekly*, 4 March 1950; quoted in Phillips p. 48

p. 112: **acronym-based slang**
'*Mukl*' stands for '*muž určeny k likvidaci*'.

p. 119: **'I keep quiet, or else they would lock me up.'**
Quoted (disapprovingly) in Emil's military service records (1. Část, pp. 15–18) – in which the reported misdemeanours that follow are also recorded. Most of this information presumably came from StB informers but it has not been preserved in the StB archives. The secret service reports on Emil's political behaviour and attitudes in this chapter all come from his personal file in his military service records. The StB eventually developed a formidable filing system, but record-keeping in its earliest years was more haphazard.

p. 119: **he claimed that his application had been held up**
This explanation appears more than once in his service records. Emil claimed that he had applied to join the party in Stará Boleslav in June 1948 but was told to apply again when he had a permanent posting; and that by the time that happened new members were not being accepted. He finally applied on 11 October 1951 – after an interval during which it seems to have been generally assumed that he must already be a member – and was accepted on 10 December 1953. The revealing thing is Emil felt obliged to explain all this to his military superiors. It was highly unusual for an officer not to be a Party member. Even Colonel Antonín Ingr had joined by 1948.

p. 120: **'He who does not have a positive attitude cannot serve as a commander.'**
Quoted in *The Soviet Union and the Czechoslovak Army, 1948–1983*, by Condoleezza Rice, p. 75.

p. 122: **he preferred to 'bend'**
Quoted in Emil's military service records (Ministerstvo národní obrany – Osobní spis, 24503: Zátopek Emil, 1. Část, p. 22).

p. 123: **Emil considered himself to be in the latter camp**
Quoted in Kosatík, p. 218.

p. 123: **to learn to behave as a domesticated animal**
Jak to bylo, by Luděk Pachman (1974), p. 282.

p. 125: **accepts 'each of his races as a complete test . . .'**
'But only on Sunday', by Kenny Moore, *Sports Illustrated*, February 1973.

p. 125: **that still brought tears to his eyes**
Running with the Legends, by Michael Sandrock, p. 13.

p. 126: **A Finnish newspaper hailed him**
The Finnish and Belgian newspapers are quoted in Kožík, p. 133; the other quotation is from *The Times*, 22 August 1950, p. 2.

p. 128: **the nickname 'the Czech locomotive'**
For an exhaustive study of contemporary media coverage of Emil, see: *Hrdina v totalitních médiích: srovnávací analýza olympijských vítězství Emila Zátopka (1948, 1952)*, by Petr Dušek (Univerzita Karlova v Praze, 2010).

p. 129: **a rather average physical specimen**
Details of Emil's physiology in this and the following paragraphs are taken from, among other places, 'Emil Zátopek from a Medical Point of View', by Dr Zděnek Hornof, published in *Zátopek in Photographs*, by František Kožík, pp. 69–70; 'Emil Zátopek', by J. Armour Milne, *Athletics Weekly*, 12 May 1951, pp. 8–12; 'O největším vytrvalci všech dob – Emilu Zátopkovi', by Dr Ladislav Fišer (a trainer at Dukla Praha), *Práce*, 6 June 1954, p. 10; Phillips, pp. 57–8; and 'L'apport de la science dans l' entraînement sportif: exemple de la course de fond', Véronique Billat, Université Lille 2, *STAPS 2001*, p. 36. The slow-motion analysis can be found at: https://archive.org/details/

Emil_Zatopek, with comment by Dr Nicholas Romanov of Posc Tech (also at https://www.youtube.com/watch?v=XdYHCSAMDr4).

p. 131: **'poor – or non-existent'**
The Lonely Breed, by Ron Clarke and Norman Harris, pp. 107–8 – also the source of the 'ran too eagerly' quote. Clarke's subsequent comments come directly from him, in a telephone interview in September 2014. Fred Wilt's 1956 book, *How They Train*, supports Clarke's analysis.

p. 131: **'I am not particularly interested in beating my opponents'**
Kožík, p. 125.

p. 132: **'Zátopek is always to be found in his office or visiting an Army unit'**
Armour Milne, writing in *Athletics Weekly* in early 1955; quoted in Phillips, p. 108. See also *Stars of Czechoslovak Sport*, by J. Armour Milne (Orbis, Prague, 1956), p. 24; Kosatík, pp. 113–15; and *MTZ*, p. 33.

p. 133: **'There are certainly few top-class athletes in this country who would have difficulty in finding a firm to "carry" them for a few years.'**
'The stresses of international competition', by Christopher Chataway, in *Modern Athletics*, ed. H.A. Meyer (OUP, 1964), p. 98.

p. 133: **'his training methods seemed quite fantastic'**
Pirie, pp. 49–50.

p. 133: **'No athlete would be wise . . .'**
Athletics Weekly, 4 March 1950; quoted in Phillips, p. 49.

p. 134: **'it is simply more than we could stand'**
Quoted in *The Perfect Mile,* by Neil Bascomb, p. 168.

p. 134: **'misplaced intellectual arrogance'**
Quoted in Bryant, p. 214.

p. 134: **'making life agreeable for those around him'**
Stars of Czechoslovak Sport, by J. Armour Milne (Orbis, Prague, 1956), p. 21.

p. 135: **He spoke many languages – eight, ultimately**
With Dana's help I compiled the following list: Czech, German, Russian, English, French, Spanish, Finnish, Indonesian. There were

others (e.g., Hindi, and perhaps Polish) in which he was happy to have a go. This can-do attitude was clearly part of his secret.

p. 135: **'a story about a trip to Paris'**
The footage appears in *Z televizního alba Emila Zátopka*, Česka televizé (2003).

p. 136: **'the gayest and merriest home I ever visited . . .'**
Quotes from Pirie and Clarke are taken from, respectively, *Running Wild* (p. 50) and 'All-Time Greats', an article by Clarke in *Athletics Weekly*, 5 November 1987, p. 19. Jamnická and Hainová both gave their accounts in *Pohádkový Péťa* (2002).

p. 137: **'he takes the craziest risks with his precious limbs'**
Milne (*SCS*), p. 21.

p. 137: **'Physically he was more machine than man'**
Clarke & Harris, p. 108.

p. 137: **'I sing out of key, but I sing . . .'**
Quoted in an interview broadcast posthumously in the Česka televize documentary, *Nejen zlaté vzpomínky*, 3 October 2014.

p. 140: **'soft and squishy, easy rhythm, thinking of other things'**
Quoted by Kenny Moore in his foreword to *Running with Legends*, by Michael Sandrock, p. viii. Other authors – including Pirie (p. 50), Nelson (p. 61) and Corrigan (p. 40) – suggest that this was a regular occurrence. But this seems improbable, given the horror with which Dana greeted the resulting flood. In a later interview with Sandrock, Emil seemed to imply again that it had been a one-off (*Running with Legends*, p. 12). On balance, I would advise not trying this at home.

p. 141: **'I eat when I am hungry'**
Emil, talking in *Jeden ze štafety*, dir. Jaroslav Mach (Československo, 1952).

p. 141: **he would buy rolls, butter and a litre of milk on the way to work**
'Emil Zátopek', by J. Armour Milne, *Athletics Weekly*, 19 May 1951, pp. 8–12.

p. 141: **Emil revealed that he had been eating the leaves of a young birch tree**
J. Karel Bártů, speaking in *Pohádkový Péťa*.

p. 141: **similar experiments involving dandelions and . . . vast quantities of garlic**
Kosatík, pp. 89–90.

p. 141: **self-medicating with vodka**
Ludvík Liška, speaking in *Pohádkový Péťa.*

p. 142: **often ran his laps on the grass outside the track**
'Emil Zátopek', by J. Armour Milne, *Athletics Weekly*, 19 May 1951, p. 9.

p. 142: **'You must listen to your body. You must feel hard, and you must feel easy.'**
Sears, p. 217.

p. 142: **'not mad . . . just utterly absorbed, with every fibre of his explosive body'**
Brasher & Elliott, *Observer*, 27 September 1964.

p. 144: **his best times over shorter distances were many years behind him**
Emil's career-best middle-distance times were set as follows: 1:58.7 for 800m in 1943, 3:52.8 for 1,500m in 1947, 8:07.8 for 3,000m in 1948.

p. 145: **'Zátopek could run twenty kilometres in one hour'**
Quoted in Nelson, p. 61; Kožík, p. 143.

p. 146: **twenty kilometres north-east of Prague**
Svět v obrazech, September 1951. The cutting is in the Zátopek archive at the Technical Museum Tatra in Kopřivnice.

p. 146: **Emil would eventually set eight world records here**
The eight were: at 6 miles (1 November 1953), 10,000m (1 November 1953), 10 miles (29 September 1951), 20,000m (29 September 1951), 15 miles (26 October 1952), 25,000m (26 October 1952), 30,000m (26 October 1952) and One Hour (29 September 1951).

p. 147: **'the closest I'll ever come to knowing what it's like to have a baby'**
Sir Bradley Wiggins, quoted on telegraph.co.uk, 7 June 2015.

p. 148: **'The continuous pain increased with every lap . . .'**
Emil's descriptions are taken from *BZ*, pp. 53–6.

p. 149: **'indescribably cordial and enthusiastic'**
Rudé právo, 30 September 1951, p. 1.

p. 150: **'Today I really had more than enough'**
Quoted in Kožík, p. 146.

p. 150: **fifty-two beats per minute**
Phillips, p. 61.

p. 150: **'To boast of a performance which I cannot beat is merely stupid vanity'**
Kožík, p. 121.

p. 151: **'belted the living daylight out of two tremendous world records'**
Quoted in Phillips, p. 60.

p. 152: ***One of the Relay*, an hour-long propaganda film**
Jeden ze štafety had its première on 25 April 1952.

pp. 154–5: **did worse than any other athlete involved in a test to measure the force of runners' strides**
Pavel, p. 27.

p. 155: **'it was worth asking if I should even start the 5,000 metres'**
DEZ, pp. 102–3.

p. 155: **'I will focus my training and performance . . . to win two gold medals'**
Quoted in 'Emil Zátopek: Osamělost přespolního běžce', by Pavel Malik, published in *Lidové noviny*, 28 July 2012.

p. 155: **made to become a truck driver as a punishment**
See 'Jan Veselý's Perič bicycle' at www.sterba-bike.cz.

pp. 156–7: **'We are aware of how greatly we are honoured by the confidence . . .'**
Rudé právo, 9 July 1952, p. 4. See also: Kožík, p. 152.

p. 157: **He was filmed as he spoke these words**
I have not seen the footage, but you can see him being filmed in *Zátopek in Photographs.*

p. 159: **where, to his surprise, he was not arrested**
I have based these details on Emil's account, quoted in Macák, Žurman & Jirásek, p. 21; Emil also described the incident in much the same terms in, among other places, an interview with Frantisek Bouc, 'The legend lives on', *Prague Post*, 29 December 1999.

p. 159: **The pair then flew to Helsinki on a later plane**

Readers wishing to do their own detective work may wish to consult versions given by the following: *Rudé právo*, 12 July 1952, p. 4; *Kdo byl kdo v České atletice*, by Jan Jirka *et al.* (Praha Olympia 2004); 'The legend lives on', by František Bouc, *Prague Post*, 29 December 1999; the interview with Emil Zátopek shown in the Inventura Febia TV documentary *Emil Zátopek a Věra Čáslavská*, (dir. M. Mináč a O. Sommerová), Česka televize, 20–22 September 2011; and Part 1 of *Životopisy: Emil Zátopek*, Pavel Krejčí's radio series for Česky rozhlas (first broadcast on 1 May 2012). Dana Zátopková spoke to me of a three-day delay, as she did when interviewed by Daniela Lazarová for Radio Prague, on 19 July 2012; in an interview with Karel Tejkal for vitalplus.org, 21 June 2010, she insisted that she cried for two days. Emil, talking in the Česka televize documentary 'Z televizniho alba Emila Zátopka', also describes a three-day stand-off. Zdeněk Fator told me that Emil and Standa flew in a third plane. Naudin (p. 136) says that the plane didn't arrive until Sunday, 13 July.

p. 161: **plus forty from China**

Only one of the Chinese athletes actually competed.

p. 161: **Les Perry . . . 'waltzed' past the guards**

For the fullest account of Perry's visit, see *Why Die? The Extraordinary Percy Cerutty, Maker of Champions*, by Graem Sims, p. 124, where the quotes used in this paragraph originally appeared. See also *The Perfect Mile*, by Neal Bascomb, p. 64.

p. 162: **Emil's tongue 'hanging out like a dog's'**

The World in My Diary, by Norman Banks, p. 61.

p. 162: **'open and honest and willing to share his training ideas with anyone'**

Quoted in *3:59.4*, by John Bryant, pp. 212–13, where you will also find the statement that John Landy left with his 'notebooks crammed' with details of Emil's methods.

p. 162: **Bénigno Cacérès enthused about the excellence with which Emil spoke to him in French**

La XVième Olympiade, by Bénigno Cacérès (ed. du Seuil), quoted in Naudin, p. 135. It is possible that Emil was actually speaking to the Poles in Czech: the two languages are said to be mutually intelligible.

p. 163: **thousands of Finnish fans had turned out in the hope of seeing Emil arrive**
František Brož, quoted by Adam B. Ellick in his obituary of Emil in *Running Times*, 1 March 2001.

p. 163: **'I get a bigger welcome here than on Czech tracks'**
Quoted in *Miami News*, 25 July 1952.

p. 163: **an official came looking for Emil, found Cerutty instead, and made a scene**
Cerutty's visit is described in detail in Sims, p. 125; Emil's account of it is quoted in Macák, Žurman & Jirásek, p. 24. Emil describes the visit, but not the sleeping arrangements, in *DEZ*, p. 110.

p. 164: **Cerutty . . . described the encounter in an effusive letter to a friend in Melbourne**
Cerutty's letter, dated 17 July 1952, was not only reproduced in the *Melbourne Guardian* but also quoted at length in the Sydney *Tribune* (6 August 1952, p. 5; and 20 August 1952, p. 6). I suspect that its publication was what gave rise to the much-repeated tale that Emil gave his bed to an Australian journalist the night before the 10,000m final – a story for which I have yet to track down a primary source or even an alleged subject. Roger Bannister shared the 'journalist' version with his team-mates while in Helsinki (see *The First Four Minutes*, p. 131), but Bannister was merely passing on a story he had heard. It is possible that this was a garbled version of the Cerutty incident. Or perhaps I am doing Emil an injustice, and he gave his bed up to an Australian not once but twice in the run-up to the Games; in which case all I can say is that, for an athlete who placed considerable value on getting a good night's sleep, this was generosity taken to almost lunatic extremes.

p. 165: **'The only thing we can hope for is that Zátopek breaks a leg'**
Fred Wilt, quoted in the *Sarasota Herald-Tribune*, 29 June 1952, p. 13.

p. 166: **One British commentator saw this as a reason to dismiss Emil, snootily, as a 'robot runner'**
Olympic Games 1952: Official Report of the British Olympic Association (published by World Sport), p. 23.

p. 166: **his Finnish admirers . . . had modified his name to 'Satu Peka'**
The play on words works better for Finns, for whom 'Peka' is the name of a character in many folk tales – perhaps roughly comparable to the British 'Puck'. But the Czech equivalent is 'Péťa' – with Emil's full Finnish nickname thus translating into Czech as 'Pohádkový Péťa' – and the English equivalent of 'Péťa' is 'Pete'. So 'Satu Peka' translates into English as 'Fairy-tale Pete'.

p. 166: **'an oblivion of fatigue'**
Pirie, p. 93.

p. 167: **'a pitiless race of elimination' . . . a 'battle conducted by Zátopekian fury'**
Gaston Meyer is quoted in Phillips, p. 67; Jacques Goddet is quoted in Naudin, p. 139.

p. 169: **'Sasha, come on, we must get a move on'**
Quoted in Nelson, p. 63.

p. 169: **'Come along, Stone, if you want to qualify'**
Quoted in Nelson, p. 63. Others, such as Krise and Squires, give the quote as 'Come along, Stone, or you'll miss the bus' – which wouldn't be out of character for Emil. It seems sensible, however, to prefer Nelson's version, which was published twelve years earlier.

p. 169: **Perry thought it was a wave of encouragement to him**
See: Sims, p. 129.

p. 170: **Talk of 'the race of the century'**
Kožík, p. 161.

p. 171: **'the atomic bomb of the Games'**
Gaston Reiff, quoted in *L'Équipe*, No. 1,957, 23 July 1952, p. 1.

p. 171: **reports that people had been hanging on to the outside of heaving trams**
Lovesey, p. 141.

p. 171: **the consensus among commentators**
Based on surveys by *Athletics Weekly* and an unnamed Swedish newspaper quoted in, respectively, Phillips, p. 65, and Kožík, p. 161.

p. 172: **had taken the lead purely out of sportsmanship**
See *BZ*, p. 59; and Pavel, p. 40. Pavel gives this account of Emil's thinking: 'Better not to win at all than to win like this' (i.e., unsportingly allowing Schade to do all the work). Les Perry's interpretation was quoted by Ron Clarke in an article in the 'All-time Greats' series in *Athletics Weekly*, 5 November 1987 (p. 19).

p. 172: **at 3,500m, Reiff detonated an explosive attack**
See Kožík, p. 164; *et al.* The *Official Report of the Organising Committee for the Games of the XV Olympiad, Helsinki 1952* (p. 252) seems to be alone in suggesting that Reiff's move didn't come until 4,400m – which would be hard to reconcile with Reiff dropping out with 600m to go. See also: Macák, Žurman & Jirásek, p. 69.

p. 173: **fuelled by the thought that he would never again allow gold to slip from his grasp . . .**
Emil is fairly explicit about this motivation in *EZVžs*; he reckoned that he could have won the Olympic 5,000m in 1948, if he had only started his final sprint a bit earlier.

p. 174: **'There is no medal for fourth'**
Quoted in Macák, Žurman & Jirásek, p. 70; *et al.*

p. 174: **One journalist described him as looking like 'a tortured wreck'**
'Czech and Double Czech', by Red Smith, *New York Herald Tribune*, 24 July 1952; collected in *Views of Sport* (1954).

p. 174: **Did it not follow, then, that they were likely to tire?**
In chapter 31 of *The Official History of the Olympic Games and the IOC – Part II: The Post War Years (1948–1980)*, by David Miller, Emil said: 'I was experienced enough to know that the sprint by the other three . . . would produce quick fatigue.'

p. 175: **'I ran like the wind'**
Quoted in Macák, Žurman & Jirásek, p. 70.

p. 175: **sometimes spiced with an expressive 'Grrrrr'**
Quoted in Macák, Žurman & Jirásek, p. 21. See also a charming account on YouTube by Michael Sandrock, in which he describes

turning up uninvited on Emil's doorstep and being welcomed, invited in and entertained for hours with accounts of triumphs gone by.

p. 176: **'The track seemed to be flying past beneath me . . .'**
Emil's account in *EZVžs*; the 'I could already see the gold medal' remark is quoted in Macák, Žurman & Jirásek, p. 70.

p. 176: **'Mimoun . . . But Zátopek finishes wonderfully . . .'**
You can hear parts of the commentary at Radio Praha (http://rebel.radio.cz/mp3/podcast/en/archives/111126-emil-zatopek-a-czech-sporting-hero.mp3); or in the first part of Pavel Krejčí's radio series, *Životopisy: Emil Zátopek*. But the best place to listen is in Kopřivnice, at the Expozice Emila a Dany Zatopkovych in the Technické muzeum Tatra – where the radio commentary has been synchronised with (non-Czechoslovak) film footage. I have made it sound more coherent than it is.

p. 177: **even going so far – according to one account – as to offer to give him his medal**
Pavel, p. 42; *Zátopek a ti druzí*, by Zvonimír Šupich, p. 72.

p. 177: **Percy Cerutty's verdict**
See note to p. 164; the letter was subsequently republished at least once.

p. 177: **'The name Zátopek has become synonymous with the idea of speed . . .'**
Otakar Mašek, quoted in Kožík, pp. 167; I have not been able to track down where these words were originally published.

p. 178: **An English journalist, Guy Butler, had almost been hit by a javelin**
See: 'Czech and Double Czech', by Red Smith.

p. 178: **Eventually she managed to get a passing Soviet trainer**
Dana has given many accounts of this episode, including a detailed one in an interview with Daniela Lazarová for Radio Prague on 19 July 2012. The trainer is sometimes identified as Markov and sometimes as Romanov. See also: 'A Bridge to Long Ago', by Leigh Montville, *Sports Illustrated*, 26 March 1990; and Šupich, p. 72.

p. 179: **'pleases me more than all the others'**
Kožík, p. 167.

p. 179: **'I will never forget the way he looked at me'**
Dana Zátopková, interviewed by Daniela Lazarová on Radio Prague, 19 July 2012.

p. 179: **'If he could improve his behaviour, he could be a good example to our youth . . .'**
I have heard this incident described, several times: by Emil's team-mate, Ludvík Liška (to me); and by Emil himself, in *Nejen zlaté vzpomínky*, a Česka televise documentary broadcast 3 October 2014. I have taken the precise wording of Jula Torma's quote from an interview with Dana Zátopková by Karel Tejkel for vitalplus.org, 21 June 2010. Torma's words are given thus: '*Kašli na něj, Emilku, veď je to kokot.*'

p. 185: **with what he later described as Cockney defiance**
Quoted in Sears, p. 198.

p. 185: **'like a boxer after the third round'**
Emil Zátopek, talking in *Pohádkový Péťa.*

p. 186: **He had bought some new shoes specially for the race – some say Karhu (a Finnish brand), others Adidas (disguised for political reasons)**
I find the Adidas theory unconvincing. (See note to p. 97.) However, it does seem plausible that, when Emil did eventually start competing in Adidas shoes, he would have removed or disguised the stripes, so that his use of a Western product would be less conspicuous.

p. 186: **to soften them in advance with cooking grease**
Lovett, pp. 57–62.

p. 188: **'The finish line was a long way off. I was alone, and my strength had gone'**
Quoted in Macák, Žurman & Jirásek, p. 70.

pp. 188–9: **'If you want to enjoy something,' he said later, 'run 100 metres. If you want to experience something, run a marathon.'**
This quotation has been repeated many times, in many forms. Dana insists that the most common form – typically along the lines of 'If you want to win something, run 100 metres. If you want

to experience another life, run a marathon' – is a mistranslation. Emil's aphorism depends on the play between the Czech words 'užít' ('enjoy') and 'zažít' ('experience'). My wording reflects this advice.

p. 189: **the next day, he had to hobble downstairs backwards**
Macák, Žurman & Jirásek, p. 24.

p. 189: **'My legs were hurting up to my neck'**
Emil talking in *Sláva vítězům: Emil Zátopek*, dir. Simona Oktábcová, Theodor Mojžíš, first broadcast on C2 and C1 on 10 December 2001.

p. 189: **Mimoun, Reiff, Pirie – cheering him on from the roadside**
See Pavel, p. 47; *BZ*, p. 65; *Zátopek in Photographs*, p. 56; *et al.*

p. 190: **the first moment in the race when he felt happy**
Emil talking in *Pohádkový Péťa.*

p. 190: **'but my legs would not listen'**
Personal communication from Emil's former colleague, Václav Bednář, to whom he told this, August 2015.

p. 190: **'I tried to balance my steps and started to smile . . .'**
Macák, Žurman & Jirásek, p. 70.

p. 192: **an example of what a 'decent socialist' could achieve**
Ladislav Kořán, interviewed by Karel Tejkal for vitalplus.org, 21 June 2010.

p. 192: **'If you knew the relationship between me and him . . .'**
Jan Haluza, talking in *Pohádkový Péťa.*

p. 193: **'I was sorry that, already, it belonged to the past . . .'**
Emil Zátopek, talking in *Pohádkový Péťa*; Emil makes a similar point in *BZ*, p. 65.

p. 194: **Two leading poets . . . wrote epics in his praise**
'Píšen o marathonském vítezi', by Miloslav Bureš; 'Tvé jméno rodnou naši zemi . . .', by František Branislav.

p. 194: **a new, hagiographic mini-biography**
Emil Zátopek, by Emanuel Bosák & Josef Pondelik (Artia Prague, 1953). This was the same Bosák who had criticised Emil's behaviour at that team meeting in Helsinki.

p. 194: **almost certainly staged**
According to the Czech National Film Archive of the Czech Republic, *Jeden ze štafety* is part-documentary and partly dramatised. It is often, but not always, obvious which scenes are which.

p. 195: **'unique breed of conscientious athlete . . .'**
Květy, 7 August 1952, p. 2; the *Rudé právo* quote is from 28 July 1952.

p. 195: **the Order of Work**
Other honours received by Emil over the years included the Order of the Republic, the Medal for Services to the Nation, the Order of Merit for the Defence of the Homeland, the title Merited Master of Sport, the Czechoslovak Peace Prize and, at the end of his life, the Order of the White Lion.

p. 196: **General Kratochvíl looked again at the recommendation for punishment, dismissed it as 'nonsense' and tore it up**
Emil told this story many times. The fullest version I have seen is in *Sláva vítězům: Emil Zátopek*. Emil is also quoted at length on the subject in Macák, Žurman & Jirásek, p. 24.

p. 197: **Emil addressed an audience of 2,500 at a peace rally**
See: 'Letter from Helsinki', by A.J. Liebling, in *The New Yorker*, 23 August 1952. Emil is quoted as saying: 'The burden that is hanging over this year's Olympics is like a heavy shadow – the fact that the war adventure carried on for more than two years by foreign-intervention troops under the command of American generals against the Korean people has not been terminated, or even suspended, for the duration of these Games . . .'

p. 197: **According to apologists for the regime**
See: *Czechoslovak Sport: 1945-1955*, by J. Armour Milne, p. 57. Milne, who lived in Prague, was a committed Communist.

p. 198: **their highest rate of coal extraction**
See: Bosák & Pondelik, pp. 12–13; and Naudin, p. 124.

p. 198: **'chased like a bloated goat'**
Věra čáslavská: život na Olympu, by Pavel Kosatík, p. 43. I don't pretend to know what 'like a bloated goat' means. In Czech, it is: '*jak nadmutou kozu*'.

p. 199: **life-lessons-drawn-from-sport**
See Kožík, p. 93 and p. 124.

p. 200: **Koščák . . . while Černý**
See: *DEZ*, p. 72.

p. 200: **'the new man: Socialist Man'**
L'Humanité, 28 February 1953 ('C'est cela l'homme nouveau, l'homme du socialisme').

p. 201: **'As a good soldier, he must obey . . .'**
Czechoslovak Sport: 1945–1955, p. 20.

p. 201: **' . . . the greatest sportsman I have ever met'**
Pirie, p. 51.

p. 202: **reports of forged tickets led to a police investigation**
'Lidé utíkali z práce, přijel Zátopek', iDNES.cz, 12 April 2006.

p. 203: **evidence from his later life**
See, for example, Emil's remarks about his own possible defection after 1968, and his falling-out with Luděk Pachman (chapters 15–17).

pp. 203-4: **mourning . . . 'a great teacher of Soviet sport'**
'Učíme se z myšlenek a díla soudruha Stalina', by Emil Zátopek, in *Mladá fronta: Deník československého svazu mládeţe*. 1953, r. 9, č. 58, s. 3.

p. 205: **The next finisher was fifteen minutes behind**
Phillips, p. 77.

p. 205: **'OK, we'll throw her a little bit further . . .'**
Kožík implies that Dana jumped in of her own accord – presumably to avoid the suggestion that a Communist hero such as Emil could have been so reckless and stupid.

p. 206: **the best ever 5,000m time by an Australian**
The Australian authorities refused to ratify it as an Australian record, because of the circumstances in which it was run.

p. 208: **'You must not expect too much of me in future . . .'**
Quoted in Phillips, p. 88–9.

p. 209: **No transcripts of his debriefings survive**
A summary in the StB archive suggests that Emil's trip to Algiers for Christmas 1947 produced some eight pages of debriefing in January 1948. (The StB was founded in 1945 and, like the Ministry of the Interior from 1946, was controlled by the Communists. It is not hugely surprising that Emil, as a soldier as well as an athlete,

was ordered to give debriefings even before 'victorious February' in 1948; in *Běží Zátopek* he reports that the Czechoslovak team were accompanied by a 'sharp eye' to the European Championships in Oslo in 1946 – and tampered with her notebook as a joke.) Emil's debriefing is said to have included his accounts of 'interviews' with visiting and local athletes, an account of a visit to the Baťa factory in Algiers, four pages of his own 'observations' – and the excuse that he could not do more because there was not enough time. It is possible that some of those he spoke to would have been surprised to have their encounters written up in this way – but perhaps no more than Emil would have been by many Western journalists' write-ups of their meetings with him. I suspect that Emil may have recycled some of his observations for his published writings, in which foreign trips, including this one, are described at length. (See: Archiv bezpečnostních složek, ZS GŠ, č. 37843; and *DEZ*, pp. 69–70).

p. 210: **'To stand on the starting line . . .'**
Quoted in 'Zatopek now runs with pupils', AP (Prague), 10 April 1962 (printed in the Milwaukee Sentinel, part 2, p. 5, 11 April 1962).

pp. 210–11: **His training diary recorded . . . 100 laps a day**
See: *MTZ*, pp. 56–7; see also Sandrock, p. 25. The 1,845km figure is calculated from figures recorded by J. Armour Milne in *Athletics Weekly*, quoted in Phillips, p. 106.

p. 211: **catch-Reiff-or-die sprints**
See: Steffny, pp. 54–5. It is not absolutely clear which year Steffny has in mind, but his suggestion seems to be that, in these later years, Emil might do a set of fast 200s (30–35 seconds), some sub-racing-pace 400s (80–90 seconds), some fast-as-possible-in-the-circumstances 400s (70 seconds), some more sub-racing-pace 400s (80–90 seconds) and some more fast 200s (30–35 seconds). My own view is that it would be a mistake, from this distance in time, to get too hung up about the numbers: we cannot even be certain that the distances quoted were exact.

p. 212: **specific, public pledges . . . displayed in a shop window in Wenceslas Square**
Described in the *Guardian*, 8 April 1954.

p. 212: **The French athletics federation . . . had forbidden French athletes to take part**
For this and other details of *l'affaire de Colombe*, see: 'Emil Zátopek dans la Guerre Froide: de la soumission à la rébellion (1948–1968)', by Yohann Fortune, in *Sciences Sociale et Sport, 2012/1 (No.5)*, pp. 264ff.; '1954: l'indésirable Zatopek triomphe à Colombes', by Jocelyn Lermusieaux, *L'Équipe*, 20 May 2014; Naudin, pp. 179ff.; Phillips, pp. 92–5; and Christophe Wyrzykowski's interview with Emil in *L'Équipe*, 4 August 1998.

p. 212: **'the Paris of junk literature, the Paris of pornographic revues and magazines'**
Quoted in *Figaro*, 29 and 30 May 1954.

p. 213: **'horse dosage, every day'**
Quoted in part 4 of Pavel Krejčí's radio series, *Životopisy: Emil Zátopek*.

p. 214: **those who found their foreign office's stance embarrassing and those who suggested that Emil was a 'Communist fanatic'**
See: *L'Équipe*, 29 May 1954; *Figaro*, 29 May 1954; and *L'Aurore*, 31 May 1954.

p. 215: **'*admirable réponse*' . . . '*incroyable stupidité*'**
Respectively from *L'Équipe*, 31 May 1954; and *L'Aurore*, 31 May 1954 (both quoted in Naudin, pp. 184–6).

p. 216: **made a low(ish) bow to him**
Československý filmový týdeník, Archiv ČT24. The footage makes a nonsense of Kožík's claim that this was a 'deep' bow.

p. 216: **'The delight in work, the conscientiousness, the courage, the feeling of responsibility of a Zátopek'**
Quoted in Kožík, p. 167.

p. 216: **Athletes also received a 'nutrition allowance' . . . rumours of cash bonuses for Olympic medallists**
See: *The Rings of Destiny*, by Olga Connolly, p. 102.

p. 219: **'capable of being beaten by younger, speedier runners'**
Jimmy Green, writing in *Athletics Weekly*, October 1955 (quoted in Phillips, p. 112).

p. 219: **'I am not fast enough for the 5,000 metres'**
Reported in the *Manchester Guardian*, 12 October 1955.

p. 220: **single-handedly started an Indian running boom**
See: 'The Haves and the Have-Nots', by Ashwini Kumar and Ashwani Kumar, *India International Centre Quarterly, Vol. 9, No. 2: Sports through the looking glass* (June 1982), p. 122. For more details of this trip, see: *The Illustrated Weekly of India*, Volume 107, Issues 1–13, p. 52; and *Emil Zátopek: earth's tearing cry and Heaven's beaming smile*, by Sri Chinmoy (Agnes Press, 1980).

p. 220: **incorporating wife-carrying into his training regime as a regular feature**
Reputable sources in which this assertion can be found include: *Olympic Marathon: A Centennial History of the Games' Most Storied Race*, p. 64; Macák, Žurman & Jirásek, p. 25; 'A Bridge to Long Ago', by Leigh Montville, *Sports Illustrated*, 26 March 1990; *The Lonely Breed*, by Ron Clarke and Norman Harris, p. 106 (where the wife-carrying is supposed to have happened in the snow); *Praha Velké osudy: Emil Zátopek*, a radio programme by Karel Tejkal for Česky rozhlas, first broadcast on 27 October 2009 (which mentions the bony shoulders and the tree-root). J. Armour Milne's description appears in *Stars of Czechoslovak Sport* (pp. 22–3).

p. 221: **'Do anything they ask of you . . .'**
Connolly, p. 16. Connolly (who in those days was Olga Fikotová) adds that, nonetheless, Emil would often skip on the spot during interviews, so that the time wouldn't be entirely wasted.

pp. 222–3: **'To have this sudden shadow of strife and misery cast over the whole affair . . .'**
Quoted in *The Argus* (Melbourne), 10 November 1956, p. 24; the 'probably the whole field' quote at the end of the paragraph is from the *Manchester Guardian*, 10 November 1956, p. 3.

p. 223: **a case of Pilsner Urquell beer**
Yet another colourful detail that appears in *The Rings of Destiny* – which is worth reading in its own right for its compelling account of Olga Fikotová's romance with Harold Connolly.

p. 224: **'He was a wonderful, affable fellow . . .'**
Quoted in 'The Man Who Taught Me Everything', a tribute to Kelley by Amby Burfoot, published in *Runner's World*, May 2007.

p. 226: **'against his better judgement'**
Leading article marking Emil's retirement in the *Manchester Guardian*, 8 March 1958.

p. 226: **'Men, today we die a little'**
The words have been endlessly quoted, nearly always with a confident attribution to the starting line of the Melbourne Olympic marathon. A random selection of reputable sources from around the world might include the following: Ian O'Riordan's interview with Olympic marathon runner Frank Murohy in the *Irish Times*, 29 November 2014; the *Troy Messenger*'s obituary of Nicholas Costes (to whom the remark was allegedly addressed), 13 April 2003; *Modern Training for Running*, by Ken Doherty (Prentice Hall, 1964), reporting Dean Thackery's version of the remark; 'Profiles: Emil Zátopek' at runningpast.com; *László Tábori: a Biography*, by András Kő, chapter 15; *The Gigantic Book of Running Quotations*, by Hal Higdon (2008); *Zátopek* magazine, No 26, May/June/July 2013, p. 42; *et al.* But I confess to being slightly perplexed as to who first reported the remark in this form. The nearest I have seen to a primary source is a letter from John J. Kelley to the director Benjamin Rassat, written more than half a century later (and published in 2011 by Pat Butcher on his website, globerunner.org), in which Kelley remembers a 'playful' Emil saying 'Today we die' on the starting line. It is possible that the other three words are a later invention – but I can't quite bring myself to discard them. They seem a strange piece of embroidery for someone simply to make up.

p. 227: **'Alain . . . I am not good. Don't stay with me.'**
Emil's account, quoted in Sandrock, p. 28.

pp. 227: **One television commentator was already describing him as 'in trouble'**
Unidentified American footage, viewed here: https://www.youtube.com/watch?v=NSQPWA915-c.

p. 228: **causing the crêpe to disintegrate into little pellets**
See: *BZ*, p. 86. Martin Řehák's comments were reported to me by Dana Zátopková. See note to p. 97.

p. 229: **no longer able to accelerate even a little bit**
See *DEZ*, p. 151 – although Emil confuses Lee with Kawashima of Japan.

p. 230: **'as if he were waking from a dream'**
Mimoun described these moments when interviewed in William Johnson's article, 'After the Golden Moment', in *Sports Illustrated*, 17 July 1972. Ron Clarke, who was watching close to the finishing line, gave a very similar account to me in a telephone conversation in September 2014. See also: *The Legend of Alain Mimoun*, dir. Benjamin Rassat, TV5 MONDE; Butcher, p. 26; 'Alain Mimoun: Athlete who ran in the shadow of Emil Zátopek', by Emily Langer, *Washington Post*, 9 July 2013. Emil gives a slightly different account in *DEZ* and *BZ* – focusing more on the detail that Mimoun passed on the news, of which he had just been made aware, that he had just become a father.

p. 230: **'Great is the victory . . . but the friendship of all is greater'**
Quoted in Kožík, p. 183. This appears to be the original source for the endlessly recycled quote. It is not attributed to Emil.

p. 231: **'It was too much for an old man . . .'**
The Argus (Melbourne), 3 December 1956, p. 20.

p. 232: **They shared the ship, the *Gruzia*, with the Soviet team**
The voyage is described in *DEZ*, but the most colourful details in this and the next paragraph come from *The Rings of Destiny*. Olga Connolly was on board. There is also a good description of the voyage in 'Emil Zátopek na cestě domů z Melbourne – část první: plavba lodi 'Hrůzia'', by Dav Schovánek, at bezeckaskola.cz.

p. 233: **in times that were respectable rather than world-beating**
At 5,000m Emil's times in 1957 ranged from 14:06.4 to 14:36.2, at 10,000m from 29:23.8 to 30:31.0.

p. 233: **escorted by an official called Jan Jirka, an old friend**
Jirka – who worked in broadcasting but should presumably be thought of, in this context, as a 'sharp eye' – described the trip in 'Olympijští vítězové Emil Zátopek a Dana Zátopková a jejich vztah k Přerovu', *Sborník Státního okresního archivu Přerov 2006*

(p. 137), from which several details in my description are taken. Other sources I have used include 'Zátopek Brillante Vencedor del III Gran Premio Internacional', by Miguel Vidaurre, first published in *La Voz De España*, 28 January 1958, and collected in *Retazos de la vida de Lasarte y Orla del siglo XX a través de la prensa*, pp. 192–9; and Adam B. Ellick's obituary, 'Emil Zátopek, 1922–2000', published in *Runner's World*, 1 March 2001 – in which Jirka is interviewed. Emil's own account (in *DEZ*, pp. 153–4) is tame by comparison.

p. 234: **made to do a stint as a barman**
See: 'Veía boinas por todas partes', a blog by Ander Izagirre, Patxi Alcorta's nephew, 16 May 2009 (see: http://www.gentedigital.es/blogs/anderiza/22/blog-post/1695/veia-boinas-por-todas-partes/).

p. 235: **'But . . . the dog didn't even speak Czech'**
Quoted in Adam B. Ellick's *Runner's World* obituary – which also features a delightful picture of Emil, Jirka and Jurek standing at the airport in Paris alongside a bulging kit-bag that looks very much as though it contains a puppy.

p. 236: **asked if, on their return, he could be taken straight to the training retreat at Stará Boleslav**
An informer's report in the StB archive (č: 648808 MV) describes this episode at length.

p. 236: **The problem may have originated with a bout of peritonitis**
13. komnata Dany Zátopkové, interview by Susan Burešová, Česka televize documentary first broadcast in 2011.

pp. 237–8: **'I can't run until my death' . . . one final appearance**
Manchester Guardian, 8 March 1958, p. 7.

p. 238: **joining the celebrated writers Jiří Hanzelka and Miroslav Zikmund on their travels**
Informer's report in the StB archive (č: 648808 MV). Hanzelka was from Štramberk, just a few miles outside Kopřivnice, and was related to the Zátopeks, via Emil's mother. Emil's father had helped Hanzelka create Kopřivnice's folk museum, which Emil also supported. This would not be the last time that Emil fantasised about joining Hanzelka and Zikmund on their travels.

p. 239: **'to be in the military in peacetime is heaven on earth'**
Süddeutsche Zeitung, 24 November 2000.

p. 239: **ordered out at gunpoint by some soldiers**
Pirie, p. 133.

p. 239: **Emil put him at his ease by saying: 'I can do that too'**
One of the conscripts, Milan Středa, described this episode to the ourCollective Memory Project, March 2009.

p. 240: **Coaching athletes, he liked to jog along**
'Emil Zátopek only chugs now', AAP report, printed in *Miami News*, 8 April 1962, p. 13.

p. 240: **Supervising marches . . . supervising artillery exercises . . .**
Milan Středa, talking to the ourCollective Memory Project, March 2009.

p. 241: **'and return home to a country where time has stopped'**
Emil, interviewed by Frank Csongos for Radio Free Europe/Radio Liberty, 9 June 1996.

p. 242: **'put in a kind word'**
The best source for this episode is Olga Connolly's own account, *The Rings of Destiny*, which includes a detailed account of her audience with Zápotocký. However, I have also drawn from an interview with Connolly by Ian Willoughby for Radio Prague, 1 May 2008; an interview with Dana Zátopková quoted in 'Olympic gold medalist Olga Fikotová-Connolly celebrates eighty' in *Sport iDnes*, 13 November 2012; an extensive obituary of Harold Connolly, by Frank Litsky, in the *New York Times*, 19 August 2000; and an account by Denzil Batchelor, 'Two gold medals and a gold ring', *Picture Post*, 8 April 1957, pp. 12ff.

p. 244: **On a sunny Saturday afternoon early in 1961**
Much of the detail in my account of Emil and Dana's creation of their Troja home is taken from 'Danešek, Ťopek and Zadní Ovenec', an article by their close friend Karel Engel for the journal of the Czech Olympic Committee, August 2009. Karel has been almost as tireless and tolerant as Dana in indulging my insatiable curiosity about Emil's life.

p. 246: **a post-retirement 10,000m . . . 5,000m**
See: Phillips, p. 125; *DEZ*, pp. 161–84.

p. 247: **even tried taking up smoking**
Emil made this startling admission when interviewed for *Emil Zátopek: Die Lauflokomotive*, a television documentary by Hagen Bossdorf for ARTE television, first broadcast 3 October 1995.

p. 247: **'Dana's javelin training is paying off'**
Quoted in 'Emil und die Detektive', *Der Spiegel*, 23 September 1968.

p. 248: **'After two hours . . . I had flickering in front of my eyes'**
Pavel, p. 26.

p. 248: ***Warmflaschenizolation***
Interviewed about this in *Mozaika* in February 1995 (p. 6), Emil and Dana even supplied the magazine with an architectural diagram, which explained in a marginal note that the bottles were 'unfortunately empty'.

p. 249: **'You honour opponents in a different way than the friends in the street'**
Emil talking in *Emil Zátopek: Die Lauflokomotive.*

p. 249: **'too sad to live without her'**
This comment came from Dana Zátopková, Emil's niece.

p. 251: **Hana Trejbalová**
See: 'Medvídek Emila Zátopka', by Leoš Pernica, in *Kulturní přehled*, 7/1968, pp. 16–17 (quoted at hamelika.cz/?cz_emil-zatopek-(1922-2000),313). See also: 'Steroids linked to early deaths of athletes', by Maggie Lawson, *Prague Post*, 31 July 1996; 'Československý doping: Byl to podvod, přestože nevraždil', by Václav Pacina, in *Mlada fronta/Dnes* (undated; published on svet.czsk.net/clanky/publicistika/csdoping.html).

p. 251: **'It was my dream to give a good example to children and get them started'**
Quoted by Cart, *Los Angeles Times*, 29 April 1991.

p. 254: **Luckily, Allen was not so negligent, and wrote it up for *Times* readers**
The Times, 24 March 1967.

p. 256: **'Look after this, because you deserve it . . .'**
I am tentative about the phrasing because no one really knows. Clarke, writing more than twenty years after the event, phrased it

as 'because you deserved it'; but much earlier accounts (for example, by Neil Allen and Kenny Moore), based on conversations with Clarke, use 'deserve' – which was also how Clarke phrased it when I spoke to him in 2014. It is hard to imagine Emil saying 'deserved' in the context. Similar confusion applies to the precise time and place of Clarke's opening of the gift. See: 'A witness to change – 40 years of Olympic reporting', by Neil Allen, 20 June 1997 (published in *Society's Watchdog – or Showbiz' Pet? Inspiration to Better Sports Journalism*, Danish Gymnastics and Sports Associations 1998). For other relatively contemporary accounts, see 'But only on Sunday', by Kenny Moore, first published in *Sports Illustrated* in February 1973 and collected in *Best Efforts* (Doubleday, 1982); and 'A gold medal to Ron Clarke', *Sydney Morning Herald*, 18 July 1976, p. 60. Clarke's own account was published in *Athletics Weekly*, as part of the 'All-time greats' series, on 5 November 1987, p. 19.

p. 258: **After a brief spell in a museum**
Clarke lent the medal for a while to the Gold Coast Sporting Hall of Fame in Southport.

p. 260: **Vaculík's address to the Fourth Congress of the Union of Writers**
Published as *The Relations Between Citizen and Power*, by Ludvik Vaculík (Liberal International British Group, 1968).

p. 261: **It can't really have been that good**
A Czech academic who very kindly read my manuscript before publication made a marginal note at this point: 'It really was that good.'

p. 262: **'threatening the foundations of socialism'**
The idea was used most pointedly in the notorious 'Warsaw letter', sent to the Central Committee of the Communist Party of Czechoslovakia on 15 July 1968, drafted under Soviet guidance by the leaders and senior Party members of the USSR, Bulgaria, the Germany Democratic Republic, Poland and Hungary in the course of a two-day conference in Warsaw. 'We are convinced,' said the letter, 'that a situation has arisen in which the threat to the foundations of socialism in Czechoslovakia also threatens the common vital interests of the other socialist states.'

p. 265: **by the end of the year, the civilian death toll had reached at least 108**
Victims of the Occupation: the Warsaw Pact Invasion of Czechoslovakia: 21 August – 31 December 1968, by Milan Bárta, Lukáš Cvrček, Patrik Košický and Vitězclav Sommer (Ústav pro studium totalitnich režimu), itemises the deaths.

p. 266: **'All further statements will not be issued by—'**
Some English language reports phrase the bulletins differently; I have relied for the wording on Jan Krčmář, who actually wrote and issued them.

p. 266: **'No sooner had the great mailed fist clanged down . . .'**
'How the coup went wrong', by Cyril Dunn, Laurence Marks and Andrew Wilson, *Observer*, 25 August 1968, p. 2.

p. 266: **'Emil was clearly the dominant figure'**
Checkmate in Prague, by Luděk Pachman (Faber & Faber, 1975), p. 91.

p. 267: **'They didn't want to listen . . .'**
Montville, *Sports Illustrated*, 26 March 1990.

p. 268: **'the most dramatic case of non-violent action against foreign aggressors that the world has ever known'**
'Civilian Resistance as a National Defence: Non-Violent Action Against Aggression', ed. Adam Roberts (Penguin, 1969) p. 7 (quoted in *The Prague Spring and its Aftermath: Czech Politics 1968–1970*, by Kieran Williams, p. 42).

p. 268: **'addressed the crowd under the muzzles of Soviet cannon . . .'**
'Olympic ban demand by Zátopek', by Neil Allen, *The Times*, 23 August 1968, p. 5.

p. 269: **'called on the Russians to leave . . .'**
Untitled report by Reginald Peck, *Daily Telegraph*, 23 August 1968.

p. 269: **'We must develop a new citizen tactic . . .'**
External Affairs Review, Volume 18, p. 29.

p. 269: **may have been involved in facilitating this form of pirate broadcasting as well**
See: *Televize v srpnu 1968*, by Václav Kolář and Ladislav Kejha (ČT, 2001); also Kosatík, p. 233. The 'secret television' project was based in Petřiny.

p. 269: **'Do not give them a provocation'**
UPI report (New York), printed in *The Argus* (Fremont-Newark, California), 23 August 1968, p. 1.

p. 269: **'our good friends' . . . were waiting for them**
Mit blossen Händen, by Erich Bertleff, p. 152.

p. 270: **'without even noticing that just a couple of steps away from him was a soldier with an assault rifle'**
Pachman, p. 94.

p. 271: **'anger leads to bloodshed'**
'Shots as crowds taunt soldiers', by David Leitch, *The Times*, 28 August 1968, p. 1.

p. 271: **'It's over'**
Prague, l'été des tanks, by Vaclav Byk (Paris, 1968); quoted in Fortune, pp. 53–86.

p. 272: **'Every race has its finish line . . .'**
Stadión, September 1968, quoted in 'Osamělost přespolního běžce', by Pavel Malík, *Lidové noviny*, 28 July 2012.

p. 273: **'If they punish me, they will discredit themselves'**
Interview with Johan Struye in *Express* (Austria), August 1969; quoted in Naudin, p. 196.

p. 274: **'We love our country too much to live anywhere else'**
Naudin, p. 194.

p. 274: **'If I had left my country at that time . . . I did not want to leave my country like a rat . . .'**
AP reports from Prague (23 April) and Stockholm (27 April) (printed in the *Bridgeport Post*, 24 April, and the *Danville Register*, 27 April, respectively); the latter draws from an interview published in *Aftonbladet* on 26 April 1969.

p. 274: **'The Russians . . . were acting out of fear . . .'**
'Zátopek recalls invasion', by Will Grimsley, Associated Press report, 9 October 1968.

p. 275: **'Hush, Emil. They'll hear you . . .'**
'Golden legacy of a great man', by Chris Brasher, *Daily Mail*, 23 November 2000.

p. 277: **An editorial . . . denouncing Emil as a 'traitor'**
Sovietsky sport, 1 January 1969 (quoted in Naudin, pp. 194–5).

p. 277: **'changes his convictions the way he changes his shirts'**
Friedrich Janke, quoted in Naudin, p. 195.

p. 279: **an astonishing claim about Jan Palach's death**
The claim had already been circulated in leaflets around Prague, and Nový had said something similar in a newspaper interview a few weeks earlier, but this was the fuller, more aggressive version. To hear the recording, search for 'Vilém Nový O Janu Palachovi - lež o studeném ohni'. The audience reception prompted Nový's wife to observe: 'They don't seem to like Vilém here.'

p. 281: **'conduct at variance with the relevant orders'**
See: 'Zátopek seiner Funktion enthoben', *Neues Deutschland*, 22 April 1969, section 3; Naudin, p. 195.

pp. 281–2: **'It would be quiet, and I could write without being disturbed'**
AP report, 23 April 1969 (printed in the *Bridgeport Post*, 24 April 1969).

p. 282: **'his merits will be taken fully into account'**
'"Expel dissidents" call at Czech party rally', by Michael Hornsby, *The Times*, 22 April 1969.

p. 282: **'It is better to be beaten in a fair game than to win an unfair one'**
Quoted in an AP report, 27 April 1969, printed in the *Fresno Bee* (p. 30) and the *Danville Register*, 27 April 1969.

p. 282: **'when people are leaving the country I do not want to leave'**
UPI report, 1 May 1969 (printed in the *Times Recorder*, 2 May 1969, p. 9).

p. 282: **'received a letter firing me from the Army . . .'**
Interview by Johan Struye, *L'Express*, 18 August 1969, quoted in AP (Vienna) reports, 18 August 1969; and in Naudin, p. 198.

p. 283: **'I am not a politician . . .'**
Informer's report, StB archive (č: 648808 MV).

p. 283: **The 'Ten Points'**
'Deset bodů adresovaných federální vládě, Federálnímu shromáždění ČSSR, České národní radě, vládě České socialistické republiky a ÚV KSČ', Václav Havel Library.

p. 285: **doing menial work for a doll-making co-operative**
See Szczygiel, pp. 166ff., for a haunting account of Kubišová's ordeal.

p. 285: **'counting on starving us out'**
Pavel Juráček, quoted in *The Greengrocer and His TV: The Culture of Communism After the 1968 Prague Spring*, by Paulina Bren, pp. 56–8.

p. 286: **it had cost them 180,000 crowns**
Interview in *Mozaika*, February 1995.

p. 286: **to be jobless was a criminal offence**
Under Section 188a of Czechoslovakia's Penal Code, anyone who 'avoided honest work' could be jailed for up to three years for 'parasitism'.

p. 286: **one option after another melted away**
The examples come mainly from informers' reports in the StB archives (č: 648808 MV), although Emil raised the first two in his interview with Johan Struye in *L'Express* (18 August 1969).

p. 286: **no one came to say goodbye to him**
Kosatík, p. 245.

p. 287: **'I heard the word treason used . . .'**
Květy, 6 September 1969 (quoted by UPI, 11 September 1969, and printed in *The Daily Notes*, 12 September 1969, p. 10).

p. 287: **an article in *Rudé právo***
'I pro Emila Zátopka platí stanovy strany', by Jiří Hečko, *Rudé právo*, 24 October 1969, p. 8; also reported by AP and printed in *Santa Cruz Sentinel*, 25 October 1969.

p. 287: **'He can . . . do everything – except controlling himself in press interviews'**
AP report, printed in *Kansas City Times*, 29 November 1969.

p. 288: **'No wonder the army eventually had to part company with Emil Zátopek'**

Obrana lidu, 28 November 1969; reported by AP and printed in *Kansas City Times*, 29 November 1969.

p. 288: **'violating legal norms . . .'**
ČTK news agency report, 5 December 1969, reported by AP (Vienna) and New York News Service.

p. 288: **working as a garbage collector**
The garbage collector story has been circulating since the early 1970s. Pierre Naudin repeated it (*Zátopek: Le Terrassier de Prague*, p. 19), quoting anonymous Prague-dwellers; and Brian Freemantle, quoting Emil himself, included it in his *Daily Mail* article in May 1971. But Dana denies it, as (less convincingly) did the Czechoslovak government. There is no mention of it in the archives of the StB – who were watching Emil's every move in late 1969 and early 1970. And Emil himself denied it, not just in his 'retraction' interview in *Rudé právo*, 20 July 1971 but also in an interview with Hedley Thomas, published in the Queensland *Sunday Mail* on 15 April 1990, in which he was quoted as saying: 'Was I forced to be a garbage man? No, no. I once helped a garbage man, that's all.' The sanitation department story was reported by the New York News Service, 6 December 1969 (and printed on the front page of the *Ottawa Journal*, 6 December 1969). But Dana denies it, and, again, I can find no mention of it in the archives of the security services. I suspect it was a garbled account of his actual employment, which began in early November and may well have been misinterpreted by, for example, foreign visitors in Mariánské Lázně.

pp. 290–1: **Jaromír Malák . . . Emil kept demanding a 'real job'**
Jaromír Malák was talking in *Pohádkový Péťa*, 2002; if he is still alive, I have been unable to trace him. I am grateful to Oldřich Stehlík, Stanislav Šula and Richard Händl for helping me to understand the practical details of Emil's employment at Stavební geologie, based on their own experience.

p. 291: **one was usually an StB informer**
Kosatík (p. 255) implies that this was a matter of policy; given the number of informers' reports from this period in the StB archive, this is easy to believe.

p. 291: **'could have made things quite nasty for me'**
Quoted, along with Emil's words in the two paragraphs that follow, in part 4 of *Životopisy: Emil Zátopek*, directed by Pavel Krejčí for Česky rozhlas (first broadcast 1–5 May 2012).

p. 295: **more than he earned in the army**
Quoted by Zdeněk Hrabica in *Emil Zátopek a sport objektivem – Emila Fafka a jiných*, p. 12.

p. 296: **'not seventh heaven'**
Quoted in *Životopisy: Emil Zátopek.*

p. 296: **'Is this how they treat their hero?'**
I first came across this in 'Šest let hloubil studní', by Jiří Jakoubek, *LUCIE*, September 2009; Dana and others confirm it.

p. 297: **'I am not the Zátopek who you used to know'**
Kosatík, p. 255.

p. 297: **a fleeting clip of film footage**
The short clip appears in *Pohádkový Péťa*. Emil is not actually working, but appears to be in drill-worker mode. I have spent many months trying unsuccessfully to follow up a rumour that there was once a public information newsreel that included footage of Emil and his team at work. I suspect that the footage once existed (an StB informer reported that some filming took place in early 1970), but it does not appear to have survived.

p. 299: **Pachman . . . was about to flee the country**
This was what Dana remembered, and reports in the StB files (č: 648808 MV) appear to bear it out – as does Pachman's account of the evidence Emil is supposed to have given in May 1972 (see notes to p. 309).

p. 299: **'afraid of being sent to jail for 20 years'**
Close friends who believe this to have been the case include Karel Tejkal, the journalist, and Zdeněk Fator. The StB files seem to support this. Kosatík suggests that Emil was afraid for his liberty from late 1968 onwards.

p. 300: **'as if they were about to hug each other in a "double Khrushchev"'**
Pachman, pp. 132–3.

p. 300: **'a grown man collapse like a house hit by a bomb'**
Speech by Pavel Kohout for a 'Palach evening' commemorating Jan Palach's death at the Nová scéna at the National Theatre in Prague, 16 January 2015.

p. 300: **'an example of surrender which meant the end to the solidarity of Czech society'**
'O druhém upálení Jana Palacha', by Pavel Kohout (3 March 2012), published in Kohout's collection, *Zánik trilobitů v Čechách*, pp. 121–3.

p. 301: **others would follow**
For example: Rudolf Battěk, the sociologist, and Jan Tesař, the historian.

p. 301: **not the only signatory to withdraw**
Josef Wagner, deputy president of the council of youth associations, also withdrew; see: 'Osudy a smysl petice "Deset bodů" ze srpna 1969', ed. Michal Lakatoš, Luděk Pachman, Ludvík Vaculík – in *Proměny Pražského jara 1968–1969* (Doplněk, 1993), pp. 218–310.

pp. 301–2: **'He is as great a human being as he was an athlete'**
'Why quarrel with the Prime Minister?', by Christopher Brasher, *Observer*, 28 December 1969, p. 19.

p. 302: **an article in the *Daily Mail***
'Zátopek, the will to win is crushed', by Brian Freemantle, *Daily Mail*, 31 May 1971.

p. 303: **a 3,000-word interview . . . in which Emil recanted pretty much everything he had fought for in 1968**
Rudé právo, 20 July 1971, p. 3 ('Emil Zátopek odpovidá redakci rudého práva o věcech včerejších i dnešních').

p. 304: **Emil 'got what for' . . . 'I don't think he would have done it'**
See also: 'Šest let hloubil studní', by Jiří Jakoubek *LUCIE*, September 2009; Montville, *Sports Illustrated*, 26 March 1990.

p. 305: **'Never glad confident morning again . . .'**
'The Lost Leader', by Robert Browning (1845).

p. 306: **he couldn't keep up with his workmates in the pub either**
Praha Velké osudy: Emil Zátopek, a radio programme by Emil's friend Karel Tejkal, first broadcast 27 October 2009, Česky rozhlas.

p. 309: **thought to include subversion, slandering the Republic, incitement and preparing a felony**
It is hard to say with absolute certainty exactly what took place. The proceedings were closed to the public, while the relevant court records were dispersed in the floods that overwhelmed the Prague city archives in 2002, and are now partly contained within the StB archive. This summary is based on Reuters reports printed in *The Times* ('Prague trial of former chess grand master', p. 7, 5 May 1972; 'Czech court frees Ludek Pachman after giving him a jail term', p. 5, 6 May 1972) and the Amnesty International Newsletter (Vol. 2, No. 7, July 1972). The order for his immediate release was interpreted as an attempt to prevent him from becoming an international *cause célèbre*.

p. 309: **Emil is assumed to have been called as a witness**
A Reuters bulletin reported that Emil was 'seen leaving the court . . . apparently after having given evidence at the trial'; see: 'Czech on trial for radio talk', printed in *New Nation*, 5 May 1972, p. 7. Emil's appearance is also discussed in an informer's report in the StB archives.

p. 309: **a conversation in which Pachman and the Soviet chess player Paul Keres jokingly discussed emigration**
Pachman, pp. 128–9.

p. 310: **'Where am I going to get someone to replace you for three weeks?'**
Emil's account, quoted in part 4 of *Životopisy: Emil Zátopek.*

p. 310: **a brief . . . to look happy and keep his mouth shut**
According to a report in Emil's file in the StB archive, Antonín Himl, president of the ČSTV, personally briefed Emil in July on the importance of not discussing politics in Munich.

p. 311: **'I am a simple worker and drill outside Prague for mineral water'**
'Laufen wie die Vögel fliegen: Interview mit dem Olympia-Gast Emil Zátopek', *Der Spiegel*, 4 September 1972.

p. 312: **'In my country I am just a common man – a nobody'**
The episode is described in chapter 31 of *Going Far*, by Joe Henderson (Create Space, 2012).

p. 313: **'Former Olympic champion Emil Zátopek,' reported Wortzel**
Diplomatic cable, courtesy of Wikileaks (https://www.wikileaks.org/plusd/cables/1973PRAGUE02002_b.html).

p. 315: **'Life is the most precious thing we have . . .'**
From Dana Zátopková's memoir, unpublished at the time of going to press but provisionally entitled *Jak to bylo* ('How It Was').

p. 315: **'at least we know that those who stayed are really worth something'**
Quoted by Zdeněk Hrabica in *Emil Zátopek a sport objektivem – Emila Fafka a jiných*, p. 12.

p. 316: **often degenerated into wild hilarity**
'Chtěla bych ještě jednou posedět s Ťopkem', Jiří Jakoubek, *Lidové noviny*, 16 September 2002.

p. 319: **'render unto Caesar the things that are Caesar's'**
Matthew 22:15–22; Mark 12:13–17; Luke 20:20–26.

p. 320: **'I became a sports spy'**
Montville, *Sports Illustrated*, 26 March 1990.

p. 320: **'Emil Zátopek has been welcomed back into the fold . . .'**
'Hoffman's staying power to be tested', by Neil Allen, *The Times*, 26 July 1974, p. 9.

p. 321: **a signed, limited edition print by Pablo Picasso**
I have been trying, so far without success, to contact the alleged recipient; and as a result have been unable to determine which print it was, beyond the fact that it was some kind of dove. (Picasso did several.)

p. 322: **'the great surrender'**
"Neumírat předčasně!", by Pavel Kohout (18 January 2014), collected in *Zánik trilobitů v Čechách*, pp. 278–80.

p. 322: **'political adventurers who with this Charter have tried to stick a knife into our collective work'**
Quoted in 'Anticharta, 1. mimořádné číslo' for *Revolver Revue*, by Viktor Karlík and Terezie Pokorná (eds), p. 21; and *Charta 77 v dobovém mediálním a sociálním kontextu*, by Jakub Železný (Charles University, Prague, 2010), p. 49. The footage has not survived: ČST routinely re-used old film in those days.

p. 323: **which he probably had read**
Emil said on television that he had been upset when he read *Rudé právo*'s account of the Charter – published under the headline 'Ztroskotanci a samozvanci' ('losers and usurpers') on 12 January 1977.

p. 323: **'sang English songs extremely loudly'**
'Winning is the only thing that matters', by Rob Hughes, *The Times*, 16 August 1997.

p. 324: **'beautiful' Finnish**
Pirkko Järvinen, who was supposed to be acting as Emil's interpreter, quoted in *Pohádkový Péťa*. See also Macák, Žurman & Jirásek, p. 28.

p. 324: **'Who's Zátopek?'**
Cliff Temple described this incident in his 'Sports Diary', *The Times*, 2 September 1978, p. 12.

p. 324: **George A. Hirsch . . . invited him to the USA**
Hirsch wrote two evocative descriptions of this episode: 'Zátopek should carry torch', *New York Times*, 22 April 1984, Section 5, p. 2; and, more fully, '60 Years Ago, an Olympic Trifecta of Endurance', *New York Times*, 23 June 2012, p. 11. See also: 'Zátopek lasts the political distance', an Associated Press interview with Emil, printed in *The Times*, 23 April 1982, p. 29. *The Runner* merged with *Runner's World* in 1986.

p. 325: **At the airport, Chinmoy made to shake hands with him . . .**
Salutations, numbers 1–4, by Sri Chinmoy (Agni Press, 1981; srichinmoylibrary.com/slt-2).

p. 326: **'work with him didn't even feel like working'**
Věra Čáslavská: Život na olympu, by Pavel Kosatík, p. 149.

p. 326: **'Yes, but you signed the "Two Thousand Words". You will get no more.'**
Montville, *Sports Illustrated*, 26 March 1990.

p. 327: **a special celebration at Houštka Spa**
Dana described this occasion in detail in an interview with Karel Tejkal for vitalplus.org, 21 June 2010.

p. 328: **gave his broad backing to the boycott**
Rudé právo, 14 May 1984, p. 7.

p. 328: **'all athletes who have conscientiously trained . . .'**
Quoted in a report by United Press International (Prague), 10 May 1984.

p. 328: **invited to be torch-bearer**
United Press International, 13 October 1983; *New York Times*, Section A; p. 27, 14 October 1983. See also George A. Hirsch's article, 'Zátopek should carry torch', *New York Times*, April 22, 1984.

p. 328: **'The generosity, charm and charisma that so impressed John Landy, Les Perry and the other Australians . . .'**
'50 Years of the Emil Zátopek Race', by Len Johnson, *Sydney Morning Herald*, 4 December 2011.

p. 329: **'I think he was genuinely touched . . .'**
Quoted in *The Age* (Melbourne), 13 December 1993, p. 28.

p. 333: **One of the first to call was the Australian journalist Hedley Thomas**
'Emil!', by Hedley Thomas, *Queensland Sunday Mail*, 15 April 1990. The full interview is much more entertaining than my brief extract suggests.

p. 334: **'Our hope is that all will be quiet . . .'**
Montville, *Sports Illustrated*, 26 March 1990.

p. 334: **'To live in such a place – how is it possible?'**
Cart, *Los Angeles Times*, April 29, 1991.

p. 336: **During the furore that followed . . . suggesting that one of those under suspicion was Emil Zátopek**
See: Radio Prague report, 2 November 1998; 'Spy backlash hits president', by René Jakl, 'Prague Post', 4 November 1998; 'Benda: Vyznamenáno bylo více agentů StB', *ČTK - Z domova* (str.02), 2 November 1998; 'Jak viděla StB dění na severu', by Antonín Viktora, *Severní Čechy* (str. 03), 15 November 2006, *et al.*

pp. 336–7: **Josef Frolík . . . gave evidence to a hearing**
United States Congress Senate Committee on the Judiciary, Subcommittee to Investigate the Administration of the Internal Security Act and other Internal Security Laws. *Communist Bloc Intelligence Activities in the United States: Hearing, 94th Cong., 1st–2nd Sess. November 18, 1975 [and April 12, 1976]* (Washington: U.S. GPO,

1975–1976, p. 22; LC Catalog Record http://lccn.loc.gov/76600952. LC Call Number: KF26 .J832 1975b).

p. 338: **not least in his book, *Špión vypovídá***
Frolík also published an English version of his memoirs, *The Frolík Defection* (Leo Cooper, 1975). His allegations about Emil do not appear in it, however.

p. 340: **'gangsters of the world'**
Quoted by Michael Knife in 'Prague students clean Wenceslas statue', *The Times*, 29 August 1968, p. 5.

p. 341: **reprimanded shortly before leaving for Melbourne**
Kosatík, p. 204.

p. 341: **Ladislav Kořán . . . was interrogated more than once about Emil by the secret police**
See: Kosatík, p.76.

p. 342: **Department D**
The department's activities are described in jaw-dropping detail in *The Deception Game*, by Ladislav Bittman.

p. 342: **'It is now generally accepted that Frolík was a plant . . .'**
The Intelligence Game: The Illusions and Delusions of International Espionage, by James Rusbridger (I.B. Tauris, 1991; first published by The Bodley Head, 1989), pp. 58–9.

p. 343: **'sold his soul to the Communist regime'**
'Setkávání s Emilem Zátopkem', by Stanislav Berton, *CS-Magazín*, 3 May 2009 (cs-magazin.com/index.php?a=a2009061008).

p. 343: **although others have been equally scathing about Pachman's reliability**
Several of Emil's friends spoke disparagingly of Pachman to me. Ludvík Liška, Emil's former team-mate, described him as 'a crooked man'. See also: *The Miracle Game*, a novel by Pachman's US publisher, the Czech exile Josef Škvorecký, in which a Pachman-like character, Bukavec, admits to the invention of malicious lies about people. Informers' reports in the StB files confirm the view that the eventual animosity between Emil and Pachman was personal as well as ideological; Emil particularly disapproved of the way Pachman cheated on his wife.

p. 344: **some 'sharp eyes' who took pride in being attached to such a great man**
Examples include Jan Jirka (see pp. 233–5); and, according to Ludvík Liška, a regular 'sharp eye' called Nikolaj Hrib.

p. 344: **'always as about people whom he feared'**
Kosatík, p.97.

p. 346: **people in high places who liked him**
Dana is sure that Emil's former colleagues in the Army 'tried to protect him'.

p. 346: **he felt like weeping**
Informer's report in the StB archive.

p. 347: **Luděk Pachman and Pavel Kohout, before they became liberals**
See: *Fools and heroes: the changing role of Communist intellectuals in Czechoslovakia*, by Peter Hruby, chapters 2 and 4, for a detailed account of Pachman and Kohout's pre-liberal activities.

p. 347: **starting an argument believing one thing but ending it believing the opposite**
See: Kosatík, p. 218.

p. 349: **'What good is it if someone says five or ten years after you are dead that you are a hero?'**
Quoted in Montville, *Sports Illustrated*, 26 March 1990.

p. 352: **Haluza's contribution to Emil's success**
Haluza's account of the relationship can be found, along with the blurred photograph, in *Trénoval jsem Emila*. But Dana and others insist that Haluza was less crucial to Emil's development than he claimed – and that Emil exaggerated his influence in order help him back on his feet after Jáchymov.

p. 353: **a tiny asteroid**
I understand that Zátopek, asteroid serial number 5910, can be found at these coordinates: 2.28, 0.14, 5.0. See: *Dictionary of Minor Planet Names*, by Lutz D. Schmadel, p. 473.

p. 356: **Two photographs**
Emil Zátopek a sport objektivem Emila Fafka a jiných, p. 95.

p. 357: **the last fell in 1965**
The last records to go were those for 15 miles and 25,000m, broken by Ron Hill in Bolton on 21 July 1965.

p. 357: **But attempts to mark that landmark with a special radio celebration were hampered by Emil's health**
Kosatík, p. 270.

p. 357: **'At this age . . . there is no shame in dying'**
Quoted in 'Die tschechische Lokomotive', by Karl-Heinz Bergmann, *Berliner-Zeitung*, 23 November 2000.

p. 358: **'You are a guest in my house, so we will speak in your language . . .'**
'Radcliffe has many miles to run to match true legend', by Alasdair Reid, *Sunday Herald*, 2 August 2005.

pp. 358–9: **a 'tough week full of deep depression . . .'**
Petr Krejci, head of the department of functional diagnostics and sports medicine, Prague Central Military Hospital, quoted in PA report in *iDNES*, December 7, 1999.

p. 359: **'practising for eternal sleep . . .'**
Quoted in Kosatík, p. 270.

p. 360: **'Zátopek the great' . . .**
Headlines from, respectively, *Mirror*, 23 November 2000; Agence France Press, 22 November 2000; Xinhua General News Service, 22 November 2000.

pp. 360–1: **'I am losing a brother, not an adversary . . .'**
Quoted in *L'humanité*, 23 November 2000.

p. 361: **Dana asked for it to be kept simple**
It was Emil and Dana's great friend Karel Engel, a former Olympic wrestler and now a prominent member of the Czech Olympic Committee, who arranged for the National Theatre to be made available. He knew the director's father and decided to call in a favour.

p. 361: **'Better an ugly wedding than a lovely funeral'**
See: 'Tisíce lidí se poklonily legendárnímu atletovi', by Jiří Jakoubek, *Lidové noviny*, 7 December 2000.

p. 364: **denounced on the radio . . . allegations had been raised on television**

The director of the National Gallery was Milan Knížák; the allegations were made on Katovna by Jan Rejžek; at the time of going to press Jiřina Fuchsová's blog could still be found at http://www.britskelisty.cz/0012/20001218l.html. See: *Emil Zátopek a sport objektivem – Emila Fafka a jiných*, p. 13.

p. 365: **'. . . in our country they scorned him'**

Jiří was talking in *Pohádkový Péťa.*

p. 365: **'sophisticated because he is so simple'**

Quoted in the *Melbourne Age*, 2 August 1992, p. 3.

p. 366: **'constantly pretending to be a decent person . . .'**

'How famous am I? Not very', by Caitlin Moran, *The Times* (magazine), 2 August 2014. Moran had unexpectedly found herself a role model for troubled young women, following the success of her book *How to be a Woman*, and felt obliged not to disappoint them.

p. 367: **possible that Emil 'borrowed' the incident from Ladislav Kořán**

Karel Tejkal's 2009 radio programme, *Praha Velké osudy: Emil Zátopek*, suggests that this may have been the case.

p. 369: **'proved that the ordinary man is capable of feats previously considered impossible'**

Stars of Czechoslovak Sport, p. 12.

p. 372: **'He was a simple man – a good boy . . .'**

The speakers are, respectively: Jaromír Konůpka, John Disley, Jiří Zátopek (Emil's nephew), Ludvík Liška, Olga Lišková, Marie Vlachová, Vaneesa Kořán, Zdeněk Fator; Dana Zátopková (Emil's niece).

Acknowledgements

This book could not have been written without the kindness and enthusiasm of many people. I am especially indebted to the Zátopek family, particularly (and obviously) Emil's widow, Dana Zátopková but also (less visibly) to his nephew and niece, Jiří Zátopek and Dana Zátopková.

Nor could it have been written without the tireless, patient and at times inspired support of Petr Bráník, Radka Brahová and Lewis Paines.

I am also very grateful for the support of (in no particular order): Karel Engel of the Czech Olympic Committee; Michaela Bortlová (historian and curator of the permanent Emil and Dana Zátopek exhibition in the Technical Museum Tatra in Kopřivnice); Kateřina Mikulcová; Ondřej Šalek at Kopřivnice's Muzeum Fojtství; Petr Cimala at the Hranice military academy; Šárka Kárpátiová; Radomir Michálková; Rudolf Braha, Oldřich Stehlík, Stanislav Šula and Richard Händl; Jiří Pihera and Petr Loukota; Vojtěch Franta; Dr Libor Svoboda of the Institute for the Study of Totalitarian Regimes; Steve Riley of the Faculty of Management at Prague's University of Economics; Judita Matyášová; Stephen Weeks; Jaroslav Šonka; Olga Šílová; Barbara Smit; Emily Howard; Vaneesa Kořán; Ondrej Kohout; Kateřina Moravcová; Tomáš Luňák; Jan Dufek; Petr Hájek at Krátky Film Praha; Tomáš Mrva; Jan Havlíček; Zuzana Štefunková and Eva Pavlíková at the Czech National Film Archive; Libuše Pekárková at the Archiv

ČT Praha; Ivana Roháčková at ASC Dukla; Stanislav Berton; Ian Robilliard; Glynis Nunn-Cearns; Claire Sanjuan; Alice Laurent; Alan Hubbard; Filip Paulus at the National Archive of the Czech Republic; the staff of the Czech National Library in Prague, the Archiv bezpečnostních složek, the military archive in Olomouc, the Jáchymov museum and (not least) the British Library Reading Room. I am grateful to Supraphon A.S. for permission to quote, in my own rough translation, the lines from 'A Prayer for Marta' ('Modlitba pro Martu', words by Petr Roda and music by Jindřich Brabec) on p. 261. I also owe warm thanks to Tomáš Dimter at Mlada fronta (for helping me find my feet in Prague); Alexandr Kohák (for repeatedly looking after me there); three generations of the Konůpka family; my colleagues at the (now only digital) *Independent*; and, almost certainly, several other people whose names I have forgotten to list, but to whom I am no less grateful.

I owe additional and special debts to Jon Waldron, Jon Henderson, Anna Kudrnová, Jan Krčmář and Dr Jan Čulík (senior lecturer in Czech Studies at the University of Glasgow), all of whom have encouraged me and advised me with extraordinary generosity and saved me from countless embarrassing mistakes. The embarrassing mistakes that remain are exclusively mine.

Finally, nearer home, I thank Robin Harvie, who first encouraged me to write about Zátopek; Brie Burkeman and Meg Davis, my past and current agents; Matt Phillips and Frances Jessop at Yellow Jersey, who kept faith in this book when it would have been easier not to – and cajoled me into making a far better job of it than I would ever have done unaided; and, above all, my family (Clare, Isobel, Edward, Anne), who have been patient and encouraging beyond the call of duty while I have been immersed in the world of Emil Zátopek. I hope they will forgive me for occasionally seeming reluctant to emerge from it.

I do not know what I have done to deserve so much kindness, but I suspect that much of it was initially directed at Emil: a great man in his life who continues to inspire us to find our better selves long after his death.

List of Illustrations

Index